Han Yü
and the T'ang
Search for Unity

韓愈

CHARLES
HARTMAN

Han Yü
and the T'ang
Search for Unity

Princeton University Press
Princeton, New Jersey

Copyright © 1986 by Princeton
University Press

Published by Princeton University Press,
41 William Street, Princeton, New Jersey
08540
In the United Kingdom: Princeton University Press, Guildford, Surrey

Library of Congress Cataloging in Publication Data will be found on the last
printed page of this book

ISBN 0-691-06665-5

Publication of this book has been aided by
a grant from The Andrew W. Mellon
Foundation

This book has been composed in
Linotron Bembo
Clothbound editions of Princeton University Press books are printed on acid-free
paper, and binding materials are chosen
for strength and durability

Printed in the United States of America
by Princeton University Press, Princeton,
New Jersey

Frontispiece:
Calligraphy by Professor
Chow Tse-tsung,
University of Wisconsin

For
Ch'en Yin-k'o
and
Hsü Li-yün
BOTH POWERFUL
SOURCES OF
INSPIRATION

CONTENTS

ACKNOWLEDGMENTS

This book has been a long time in the making, and many people—colleagues, friends, and fellow Han Yü scholars—have helped along the way. My parents, Wayne and Dorothy Hartman, constantly encouraged and made possible my life as a scholar. My teachers and colleagues at Indiana University, F. A. Bischoff, Michael Fish, Liu Wu-chi, and William Nienhauser, helped to nurture my early interest in Han Yü and to sustain that interest over the years. Many aspects of Han Yü studies are well-traveled ground, and I have profited from the scholarship. The notes to this volume indicate the main sources of my indebtedness. Special mention should be made, however, of the fine dissertation by Timothy Hugh Barrett on Li Ao (774-836). This work was especially helpful for its meticulous translation of Li Ao's *Writings on Returning to One's True Nature (Fu-hsing shu)* and for the overwhelming evidence it offered to confirm my own suspicions about the relationship between Han Yü and Li Ao.

In Taiwan, Lo Lien-t'ien and his students at National Taiwan University constitute a major center of Han Yü studies, and I am indebted to him for the many years he has generously shared with me his detailed knowledge of Han Yü's biography and for his constant encouragement and bibliographical suggestions. Wu Wen-chih in Peking, one of China's leading authorities on Han Yü, was gracious with his encyclopedic knowledge of Han Yü scholarship. Unfortunately, his monumental *Han Yü tzu-liao hui-pien (Compendium of Materials on Han Yü)* appeared only as my book was going to press. Three great Japanese scholars, Hanabusa Hideki, Shimizu Shigeru, and Yanagida Seizan, were instrumental in helping me obtain copies of their own and other Japanese publications on Han Yü.

ix

I am particularly grateful to William Theodore de Bary, Irene Bloom, C. T. Hsia, Robert Hymes, W. Scott Morton, and Bernard Solomon of the Traditional China Seminar and the Seminar on Neo-Confucian Studies at Columbia University; much of the material in this book was presented at their forums, and I have profited immeasurably from their comments and criticisms. My special gratitude goes to Denis Twitchett whose repeated readings of earlier drafts and whose patient support have helped me to produce a book far better than it would otherwise have been. Likewise, Victor Mair's extraordinarily careful reading of the manuscript removed numerous major and minor errors. R. Miriam Brokaw and Cathie Brettschneider of the Princeton University Press took special pains to bring order to my original unwieldy manuscript. A faculty research grant from the Research Foundation of the State University of New York enabled me to devote full attention to this work during the summer of 1981. Finally, the following individuals have all made important contributions to this book in a variety of ways: Chan Wing-ming, Ch'eng Ch'ien-fan, Ch'ien Chung-shu, the late William Hung, David McMullen, Stephen Owen, and Jerry Schmidt. All remaining errors are mine.

CHARLES HARTMAN
Thanksgiving 1984

Han Yü
and the T'ang
Search for Unity

ORIENTATIONS

"Antiquity is now."
—Chuang-tzu via Han Yü

Han Yü (768–824) ranks among the most important personalities in the history of traditional Chinese culture. Students
of classical Chinese literature appreciate him primarily as an
advocate for reform of the existing prose style known as "parallel prose" (p'ien-wen) and as the first notable practitioner of
a radically different prose called the "literature of Antiquity"
(ku-wen). But Han Yü was much more than a reformer of
style. The Chinese literati of premodern times were closer to
the mark when they looked to Han Yü as one of their tradition's most eloquent spokesmen for a fundamental renewal
of Confucian moral values, for a comprehensive reform that
was to affect all spheres of Confucian public and private life.
Han Yü crafted the ku-wen style to be an appropriate vehicle
for this message. For him, style and message formed a sym-
biotic union, each adding to the moral force of the other. But
the modern demise of institutionalized Confucian moralism
as a meaningful force in Chinese life has fragmented our view
of Han Yü's achievement. Most modern scholarship, although content to assign to Han Yü a secure place in the
history of Chinese literature, has been embarrassed by the
violence of his Confucian passions. Few have considered the
origins of these passions or contemplated the relationship between his experiences, his beliefs, and his literary voice. If
Han Yü created ku-wen to give suitable expression to his Confucian values, then an understanding of T'ang dynasty (618–
907) political and social issues and Han Yü's involvement with

them is prerequisite for an understanding of the literary force of this *ku-wen* style. This book then, through an examination of the complex totality that was Han Yü, attempts to present the case for a deeper appreciation of his full stature as a literary artist.

Han Yü's own life and personality as well as recent advances in our understanding of T'ang history have made this process more feasible than it would have been half a century ago. Han Yü is among the most personal and at the same time the most open of Chinese authors: he writes often and frankly about his own life, his feelings, his career, his friends. Accordingly, almost 95 percent of his writings can be securely dated and then read against the political history of the time.[1] The result is a remarkably clear picture of Han Yü as an active participant in the political life of his age.

This narrative is presented in chapter one, both for its own interest as biography and for its ultimate value as context for Han Yü's writings on political and social thought, which are discussed in chapter two. These then provide a larger context for Han Yü's philosophical writings discussed in chapter three; and all three chapters coalesce as context for the concluding chapter on Han Yü as man of letters. The basic framework of the book is thus an ever-widening spiral of text and context, arranged so that the explication of one text provides context for the text that follows. This sequence of text and context begins with the clear relation between political tracts and political action and concludes with the subtle, almost imperceptible relation between intellectual persuasion and literary style.

From its beginnings, the Confucian tradition has esteemed those who faithfully transmit its values: "I transmit but do not innovate" said Confucius (*Analects* VII.1). Han Yü's pivotal position in the Confucian tradition is thus the strongest measure of his success as a transmitter of these values. I have thus chosen in this study to focus on his role as a key transition figure in Confucian and in T'ang culture. More than the work of any other author, Han Yü's works mark a transition between the backward-looking first half of the T'ang—its political, social, and cultural roots in the Six Dynasties period

(265-589)—and the forward-looking latter half, in so many respects the forerunner of Sung times and of modern China. This focus owes much to the extraordinary scholarship of the late Ch'en Yin-k'o (1890-1969) on T'ang society and culture. My serious consideration of Han Yü began with a reading of his trenchant 1954 article "On Han Yü," and this book is partially an attempt to document this article's premises and develop its many seminal observations to their logical conclusions.[2]

Among the most fundamental assumptions of Ch'en Yin-k'o's "On Han Yü" was its understated realization that this task of transmission is different for each age: given the constant flux of political and social conditions, the crucial choice of what and how to transmit becomes itself a supremely innovative and creative act. Modern scholarship has partially lifted the Neo-Confucian veil over T'ang history to reveal that the T'ang was in all essentials a Buddhist state. Perhaps at no other time did the Confucian tradition come closer to extinction as a meaningful force in Chinese life. Han Yü himself lamented that "the great classics are lost beyond recovery; the great doctrines decayed beyond recognition. Only one part in a hundred remains of what once was. . . ."[3] The formidable task of transmitting Confucian values to an uncomprehending and unsympathetic age accounts for much of the martial tone in Han Yü's writings. Indeed, his son-in-law and literary executer Li Han (c.790-c.860) resorted to military metaphors to describe this struggle: "expressed as a military exploit, it was heroic and extraordinary."[4] It is necessary to remember, however, that this martial tone was the product of the age and is not itself the message of Han Yü's Confucianism.

Ch'en Yin-k'o pointed out that in this struggle Han Yü drew inspiration and example from the Ch'an school of Buddhism, which arose in the decades following the An Lu-shan rebellion (755-763) as a challenge to the state-supported Buddhist monastic schools. Although Ch'en's idea was furiously attacked at the time and continues to draw skepticism from many quarters, recent Japanese scholarship on Ch'an has vindicated his hypothesis by demonstrating the antiestablishment character of Ch'an and its many parallels to the Confucian humanist revival of the eighth and early ninth centuries.[5] Common to both Ch'an and the *"ku-wen* movement" was a drive toward a more human (and more humane) actualization of life: the urge to bring human intellectual concerns into closer contact with the actualities of daily existence. A leading scholar has written that the period after the An Lu-shan rebellion was marked by "its seriousness, its concern, even when dealing with theoretical problems, for applications to the present day—its activist (*yu-wei*) tone."[6] Ch'an and Confucian humanism share this activist, positive spirit, and both manifest a bilateral concern with similar issues.

The first and most obvious point of convergence is the supposition, common to both, that human nature is ultimately good. The idea is pervasive in the writings of the great ninth-century Ch'an master Lin-chi (d.867) and finds even earlier expression in the *Platform Sutra of the Sixth Patriarch*: "man's nature is of itself pure, but because of false thoughts True Reality is obscured."[7] This notion foreshadowed the Confucian revival of interest in the text of *Mencius* and its teaching that human nature is essentially good. A second and related tenet of both movements was that every being possessed the potential for sanctity. The *Mencius* also records the comment of a Confucian disciple on the great sage-ruler Shun: "he was a man and I am a man. Why should I be in awe of him?"[8] Less strident but identical in spirit is a story told of the Ch'an master Pai-chang Huai-hai (749-814):

> When the master was a child, he went along with his mother into a temple to pay respects to the Buddha. He pointed to the statue and asked his mother, "Who is this?" His mother said, "He is a Buddha." The boy said, "His features are the same as a man's—later on I too shall be one."[9]

A third point of similarity is the concern of both movements with the direct appeal to "mind" (*hsin*) as the basis of wisdom. "There is no Buddha but Mind; there is no Mind but Buddha.

6

. . . The Triple World is nothing more than one's mind,"
proclaimed the early Ch'an master Chiang-hsi Tao-i (709-
788), better known as Ma-tsu.[10] This appeal to mind is ultimately directed against the Chinese passion for bibliolatry and
adulation of the written word and is ultimately related to the
previous points of rapprochement between the two movements: it freed the student from the bondage of commentary
and placed the burden of wisdom directly on the individual.
Both movements accordingly manifest, each in its own way,
a humanistic and iconoclastic attitude toward scripture: the
Ch'an masters spurned the "doctors of scripture" and posited
a "special transmission outside the teaching"; the new Confucian humanists spurned the orthodox commentarial tradition of K'ung Ying-ta (574-648) and subjected the Confucian
classics to a fresh reading in light of their own concerns and
issues. Both attitudes were antiestablishment and spiritually
innovative. In chapter three, I have attempted to demonstrate
that Han Yü participated significantly in this effort to rethink
the Confucian canon. In this attempt, I have made use of the
evidence contained in the *Random Notes on the Analects (Lun
yü pi-chieh)*, a fragment of commentary attributed to Han Yü
and Li Ao (774-836), which has hitherto attracted little attention from Han Yü scholars.

The last convergence between Ch'an and Confucian humanism of the mid-T'ang is the most subtle and perhaps the
most important. Fundamental to Ch'an is the postulation of
mind (*hsin*) or nature (*hsing*) (the two being ultimately the
same) as a basic ontological first principle. This first principle
is manifested through a number of false dualities—"substance" (*t'i*) and "function" (*yung*), "reality" (*shih*) and "va-
cuity" (*hsü*), "theory" (*li*) and "action" (*hsing*)—that are simultaneously identical and nonidentical. The student who can
personally embody this first principle through direct realization of the essentially false nature of these dualities becomes
enlightened (*wu*). Having achieved this state, the student must
continue to "maintain" (*pao-jen*) by realizing that the ultimate
pseudo-reality is that between the spiritual plane (*sheng*) that
one has achieved and the mundane world (*fan*) in which one

lives like everyone else ("Shun was a man . . .").[11] The central notion here is the transcending of dualities—Paul Demiéville calls it a "dépassement des contraires."[12]

There is in Han Yü and other ku-wen authors an adulation of "Antiquity" (ku) that at times comes close to investing the concept with spiritual if not metaphysical qualities. "Antiquity" is a state of mind, what the ku-wen (literature of Antiquity) author was striving to achieve; yet it is not fundamentally different from "modernity" (chin). These two poles form yet another pseudo-duality, realization of whose falseness constitutes a kind of Confucian enlightenment. Thus the search for "Antiquity" (ku) is actually a search to understand the realities of the present (chin). As the spiritual quest in Ch'an is ultimately "this worldly," so is the quest of the Confucian humanist. We will have occasion later to examine examples of this attitude in Han Yü; but none is more vivid than his youthful description of his friend Meng Chiao (751–814):

> Master Meng is a scholar of rivers and seas;
> ancient in mien, ancient in mind.
> He has read the works of the ancients,
> and of him it can be said, "Antiquity is now."[13]

This poem, written in 792, is among Han Yü's earliest; and the notion here—no less than the actualization of Antiquity—was to be a major theme throughout his life as a thinker and man of letters.[14]

A striking feature of the Neo-Confucian outlook is its desire for all-inclusiveness, its drive to encompass all the world and its parts in a comprehensive system of thought, thus making possible the formulation of a complete agenda for human action. Earlier Confucianism seems to have lacked this urge, content to concede control over large areas of the human spiritual endeavor to Taoism and shamanism. But gradual exposure through the Six Dynasties and early T'ang to the holistic thought systems of the Buddhist schools plus the emergence of Ch'an, the first fully sinicized Buddhist school, seem to have sparked a Confucian search for a unified system that would incorporate the realms of both thought and action.[15] This book examines Han Yü as an early articulator of this Neo-Confucian unity in three spheres—political and social, philosophical, and literary.

An important political consequence of the An Lu-shan rebellion was the erosion of central power vested in the house of T'ang at Ch'ang-an and the corresponding growth of regional, often autonomous, centers of provincial authority. Specifically, the northeast provinces in modern Hopei, where Turkish ethnic and cultural influence was especially strong, maintained a fierce spirit of separatism and independence from Ch'ang-an. Ch'en Yin-k'o has emphasized that the northeast after the An Lu-shan rebellion became so culturally divergent from Ch'ang-an that this region is best considered virtually a separate state.[16] The T'ang dynasty was in effect a multiracial empire, held together by the hybrid Sino-Turkish origins of its founders and the pluralistic cultural policies of these rulers. But the fragile balance the founding generation had struck between "Chinese" or Hua and "non-Chinese" or Hu values could never have long survived. Thus, although the political and social imbalances that culminated in the An Lu-shan rebellion posed for some adherents of central power the need to reconquer the separatist provinces and reestablish the political unity of early T'ang, the deeper question was how to formulate a cultural unity from so diverse an empire once the military reconquest was complete.

Active support for Emperor Hsien-tsung (778-820; r.805-820) and for this monarch's struggles to restore T'ang political unity dominated Han Yü's political life. The rewards and recognition that came to him in 817-818 following the government's conquest of the separatist province of Huai-hsi marked the apex of his professional career as a T'ang civil servant. Yet already at the beginning of Hsien-tsung's reign, Han Yü had considered this larger, underlying question of cultural and social unity in his "Essentials of the Moral Way" (*Yüan tao*). This great treatise set out to determine which of the multifarious and conflicting spiritual, social, and intellectual elements of the T'ang empire were to be considered

9

Chinese: to form a definition of Chinese civilization for the early ninth century.

Han Yü's attempt to base these determinations on Confucian criteria and to formulate the results in Confucian terms was a radical innovation in an intellectual atmosphere dominated by Buddhist and Taoist thought.[17] Although a major concern of Han Yü's treatise was how a man can develop his own humanity to the fullest, an equally central message was that such development is possible only in a world governed by Confucian values. The vehicle for this message is the strategically placed quotation from the *Great Learning (Ta hsüeh)* section of the *Record of Rites (Li chi)*:

> In Antiquity those who wished to radiate their bright strength through the empire first brought order to their own states. To bring order to their own states, they first regulated their own households. To regulate their own households, they first cultivated their persons. To cultivate their own persons, they first set their minds in order. To set their minds in order, they first made their intentions sincere.[18]

This seemingly innocuous catenation selected from a then little studied chapter in the *Record of Rites* provided a crucial framework for the reconstitution of Confucian values: it posited the ultimate equation of thought and spiritual endeavor (the sphere of the mind, the supramundane) with action and political success (the mundane). Personal spiritual cultivation brings order to the self; this ordered self brings order to the family; ordered families bring order to the state; ordered states bring order to the empire, the world. No one link can be pursued independently of the others; to perfect one goal is to help perfect the others. Han Yü's citation of the linkage between these goals was a direct attack on monastic celibacy, both Buddhist and Taoist, and its assumption that personal cultivation can occur only apart from the mundane world. On the contrary, the new Confucian was to take the real world of political action as the arena for spiritual development: politics becomes for the Confucian the supreme expression of the inner moral life.[19]

Han Yü's actions and writings confirm his support for a radically new structuring of real political power based on these insights from the *Great Learning*. He favored a bipartite system of power, consisting of rule by a vigorous monarchy and government by a career bureaucracy. He opposed contemporary elements or groupings—the hereditary aristocracy, the eunuchs, the Buddhist and Taoist ecclesiastical establishment, and the independent military—that took power from either emperor or mandarin. Certainly, the First Emperor of Ch'in (259-210 B.C.) had evolved an earlier prototype of this bipartite system of government, and Han Yü's respect for this monarch and interest in certain "Legalist" thinkers testify to this influence on his political thinking. But the crucial linkage provided by his new emphasis on the *Great Learning* catenation, which unified the private spiritual goals of the individual mandarin and the public governmental goals of emperor and state, cloaked this old conception of power in a new humanistic and Confucian guise. The family became the model for the world; the local magistrate in his small district became the microcosm of the Son of Heaven and the empire and participated in their majesty.

> You have brought forth our Great Tranquillity
> which shall prevail without cease forever;
> for a myriad years and for eons
> you shall be father and mother to all.[20]

The rhetoric is old, but the conception is fundamentally new; for now, each mandarin who brings about his own personal tranquillity assists the Son of Heaven as "father and mother to all." To reflect is to rule, and all beneficial endeavor assumes a meaningful place in the unified polity.

It should already be apparent that Han Yü's concept of a new Confucian polity entailed an updated definition of that Confucian paragon, the *chün-tzu* or "superior man." Han Yü was an active participant in the mid-T'ang effort to reevaluate the old Confucian canon and to formulate from this material a new and more concise canon that would speak more directly to contemporary concerns. Enough evidence remains to suggest that Han Yü and Li Ao (774-836) had already conceived of the *Four Books* (the *Great Learning, Doctrine of the Mean, Analects,* and *Mencius*) as such a compact Neo-Confucian canon and that they had planned and perhaps begun a joint commentary on these texts. A major task of this exegesis was to present a new image of the Confucian Sage (*sheng-jen*), an image created by fusing the old Buddhist concept of the Sage as *bodhisattva* who progressed through ten stages to spiritual and inner perfection with the old Confucian concept of the Sage as teacher, administrator, and ultimately as sovereign. This image of the Confucian paragon was the first step in the Neo-Confucian synthesis of Buddhist metaphysics and Confucian ethics.

For Han Yü, the climax of the *Great Learning* catenation was to "make intentions sincere" (*ch'eng ch'i i*). "Sincerity" or better "integrity" describes that quality of the mind of the Sage in which there is a perfect integration of inner spiritual and outer public life. "Integrity" is the realized unity of thought and action, of theory and practice. It is the root of all inner and outer, all lesser and greater tranquillity. The Ch'an parallels to these concepts are obvious, and probably the ubiquity of such ideas in the late eighth century directed the search for passages in the traditional Confucian canon that would lend themselves to similar interpretations. Once again, the heterogeneous *Record of Rites* provided fruitful material in its section titled the *Doctrine of the Mean*, whose discourse on "integrity" comes closer to metaphysical speculation than anything else in the old canon.

> Integrity is the Way of Heaven. To attain to that integrity is the Way of human beings. The man of integrity without effort hits upon what is good and without thought perceives it; naturally and easily he embodies the Way: he is the Sage. . . .
>
> Only he possessed of the most complete integrity (*chih ch'eng*) under Heaven can develop his nature to perfection.

He who can develop his nature to perfection can perfect
the natures of other men. He who can perfect the natures
of other men can perfect the natures of all things. He
who can perfect the natures of all things can assist Heaven
and Earth in their transforming and nourishing. And he
who can assist Heaven and Earth in their transforming
and nourishing forms then with Heaven and Earth a
triad.[21]

This definition of the Sage, couched in the same rhetorical
catenations as the previous passage from the *Great Learning*,
articulates in metaphysical terms the same hierarchical progression from the individual self to world harmony and unity.
Both texts suggest the ultimate identity of the private and
public spheres of human endeavor and the ultimate unity of
theory and action. Similar passages could be found in *Mencius*,
and Han Yü quoted several times the most concise of these:
"the myriad things are complete in ourselves; and through
self-examination we are made true (*ch'eng*)."[22]

There are at least two reasons why Han Yü is better known
as a writer than as a political theorist or philosopher. First,
awareness of his achievements in these latter fields has always
remained within the domain of specialists in T'ang history
and thought. The quality and appeal of his literary work,
however, are immediately apparent to the broadly educated.
Second and more important, although Han Yü's political and
philosophical speculations represented the dynamic spirit of
a new age, other like-minded contemporaries shared similar
views. Politically and philosophically, Han Yü was in the
minority; but he was not alone. As a writer, however, Han
Yü was an original, an innovator whose unique and startling
genius created a style that attained the moral force and urgency
of the new ideas it conveyed. A goal of this book is to demonstrate first the connection between this contemporary intellectual spirit and Han Yü's literary style and second to
maintain the uniqueness of his creation in light of the contemporary literary scene.

The *ku-wen* style, as created by Han Yü, is an attempt to

manifest in words that quality of the Sage's mind described as *ch'eng* "sincere, integral." If, as was maintained above, *ku* "Antiquity" can be understood as a spiritual state roughly synonymous with *ch'eng*, then the term *ku-wen* itself defines the attempt to express this state of Confucian enlightenment. *Ku-wen* is a unified style, or better group of styles, that derives from and thus mirrors the relative perfection, "integrity," and unity of the author's mind. As that mind encounters the diverse phenomena of the mundane world, it formulates language appropriate to each occasion. In Western terms, *ku-wen* presupposes the unity of form and content and may manifest itself in a variety of diverse styles. For Han Yü, poetry as well as prose is *ku-wen*. As the mind of the Sage encompasses all things, so *ku-wen* can embrace all subjects, styles, and genres. And because *ku-wen* mirrors the mind of the Sage thinking, it acquires the Sage's authority and moral force. In other words, the writings of a man whose mind has attained to unity with the outside world express a universality that speaks to all men. In Han Yü's terms, there is a unity between *wen* (literature) and *tao* (the moral Way) whereby the quality of written works becomes a measure of the moral quality of the author's mind.[23]

This concept of *ku-wen* is a major contribution to Confucian theories of literature and stands in marked contrast to contemporary Buddhist and Ch'an notions that ultimately denied the possibility of language to articulate adequately the enlightened mind. Han Yü's bold equation of *wen* and *tao*, which is perhaps related to his philosophical equation of thought and action, constituted a dramatic lift for the status and role of literature in a Confucian society. It demanded for the writer a position on par with the administrator. Artistically valid literary expression was no longer a polite accouterment of the civil servant but rather became a basic requisite for great political success. Of course, this ideal was not actually attained until the political/literary leaders of the eleventh century— Ou-yang Hsiu, Szu-ma Kuang, Su Shih, Wang An-shih— combined these dual achievements in their own persons. But perhaps because realization of this goal was so difficult, although *ku-wen* became the standard literary voice of Neo-Confucianism, Han Yü's concept of the unity of *wen* and *tao* was abandoned. The formulation of Chou Tun-i (1017-1073) that "literature is a vehicle for the Way" (*wen i tsai tao*) signaled the separation of this unity and the subordination of *wen* to *tao*. This tendency manifested its logical conclusion in the later Neo-Confucian discomfort with literature and accordingly colored their understanding of Han Yü's concept of literary art.[24]

Finally, I would like to caution the reader that although the works of Han Yü clearly posit the case for "unity" in each of these three spheres—political, philosophical, and literary—the connections between these spheres and thus the notion of an all-encompassing "T'ang search for unity" is my own attempt to impose order on my material. I believe, however, it is an order Han Yü would find natural and compelling. Our scholarly training in the West encourages us to mark out boundaries that divide the human intellect into disciplines and subdisciplines. Our better instincts tell us this process serves no higher purpose than to foster academic posturing and to assist us in dividing our books into chapters. These instincts must be allowed free rein when the subject is an exemplar of a traditional culture that has long maintained the interrelatedness of all things and the holistic nature of human activity. If Han Yü nowhere explicitly states these interconnections, it is certainly because he held with the *Book of Changes* that "all movement under Heaven is regulated by unity."

CHAPTER ONE

The Life of
Han Yü

But we must remember, for one
thing, that we tend to think of
an Age in terms of the man
whom we take as representative
of it, and forget that equally a
part of the man's significance
may be his battle with his age.
—T. S. Eliot
"Goethe as the Sage"

I Ancestry

Fragments of an official genealogy compiled during Han Yü's
lifetime trace the origin of the Han surname to the feudal
principality of Han, which became independent when the he-
gemony of Chin was partitioned in 376 B.C. The Ch'in empire
conquered and incorporated the Han statelet into its Ying-
ch'uan prefecture in 230 B.C. The earliest Han ancestor listed
in this genealogy is Han Hsin, whom Liu Pang enfeoffed as
King of Ying-ch'uan in 202 B.C. for services rendered in the
epic struggle against Hsiang Yü. Han Hsin later defected to
the Hsiung-nu, but Han forces eventually captured and executed him in 196 B.C. His sons finally submitted to the Han

in 168 B.C. One can only surmise what Han Yü thought about Han Hsin as his official progenitor.[1]

Han Yü himself claimed descent from one Han Ch'i, a native of An-ting in Kansu, who defected in A.D. 409 from the Hunnish kingdom of Ho-lien P'o-p'o to serve Emperor Ming-yüan of the T'o-pa Wei dynasty. His son, Han Mao (d.456), caught the attention of the emperor and established the fortunes of the family when he distinguished himself in battle against the Ting-ling at age seventeen by holding his standard high in the air on a windy day. He was present at the destruction of the Hsia kingdom in 431 and was ennobled as King Huan of An-ting. The official history of the Wei dynasty recorded that Mao "was both resolute and straightforward. Although he was without literary knowledge, his opinions were rational. As a general, he excelled in providing for the populace. He was the bravest man of his time and was praised at court."[2]

Han Yü's grandfather, Han Jui-su, served as chief administrator in the government-general of Kuei-chou, where, in Han Yü's words, "he brought civilization to the South." He had four sons; Han Yü's father, Han Chung-ch'ing (d.770), was the oldest and probably entered government service through the yin or hereditary privilege available to the son of a mandarin of the fifth degree or above.[3]

Almost the only source of information about Han Yü's father is the "Inscription Commemorating the Departure of Magistrate Han of Wu-ch'ang" by the famous poet Li Po (701-762).[4] Wu-ch'ang county, part of the prefecture of O-chou situated at the confluence of the Yangtse and the Han rivers in modern Hupei province, had rich deposits of iron, silver, and copper ores, which were used to mint coins. In addition to being the site of a major mint, O-chou was also the collection point for tax revenues from the South destined for Ch'ang-an via the Han River valley. Han Chung-ch'ing had apparently just been appointed magistrate of Wu-ch'ang when the An Lu-shan rebellion broke out on December 16, 755. The fighting soon closed the Pien Canal, the main transportation link to the South, and the Han valley route via O-

chou became crucial to the government's continued access to
its southern revenues. To further complicate matters, refugees
from the North tripled the population of the O-chou area by
757.⁵

Under these difficult circumstances, Han Chung-ch'ing
eliminated corruption and improved the organization of the
Wu-ch'ang minting operations, forwarding the increased output to the beleaguered government-in-exile northwest of
Ch'ang-an. In recognition of these services, the Prime Minister Ts'ui Huan (730-791) recommended him for a special
citation and transferred him to the magistracy of P'o-yang
county in Jao-chou, also the location of a government mint.

Li Po ascribes to Han Chung-ch'ing that fragile combination of severity and compassion so cultivated by the civil
servants of traditional China. "When he arrived to begin his
appointment as magistrate of Wu-ch'ang, before he descended
from his carriage, the people feared him; but as soon as he
had descended, they liked him. His kindness was like a spring
breeze, and in three months there were major reforms. The
rapacious officials were held at bay, and the powerful families
eyed him askance."

There is some evidence that Han Chung-ch'ing also had
literary inclinations. According to a legend current in later
times, the famous poet Ts'ao Chih (d.232) once appeared to
Han in a dream and requested that he write a preface for
Ts'ao's collected works. Although neither this preface nor
any of Han Chung-ch'ing's other writings survive, the father
of Han Yü finished his career as a secretary in the imperial
library, obviously a post requiring some literary ability.⁶

It is worthwhile noting that several features of Han Yü's
ancestry probably influenced his thinking on social, cultural,
and literary matters. First, there is the question of race. Eth-
nically, the T'ang was easily the most heterogeneous state in
China before the Yüan (1260-1368), and, as we shall see, much
of Han Yü's political and social thought attempted to establish
a cultural unity in the face of this ethnic diversity. It is thus
useful to remember that Han Yü was not descended, as were
many of his contemporaries such as Yüan Chen (779-831),

from the non-Chinese, mainly Turkish, settlers of northern China. Han Yü's lineage was Chinese, dating as fact from the early fifth century and as legend through a founder of the Han dynasty back to the mythical beginnings of Chinese civilization itself. Second and just as important, Han Yü's forefathers were northerners, and northern traditions of classical commentary and literary expression played an important part in the revitalization of latter eighth-century T'ang letters. We should also note the military origins of Han Yü's lineage. Throughout his life, Han Yü worked with the professional military in a variety of capacities and prided himself as a military strategist. This pride was apparently not unfounded: he was entrusted late in his career with a number of sensitive missions demanding a considerable understanding of late T'ang politico-military realities.

Finally, Han Yü's entire background, his ancestry and early life, identify him as a member of a *chün-wang* or "locally prominent clan." Although these clans were not among the elite aristocracy of the T'ang, they were part of a "much larger and more fluid group of lineages whose . . . social and political influence was essentially provincial rather than national."[7]

The provincial base of Han Yü's family was located in the area directly north and east of Lo-yang. The family owned land on both sides of the Yellow River, and its ancestral tombs were located on the northern bank of the river, slightly over three miles west of the modern city of Meng-hsien in the Huai-ch'ing district of Honan province. In the T'ang, this area was Ho-yang county, under the jurisdiction of the prefectural authorities at Lo-yang.[8] The northern bank of the river around Ho-yang was a frequent battleground during the T'ang due to its strategic location on the northern approaches to Lo-yang. More than once, invasion forces from the separatist provinces in the northeast attempted to cross the Yellow River via the famous Ho-yang Bridge and capture Lo-yang. In the summer of 756 the great general Kuo Tzu-i made a desperate defense of the city here, and the old woman in Tu Fu's "Recruiting Officer at Shih-hao" offered to go herself to "answer the urgent call from Ho-yang."[9] To prevent a repeat of this tragedy, the special military district of Ho-yang san-ch'eng was created in 781. Its military governor used the tax revenues of Ho-yang and neighboring counties for the support of a standing army in the area, although the prefect of Honan in Lo-yang still handled civil matters.

2 Early Life

Han Yü was born in 768, probably in the eastern capital of Lo-yang where his father seems to have had a house either in the city or on the family's lands to the northeast.[10] A poem written in 807 relates that on the evening of his birth the moon was in the constellation of Sagittarius. According to T'ang astrological lore, people born on this day were fated to suffer unduly during their lifetime from slander and calumny.[11]

Two months after his birth, Han Yü's mother died. When his father died two years later in 770, the orphan was taken in by his older brother Han Hui (739-780?), then aged about thirty, and his wife, nee Cheng (d.794). Since Han Hui was in mourning for his father, the next several years were probably spent at home in Lo-yang. Han Yü described these early years and the importance of his sister-in-law:

> My birth was not auspicious. I was orphaned at two and raised by my older brother. But it was actually my sister-in-law's kindness that rescued me from death to life. Before I was seven, my brother received a government post, so we left Lo-yang to live in Ch'ang-an. When I was cold she clothed me, when I was hungry she nourished me, so that neither illness nor misfortune befell me.[12]

Since most knowledgeable scholars agree Han Hui and his uncle Han Yün-ch'ing exerted a strong personal influence on Han Yü's early intellectual and literary development, it is important to understand as much as possible about their backgrounds and thinking.[13]

Five works by Han Yün-ch'ing survive, all of them stele inscriptions dating between 761 and 777. Writing in 759-760, Li Po already mentioned Han Yün-ch'ing's renown as a man of letters. There is little doubt this renown was the beginning of the Han family's literary reputation. Han Yü himself wrote:

> My uncle's writings were esteemed at court during the Ta-li period (766-780). All who wanted to engrave the merits of their ancestors so as to have them believed by later generations repaired to the Han family.[14]

In the wake of the An Lu-shan rebellion, most of the Han family seems to have fled its northern homestead along with many other intellectuals of the time and taken refuge in the region south of Yang-chou. Some, like Han Shen-ch'ing, another of Han Yü's uncles, found local employment.[15] But others like Han Hui seem to have used the forced leisure to develop intellectual and potentially useful political contacts. Typical was the group known as the "Four K'uei" active about 765 in Shang-yüan county of Sheng-chou (modern Nanking):

> Ts'ui Tsao, Han Hui, Lu Tung-mei, and Chang Cheng-ts'e were friends, all living temporarily in Shang-yüan. They liked to discuss plans for managing the world and allowed that they themselves could serve as ministers to princes. Their contemporaries called them the "Four K'uei."[16]

K'uei was the legendary director of music whom the sage-emperor Yao entrusted with the task of educating his "descendent sons" through the use of poetry.[17] Thus when another text claims that Han Hui's prowess at "singing" made him the leader of this group, this implies that he was capable not only of serving as a minister but also of fulfilling the ancient ideal of making literature an instrument of political reform.[18] This ideal is also implied in Han Yü's own statement that Han Hui's "virtue, his actions, and his words were models for the age."[19]

More difficult to gauge is the extent of the Han family's

relations with other leading literary figures of the period. One of Han Yü's own poems shows that in his youth he knew Hsiao Ts'un, son of Hsiao Ying-shih.[20] Han Yü also had a much deeper acquaintance in his early Ch'ang-an days with Li Kuan (766-794), son of Li Hua.[21] But, given the lack of contemporary evidence, there is no way to substantiate the contacts the Sung sources allege between Han Hui and Han Yün-ch'ing on the one hand and Li Hua, Hsiao Ying-shih, Tu-ki Chi, and Liang Su on the other.[22]

The "Four K'uei" caught the attention of Li Hsi-chün who early in 768 was appointed regional inspector of Che-hsi with headquarters at Jun-chou. Li entered the Censorate in 771 and recommended Ts'ui Tsao (737-787), who later indeed became prime minister. In 774, the mourning period for his father now completed, Han Hui was appointed diarist of activity and repose, probably also on the recommendation of Li Hsi-chün.[23] There is no question that during these years in Ch'ang-an Han Hui belonged to the faction surrounding the powerful prime minister Yüan Tsai (d.777), the dominant figure at court during the reign of Emperor Tai-tsung (r.763-779). Unfortunately, the historical sources are so biased against Yüan Tsai it is difficult to form an accurate assessment of his policies. It is certain, however, that strong dictatorial control over the central bureaucracy and open patronage of Buddhism were central to his administration.[24] Han Hui's participation in this faction embarrassed the Sung historians and is probably why they excluded him from the *New T'ang History*. When Yüan Tsai fell from power in the spring of 777, Han Hui was exiled with the rest of the Yüan party.[25]

Han Yü was eleven when his brother arrived to assume his post as prefect of Shao-chou. He had begun to read and memorize the classics at the age of six when his family first moved to Ch'ang-an, and even then "he was fond of study and could compose orally."[26] It was during these several years in Shao-chou that the young scholar began to compose serious compositions and to participate in adult literati society. It is certainly significant that Han Yü spent this important period of intellectual puberty at Shao-chou, the legendary site of the preaching of the *Platform Sutra* by the sixth Ch'an patriarch Hui-neng and a major Ch'an center in later years.[27]

Han Hui died in late 780 or early 781, and his widow, now in charge of the family, undertook the arduous journey north to bury her husband in the ancestral cemetery at Ho-yang. This task completed, Madame Cheng apparently hoped to settle on the Han lands east of Lo-yang. The outbreak of hostilities between the court and the separatist provinces of the northeast, however, forced her to abandon this plan. Once again, the Han family headed south of the Yangtse, this time to an estate in Hsüan-ch'eng county of Hsüan-chou, probably acquired by Han Chung-ch'ing or Han Hui following the An Lu-shan rebellion.[28]

The next four or five years were probably among the most tranquil of Han Yü's life. While warfare raged across the northern plains he lived in the secluded security of the Anhwei countryside and concentrated exclusively on his studies. He later wrote of these years that "carrying forth the work of my forefathers, I knew not the burden of weapons or plowshares, but I read and I wrote."[29] And so it continued, year after quiet year until Han Yü was eighteen and ready to leave for the capital in pursuit of an official degree. In 786 the prospects for such a move probably looked bright. The central government had come to terms with the separatists, and Ts'ui Tsao, Han Hui's old friend from the "Four K'uei," had indeed become a prime minister. And Han Yü was ready, too. The period of adolescent memorization and preparation was over; the search for meaning and the hard road toward intellectual and literary maturity were about to begin. But large parts of what was later to become a program for reform of the national letters had already taken shape in Han Yü's mind, or so some scholars conclude from the following enigmatic lines from the "*Fu* on Renewing my Purpose," composed over ten years later in 797:

> Because there were troubles on the central plains,
> we went south of the River to live,
> and there I began solely to focus on study,

putting my mind only to the precepts of the ancients.
I spied the traces these former spirits had left behind
and rose high and alone to search out their depths.
When once I saw my road, I pulled swiftly ahead,
never realizing I lacked the strength.
Probing the raiment of the ancients,
lamenting the dull garb of the moderns,
suddenly I forgot my lack of worth
and thought I could pick from the highest posts:
brightest are those who know themselves
and so the reason for my own delusions.
A good day chosen, I headed west
and in time arrived at the capital city.[30]

3   The Examinations

The Ch'ang-an that Han Yü saw in 786 was certainly much
changed from the city he had left as a boy almost ten years
earlier. Although the court had returned in the summer of
784 after a year in exile, the last of the separatist rebellions
lingered on until May of 786, and Han Yü probably did not
arrive in the city until late summer or autumn. By his own
estimate, about a million people lived in Ch'ang-an, but it
seems there was no one to whom he looked for assistance or
companionship. Han Yü probably knew few people. Ts'ui
Tsao and his reform party, a distant connection at best, had
fallen from power by the end of the year. But as Han Yü later
admitted, his own arrogance was mainly responsible for his
isolation:

> The first year I lived in the capital, I did not go even
> once to the doors of the highly-placed. I disdained what
> others rushed toward. If someone got along with me,
> then I associated with him; but if not, then even though
> he visited my lodgings, I would not even sit with him.[31]

A poem written during this first year in the capital suggests
the reason for his arrogance was the eighteen-year-old's confidence in his literary training and ability:

OUT PAST THE DOOR

Ch'ang-an has a million people,
but past my door there's nowhere to go.
It's not that I like the seclusion,
it's actually the world that's at odds with me.

The ancients are long dead, but
written in books are the words they left.
I open my scrolls, then read and think—
like meeting through a thousand years of time.

Past the door, for each there's a way,
my way is not easy just now,
but if I rest here awhile,
fortune cannot betray me.[32]

The poem shows a bookish young man aware of the power of literary scholarship to ward off loneliness and also confident that the "way" of literature—"way" here means both commitment to an intellectual way of life and the road or path of one's career—will ultimately lead to success and renown.

Han Yü had scarcely begun his quest for success at the civil service examinations when events on the distant Sino-Tibetan border culminated in a personal tragedy that profoundly altered his life. As a consequence of the Sino-Tibetan treaty of 783, Tibetan forces had joined Chinese government troops under General Hun Chen (736-799) and inflicted a decisive defeat on separatist armies at Wu-kung on March 3, 784. In return for their services, the Tibetans were promised large territorial concessions, but Emperor Te-tsung reneged on these promises, and hostilities resumed in late 786. At this point, the Tibetan master strategist Żan Rgyal-bcan (d.796) devised a plan to capture or destroy the careers of the three leading Chinese commanders guarding the Tibetan frontier: Hun Chen, military governor of Ho-chung; Li Sheng (727-793), military governor of Feng-hsiang; and Ma Sui (726-795), military governor of Ho-tung. Taking advantage of the jealousies among these commanders and spreading disinformation among them through their own spies, Rgyal-bcan first invaded the territory of Li Sheng but then withdrew without plundering the area. The court suspected Li Sheng of collaboration, and he was removed from his post in early 787. At the same time, Rgyal-bcan bribed Ma Sui to intercede at court for the Tibetans. Accordingly, Ma Sui, who seems genuinely to have believed the Tibetan desire for peace, arrived in Ch'ang-an in the spring of 787 with the Tibetan ambassador to request a renewal of the 783 treaty. Based on Ma Sui's assurances of Tibetan good faith, Te-tsung agreed to renew the treaty at P'ing-liang outside Ching-chou on June 5, 787. Hun Chen was to lead the Chinese delegation. His secretary was Han Yen (753-787?), second son of Han Yün-ch'ing and cousin of Han Yü.

The Tibetans planned first to ambush and capture Hun Chen and thereby to discredit Ma Sui and destroy his influence at court. The plan almost succeeded. Hun Chen alone managed to collar a strong horse and fled the ambush galloping away bareback through volleys of Tibetan arrows. But sixty top-ranking members of his party were captured and held for ransom, and renegade Tibetan soldiers killed several of Hun Chen's retinue. This debacle shocked the nation and aroused the emperor's sympathies for the families of the captured and the slain, on whose sons he conferred mandarin ranks. The fate of Han Yen was unknown for a number of years. He was not among those released by the Tibetans and by the early 790s seems to have been presumed dead.[33] Since he left only a sixteen-year-old wife and seven-month-old daughter, his majesty's largesse did not profit the Han family.[34] Han Yen had obtained the *chin-shih* degree in 783, the first of the Hans to do so.[35] His tragic disappearance deprived the clan of its most promising leader and deprived Han Yü at a critical juncture in his life of yet another family mentor.

Ma Sui retained his court positions but was relieved of field command and forced into semi-retirement. Perhaps guilt over the fate of Han Yen, for which he was indirectly responsible, combined with sympathy for his unfortunate cousin prompted Ma Sui to help Han Yü:

> Long ago, when I had just come of age (nineteen), I
> was in the capital to sit for the *chin-shih* examinations. I

was poor and unable to support myself. Because his youngest son was my friend, I did obeisance before the horse of the Prince of Pei-p'ing (Ma Sui). He listened and commiserated with me, and so I was received at his mansion in the An-i ward. The prince was distressed at my poverty and gave me food and clothing. He sent for his two sons and ordered them to treat me as a guest. . . . He was like a towering mountain, a deep forest, a great valley, like a dragon or tiger whose permutations cannot be fathomed—a man of outstanding stature.[36]

Ma Sui was among the richest men of his day, and if Han Yü indeed lived permanently or intermittently during his Ch'ang-an years at the Ma mansion, he lived among the most opulent surroundings in the empire.[37]

Late in 786 Han Yü took and passed the provincial examination, perhaps in his native Lo-yang but probably in Ch'ang-an. He was thus qualified to sit for the metropolitan *chin-shih* examinations of 788.[38] The examiner was the Vice-President of the Ministry of Rites Liu T'ai-chen, who had once been a student of Hsiao Ying-shih. Thirty-one candidates passed, but Han Yü was not among them. The following year, Han Yü again sat for the examination, Liu T'ai-chen was again the examiner, and again Han Yü failed. Among those who passed this year was P'ei Tu (765-839), Han Yü's great patron of later years. When the results were announced in the spring of 789 it was determined that Liu, a timid and cowardly man, had allowed his subordinates to give special consideration to relatives of the powerful prime ministers and provincial governors. Liu was demoted to governor of Hsin-chou in April 789 and died shortly thereafter.[39]

The experience was certainly unsettling for Han Yü who decided to forego the 790 examinations and return to Hsüan-ch'eng. He paused at P'u-chou on the bend of the Yellow River long enough to deliver an encomium for Hun Chen, Han Yen's former superior, now military governor of Ho-chung. From an inn at Cheng-chou at the head of the Pien Canal he sent a flattering cover letter and fifteen of his compositions to the famous geographer Chia Tan (730-805), governor of Hua-chou and the I-ch'eng military district.[40] The young scholar, now certainly much less arrogant than when he first arrived in the capital three years ago, was attempting to strengthen old contacts and forge new ones among the nation's military governors. These men, the holders of actual provincial power in late eighth-century China, recruited their staffs from the large pool of hopeful and even recently successful candidates. The young scholars provided the governors with expert administrative and clerical services and added a literary and metropolitan aura to the otherwise military provinciality of these "minor courts." The governors, in turn, were often former or soon-to-be prime ministers. Following his patron's fortunes, the provincial secretary of today might well find himself an important Ch'ang-an post tomorrow, or as in the case of Han Yü's cousin, a violent death on a far frontier.

Even under the best of circumstances, passing the *chin-shih* examinations in the mid-T'ang required the candidate to combine his literary ability with a personal connection to the examiners. Han Yü had been unable to affect this combination in 788 or 789 when the pusillanimous Liu T'ai-chen administered the examinations. Late in 790 he returned to Ch'ang-an to register for the 791 examinations but was apparently unable to develop a connection to the chief examiner Tu Huang-shang (737-808), a "representative of the mainstream of conventional statecraft," and he failed again.[41] In 792 the situation was different. The chief examiner was the famous finance specialist Lu Chih (754-805), officially assisted by Liang Su and Wang Ch'u. A description of the 792 examination preserved in the *Collection of Essential T'ang Documents (T'ang hui-yao)* emphasizes this delicate relationship between ability and influence:

> In 791 the Vice-President of the Ministry of War Lu Chih was appointed acting chief examiner. At that time, Ts'ui Yüan-han and Liang Su were preeminent in literary talent. Lu Chih put faith in Liang Su who, together with Ts'ui Yüan-han, recommended scholars with real ability.

When the results were announced, many were dissatis-
fied. But of the top fourteen or fifteen who passed, over
ten held important posts within several years.[42]

The mention of Ts'ui Yüan-han is significant. Ts'ui had served
as Ma Sui's secretary in the 780s and was involved in Han
Yü's fortunes at the 793 Placing Examination the following
year. Han Yü's own account of his 792 *chin-shih* success is
best read in the light of the *T'ang hui-yao* text:

> When the Prime Minister Lu Chih supervised the ex-
> aminations, he examined the papers very carefully. I was
> fortunate at that time to be among the successful can-
> didates but did not realize how well Lu had chosen. Sev-
> eral years later those who had passed with me all made
> names for themselves, and the reason was because Liang
> Su and Wang Ch'u had assisted Lu. Liang recommended
> eight candidates, and all passed. The rest Wang arranged.
> That Minister Lu examined the papers carefully, that he
> relied on and trusted Liang and Wang, and that their
> recommendations were so appropriate—all this has con-
> tinued to be lauded to this day.[43]

The Ts'ui Yüan-han connection is important because it
counters the implication, found as early as Han Yü's biography in the *Old T'ang History*, that Liang Su's recommendation of Han Yü in the 792 examinations was an affirmation
of Han Yü's literary principles and a furthering of the "*ku-
wen* movement." No contemporary T'ang text admits of such
an interpretation. Han Yü's own "*Fu* on Clear Water" written
for the 792 *chin-shih* is hardly *ku-wen* and was excluded from
his collected works.

Receipt of the *chin-shih* degree conferred mandarin rank of
the ninth degree but no actual position. To obtain employment, the *chin-shih* could wait for assignment through the
Ministry of Personnel, a process that could take up to ten
years, or he could pass another examination on "vast erudition
and grand composition" (*po-hsüeh hung-tz'u*).[44] Han Yü sat
for his examination in 793, 794, and 795. In 793 Ts'ui Yüan-

han again recommended him and Han Yü was among three passing candidates from a field of thirty-two. A prime minister, however, removed his name from the list, probably as a consequence of the political infighting between Han's official patron Lu Chih and P'ei Yen-ling (728–796).[45]

During these years Han Yü was often on the move, searching for a position or attending to family matters. In the summer of 793 he traveled to Feng-hsiang, headquarters of the military district defending the western approaches to Ch'ang-an, to seek employment from the military governor Hsing Chün-ya (728–798). He blatantly advertised his literary services:

> I have observed that your excellency's achievements are insufficiently recorded on bamboo and silk, that your excellency's manner is insufficiently praised on metal and stone. I am a scholar of humble origin. At six, I could read; at twelve, compose. I received my *chin-shih* at twenty-four and became known for my literary ability. I have been attentive to the lessons of the past and most concerned about the events of the present.[46]

The general was apparently not interested in having Han Yü preserve his exploits for posterity, and nothing came of the trip. In the late spring of 794 Han Yü returned to Ho-yang to observe the annual ritual cleaning of the ancestral tombs and to bury his recently deceased Aunt Cheng, wife of Han Hui.

After his third failure to pass the *po-hsüeh hung-tz'u*, Han Yü did an extraordinary thing. On February 21, 795 he wrote directly to the prime ministers and asked for employment. The letter begins with a meditation on the text "when the ruler develops and nourishes men of talent, then all under heaven rejoice and are glad," which is the traditional Mao interpretation of *Book of Poetry* ode 176 "Fair, Fair the Artemisia." Skillful quotations from *Mencius* and the *Book of Documents* implicitly introduce the notion that the minister who fails to discharge this duty to nurture talent in public service does not, according to the Confucian concept of the "rectification of names," qualify to serve as minister. After a brief account of his own background, his dismal record at the examinations, and his present plight, Han Yü again emphasizes that the prime ministers are personally accountable for each member of the state. Fusing quotations from the *Book of Documents* and from *Mencius*, he alludes to the sage-minister Yi Yin: "if even a single person did not find his desire, it was as if he himself had pushed him into the gutter." He argues that one should return to the ancient practice of "self-presentation" (*tzu-chin*) whereby dispensers and seekers of office entered into direct contact: "those seeking men and those seeking office see one another and actually have the same goal." He notes "His Majesty has lamented that scholars have secluded themselves in the mountains and forests and has often ordered his officials to search between the four seas for them." The Ministry of Personnel and the examination system separate these two groups:

> There one is examined in the literature of embroidered silk and carved and polished jade, tested in the correctness of his tonal patterns and the length of his phrases. The one who succeeds in these standards may then join the ranks of petty officials. Although he may have a plan to transform the masses or a stratagem to pacify the borders, if he does not follow these standards, he has little chance of passing—not one in ten thousand.

And finally comes the plea:

> Now if it were known that one had written to the prime ministers seeking a position, that they were not outraged but instead recommended him to the Son of Heaven, conferred a charge upon him, and published his letter, then those scholars exhausted and dejected but eminent and learned would certainly be moved and excited and would tie their official hats high and hurry to come forward.

Perhaps fearing just such a result, the ministers declined Han Yü's gambit. Two later letters of March 11 and April 8 also

went unanswered.[47] Han Yü had gambled and lost. Although
traditional scholars have rightly remarked that these letters
betray a political naiveté, they also contain a strong element
of coercion. Han Yü indirectly charged the ministers with
shirking their duty to the emperor, to the state, and to the
people. The letters placed Han Yü in open conflict with the
government. If they had resulted in a position, it would have
been a political and social *tour de force*. When they did not,
Han Yü could do little but depart with as much grace as he
could still muster. And so he left the capital on May 24, 795,
heading for the homestead at Ho-yang where he spent the
summer.[48]

Han Yü expressed the psychological tensions of these
months and his enormous sense of frustration in the following
composition, the first great poem of his life:

OCCASIONAL POEM

Ancient annals strewn left and right,
Poetry and *History* placed front and back,
How do I differ from a bookworm,
From birth to death encased in words?
The ancient way dulls and stultifies
Ancient words cage and fetter.
Modern times differ indeed from antiquity,
Who today can share such pleasures?

Hand in hand along with Master No Speech
We mount together the K'un-lun peaks.
Distant winds flapping lapels and hems
We rise and soar the lofty vault.
Below we sight the nine domains of Yü—
A dust speck held on a brush tip.
We tour in delight just a while—
Eons of years elapse below.

The loud disputants of yesterday—
A myriad grave mounds weight their skulls.
Sad the perverse clutch to opinion,

They could not separate white from black!
My indignation cries out in anguish
Tears surge like the Nine Rivers.
With faultfinders mutually accusing, slurring,
Even to return today, who would befriend me?
Nimbly gliding we drop to the Great Expanse
Hair flying, galloping on unicorns.[49]

The poem is better read as a record of the poet's own exhaustion than as an attack on his political tormentors, although both motifs are present and reinforce each other. The first eight lines delineate the poet's circumstances in terms of two related yet unresolved conflicts. As a bookworm eats the pages of books to live and yet begins and ends his life a prisoner "encased in words," so the poet is bound to books for his life sustenance. Also in conflict is the goal of an ideal antiquity and its pedantic and lifeless exposition in official commentary. It is the "ancient way" in both senses—the difficulty of transforming the essence of the classics themselves into a living reality and the drudgery of mastering the exegesis required by the examinations—that "dulls and stultifies." Antiquity and its study should not be dead scholastic exercises but rather must be shaped into vital entities that exert a positive force on contemporary life. The poet of these lines has articulated such a vision but has exhausted himself trying to achieve it. More than one commentator has seen here a parallel to the despair of Goethe's protagonist in the opening scene of *Faust*.

The two remaining sections of the poem also present a contrast. Master No Speech (*wu-yen tzu*) personifies silence, that quiet lack of assertion behind genuine understanding, and represents the essence of the classics of antiquity. The term itself is a Han Yü coinage, but the heart of the term, "no speech" (*wu-yen*), can be traced to Confucian, Taoist, or Buddhist texts.[50] This intentional ambiguity of reference reinforces the catholic progression of allusions in the following lines. "The nine domains of Yü" is Confucian, the "dust speck held on a brush tip" is Buddhist, the next couplet is Taoist. As space and time are relative when viewed from the vantage point of true wisdom, so the true scholar with a command of literature and Antiquity is above space, time, and partisanship.

This partisanship is the subject of the closing section. "Loud disputants" attempts to translate *k'ua-to tzu*, another Han Yü coinage parallel to *wu-yen tzu*, meaning literally "those who demonstrate and refute." This refers to scholars of the distant and recent past who insist loudly on their own interpretation of minutiae but cannot "separate white from black," distinguish what is trivial from what is important in the tradition.[51] The poet has fled in indignation from such people and to return now would be unthinkable. They were there "yesterday," and "even to return today, who would befriend me?" he asks, rhetorically echoing Ch'ü Yüan's conclusion of the *Li sao*: "Enough! There are no true men in the state: no one to understand me."

The final couplet accentuates the iconoclastic sentiment of the whole poem. The poet and his guide Master No Speech gallop on unicorns to the Great Expanse, the mythical mountains where the sun and the moon set. The sense of despair and isolation is complete. But it was also to be temporary. Whatever the attractions of the ancient Taoist or T'ang Ch'an notions of "silence," Han Yü was to be "from birth to death encased in words."

4 "On Duty"

In the autumn of 795 Han Yü left Ho-yang for Lo-yang where he spent the winter. Sometime following the receipt of his *chin-shih*, Han Yü married. His wife was the daughter of one Lu I, a member of the socially prominent Lu clan of Fan-yang. Lu I was established in Lo-yang where he was on the staff of the prefect of Honan.[52] Han Yü's marriage into this aristocratic family was probably arranged by Ma Sui, whose son, Ma Ch'ang (762-812) had taken a wife from the same clan. Han Yü remarked in his epitaph for Ma Ch'ang's wife that the girls of the Lu clan were noted for their proper upbringing, education, and affability. One is tempted to read these lines as a description of Han Yü's own wife.[53]

On April 28, 796 the ex-Prime Minister Tung Chin (724-799) was appointed viceroy of the eastern capital at Lo-yang. Now over seventy, Tung Chin was one of the great lords of the empire. As a young scholar, he distinguished himself at the exile court of Emperor Su-tsung in 756 and was appointed to the Han-lin Academy. He served long years in the provinces, had firsthand experience of foreign affairs, and was prime minister from 789 to 793. It is not certain if he knew Han Yü before arriving in Lo-yang or whether he met him there. At any rate, on August 13 when Tung Chin was appointed prefect of Pien-chou, military governor of the Hsüan-wu district, and regional inspector of the prefectures of Pien, Sung, Po, Ying, and so forth, he gave Han Yü his first job. The position was that of "judge" (*t'ui-kuan*) attached to the office of the regional inspector. Since this position did not require mandarin rank (*p'in*), which Han Yü already had as a *chin-shih*, he was concomitantly appointed a collator of texts in the imperial library and given the lowest possible rank, ninth degree fourth class.

Pien-chou, headquarters of the Hsüan-wu military district, was the most important provincial city in the east, where it defended the Pien Canal, the government's major transportation link to the Yangtse delta area. Because of this strategic importance, the garrisons at Pien-chou had been increased to 100,000 troops during the 780s. Maintaining control over these haughty and potentially rebellious soldiers and ensuring their loyalty to the central government demanded from the commander delicate mixtures of discipline and looseness, impartiality and tolerance, grandeur and comradery. Failure to achieve the proper balance in rapidly changing circumstances could result in mutiny and violent death. As a result, transitions of such governorships were fraught with political and personal tensions. Rather than risking a mutiny, the central government often allowed the troops to choose their own commander in return for a guarantee of good behavior. Such arrangements had been sanctioned in the Hsüan-wu district in 792 and 793, and the government was now anxious to restore direct control over this vital command.

In the summer of 796, the then military governor suffered a stroke, and a struggle over the succession ensued between his son and a subordinate general, Teng Wei-kung. The local eunuch supervisors and the general imprisoned the son, and Tung Chin was appointed governor. But the following day, the old governor died, and Teng Wei-kung proclaimed himself governor. It was urgent that Tung Chin hurry to Pien-chou and assume control before Teng Wei-kung could solidify his authority over the troops. Tung Chin rushed to Cheng-chou, about fifty miles east of Pien-chou, with only a small unarmed staff that included Han Yü. When no one arrived from Pien-chou to welcome the new governor, Tung was urged to remain in Cheng-chou and await developments. But he pushed to within three miles of Pien-chou and made camp. The next day Teng Wei-kung and the other generals, caught off guard by Tung's haste, were forced to ride out and receive his party. Tung did not require the recalcitrant general to dismount his horse but treated him affably and allowed him to retain his command. This largess won Tung Chin the admiration of the troops.[54]

These dramatic events must have staggered the twenty-eight-year-old "judge" on his first assignment. Severe depression over his joblessness followed by the tensions of assuming duties at Pien-chou probably best explain why 796 is the only year of Han Yü's adult life from which there are no datable writings. A month later the rest of Tung Chin's staff arrived, headed by Lu Ch'ang-yüan (d. 799), a punctilious administrator whom the court had sent to assist the aging and permissive governor. Among Han Yü's duties in Pien-chou was the supervision of the provincial examinations each autumn. This position made him a man of importance in local literati circles and together with his own innovative and unorthodox ideas about literature began to attract like-minded scholars of all ages to the Pien-chou garrison. The first to arrive was a man in his early twenties named Li Ao (774-836), who came from neighboring Hsü-chou late in 796 to "study" with Han Yü.[55]

Next year Meng Chiao (751–814), who had just passed his *chin-shih*, arrived to stay with Lu Ch'ang-yüan, whom he had met on a trip south in 793. Han Yü and Meng Chiao had known each other at least since 792 and had developed a close literary and personal relationship.[56] Finally, in the winter of 797 Chang Chi (766–829?) came to Pien-chou to study with Han Yü and to take the provincial examinations there. Han Yü passed one of his best "students" and his severest critics in 798, and the following year Chang Chi obtained the *chin-shih* in Ch'ang-an.[57]

Although evidence indicates that the dearth of writings from Han Yü's two and a half years at Pien-chou was intentional, there is no doubt the intellectual stimulus of this literary coterie afforded him several of the most fruitful years of his intellectual life. During a brief illness in the autumn of 797, he composed the "*Fu* on Renewing My Purpose," which articulated his intention to recover from his earlier depressions. The 798 correspondence with Chang Chi reveals a man once again engaged in intense debate on the important intellectual and literary questions of the day. In the "Letter to Feng Su Discussing Literature" written in 798, Han Yü describes how his innovative writings affected his contemporaries. The sense of isolation and frustration is still present and perhaps explains his diminished output during this period, but the overall tenor of the letter reveals a man convinced he is on the right track:

> The "*Fu* on the First Oracle" you have shown me is indeed interesting. If you merely use a little effort the Ancients can be attained without difficulty. But I do not know how something that looks exactly like the Ancients will be accepted by the moderns.
>
> I have been writing for a long time. Whenever I think in my own mind that a piece is well done, others think it's bad. If I am only slightly content with a piece, then others will think it only slightly outlandish. But if I am really content with a piece, then others will think it really outlandish.

Often I have been forced to write in the current style, and from the moment I began it was embarrassing; but when I showed such works to people, they thought they were good. When I was only slightly embarrassed, they would praise the work only slightly. But when I was really embarrassed, they would really praise it.

I do not know if *ku-wen* will ever actually be used in our times. I am simply waiting for those who know to find out. When Yang Hsiung wrote the *Great Mystery*, people laughed at him. But he said, "That my age does not know me causes me no harm. In later ages there will again be a Yang Hsiung, and he will praise it." It's a pity that a thousand years after his death there is still no Yang Hsiung.

From this it is clear that writers do not beg people to know them; they wait without doubting a hundred generations for a sage. . . .

Li Ao is now studying composition with me. He's not bad; but he has financial and family problems and has not been able to finish his studies. A certain Chang Chi, who is older than Li Ao, is also here studying with me, and his writing is about the same. If he works for another year or two, he should succeed.[58]

Almost the only poem from these years, aside from some obligatory social verse, is "Drunk, Detaining Tung-yeh," probably written to see off Meng Chiao when he departed Pien-chou in late 798. It is "outlandish" even by today's standards:

Ever since I read long ago the poems of Li Po and Tu Fu
I've always regretted that those two couldn't be together.
You and I were born in the same age
yet we're treading in their tracks again.

You don't have a job
    a white head vaunting dotage
I'm a little smarter
    but I'm ashamed
to be a green vine leaning on a tall pine.

I lower my head and I bow to you
wanting to be forever like hand and glove,
but you won't even turn your head—
like a blade of straw beating a great bell.

I want my body to be a cloud
and you to turn into a dragon
and all around and up and down
    I'll chase you
so although we part here
    yet shall we meet.

The sentiments of the poem are so direct they almost shock. The structure is also unusual—a mixture of five-, seven-, and nine-word lines with a fluid rhythm and elements of colloquial diction. Although a good example of the seemingly light-hearted experiments that drew criticism from Chang Chi and P'ei Tu about this time, this poem illustrates a fundamental characteristic of Han Yü's poetry: as the nineteenth-century critic Chang Hung remarked, "its conception and its diction are both unusual (*ch'i*). In poetry and in prose, his style proceeds from the same principles."[59]

The lighthearted experiments came to a rapid halt on March 13, 799 when Governor Tung Chin died. His subordinate Lu Ch'ang-yüan assumed temporary command. But Lu was an arrogant literatus and openly disdained the military. His subordinate, Meng Shu-tu, in addition to being harsh and insulting toward the troops, was renowned for his licentious carousing among the garrison prostitutes. Tung Chin's death removed the authority and stability that had prevented the frictions between his officials and the troops from exploding into disaster. Lu exacerbated the situation by proclaiming that "both officers and soldiers have been lazy too long; I shall discipline them according to the statutes." When the soldiers requested cloth rations for new uniforms as was customary during a change in command, the request was denied, but Lu granted the cash value of the cloth to be paid in salt. Meng Shu-tu saw the opportunity for quick profits and raised the salt versus cloth exchange rate. As a result, each soldier re-

ceived only several pounds of salt. This chicanery further
incensed the troops, but Lu retorted, "Am I some Hopei rebel
that I must buy soldiers to obtain my command?" By March
21, the soldiers could stand no more. They seized Lu, Meng,
and the other staff officials, sliced them alive, and ate them.[60]

Han Yü only narrowly escaped the same fate. He had left
Pien-chou several days earlier with the cortege delivering
Tung Chin's body to Lo-yang. As the party reached the outskirts of the city, it received word of the uprising at Pien-
chou. Tung Chin's sudden death had prevented Han Yü from
making preparations to move his family from Pien-chou. His
household numbered over thirty people. There were several
daughters, and his wife was pregnant with his first son, Han
Ch'ang (799-855). Han Yü hurried eastward, fearing the worst
as the grisly details of the mutiny became known. The news
arrived shortly, however, that his family had escaped by boat
down the Pien Canal to Hsü-chou. He found them quartered
in the village of Fu-li on the bank of the Sui River in Hsü-
chou, where he arrived in early April 799.[61]

The decision to seek refuge in Hsü-chou was not accidental.
The military governor there was Chang Chien-feng (735-
800), a protégé of Ma Sui, who had recommended Chang to
the court in the early 780s. Chang had known the Han family
for almost half a century. When he was appointed to his post
at Hsü-chou in 788, Han Yü, then only twenty, wrote him
recommending one Hsieh Kung-ta (763-809).[62] Chang provided the Han family with a house, clothing, and food. Thus
freed from momentary anxieties, Han Yü devoted the summer to compiling a literary record of the previous months.
He completed the "Life of Tung Chin" and "How Sad This
Day: A Poem Sent to Chang Chi," a carefully crafted and
moving account that marks an important stage in the development of Han Yü's narrative verse. He also wrote "Two
Poems on the Pien-chou Rebellion," which both traditional
and modern critics read as criticism of Emperor Te-tsung's
appeasement policy toward recalcitrant military authority.[63]

In the autumn of 799 Han Yü accepted an official appointment as *t'ui-kuan* or "judge" in Chang Chien-feng's provincial

government, the same post he had held in Pien-chou. Chang was a haughty and aristocratic master, jealous of his literary pretensions. It is significant that although Han Yü was acquainted with Chang since childhood, he never sought a position from him. There was an obvious clash of personalities. Han Yü did not want a position but rather a recommendation from Chang for a Ch'ang-an post, preferably in the Censorate. In late August 799 the Yellow River overran its banks and flooded the prefectures of Cheng-chou and Hua-chou with extensive loss of life. Han Yü fused the dark moral and political implications of this disaster with his own desire for a court position in "Craven," a poem best read as a private meditation rather than as a direct appeal to "His Lordship" Chang Chien-feng.

> Craven are the scholars of this age,
> anxious only for their own existence,
> one sees the poor grieving
> never hears the rich sighing.

> The task of the great sage is different,
> he embraces wide an uncommon outlook:
> to serve the state his heart is pure,
> concerned for the times his tears flow forth.

> Seductive ladies seated round,
> soft fingers playing sad tunes,
> and wine and food in daily display,
> but thus inflamed, how could I enjoy these?

> Autumn clouds have belied the bright sun,
> and oozing mud-flats have not begun to dry;
> Yellow River dikes broke at Hua-chou
> and raging floods swept away the aged and young.

> Heaven indeed intends a purpose here,
> yet who dares question his reasons?
> I wish to be favored with his Lordship's referral
> and obtain a censorial post at Court.

I would part the clouds and shout at Heaven's gate,
I would bare my heart and present my precious stones;
I am not without arts to assist my Prince,
yet to present myself is in truth too hard.[64]

The frustration of the poet is evident. Because the "scholars of this age" are craven and concerned only for their own welfare, the emperor, "my Prince," is not properly advised, or as Han Yü metaphorically writes, "Autumn clouds (literally "autumn *yin*") have belied the bright sun." The third stanza expresses the poet's inability to participate in the enjoyment of such pleasures when the mismanagement of the state is so obvious. His specific frustration is reserved for the conclusion: four years after the unsuccessful letters to the prime ministers, Han Yü now realizes the futility of trying "to present myself" (*tzu-chin*).

Instead of a recommendation that would have released him from Hsü-chou, Han Yü encountered quite something else and on October 4, 799 protested to the governor:

> The day after my appointment I was in attendance at your office when a minor functionary presented me with a list of over ten office regulations. Among them was one quite impossible for me: from the ninth lunar month through the second month of the following year daily office attendance from dawn to dusk is mandatory except in case of serious illness.

Han Yü proceeds to explain that adherence to this regulation "will certainly cause me to lose my mind," in which case he will be of no use to Chang or to himself. In a fascinating glimpse of what must have been considered favorable T'ang working hours, he asked to be allowed to attend the office from five to nine in the morning and again from five to seven in the evening.[65]

Whatever the outcome of this request, relations between the two did not improve. The governor was fond of polo, which the T'ang military viewed as a form of training for the cavalry. But Han Yü protested in both verse and prose that the governor's addiction to the game was exhausting him and his troops and diverting them from their real purpose of defending the empire and "killing rebels."[66]

Han Yü continued his literary experimentation in Hsü-chou despite the absence of his Pien-chou coterie of Meng Chiao, Li Ao, and Chang Chi who were all in the south. An extreme example is the following attempt to blur the distinction between verse and prose:

How Abject

> How abject it is I have never known what the pleasures
>   of life are;
> I wish to flee from here, but have not the means.
> Why can't long-feathered pinions large as clouds grow
>   from my body
> so I can mount the wind on wings, soar past the empy-
>   rean, and leave this floating dust?
> Life and death, joy and sorrow I'd renounce them both;
> right and wrong, success and failure consign to idle
>   men.[67]

This text, which comes as close as anything in Chinese to being an actual prose-poem, is composed of lines containing eleven, six, eleven, ten, seven, and seven characters respectively. This *vers libre* form intensifies the poet's expressed desire to "flee" the circumstances that constrain him. Critics have found the imagery similar to the "Occasional Poem" of 795 and duly noted the "influence" of Li Po.

A respite for both parties came in the winter of 799 when Han Yü traveled to Ch'ang-an as Chang Chien-feng's representative at the New Year celebrations. While in the capital Han Yü met Ou-yang Chan, his classmate from the *chin-shih* of 792, now an assistant professor at the imperial university. Ou-yang prompted his students to lobby for a university appointment for Han Yü, but the effort seems to have encountered legal complications and came to naught.[68] On the journey back to Hsü-chou Han Yü composed "Returning to

P'eng-ch'eng," his most virulent attack on the government and a poem often quoted to demonstrate his concern with "social" issues.[69]

A respite from the bureaucratic tedium of Hsü-chou must have been Li Ao's arrival in the spring of 800 and his marriage to Han Yü's niece, the daughter of Han Yen.[70] At the end of May an ailing Chang Chien-feng dismissed Han Yü, who left immediately for Lo-yang, traveling in a leisurely fashion with his family and the very new family of Li Ao. On June 9, 800 the two scholars were in the vicinity of Sung-chou where they visited the historical sites in the company of Wang Yai and Hou Hsi (d. 823), a new acquaintance.[71] The timing was providential. Chang Chien-feng died on June 8, 800, and the Hsü-chou garrison mutinied two days later during a struggle to determine his successor.

5 Back to Ch'ang-an

Han Yü, jobless again, returned to his home base in Lo-yang. During the winter of 800-801 he traveled to Ch'ang-an to participate in the annual "levy" (*hsüan*), a general examination open to officials of the sixth rank and below who wished to obtain or change a position.[72] Han Yü obtained nothing and returned in the spring to Lo-yang, where he continued to attract and cultivate a following of like-minded adherents who were hopeful that association with him would bring the literary training and reputation necessary to pass the *chin-shih* examination. On September 3, 801 Han Yü and three of these followers, including Hou Hsi and Yü-ch'ih Fen, undertook a fishing excursion along the Lo River and stayed overnight at the Forest of Wisdom Temple (Hui-lin szu), a famous Ch'an establishment north of Lo-yang.[73] Two of Han Yü's poems relate to this occasion. "To Hou Hsi" is a subtle fusion of humor and despair that develops as a variation on the traditional metaphor of catching a fish as an analogy for seeking a position. Han Yü catches a fish so small "one can barely distinguish its scales from its fins." He concludes, "if you

want to catch a fish, you've got to go far away; / would a
big fish ever consent to live in such muddy ooze?"[74]

The second poem is "Mountain Boulders," well known to
readers through its inclusion in the anthology *Three Hundred
T'ang Poems*:

Mountain boulders in jagged profusion
    a walking trail concealed,
In yellow twilight we reach a temple
    bats swarm above.

We climb to the hall, sit on the stairs,
    plenteous the recent rains,
on the banana tree big leaves
    flush jasmine flowers.

A monk speaks of ancient murals
    fine paintings of Buddha,
Brings a torch to illume
    things wondrous and rare.

He spreads bedding, shakes out the mats,
    serves broth and rice—
Though coarse and simple food
    it serves to quell our hunger.

In deep night a quiet sleep
    sounds of insects cease.
A clear moon exits the ridge
    light enters the door.

As sky brightens, we leave alone
    no road to follow
In and out of heights and lows
    exhausting the trailing mist.

Red mountains jade-blue rills
    confused gleaming surging
We see evergreens and oaks
    ten spans around.

45

Standing in the flow with bare-red feet
　　we wade the rill on stones
Water surges around
　　clothes swollen with wind.

That human life can be like this
　　we should surely rejoice,
Why bend and cramp ourselves
　　taking the bit from others?

Oh, my chosen companions,
　　my favored friends,
Why not stay here till old age
　　and never return?[75]

Critics have appreciated the uncontrived lucidity of the poem's diction that articulates the poet's emotion through a progression of clearly realistic and easily visualized pictures. More than one critic has compared the vivid realism of the poem to the scenes of a landscape album. The first two stanzas depict the twilight arrival at the temple, the third and fourth narrate the encounter with the monk and the evening meal, the fifth describes the still night, and the sixth, seventh, and eighth, the early morning departure. The last two stanzas are the poet's comment on the emotional and psychological truths the poem describes. It has been observed that, as in a good landscape album, the first scene contains the seeds of all major elements later developed in the narrative. The boulders and the recent rains are the essence from which the central experience of the poem unfolds: the sound of the morning stream, swollen with rain, rustling against the mountain boulders and the direct touch of the cold water on the poet's bare feet spark an instant, almost Ch'an-like realization that "human life can be like this." The refreshing contact with the mountain stream is contrasted to the author's usual life where he must "take the bit from others." A critic has also noted the skillful use of "heavy" (*nung*) and "light" (*tan*), or in modern terms paratactic and hypotactic syntax to express respectively "scene" (*ching*) and "event" (*shih*). Stanzas one, two, five, six, seven, and eight are "scene," the others are "event." The translation attempts to preserve this essential distinction within the poem. This alternating and contrasting syntactic structure coupled with the poem's narrative cinematographic quality constitutes a major advance on Hsieh Ling-yün's narratives of mountain travel and was a powerful model for Ou-yang Hsiu and Su Shih in the Sung. The well-known and widely anthologized "Preface Seeing Off Li Yüan on His Return to Winding Valley," which Ou-yang Hsiu considered among the best prose of the T'ang, antedates "Mountain Boulders" by several months and is fundamentally identical to the spirit of the poem.[76]

Sometime shortly after this "fishing" excursion Han Yü indeed obtained his first regular post in the bureaucracy of the central government at Ch'ang-an. Probably as a result of the levy of 801 he was appointed to a two-year term as professor in the College of the Four Gates at the University of the Sons of the State.[77] The civil service rank of a student's father determined which of three colleges in the university he could enter to prepare for the *chin-shih*. The College of the Four Gates was the lowest of the three and accepted students from the bottom echelons of the bureaucracy and from the general populace. The college had six professors, six assistant professors, a variety of lesser instructors, and about a thousand students. Han Yü's affiliation with the University of the Sons of the State, a major T'ang educational and cultural institution, was to continue until the end of his life.

Han Yü was eminently suited for his new duties, the goal of which was to secure the *chin-shih* for his students. The examiner in 802 was Ch'üan Te-yü (759-818) assisted by Lu Ts'an (748?-802), an acquaintance of Li Ao, who had met him in the south in 799 and at whose instigation Li had composed his three "Writings on Returning To One's True Nature"(*Fu-hsing shu*). Han Yü wrote to Lu Ts'an recommending ten students. Of these then, four, including Yü-ch'ih Fen and Li I, passed in 802, and five more, including Hou Hsi, passed within the next five years. This phenomenal record created a demand for Han Yü as a teacher and brought him overnight renown. The *Supplement to the State History of the T'ang (T'ang kuo-shih pu)*, completed in 825, records laconically and with a touch of sarcasm:

> Han Yü recommended his juniors and helped them succeed in the examinations. There were many who sent him compositions and sought his advice. People call them "Han's disciples" (*Han men ti-tzu*). Once Han Yü attained high position, he did not do this any more.[78]

The contents of Han Yü's prose output during his two years in the college clearly reflects the demands of his new profession as teacher. The "Letter in Reply to Li I,"[79] the largest and most systematic exposition of Han Yü's ideas on literary creativity, dates from 801, as does the similar although more concise "Letter in Reply to Yü-ch'ih Fen."[80] It is clear that the ideas in these letters represent long years of literary practice and meditation on the philosophy of literature and its function in society. Han Yü was simply summing up ideas that had been germinating for almost twenty years. For another student, Li P'an, who received his *chin-shih* in 803, Han Yü summarized his thoughts on his profession as a whole in the justly famous "Discourse on Teachers."[81]

6 Disaster

The early years of the first decade of the ninth century were difficult times for the Confucian civil servant to actualize the best of his political traditions. For a quarter century the regular bureaucracy had lost ground on the one hand to the growing power of the court eunuchs and on the other to provincial authorities. In the countryside severe deflation had impoverished a peasantry whose taxes were assessed in cash and paid at outdated cash-versus-commodity exchange rates. The aging and increasingly cantankerous Emperor Te-tsung, who had ruled since 779, devoted less time to administration, and the routine mechanics of government were often interrupted. Such conditions encouraged both reformers and opportunists, sages and scoundrels, and the first requisite of political survival was the often impossible task of distinguishing the one from the other.[82]

In the spring of 803 Han Yü obtained leave from the university to return to Lo-yang and make arrangements to bring his family to Ch'ang-an. During this trip an event occurred that probably puzzled his contemporaries and certainly troubled later admirers. The basic account is the following entry in the *Supplement to the State History of the T'ang*:

> Han Yü was fond of the unusual. Together with several travelers he climbed to the highest peak of Hua Mountain and then figured he would be unable to get back down again. After making out his will, he became deranged and wept bitterly. The magistrate of Hua-yin, using a hundred stratagems, finally reached him, and they descended.[83]

This account not only presents a discomforting image of the great sage deranged at the imminence of his own demise; more alarmingly it portrays a Confucian hero whose pursuit of the "unusual" had led him to violate the basic Confucian injunction against willingly placing one's body in physically dangerous situations. Some have argued the incident never took place, but a passage in a later poem refers unambiguously to this event.[84] A short tract titled "The Significance of the Ascent of Hua Mountain" by the late T'ang scholar Shen Yen, however, suggests a fascinating interpretation:[85]

> I once read Li Chao's *Supplement to the State History of the T'ang* where it says that when Han Yü ascended to the summit of the Hua peak he looked down at the precipice, became afraid, and figured he would be unable to descend. Then he became deranged and wept and was about to lower his last will down on a rope as a farewell. The story thus ridiculed Han Yü's excessive fondness for the unusual.
>
> But I maintain that this interpretation does not reveal Han Yü's intentions. When Confucius grieved over the

unicorn, he was not grieving at the unicorn itself. When Mo-tzu wept over the silk, he was not weeping because of the silk itself. And when Juan Chi allowed his carriage to wander along the road, and the road ended, and he burst out weeping, he did not only just then begin to think he might not arrive. All of these were using action to criticize their times, and therein is the meaning they convey.[86]

Now how could the Way of the former and the latter sages differ greatly? Han Yü was incensed at those who scramble after glory and covet position as if they were climbing a cliff. When it becomes so steep they cannot stop, this causes them to endanger their persons by toppling over. Afterwards they lament they did not know how to arrive at a place where they could halt their carriages. I grieve that if it were not for me Han Yü's intentions would almost have been lost.

Shen Yen understands Han Yü's ascent of Hua Mountain as symbolic or allegorical action. Han Yü's intention, the true "significance" of the event, lies outside the narrative of the actions themselves. Proper comprehension requires that the observer or later reader link the ascent with a supposed tradition of social comment through symbolic action. Shen Yen traces such a tradition back to Confucius and suggests such actions are part of the universal Way of all sages.

Although the obviously apologetic nature of Shen Yen's explanation should not be overlooked, Han Yü's entry into the Ch'ang-an political scene in 801 did force him to rechannel his political and social criticism into a less strident and more traditional mold. Open criticism of Chang Chien-feng, provincial magnate and family friend, for excessive polo playing could be tolerated as a quirky display of Confucian enthusiasm; open criticism of key figures in the Ch'ang-an government was dangerous. Critics have linked Han Yü's ascent of Hua Mountain with an enigmatic poem titled "An Ancient Idea," which, like Shen Yen's interpretation of the ascent itself, makes the best sense when read as a political statement.

The poem is Han Yü's first use of the traditional metaphor of the mountain as a figure for the state and the body politic, a figure that later provided the central structure for his masterpiece, the "Poem on the Southern Mountains." "An Ancient Idea" is structured on the Taoist legend that there exists on the summit of the Hua Mountain a pool containing a variety of giant lotus, ingestion of which enables the devotee to become a transcendent.

> On the summit of the Great Hua
>   the lotus of the jade well
> have blossoms that open a hundred feet
>   and leaves like boats.
> Cool as snow or frost
>   and sweet as honey,
> when a single slice
>   enters the mouth,
> the severest illness
>   is cured.
> I set out to seek them,
>   not fearing the distance,
> but the roadless green walls
>   made the climb too hard.
> Why couldn't I get a long ladder
>   to go up and pluck their seeds,
> then plant them in the seven lowlands
>   below, their roots intertwining?[87]

The social import of the poem is obvious enough: the poet wishes to make the benefits of those at the top of the mountain accessible to those below in the "seven lowlands." His inability to reach the summit, however, frustrates this desire, which is the "ancient idea" or rather ideal of the poem.

During the entire spring and summer of 803 a severe drought affected the capital area. On July 17, 803 it was officially decreed that "because there has been no rain from the first of the year until now, prayers should be made at mountains and streams."[88] On July 31 the upcoming examinations for the year 803–804 were canceled, ostensibly because of a shortage of food in the capital. Han Yü, although still on the university faculty, memorialized against the cancellation. He argued that the previous harvest was a good one and there was sufficient food on hand to feed the five to seven thousand people expected to attend the examinations. Cancellation would cause a general panic and result in a loss of jobs. Han Yü concluded by attributing the drought to an imbalance in the relationship between the ruler and his advisors. "The sovereign is *yang*. The minister is *yin*. When there is only *yang*, there is drought. When there is only *yin*, there is flood. We now have an enlightened sovereign, the equal of Yao and Shun. But the wisdom of his ministers does not measure up to Antiquity; they do not devote total attention to the state. . . . There is a sovereign but no ministers, and thus this prolonged drought."[89] It has been plausibly suggested that Han Yü wrote his memorial at the request of the then Prime Minister Tu Yu (735-812).[90] Han Yü had wanted at least since 799 a position in the Censorate, and this memorial is best understood as part of a political arrangement to secure such a position, which could come as a direct appointment by the president or vice-president of the Censorate. In the autumn of 803 the Vice-President of the Censorate Li Wen (d. 804) appointed Han Yü censor in the court of outside inquiries.[91] When he reported for duty, he found an illustrious array of colleagues all newly installed: Chang Shu (758-817), Liu Tsung-yüan (773-819), and Liu Yü-hsi (772-842).[92]

From the autumn of 803 until the autumn of 805 the nation's political life was dominated by Wang Shu-wen (735-806), one of the most controversial figures in T'ang history. In the last years of the eighth century Wang organized a small group of mostly young officials interested in reforming the governmental abuses of the times by decreasing the tax burden on the population and curbing the power of the eunuchs. The heir apparent to the throne, Li Sung (761-806), supported these goals and Wang Shu-wen. As the demise of the old emperor became imminent, the Wang group assumed the character of a government-in-waiting and attracted a talented yet diverse collection of individuals, each with his own reasons for joining the group. Wang himself was not a member of the regular bureaucracy but rather acquired power through his personal acquaintance with Li Sung in the Han-lin Academy where he was retained for his skill at chess. Although the majority of thoughtful men probably sympathized with the basic goals of the reform, most members of the regular bureaucracy ultimately came to view Wang Shu-wen as a social upstart and the unorthodox demands of the group as a threat to the status quo and to their own careers.[93]

Han Yü certainly knew, although not closely, the literary members of the Wang group, Liu Tsung-yüan and Liu Yü-hsi, who were now his colleagues. Control of the Censorate, the investigatory agency of T'ang government, was vital to the success of the Wang group. The two Lius sounded out Han Yü and their other colleagues about Wang Shu-wen without revealing their own association with the group. Han Yü's response to these overtures can be read in a scathing satirical poem "Inscribed on the Temple at Coal Valley Tarn." The traditional interpretation of this poem as a satire against the Wang clique seems quite plausible. Like the previous "An Ancient Idea," the poem describes the author's ascent to a mountain pool. In this case, however, the tarn is inhabited by a dragon maiden, the Lady of the Pure Source (*Ch'eng-yüan fu-jen*) whose temple is beside the pool. Such a temple actually existed in the Southern Mountains about twenty miles south of Ch'ang-an and seems to have been the site of a local rain divinity cult. In the poem the dragon is maleficent because, ignoring its role as a rain-producing deity, it has subjected the country to a serious drought. In political terms the dragon would be a figure for Wang Shu-wen, who has usurped the *yin* function proper to a minister, thus causing a political "drought." The paraphrase accompanying the following translation attempts to convey the main outlines of the traditional interpretation of this poem as a political satire against Wang Shu-wen.

The myriad beings reside in the sun's light,
but ghosts dwell in deep darkness;

such skill alone has the dragon
to move among ghosts and humans alike.
> (Wang Shu-wen has the ability to move in all
> circles of government, both orthodox and
> unorthodox.)

I don't know who helps him, it's as
though he held the creator's secret itself.
Tired of living in the waters of the plains,
he nests in the mountains that pierce Heaven,
> (I suspect this ability comes from the support of
> the heir apparent. With this support, Wang has
> been able to rise from nowhere and extend his
> influence into the highest levels of government.)

where from peaks assembled like fingers together
a stone basin round like a ring looks up.
The Great Spirit cups high in both hands
and protects this stingy palm-full of water.
> (Wang has used this support and influence to
> form a faction, which enjoys powerful
> protection.)

Its dark depths hidden and concealing
were made for amassing watery evil.
Fish and terrapins find refuge and shelter there,
sporting together vaunting their ignorance at Heaven;
and swarms of birds flock there to rest
hovering around in easy flight.
> (This faction is a gathering place for those with
> dark intentions. All kinds of lesser creatures
> have associated themselves with Wang because
> he provides them with a safe political haven.)

The woods are thick and forever in darkness,
for never through the year can a tree be cut.
Delicate blossoms mixed with radiant fruits—
small stars in patches of yellow and red.
The stone steps are steep and slippery,
fall on the way up and there's nowhere to hold fast.

(The members of the Wang faction are free
from outside scrutiny; they are dilettantes—arrogant and useless. Associating with such people
is dangerous. One false step and you are lost.)

The idol in the temple hall is like real,
choicest jade turned round in misted tresses;
the grotesque assembly attend with awe
the grace and majesty mirrored in her face.
   (Wang Shu-wen looks like the real thing; his admirers adore him.)

Though I arrived with the sun exactly at midday,
trembling with fear I thought to go back at once,
but stood fast on my small patch of earth,
not daring to speak of the hardships of the coming road.
   (When I encountered the Wang faction, I
   wanted nothing to do with them, but hesitated
   because I knew refusal to cooperate would mean
   trouble for me.)

I grieved I had no hair-sharp blade
to bloody red this ox-hoof pool,
where even now widows and old men
come to drum and dance for rain.
   (I wanted at that point to do something to destroy Wang Shu-wen who will be the ruin of
   the country, but I had no means to do so.)

The fledglings of this motley lair swarm together,
the allotted lodgings already assigned.
But I quit them and leave; for what can I do?
I choose not to die among couch grass and quitch.⁹⁴
   (His underlings are busy staking out their territory. I will not join them. I believe the faction
   will fail, and they will all die in exile.)

If the two Lius were indeed sounding out Han Yü on his
opinion of Wang Shu-wen, there can have been little doubt
as to his position.

At the end of 803 Han Yü and two other censors submitted "A Memorial from the Censorate on the Subject of the Drought and Famine."[95] They noted that the combined effects of the drought and an early frost had reduced the normal harvest by ninety percent, so even though the tax revenues were small, their collection imposed severe burdens on the populace who were forced to abandon children and to dismantle houses and fell trees to obtain money to pay taxes. The starving and dead fill the gutters. His Majesty, a humane and compassionate sovereign, has not been informed of conditions by his ministers. The capital area is the base of the empire; its people are deserving of special commiseration. Since the winter's snowfall has been abundant, next year's harvest should be good. It would therefore be prudent to be lenient now. The memorial recommends a cancellation of winter taxes in the capital area. In addition to obvious concern for the populace, this memorial also constituted an indirect attack on Li Shih (d. 806?), then metropolitan prefect of Ch'ang-an, whose harsh administration was chiefly responsible for the continued collection of taxes.[96] As a result of this memorial Han Yü, Chang Shu, and a third censor were dismissed and demoted to obscure posts in the distant south. Han Yü was ordered to Lien-chou in Ling-nan province to serve as magistrate of Yang-shan county. He was thirty-five.

Han Yü himself was uncertain of the real reason for his exile. He knew the memorial and the resulting ire of Li Shih were major factors but suspected also that Liu Tsung-yüan and Liu Yü-hsi had somehow been involved.[97] Autobiographical passages in subsequent poems make it possible to follow Han Yü's own understanding of the political trap into which he had fallen. When the two Lius, acting probably as secret agents for the Wang group, reported Han Yü's dislike of Wang Shu-wen (probably by revealing "Inscribed on the Temple at Coal Valley Tarn" or similar poems written in confidence), Wang, fearing Han Yü's independence and outspokenness, decided it was necessary to remove him and any like-minded colleagues from the Censorate.[98] The Wang-controlled faction in the Censorate then prompted Han Yü and

Chang Shu to submit a memorial attacking Li Shih, whose removal from office was a goal of the entire Censorate. If the memorial succeeded, Wang Shu-wen would be rid of Li Shih; if not, he would be rid of Han Yü. After the collapse of the Wang Shu-wen government in the summer of 805, Liu Yü-hsi and the other literati members of the group publicly placed the blame on Wang and his immediate associates, probably in an effort to save their own lives.[99] After Han Yü met with Liu Yü-hsi at Chiang-ling in the winter of 805, he wrote "The Events of the Yung-cheng Period (805)," which reiterates this "public" view that Wang Shu-wen and his immediate accomplices were petty men who usurped the imperial authority. The literati members of the group were innocent victims simply doing their jobs.[100] We will never know how much Han Yü actually believed this account; the poem is best read as an attempt to help his former colleagues whom he seems to have forgiven for their part in his exile of 803 and who were now on the road to even more frightening exiles of their own.

7 In Exile

Traveling with Chang Shu, Han Yü left Ch'ang-an early in 804. Crossing the Ch'in-ling range south of the capital, they descended by boat down the Han River to where it joins the Yangtse at modern Hankow. From there they proceeded up the Yangtse and across the great Tung-t'ing Lake to the Hsiang River. Passing modern Ch'ang-sha, they ascended the Hsiang to its headwaters in southern Hunan, then crossed over the mountains into northern Kwangtung. Chang Shu proceeded to his post at Lin-wu in Ch'en-chou, and Han Yü continued to Lien-chou on the upper reaches of the furious Huang River and then by boat downstream to his post at Yang-shan, where he arrived in early April.[101]

The slow journey over the waterways of central China gave the exiles much time to compose verse. Han Yü later wrote that he and Chang Shu wrote over a hundred poems during the trip. "Answering Chang Shu," one of Han Yü's ten seven-word regulated verses, the verse form at which Tu Fu excelled, was written as the poets traveled up the Hsiang River. Han Yü is imitating the style and mood of Tu Fu's later poetry.[102]

> Bright mountains, the broad river
>   through water the bottom shows,
> from where wailing gibbons cry
>   are several houses.
> Giant bamboos contend for height
>   among delicate sprouts,
> red azaleas bloom in silence
>   profuse with flowers.
> Unreturned is yet the imperial favor
>   unknown my place of death,
> so let not these steaming miasmas
>   convey me to the edge of life.
> Finished chanting your poem
>   I look at my temples in the mirror
> and suddenly realize my greying hair
>   is twice what it was before.[103]

Han Yü's poem is a mirror image of Tu Fu's and a good example of the technique known as "reversing the case" (*fan-an*). Tu Fu's river is deep; Han Yü's is so shallow one sees the bottom. Tu Fu's houses are in the midst of a quiet bamboo grove; Han Yü's are surrounded by wailing gibbons, his bamboos are a jumble of contention. For Tu Fu the future is certain; for Han Yü it remains unknown. These contrarieties culminate in the phrase *sung sheng-ya*, for Tu Fu "to speed life on its course," with pleasant connotations of living out his years in happy surroundings; for Han Yü "to convey me to the edge of life," with ominous connotations of ending his life languishing in southern exile.

Yang-shan was apparently a fine place to languish. Han Yü has left a vivid description in his "Preface Seeing Off Ou Ts'e" composed slightly before the New Year of 804-805:

Yang-shan is among the most desolate places on earth. There are treacherous crags invested with tigers and leopards. The river flows with violent force, and rocks that bisect the current are sharper than swords and halberds. Boats heading up and down the river often go out of control and break up, and many are drowned. No one lives on the outskirts of the town; there is neither a deputy magistrate nor a constable. About a dozen families of local officials live in the bamboo thickets that flank the river. They speak like birds and look like barbarians. When I first arrived, there was no way to communicate, so I wrote characters on the ground to announce the collection of taxes and the scheduling of meetings. There is of course no reason for guests or travelers to come.

I had been awaiting my punishment here for six months when Mr. Ou came up by boat from Nan-hai to make friends with me. As he ascended the stairs, his manner was dignified. And when we sat down to talk, the intelligence of his opinion was outstanding. Chuang-tzu said, "A man who has fled into the wilderness . . . will be delighted if he hears so much as the rustle of human footfall." How much more delighted will he be to find a man like Mr. Ou! He entered my house and listened to me talk about the *Poetry* and *History*, about the sense of humanity and justice (*jen i*); he was delighted and seemed really to be interested. Together we often took shade in a pleasant grove or sat on rocks by the water's edge and fished with our poles, cheerful and happy as if it were possible to forget fame and fortune and not be oppressed by our poverty and lowliness. He will now return home to visit his parents for the New Year, so after drinking a jug of wine, I have written this to mark his departure.[104]

Han Yü, like most northern literati, had nightmares of spending his life in the south, but the unremitting feeling of desolation that infuses the first half of this preface is best understood as hyperbole to enhance the appearance of Ou

Ts'e on an otherwise drab scene. There are many indications Han Yü was sensitive to the opportunities Yang-shan afforded for quieter pursuits:

READING IN THE COUNTY LIBRARY

Come an official to this mountain-river district
I read books in the pine-cassia grove,
in the solitude leave drudgeries behind,
by fortune find my first mind again.
Wailing gibbons sober trite-filled ears,
clear springs purge dusty souls.
Poems completed are read together,
wine when finished is never poured alone.
Green bamboo time for quiet fishing,
white clouded days for secluded searches.
Southern regions forever teem with venoms,
the Northern visitor always fears their influx.
Dishonored-dismissed yet content to hold my own
with lingering-waiting the shame is harder to bear.
I offer this verse as a white silken sash
and await the reply to surpass precious gold.[105]

Although Han Yü was isolated in Yang-shan, he was not alone. Several students, like Ou Ts'e, took advantage of his southern exile to contact the master in hopes of ultimate success in the capital.[106] And Han Yü, as usual, maintained contacts with local Buddhist monks. The spiritual tenor of this poem, the sense of exhilaration at finding the "first mind" again, and the contentment derived from mindful performance of otherwise mundane activities suggest that Han Yü's experiences with the local Ch'an monks were more than social.[107]

On February 8, 805 the aging Emperor Te-tsung died, and three days later Shun-tsung ascended the throne as the tenth emperor of the T'ang. A month later a general amnesty was issued "for all crimes however grave or slight, and for all those persons not freed by ordinary pardons." At the same time, a recruitment of unused official talent was to be stepped up by soliciting recommendations from metropolitan and provincial authorities.[108] This amnesty removed Han Yü's status as an exile and made reassignment possible. He left Yang-shan in June 805 and traveled north to Ch'en-chou in southern Hunan to join Chang Shu and await developments. During his three-month stay in Ch'en-chou, Han Yü was the guest of the Prefect Li Po-k'ang (743-805). It has been suggested that he wrote his famous "Essentials of the Moral Way" (*Yüan tao*) during these months.[109]

During this same period, in the capital the new government of Shun-tsung administered by Wang Shu-wen was crumbling under the combined opposition of Li Shun (778-820, the future Emperor Hsien-tsung), the more conservative elements in the central bureaucracy and the provincial administration, and a eunuch faction loyal to Li Shun headed by Chü Wen-chen.[110] Since the imminent fall of Wang Shu-wen betokened a rise in Han Yü's political fortunes, he made sure to document his negative opinion of Wang Shu-wen in a series of political satires. A good example is the following lyric, which traditional critics read as an account of the imminent demise of the Wang group. The sun about to rise is a figure for the elevation of Li Shun to the status of heir apparent on April 26; the bright stars are two prime ministers driven from office by Wang Shu-wen (the moon) and his own prime minister Wei Chih-i (c.765-807, the morning star). Growing discord between these two, however, portends their extinction at full sunrise.[111]

Semilumescent the eastern horizon,
    the bright stars are gone
and only the morning star
    attends the waning moon—
Alas waning moon,
    be not distrustful,
shine together, share the shadows
    yet a while—
Glimmer on waning moon

sparkle forth morning star—
the cock crows thrice
the fifth watch sounds.[112]

This is a fine poem and has been compared with the *ya* sections of the *Book of Poetry*. The great Ch'ing critic Chu I-tsun (1629–1709) remarked that "although it seems dry and bland, its flavor is quite pronounced and its style very refined." The breaking dawn about to dispel the dark creatures of the night and bring light and order to the world is a figure for Emperor Hsien-tsung and occurs in other satires written in the summer of 805.[113] Sometimes, unlike in "Semilumescent," which is a grave poem, Han Yü molds his satire in a humorous vein, thus magnifying his contempt for Wang Shu-wen. In "After Being Drunk," for example, the sun is about to rise on a group of dissentious drunks stumbling home in the early dawn (the Wangs), their clothes soiled with wine, writing characters upside down. The dawn in these poems is Han Yü's first reference to Emperor Hsien-tsung. Han Yü's devotion to this monarch would shortly escalate into the central concern and driving inspiration behind some of his greatest poetry.

8 *Annus Mirabilis*

On September 5, 805 Li Shun ascended the throne as the eleventh emperor of T'ang. The news reached Ch'en-chou on September 10, one day before the Mid-Autumn Festival. A poem Han Yü wrote that evening as he and Chang Shu viewed the moon from the river bank describes the events of the previous day:

ON THE NIGHT OF THE FIFTEENTH OF
THE EIGHTH MOON: TO CHANG SHU

Faint clouds roll away,
    the River of Heaven is gone,

clear winds blow across the sky,
 the moon spreads its waves.
River-sand is smooth, the water is still,
 sounds and shadows cease:
We toast each other with a glass of wine
 and you compose a poem,
but the sounds of your song are sad,
 the words so bitter
that before I can hear it to the end,
 my tears are like rain:
"Where the Tung-t'ing Lake merges with Heaven
 and the Nine Doubts tower,
krakens and dragons emerge and fade
 amid screeching of bats and macaques.
Nine of ten officials exiled here
 die before reaching their posts;
I live withdrawn in hushed seclusion
 like a criminal in hiding.
Rising from bed I fear snakes,
 eating I fear poisons;
the humid climate is fetid and damp,
 fouls fish and meat.
Yesterday in front of the provincial office
 a great sounding of drums:
a new emperor has assumed the throne
 and appointed wise ministers.
In a single day the writ of pardon
 traveled a thousand *li*,
criminals to suffer capital punishment
 had sentences commuted,
demoted officials were recalled home,
 the exiles were to return
cleansed of blemish, washed of stain,
 to brighten the ranks at Court.
The prefect submitted our names, but the inspector
 refused to forward them on,
and so unfortunately all we could get
 was a move up to Chiang-ling,

there to serve as minor police officers,
    petty beyond mention,
who can be flogged and left in the dust
    for the least transgression.
Our colleagues of like age have all
    ascended the way,
but for us the road to Heaven is steep
    and hard to climb."
Leave this song of yours now
    and listen to mine,
my song now so different
    from yours:
"In all the year, the moon tonight
    is brightest;
fate and nothing else controls
    our human lives,
so, if this wine is not drunk tonight,
    then what is the moon's brightness for?"[114]

Han Yü's bid for a place in the new government was thwarted by Yang P'ing (c.750-815), then regional inspector for Hunan. The motive was purely factional. Yang was the father-in-law of Liu Tsung-yüan and a sympathizer of Wang Shu-wen; he obviously saw no reason to further the careers of two of Wang's most outspoken critics. Instead of a post in the capital, Han Yü received appointment as administrator of judiciary services in the prefecture of Chiang-ling, a major administrative center on the Yangtse upriver from Tung-t'ing Lake. The post carried rank of the seventh degree second class. Duties included "searching out thieves and brigands and exposing extortion, corruption, and misappropriation of state property." In short, Han Yü was to be, as he himself succinctly described it, "a petty policeman."[115]

A short bout with malaria delayed departure from Ch'en-chou for several weeks, but in early October Han Yü and Chang Shu set out for Chiang-ling. Although not traveling to Ch'ang-an, they were at least headed north, and the mood of the trip was relaxed and optimistic:

On the Hsiang River, Responding
to Chang Shu

Let us cease these thousand streams of tears
    shed in foreign lands
and float our single skiff together
    down the clear Hsiang waters,
where today mountain gibbons join
    southern birds in song,
and rejoice that listening together
    we know no sorrow.[116]

The leisurely two-month trip north to Chiang-ling was the beginning of the most productive year in Han Yü's life—the *annus mirabilis*. Now thirty-seven, he was at the peak of his intellectual and creative powers. The long days in exile had provided ample time to sharpen his literary skills, and the exhausting psychological experience of exile and travel through the length of the empire provided the emotional impetus to composition. The major prose texts outlining his political and ethical positions had probably just been composed. And finally, the government organizing itself in Ch'ang-an advocated policies Han Yü for the first time in his life could recognize with some honesty as compatible with his own political philosophy. Yang P'ing was a minor obstacle that would soon be removed. Han Yü's own political dawn was breaking; and he knew this as he wrote during the *annus mirabilis*.

The two poets halted their journey to visit the sites at the famous Heng-shan, the south's official sacred mountain. It was here that Han Yü wrote the magnificent "Composed on the Monastery Tower Where I Lodged After Visiting the Heng Mountain Temple."[117] A less ambitious poem but one using the same motif of mystical ascent is "Chü-lü Mountain," so named after the main peak in the Heng-shan range. According to a legend that seems to date from the Eastern Han, during his efforts to control the floods the mythical Emperor Yü left a stone inscription on the summit of Chü-lü Mountain. Han Yü's poem records his search for this legendary inscription:

Chü-lü Mountain

On the summit of Chü-lü Mountain
    is the stele of the divine Yü,
emerald characters in red marble,
    marvelously shaped:
tadpoles bending their bodies,
    leeks spread upside down,
simurghs soaring, phoenixes resting,
    tigers and dragons contending.

So grave was its text, so hidden its form,
    even the spirits espied it not;
yet once a man of the Way ascended alone
    and saw it by chance.
I came sighing in admiration
    tears swelling into ripples,
looking, searching, seeking everywhere
    for the place it might be—
in thick forests of green trees
    gibbons wail.[118]

The stele inscription of the divine Yü of course symbolizes those idealized qualities of Antiquity for which the poet is searching. A casual reading might suggest that since the poet has not found the inscription, neither has he found those qualities it symbolizes. The Ch'ing critic Fang Tung-shu (1772-1851), however, notes that detailed description of the first quatrain gives the impression of being "real" (shih) when actually it is "unreal" (hsü). Conversely, the last five lines are discursive and "seem unreal but are real." These keen observations point toward the meaning of the poem: searching for something unreal (the stele of Yü), the poet has found the "real" significance of the stele in the pristine clarity of the green forest and the gibbons' cries. Understanding the "man of the Way" (*tao-jen*) as a Buddhist monk (as does Ch'ien Chung-lien) reinforces this Ch'an-like reading of the poem.

That Han Yü was thinking along Buddhist lines during his stay on Heng-shan is clear from the following:

PARTING FROM THE MONK YING

The mountain monk loves his mountains
    and will not come out again,
the worldly man is tied to the world
    and will not be back again.
Below the Chu-jung Peak
    I turn my head
knowing that in this life
    our parting is forever.[119]

As the two poets traveled down the Hsiang River from Heng-shan toward T'an-chou (modern Ch'ang-sha), Han Yü composed "On the Road to Chiang-ling, Sent to the Three Han-lin Scholars Wang Yai, Li Chien, and Li Ch'eng."[120] The poem is an appeal to these three scholars for political assistance and at the same time Han Yü's first and most generalized verse narrative account of his experiences in exile. After a brief stop at T'an-chou, the two proceeded across the Tung-t'ing Lake to Yüeh-chou and then up the Yangtse River to Chiang-ling.[121] Here Han Yü met Liu Yü-hsi and Liu Tsung-yüan, who had been exiled for their complicity with Wang Shu-wen and were traveling in the opposite direction. Han Yü's conversations with Liu Yü-hsi seem to have dispelled any suspicions and hostility he may have harbored concerning the role of the two Lius in his own exile of 803. The "Events of the Yung-cheng Period" places all blame on Wang Shu-wen and his colleague Wang P'ei and clearly absolves the Lius of guilt by association. The poem concludes, however, with an admonition, which is perhaps general or perhaps addressed specifically to the Lius, "to let what has gone past serve best as a warning."[122] A much shorter poem composed at the same time also expresses sympathy for his former colleagues:

67

DRAGONS MOVE

When Heaven darkened and Earth turned black
    the krakens and dragons moved on
amid furious thunder and lightning,
    females following males.
How sad the sighs of the fish and terrapins,
    parched to death,
their clear spring down a hundred feet
    turned to dusty earth.[123]

This poem returns to the metaphorical world of the "Coal
Valley Tarn," making use of the legend that this pool was
once located on the plains and dried up after its dragons moved
on the wind and lightning to the tarn in the Southern Mountains. The poem probably refers to events following the ab-
dication of Shun-tsung; "the fish and terrapins" would be the
two Lius.

Although chasing "thieves and brigands" probably deprived Han Yü of the leisure time travel had afforded for
literary pursuits, important works do date from these months
in Chiang-ling. "Four Poems Responding to Spring," the first
significant poetry of 806, are foreshadowings of the monumental "Autumn Sentiments" written later in the year and
are best read in conjunction with this longer series. On January
2, 806 Han Yü wrote to Li Sun (739-809), who had just been
appointed to assist Tu Yu in revamping the powerful Salt and
Iron Commission in Ch'ang-an, offering to put his literary
services at Li's disposal. The letter contains Han Yü's own
brief but enlightening comments on the poetry he was writing
at this time.[124]

Han Yü's final return to Ch'ang-an came as a combined
result of the new emperor Hsien-tsung's efforts to placate
disaffected literati and the thoughtfulness of an old patron
whose own misfortunes had prevented him from earlier helping Han Yü. Hsien-tsung's Act of Grace of 806 created a
hundred new positions for "students" in the Imperial University to absorb unemployed younger literati; this expansion
of the university called for additional staff. Cheng Yü-ch'ing
(748-820), then serving as prime minister, probably recom-

mended Han Yü for one of these positions. In late June he received notice to return to Ch'ang-an and assume duties as acting professor in the College of the Sons of the State.[125] He left Chiang-ling immediately and by June 27, 806 reached Hsiang-yang on the Han River where he transferred to the post road through Teng-chou and Shang-chou to Ch'ang-an. Despite his haste to return, Han Yü nevertheless took time to maintain contact with potential literary patrons among the local magnates. For instance, as Han Yü passed through Hsiang-yang, Yü Ti (d.818), military governor of the Shan-nan East district, presented him with some of his recent compositions. Han Yü replied four days later from north of Teng-chou with a detailed critique of Yü's works, and this letter is among the clearest statements of his fundamental literary tenets.[126]

During his return to Ch'ang-an Han Yü conceived of a poem that was to form these literary tenets into one of their most dazzling expositions. The great "Poem on the Southern Mountains" was probably begun as Han Yü crossed these mountains south of the capital and completed in the fall. It is also likely the "Autumn Sentiments," considered by many to be Han Yü's finest poem, was also completed in the fall of 806. The return to Ch'ang-an meant reunion with old friends, most of whom Han Yü had not seen in five years. The numerous "linked verses" (*lien-chü*) from the fall of 806 testify to long hours spent with Meng Chiao, Chang Chi, and Hou Hsi, the nucleus of the literary circle from Pien-chou. Han Yü's first poem written after returning to Ch'ang-an is an ebullient account of these poetry reunions:

DRUNK: FOR SECRETARY CHANG

When others all push me to drink
it's as though I don't hear them,
but today I'm at your house
and call for wine to push on you
so the guests at this table here
and I can each write a poem.

Your poems take on many forms
as profuse as clouds on a spring day.
Meng Chiao works to startle the pifflers
a heavenly corolla that spits rare perfume.
Chang Chi studies the ancient lucidness
a coached crane that shuns the chickens.
My nephew A-mai can't read yet, but he
writes the clerical script pretty well
so he copies out the finished poems
and serves to expand our troop.
The reason I like to drink is to
write poems waiting to get high.
The wine has a delicate clear taste
and a good strong bouquet.
Our spirits slowly turn boundless, till
laughter and joking and poems are everywhere.
This really gets at the idea of wine,
anything else is just being rowdy.

Ch'ang-an's filled with the rich,
their plates spread with flavored mutton,
who don't comprehend literary drinking
and only think of getting whores drunk.
They have their fun for a time
but are just like a pack of flying gnats.
Now I and my several friends
are really all about equally matched.
Rough words that terrify even ghosts
exalted diction that matches the Three Emperors.
The best treasures need no refining
inspired results without tilling.
Now begins an age of peace
with wise ministers assisting Yao and Shun
so with luck there'll be nothing to do
but spend our days together like this.[127]

There was, however, to be no such luck for Han Yü. The
intrigues of court politics soon intruded on this idyllic world

of wine and poetry. Li Ao's "Life of Han Yü" contains the fullest account:

> There was among the prime ministers one who admired Han Yü's writings and wished to employ him in a position that would make use of his literary ability. But there were some who fought for this priority, and they contrived Han Yü's words in order to defame him. Fearing there might be difficulties, he accordingly requested separate duty in Lo-yang.[128]

Huang-fu Shih writes even more obliquely that Han Yü "did not join with pernicious favorites and fearing of being victimized, he requested separate duty in the eastern capital to avoid them."[129] Personal matters may also have influenced Han Yü's decision to request transfer to Lo-yang. In 806, when a cousin, Han Chi (750-806), died, Han Yü took in his four children. In 807, his last surviving cousin died in K'ai-feng, and Han Yü again assumed responsibility for the five children of this family.[130] These deaths not only dramatically increased the size of Han Yü's household but also left him the eldest surviving member and head of his clan. It is quite probable Han Yü realized that a move back to his home base in Lo-yang would alleviate his present political difficulties and at the same time facilitate providing for his family and managing clan affairs. The appointment was only for two years after which he could expect reassignment. Furthermore, his patron Cheng Yü-ch'ing began in early 807 a term as mayor of Lo-yang, so Han Yü could look forward to being well received in his home town. And the teaching duties at the Lo-yang campus cannot have been onerous. In 808 the College of the Sons of the State in the eastern capital had ten students.[131]

9   In Lo-yang

Han Yü submitted to the throne his monumental "Poem on the Sagacious Virtue of Primal Harmony" in the beginning of 807. He obviously considered this among his most important works, placing it at the beginning of his collected poetry. This long poem, almost epic in stature, is the culminating expression of gratitude for his return to Ch'ang-an. Even as he presented this effusive tribute to Emperor Hsientsung and the new order, however, his detractors had managed to limit his political options to continued service at the university. The move to Lo-yang not only made good political sense and was probably necessitated by family considerations, it also made good literary sense. Meng Chiao had secured a position on the staff of Cheng Yü-ch'ing and had already moved to Lo-yang. Li Ao was also living in the eastern capital. And so when Han Yü in the late summer of 807 moved himself and his now sizable household to Lo-yang, where he had not lived since 801, he confronted a combination of old and new, familiar and unfamiliar.

Among the most significant of Han Yü's new literary acquaintances was Huang-fu Shih (777-835?), who, after receipt of his *chin-shih* in 806, was serving as chief of employees in Lu-hun county, southwest of Lo-yang. Huang-fu Shih, a nephew of Han Yü's classmate Wang Yai, achieved notoriety at a special examination in 808 at which he so severely criticized the policies of the then-Prime Minister Li Chi-fu that a scandal ensued. Huang-fu Shih addressed to Han Yü a poem called "Fire in the Lu-hun Mountains," which was probably an oblique account of these events. The poem does not survive, but Han Yü's "Fire in the Lu-hun Mountains: Following the Rhymes of Huang-fu Shih" is an imitation of its style and has been called "one of the most difficult of Chinese poems."[132]

Two other literary figures encountered during these years in Lo-yang were Fan Tsung-shih (d. 824) and Lu T'ung (d. 835). Fan, the scion of a once wealthy family fallen on hard times, was among the most prolific of T'ang writers, but his unorthodox theories and methods of composition doomed his works to oblivion. Lu T'ung on the contrary was living as a recluse in the Sung Mountains southeast of Lo-yang when Han Yü first met him. The earliest record of his acquaintance with either Fan or Lu is an inscription (*t'i-ming*) commemorating an excursion the three undertook between April 15 and April 22, 809 to the Sung Mountain.[133] One of the purposes of this trip was to call on the famous recluse Li P'o (773-831). In 806 Li Sun had arranged to have him appointed omissioner of the right, but Li P'o, despite repeated requests, refused to emerge from seclusion and assume his post. Han Yü had written him early in 809 pointing out that the new government had established an age of "Great Tranquillity" (*t'ai-p'ing*), so there was no longer any need to live in seclusion. Since everyone knows of Li's ability, his refusal to take office can only be interpreted as a maneuver for higher salary, and this perception is damaging his integrity. He should therefore accept his position as an example for others. Not to do so harms himself, the emperor, and the people.[134] As a result of this letter, Li P'o began to frequent Lo-yang, although he did not actually take office until 814. This episode is best understood as a ninth-century propaganda exercise based on the traditional political tenet that recluses will participate in genuinely good government. By enticing an obstinate but high-minded recluse into government service, Han Yü is indirectly praising Emperor Hsien-tsung and enhancing his own reputation as an articulate spokesman of the regime.

On July 25, 809, after exactly three years at the university, Han Yü was transferred to the post of auxiliary secretary in the Bureau of Prisons with separate duty in the eastern capital and supplementary service in the Bureau of Sacrifices.[135] Disregarding his brief and catastrophic service in the Censorate, this was his first central government position outside the university. The transfer thus marked an important step in his bureaucratic career and was probably obtained through the efforts of his patron Cheng Yü-ch'ing, the viceroy of the eastern capital. Han Yü's duties were to oversee the registers and account books concerning prisoners of war and convicts. The joint appointment in the Bureau of Sacrifices entailed similar duties concerning the supervision of the Buddhist and Taoist communities in Lo-yang. Since 694 the Bureau of Sacrifices compiled once every three years a list of those admitted to the Buddhist and Taoist clergy, and this practice was codified in the *T'ang liu tien* of 739. But in 807 this function was transferred to a eunuch "commissioner of merit and virtue."[136] Huang-fu Shih describes Han Yü's confrontation with the eunuchs:

> When the eunuch commissioner of merit and virtue took control of the Buddhist and Taoist monasteries of the capital, the Bureau of Sacrifices relinquished these former duties. But Han Yü went by the *T'ang liu tien* and worked hard to regain these functions. By expelling unworthy monks, regulating their activities, and forbidding noisy assemblies, he put the Buddhists in order![137]

The last statement may be exaggeration. In a report to Cheng Yü-ch'ing in late 810, Han Yü writes that his duties at the Bureau of Sacrifices "have brought me into daily conflict with the eunuchs; they wait for me to make a mistake, utter calumnies and slander against me, and create disorder among the official documents."[138] He requested an investigation, but Cheng Yü-ch'ing, perhaps not wishing to initiate a confrontation with the eunuchs, transferred Han Yü to the magistracy of Honan county.[139]

This same tenacious adherence to traditional bureaucratic procedure and insistence on doing things the "right way" that Han Yü demonstrated in his first encounter with the eunuch establishment served him in good stead during his next administrative adventure. As Emperor Hsien-tsung's policy of exerting full central control over the separatist provinces of the northeast intensified, the governors of these areas began to recruit agents for espionage and guerrilla operations in Ch'ang-an and Lo-yang. The centers for these covert activities against the central government were the hostels maintained and staffed by each military district to represent its interests in the two capitals. In Lo-yang the liaison offices of Wei-po, Yu-chou, and P'ing-lu districts were in early 811 recruiting and harboring soldiers for eventual fifth-column work. Although the local officials knew of these activities, they were too intimidated to inform the court in Ch'ang-an. Han Yü, again acting on his own authority, initiated prohibitions to forestall these clandestine activities. As soon as these became known in the city, the higher authorities, including the viceroy Cheng Yü-ch'ing, fearing the disastrous consequences of being perceived in Ch'ang-an as lax toward the separatists, hastened to add their own injunctions. The affair even reached the ears of His Majesty who is reported to have replied with pleasure, "Han Yü has helped us." The gravity of the danger was illustrated in 815 when the guerrilla forces of Li Shih-tao (d.819), governor of P'ing-lu, burned a large government tax collection depot at Ho-yin near Lo-yang and assassinated the prime minister Wu Yüan-heng (755-815) in the streets of Ch'ang-an.[140]

Early in 811 Han Yü had another brush with the eunuchs that pushed his relations with Cheng Yü-ch'ing to the breaking point. Since the late eighth century, the eunuchs directed the Shen-ts'e chün (literally "armies of the divine plan") or Palace Armies quartered in and around the two capitals. Since these were the only forces whose loyalty to the throne was absolute, they were vital to the military security of the dynasty. Consequently, these soldiers were well paid and enjoyed such attractive legal and financial advantages that wealthy merchants routinely purchased from the eunuch commanders nominal commissions as soldiers in the Palace Armies to escape taxes and other obligations due the government. This practice and the sale of monastic ordination certificates were important sources of eunuch revenue during this period. Most regular officials knew of these problems but feared to act against the eunuchs who enjoyed the direct support of the throne. As magistrate of Honan county Han Yü seized several of the most insolent of these "soldiers" and had them detained and flogged. The eunuch officers of the Palace Army protested to the viceroy and seem to have instigated some type of legal action against Han Yü. In a report to Cheng Yü-ch'ing explaining his actions and requesting his decision, he wrote, "the duty of a real soldier is to provide protection for the viceroy. If anyone who sits in the market selling griddle cakes can call himself a soldier, then who is *not* a soldier? In my opinion these are crooks who have bribed the officers, stolen Your Excellency's documents, and added their own names to the military rosters in order to lord it over the civil authorities." Han Yü concludes in a polite but forthright tone that shows the strained relations between the two men: "I am not suited for this office and have slowly come to dislike my work. If I could find a pretext, I would willingly resign without the least reluctance and with no more sense of loss than for a discharge of mucus or spittle. That I may have disappointed you by as much as a mustard seed is to me an anxiety as great as a mountain. Whether I stay or go in this office, I am totally at your command."[141] The outcome of this appeal is not known, but the patient Cheng Yü-ch'ing seems to have disposed of the case without problems; for in early summer he returned to Ch'ang-an as president of the Ministry of War, and in late summer Han Yü followed, transferred as auxiliary secretary in the Bureau of Military Affairs.

Literary activities of course continued despite the pressures of bureaucratic life. Han Yü continued to sponsor students for the *chin-shih* examination. In 810 he wrote the celebrated "Discourse on Taboo Names" to defend the right of Li Ho (791-817) to sit for the examinations.[142] A year later he met Chia Tao (779-834), with whom he maintained a literary relationship until the end of his life.[143] Good examples of poetry from these years would be "Encountering Spring in the Eastern Capital," "Two Poems on Flowering Plums,"[144] and the often-read "Song of the Stone Drums."[145] By far the greatest literary works of the Lo-yang years, however, are prose tracts—"Seeing Off Poverty," the "Preface to Linked Verses on the Stone Tripod," and "The Biography of Fur Point."

10 Back to Ch'ang-an

On the road back to Ch'ang-an Han Yü again demonstrated both impatience with perceived bureaucratic malfeasance and fierce loyalty to perceived friends and colleagues. The magistrate of Hua-yin county, one Liu Chien, had been dismissed from office by the former prefect. When the latter was about to leave for reassignment, Liu stirred up the populace who blocked the prefect's departure and demanded payment for previous goods and services rendered. The new prefect investigated the case and not surprisingly sided with the former prefect. Liu was exiled. At this point, Han Yü, who was passing through Hua-yin on his way back to Ch'ang-an, learned of the affair and memorialized the throne accusing the two prefects of collusion and exonerating Liu Chien, who in 783 had passed the *chin-shih* together with Han Yü's deceased cousin Han Yen. The court appointed a censor to investigate the affair. The official determination was that Liu Chien was guilty of embezzling government funds and that Han Yü had "examined the matter rashly." Accordingly, on March 27, 812 he was transferred back to the College of the Sons of the State as professor. Han Yü's biography in the *Old T'ang History* narrates these events then adds that "he believed his talents had often been the cause of his demotions so he composed 'An Explication of "Progress in Learning" ' in order to state his own position." After quoting the text in full, the history continues, "when those in power read this piece, they felt sorry for him, and believing he had a talent for history, transferred him to be secretary in the Bureau of Judicial Control and compiler in the Office of Historiography."[146]

This transfer occurred on April 26, 813 and was linked to changes at higher political levels. On April 15 Wu Yüan-heng (758-815) was appointed prime minister and on April 20 arrived in the capital to assume his position. Wu was also a 783 classmate of Han Yen and a friend of Li Chi-fu who had been minister since 811. Wu's protégé was P'ei Tu, the great patron of Han Yü's later years. These men formed a strong conservative influence at court in favor of adhering to regular bureaucratic procedures, and they advocated the aggressive use of force to exert central government control over the separatist provinces. There is no doubt Han Yü felt ideologically and politically at home in this group. Although the third prime minister, Li Chiang (764-830), held different opinions, he was a *chin-shih* classmate of Han Yü and is not likely to have opposed his promotion.[147]

Late in 813 Han Yü began work on the "veritable record" of the reign of Emperor Shun-tsung. Although it is probably impossible to determine how the present text of the *Veritable Record of Emperor Shun-tsung* relates to the manuscript Han Yü submitted to the throne in the summer of 815, two facts are certain. The original text related in some detail the eunuch role in the ascension of Emperor Hsien-tsung; and the eunuchs criticized this text at the time of its submission and instigated for a revision until this was accomplished about 830. Second, however much Han Yü's text may have been altered, the present work shows remains of an overall structural unity and an aesthetic awareness of the high drama of the events of 805. These literary merits are combined with an extreme subtlety of expression characteristic of the best Confucian "praise and blame" historiography. The total effect of the work tallies tolerably well with Han Yü's pronouncements on the historian's function in Confucian society and his own ambitions and self-doubts in this regard.[148]

On September 12, 814 Meng Chiao died in a small town west of Lo-yang on route to a provincial appointment on the staff of Cheng Yü-ch'ing, under whom Meng had served for many years in Lo-yang. Han Yü summoned Chang Chi, and they mourned together at Han's house in Ch'ang-an where they were soon joined by Meng Chiao's other friends. The group took up a collection to provide for the burial and support of Meng's widow, since the couple had no son. A sizable contribution arrived from Cheng Yü-ch'ing, and the funds were forwarded to Fan Tsung-shih who made the necessary arrangements in Lo-yang.[149]

A month later the prime minister Li Chi-fu died, but the loss of this patron does not seem to have affected Han Yü's career. On December 5, 814 he was transferred to be secretary of the Bureau of Scrutiny, an important subdivision of the Ministry of Personnel that maintained career dossiers on government officials, supervised an annual review of their conduct, and established performance ratings for each official.[150] In addition, on January 29, 815 he was granted the title "charged with the reduction of imperial edicts and decrees," which conferred admission to a pool of officials with superior literary talent whom the imperial secretariat could delegate to draft documents issued in the emperor's name.[151]

Among the first documents Han Yü drafted was a series of letters concerning military action against Wu Yüan-chi (783?-817), the separatist-minded governor of the Huai-hsi district headquartered at Ts'ai-chou. Late in 814, Wu Yüan-chi succeeded his father in this position and, anticipating a challenge from the central government, launched a series of raids beyond his borders to consolidate his military position. The struggle that ensued dominated court politics and Han Yü's life for the next three years.[152] Huai-hsi, unlike the other separatist provinces in the northeast, was located in the heart of the T'ang empire and at will could disrupt grain transport via the Pien Canal to the capital areas. The change of leadership there gave Emperor Hsien-tsung the opportunity to take advantage of the new "governor's" relative inexperience and thus destroy separatist sentiment in Huai-hsi. But the question of how best to achieve this goal divided the bureaucracy. Some, like Li Chi-fu, Wu Yüan-heng, P'ei Tu, and Han Yü, advocated the use of military force; others, like Li Chiang, Po Chü-i, and the new Prime Minister Wei Kuan-chih (760-821), were "antiwar" and pushed for a negotiated settlement. The sharp divisions on this issue forced the emperor to represent both sides among his three prime ministers, although personally he favored the former group.

Early in 815, the court ordered five separate commands to initiate military activities against Huai-hsi. There were few successes, however, and in June the emperor dispatched P'ei Tu on a personal inspection tour of the war area. He returned to court advising the continued use of force and recommending changes in field commanders. A long report Han Yü wrote on the Huai-hsi war was probably intended to support P'ei Tu's recommendations.[153] On July 13, 815 the prowar Prime Minister Wu Yüan-heng was assassinated in the early morning outside his residence in Ch'ang-an. The assassins also attacked P'ei Tu who was wounded in the head and fell into a culvert; a thick felt hat he was wearing had saved his life. The attacks created panic in the capital, and officials, including Po Chü-i, demanded an investigation and arrest of the guilty parties.[154] Meanwhile, P'ei Tu was convalescing under armed guard. The antiwar party tried to use this time to diminish his influence, but the emperor instead appointed him prime minister on August 4, 815. It was widely believed in the capital that the assassins had been sent from the northeast province of Ch'eng-te as a diversionary tactic to aid Huai-hsi. The emperor used this belief to open a second front against Ch'eng-te early in 816. The antiwar minister Chang Hung-ching resigned in protest on February 4, 816, and on February 15 the emperor dismissed two vocal Han-lin academicians as a warning to others in the antiwar party to tone down their opposition. One consequence of these actions was a promotion for Han Yü. On February 21 he was made imperial palace secretary, an important position that put him in regular direct contact with the emperor. The six palace secretaries (*chung-shu she-jen*) managed the flow of paperwork to and from the emperor, worked together with the prime ministers on the drafting of formal documents, and often participated in high-level deliberations.[155] The position could be a stepping stone to the highest office: on March 11, 816 the palace secretary Li Feng-chi (758-835) was appointed to fill the vacant "antiwar" ministership.

Meanwhile, the war effort, being waged now on two fronts, continued to exhaust scarce resources, increasing the tax burden on the populace and strengthening the position of the antiwar lobby. Although government forces reported sporadic successes, lack of a unified command strategy prevented the coordination necessary for a decisive victory. On June 17, Han Yü fell victim to the intense in-fighting between the two factions on the war issue. The two antiwar ministers succeeded in ousting him as palace secretary and assigning him president of the Secretariat of the Right of the Heir Apparent, a dreadful sinecure in which he was to languish for over a year while court opinion seesawed back and forth, following reports of the languishing efforts on the battlefield itself.[156] Although a major government defeat in July 816 apparently strengthened the emperor's resolve not to abandon the Huai-hsi campaign, he had first to purge the antiwar party, a process that gathered momentum through the fall of 816 when Wang Yai, a classmate of Han Yü, replaced Wei Kuan-chih as minister.

While these political changes were in progress government forces at the front were in disarray. A gradual change took place when Li Su (773-821), son of the late eighth-century general Li Sheng, assumed command of the western front. By this time, however, conditions within Huai-hsi began to deteriorate, and Li Su's lenient policy toward defectors resulted in the capture of important garrison towns on the western and northern borders of Huai-hsi. But Wu Yüan-chi quickly rallied his defenses, and the stalemate continued into its third year. In the early autumn, as the debate at court dragged on, P'ei Tu requested the emperor to send him once again as special envoy to the war zone. This request was granted on September 13, 817, and P'ei named Han Yü to a high-ranking position on his staff.[157]

On September 17 the mission departed Ch'ang-an with an escort of three hundred palace guards. His Majesty himself saw them off as far as the T'ung-hua Gate at the eastern edge of the city. Han Yü was immediately entrusted with a delicate and important mission. Han Hung (765-822), who had been military governor of the Hsüan-wu district at Pien-chou since the troubles there in 799, was an autocratic and independent-minded ruler. Although nominally loyal to the government, he had not come to court in over ten years. His district bordered on Huai-hsi, and any increase in government authority there was certain to undermine his own influence. In 815 the court had named him commander-in-chief of operations against Huai-hsi to thwart any serious countermeasure Han might take against the venture. Although he eventually sent his son with several thousand troops to join the northern command under Li Kuang-yen (761-826), the *de facto* field commander recommended by P'ei Tu, Han Hung had worked subtly to undermine the Huai-hsi campaign.[158] Han Yü hurried ahead to Pien-chou to inform Han Hung of the latest developments and to urge him to take a more aggressive military stance against Huai-hsi. As Han Yü was about to enter Pien-chou, he composed the following poem:

CROSSING THE HUNG CANAL

The dragon weary, the tiger exhausted,
    they divided the rivers and plains;
and people by the millions
    preserved their lives.
Who urged then their sovereign
    to turn round his horse
and gamble for all the world
    on a single throw?[159]

The poem is a clever application of an historical event to present realities. In 203 B.C. the future emperor Kao-tsu of the Han (the dragon) and Hsiang Yü of the state of Ch'u (the tiger) agreed to cease hostilities. The Hung Canal was to be the boundary between their territories: to the west was Han, to the east Ch'u. After Hsiang Yü had departed, Chang Liang (d. 187 B.C.) and Ch'en P'ing (d. 178 B.C.), two famous Han ministers, advised their sovereign to pursue and destroy the exhausted Ch'u forces. Kao-tsu followed this advice and shortly afterward defeated Hsiang Yü at the famous battle of Kai-hsia and founded the Han empire.[160] Han Yü is here praising P'ei Tu (and himself) by creating an analogy between their own prowar policy against Huai-hsi and the similar advice that proved so successful for Han Kao-tsu. The poem is both an encouragement to P'ei Tu, flattering his courage to go against the pacifist party, and at the same time a message to Han Hung: we have already crossed the Hung Canal (similar to crossing the Rubicon); it is not wise to oppose us any longer. The poem is thus not simply "singing the past" but rather "using the past as a model for the present."

Han Yü's mission was apparently a success, and he rejoined the main party on the road south of Lo-yang. Passing through Hsiang-ch'eng the party was attacked by seven hundred cav-

alry from Huai-hsi, a clear indication of the threat that the
P'ei Tu mission posed in the eyes of Wu Yüan-chi. It also
indicates that P'ei Tu was in actual military command. One
of his first acts upon arriving at Yen-ch'eng on October 11
was to remove the eunuch military supervisors and allow the
generals to draft strategies without interference and constant
scrutiny. Several weeks later there was another surprise attack
by the ace Huai-hsi commander Tung Chung-shih. P'ei Tu
and his top assistants again barely escaped capture.

Finally, on November 28, 817 the action began that ended
the war. Li Su, with the help of a defected general, executed
a daring overnight raid, and under cover of a snowstorm,
reached Ts'ai-chou by forced marches. He took the garrison
by surprise and the next morning captured the city and Wu
Yüan-chi.[161] On December 6, P'ei Tu entered Ts'ai-chou in
triumph, and the Huai-hsi rebellion was over.

Han Yü and his colleagues departed for Ch'ang-an on January 8, 818, leaving Ma Tsung as viceroy in Ts'ai-chou. On
the road, word reached the group that the emperor had ennobled P'ei Tu as Duke of Chin. The mission arrived in the
capital on January 26, and on January 31, 818 Han Yü was
also rewarded for his part in the expedition with the post of
vice-president of the Ministry of Justice.[162]

On February 22 the emperor ordered Han Yü to compose
an inscription to commemorate the victory over Huai-hsi. He
worked over two months on the commission and submitted
his work on May 3, 818. The controversy that ensued became
one of the legends of Chinese literature. Han Yü's biography
in the *Old T'ang History* explains that Li Su felt the text over-
emphasized P'ei Tu's role and slighted his own actions that
had actually won the war. His wife, the daughter of an imperial princess, complained within the palace that the text was
biased. The emperor ordered Han's text effaced and had the
Han-lin academician Tuan Wen-ch'ang (773-835) write another inscription.[163] Li Su was the son of Li Sheng, who, it
will be remembered, had been partially responsible for the
death of Han Yü's cousin in 787. This, combined with the
possibility that Han Yü may have felt the raid was his own

idea, plus his obvious devotion to P'ei Tu, may indeed have led him to play down the importance of Li Su in his inscription. But the latter's sense of offended military hubris was certainly the motive behind the emperor's order to efface Han's text.[164]

11 The Buddha's Finger Bone

Despite the unpleasantness over the Huai-hsi inscription, 818 must have been among the best years of Han Yü's life. With P'ei Tu as the dominant influence at court and the emperor still savoring his victory over the separatist provinces, Han Yü, now aged fifty, was at the pinnacle of his career in government service. With, however, a typically rash but passionately sincere action—immediately regretted—Han Yü himself undid the bureaucratic success he had so long coveted. Unfortunately, in the Chinese popular imagination these events came to overshadow all else in his life.

On the grounds of the Dharma Gate Monastery in Feng-hsiang about fifty miles west of Ch'ang-an was a Pagoda of the Body of Truth that Protects the State. This institution housed a relic reputed to be the finger bone of the Buddha Śākyamuni. Once every thirty years this relic was brought to Ch'ang-an and displayed at various Buddhist temples in the city. The ritual supposedly assured a bountiful harvest for the nation. Private adoration of the relic coupled with generous donations to the temples ensured the faithful of multitudinous "blessings." On February 6, 819 the emperor ordered the eunuchs to receive the relic that was venerated within the palace for three days and then passed to the Ch'ang-an temples. "Nobility and commoners alike flocked to make donations, fearing only that they would be last. People neglected their trades and exhausted their resources, then burned their heads and scorched their arms as penance, in order to make offerings to the temples."[165]

Han Yü probably wrote his infamous "Memorial on the Buddha Relic" out of concern for the popular welfare. Huang-

84

fu Shih states clearly that Han Yü feared the intense enthusiasm of the crowds posed a threat to public order in the city. The memorial asked the emperor to rescind the order to display the relic. In shaping his argument, however, Han Yü's own enthusiasm and haste led to serious rhetorical excesses not characteristic of his other official memorials. The major offense was severe *lèse majesté*. The memorial implied Hsientsung "served the Buddha," then maintained the Buddha was merely a "barbarian"; so, His Majesty had become the servant of a barbarian. Even more serious was the assertion that the coming of Buddhism to China had shortened the life spans of the emperors. Han Yü no doubt thought to utilize Hsientsung's well-known fear of death and pursuit of "immortality." But in a society that considered even the casual mention of death a serious breach of etiquette, Han Yü's suggestion that the Son of Heaven was condemning himself to an early death must have seemed an unforgivable lapse of good taste bordering on the treasonous.

The day after he received the memorial, the emperor showed the text to his ministers at their morning conference. He was angry and proposed the death penalty. P'ei Tu and Ts'ui Ch'ün replied that "Han Yü has taken severe liberties and offended your majesty. For this he truly deserves punishment. But it is only his deep feelings of loyalty and sincerity and his disregard for dismissal and reprimand that have brought matters so far. We request that you be lenient toward him and thus encourage remonstrators." His majesty, however, was not dissuaded and the two ministers were forced to marshal the opinion of the bureaucracy that the sentence was too severe and relay their sentiments to the emperor through the imperial relations. On February 12, 819 Han was exiled as prefect of Ch'ao-chou.[166]

Several aspects of this well-known event are seldom encountered in secondary literature. First, it is clear the emperor and the populace looked upon the relic as a "protector of the nation." To challenge this assumption was probably within the bounds of propriety but to advocate the destruction of the relic was actually dangerous and a clear excess. There were

85

also economic and political aspects to the memorial. The close connection between the eunuchs and the Buddhist establishment has been noted. Curtailment of activities related to the Buddha's bone would have meant major financial losses for the eunuchs. Politically, the memorial may also be construed as an attack on Huang-fu Po (755-820) and Ch'eng I (d.819), whose selection as ministers because of their effective but unscrupulous methods of raising revenue created a scandal among the orthodox bureaucracy and eventually forced P'ei Tu from office.[167]

Han Yü was ordered to depart Ch'ang-an at once; his family was to follow as soon as arrangements could be made. He left the next day, taking only his nephew Han Hsiang. The following poem was written as the pair crossed the famous Lan-t'ien Pass south of Ch'ang-an. It is among his best poems. Once again, the shock and agony of exile provided the stimulus for art.

DEMOTED I ARRIVE AT LAN-T'IEN PASS
AND SHOW THIS POEM TO MY BROTHER'S
GRANDSON HAN HSIANG

A sealed epistle submitted
    at dawn to Nine-fold Heaven—
exiled at dusk to Ch'ao-chou
    eight thousand leagues to travel

Wishing to save his Sagacious Brilliance
    from treacherous evils,
could I have cared for the years that remain
    in my withered limbs?

Clouds straddle the mountains of Ch'in
    where is my house?
snows crowd the pass at Lan
    horses will not move

I know what the reason must be
    that makes you come so far—

the better to gather my bones
from shores of miasmic water.[168]

Ch'ao-chou, located slightly inland near the modern port of
Swatow on the south China coast, was reckoned to be 7,667
li (a third of a mile) from Ch'ang-an. This distance to be
traveled was certainly on Han Yü's mind. Shortly before
crossing the Martial Pass (Wu-kuan) on his journey south, he
met a Tibetan on his way to exile in Hunan.

WEST OF WU-KUAN I MEET A BANISHED TIBETAN

Alas! my
    warlike Tibetan
        do not be sad

Hunan is near—
    a place to live
        and close your life

My sentence
    weighs heavier—
        no hope of return

Straight
    from Ch'ang-an
        8,000 leagues.[169]

One can only surmise with what mixture of memories of his
dead cousin, killed by the Tibetans over thirty years ago, and
of fear over impending death by the tropical "miasmic shore"
Han Yü crossed the Martial Pass. Clearly he expected to die.
He had survived two earlier journeys into exile; chances of
returning from the dreaded south a third time were slim.

Nor was the journey a hardship only for Han Yü. He traveled slowly to allow his family time to overtake him, but the
rigors of the trip still proved too much for his fourth daughter
Han Na (808-819). She died on March 1, 819 near Shang-
chou. Later, her body was reburied in the clan cemetery at

Ho-yang, and Han Yü composed a "Tomb Inscription for My Daughter Na."

When I was in the Ministry of Justice, I said the Buddha was a foreign ghost, that his teachings disordered the government administration, that because Liang Wu-ti served him he was defeated by Hou Ching, that we could do away with Buddhism completely and should not allow it to thrive. The Son of Heaven said these words were inauspicious and exiled me to Ch'ao-chou.

After I had departed, the authorities held that the criminal's family could not remain in the capital, so they were forced into exile also. My daughter Na was eleven. She was already ill in bed and sick with fear at the separation from her father. Furthermore, she suffered from the shaking and jolting of travel by sedan-chair and from the irregularity of the meals. She died at the Ts'eng-feng post station near Shang-nan and was buried in the hills off to the south of the road.[170]

On the very day his daughter died, Han Yü was at I-ch'eng on the Han River, at one time capital of the ancient kingdom of Ch'u. Within the confines of the post station was a well said to be sacred to King Chao of Ch'u (r. 515 B.C.–489 B.C.) who had moved his capital here in 505 B.C. Nearby were extensive ruins of the king's court and ancestral temple. Beside the latter, the local population had constructed a thatched bower where they still offered sacrifices to the ancient king. The scene inspired one of Han Yü's best quatrains.

On the Temple of King Chao of Ch'u

Grave mounds
    of princes past
        fill the view

palace spires
    in wooded wastes
        touch the clouds

Countrymen
> still honor
>> his ancient virtue

in one room
> of thatch, they
>> worship King Chao.[171]

The poem of course contrasts the former splendor of the Ch'u court and its aristocratic retainers with the present simplicity of the one-room shrine to King Chao. A more fundamental contrast is between the moral deficiency of these retainers and the virtue of the king. The former has passed away, but the latter lives on. The short poem is a powerful yet subtle encomium to Confucian royal virtue and its ability to endure as a positive force for stability in a transitory world. Han Yü is probably here again thinking analogically, positing King Chao as a cautionary exemplum for his own Emperor Hsien-tsung.[172]

Sometime later Han Yü's family overtook him, and the party proceeded along the same route as on the two previous journeys to exile, up the Hsiang River, then overland to the headwaters of the Pei River. In late April Han Yü composed "The Officer at the Rapids," certainly his most ambitious use of the colloquial in verse. By far the best poems of the journey, however, were seven-word quatrains, perfectly crafted yet intense with remorse and trepidation.

ON THE BUDDHIST TEMPLE AT LIN-LUNG

Unperceived
> 5,000 leagues
>> since leaving home

sunken and sick
> I board
>> the rapids barge

Even before Ch'ao-yang
    I can speak
        of it

sea's haze
    dark and black
        waters lash the Heavens.[173]

As the boat passed the confluence of the Pei and Shih-hsing rivers at Shao-chou, Han Yü's thoughts turned from the future to the past. Forty years before, he had followed his brother into exile here. Now, only he was left.

THOUGHTS ON PASSING THE SHIH-HSING ESTUARY

I remember
    as a child
        following my brother

now, southbound
    again, only
        I am left

Before my eyes
    the whole household
        moves again

but no one
    to talk with
        of old times.[174]

Old times must also have been on the poet's mind when a courier arrived with letters from Liu Tsung-yüan at Liu-chou sent via P'ei Hsing-li (774-820), the military governor at Kuei-lin, who also sent along some medicines. After a brief stop at Kuang-chou, the group ascended the Tung River past Hui-chou and then proceeded overland to Ch'ao-chou. They arrived May 22, 819.

He immediately wrote a long letter to the emperor, announcing his arrival and apologizing for the lack of propriety and respect in his memorial on the Buddha's relic. He adhered carefully to the line prepared by P'ei Tu and Ts'ui Ch'ün that "Your Majesty took pity on his servant's foolish loyalty but was angered at his uncontrolled directness." He reports that as the emperor's representative he has proclaimed the merits of the reign to his new charges in distant Ch'ao-chou. He describes the remoteness of the place, his age, and ill health. "Simple and rude by nature, I possess little understanding of practical affairs but instead an intense devotion to scholarship and literature, which has not left me for a single day, and which has been praised by my contemporaries. My normal writings are no better than another's; but when I describe Your Majesty's meritorious virtues, my writing is like the *Poetry* and *History*. The hymns I compose could be presented at the sacrifices to Heaven, could record the *feng*-sacrifice on T'ai-shan. . . . Place them among the pages of the *Poetry* and the *History*, I will suffer no shame. . . . Even should the Ancients themselves return to life, I would yield little to them." His Majesty has restored the fortunes of the T'ang house by subduing the "feudal lords" that attempted to seize the land in the last seventy years. His merits surpass the founders of the dynasty and should be announced to Heaven by performing the *feng*-sacrifices on T'ai-shan. Han Yü doubts he could assist much in planning this great event from such a distance and relies on His Majesty's "sympathy and compassion."[175] This appeal is basically identical to the argument Han Yü had used in letters to various patrons and grandees since his early days in Ch'ang-an: my literary talent can preserve for posterity your glorious achievements.

Also composed immediately after arriving in Ch'ao-chou was the equally infamous and usually misunderstood "Address to the Crocodiles." Informed that crocodiles were devouring the people and their livelihood, Han Yü ordered a subordinate to sacrifice to them a sheep and a pig and relate the following address: in Antiquity the former kings possessed and tamed the world, expelling all creatures harmful to humans; but less powerful sovereigns allowed these baleful creatures to reclaim their former territory. The present emperor, however, "sage in wisdom, merciful yet martial," has again established dominion over the whole world. The prefect is his representative, responsible for the people's welfare and the collection of taxes for the support of the state. "The crocodiles cannot dwell together with the prefect in this land." He admonishes the crocodiles to depart within seven days to "the great sea to the south, which can encompass all from the great whale to the tiny crab, there to live and to feed." If they do not depart, "all those who scorn the officer appointed by the Son of Heaven, who refuse to hear his words and remove themselves hence, who through folly or lack of intellect do harm the people or other creatures, shall be put to death. Archers with poisoned arrows are ready to enforce this command."[176]

Chalmers's response, though dated, is typical of modern reactions to this piece. "You smile at this rodomontade. The absurdity of the thing is extreme; and I cannot but think that Wan-kung [i.e. Han Yü] himself smiled inwardly at his own performance. But it is a curious fact, that none of his admirers, or commentators . . . seem to see the joke."[177] Indeed, with good reason, for there is no joke to be seen! On the contrary, critics as late as Tseng Kuo-fan (1811-1872) still praised the text's solemnity and high seriousness. The Chinese have always believed that imperial authority, emanating as it does from Heaven itself, relates to all nature, animal and atmospheric included. Ho Ch'o (1661-1722) notes that the Ancients established officials to oversee reptiles and tortoises, "not considering them creatures immune from civilizing influences. Han Yü, in this piece, understood this Ancient premise." The composition of ritual texts for various sacrifices to local gods and sprites was routine work for a T'ang magistrate, and Han Yü was no exception.[178] The "Crocodile Text" is exceptional only because its author has turned a routine administrative document into a political and literary *tour de force*. The text gives notice to the crocodiles that for the first time since Antiquity an emperor has manifested sufficient virtue to reclaim all the land of the ancient sovereigns. It thus extols the grandeur and achievements of Emperor Hsien-tsung more than it denigrates the evil of the crocodiles. The majesty of the text's diction and the overall structure of its rhythms, which, to quote Ho Ch'o again, "approach the Six Classics," enhances the force of the symbolic action of demonstrating imperial authority over remote Ch'ao-chou. As prefect and representative of that authority, Han Yü's text also sends a message to Ch'ang-an: I am still Your Majesty's loyal servant. Finally, the conclusion translated above makes clear what fate awaits any creature, reptilian or otherwise, who might choose to oppose the new authority.

Neither Li Ao nor Huang-fu Shih mentions the crocodile affair. To illustrate Han Yü's virtue as a provincial administrator both record that he ended child slavery in the area under his jurisdiction. It was common practice throughout the South to indenture children as security for loans. When the loan was delinquent to the extent that the interest equaled the principal, the child became the property of the creditor. In 815 Liu Tsung-yüan at Liu-chou had declared that wages must be paid the child during the indenture period, and so he made it possible for parents to redeem their children. Han Yü promoted the same measures in Ch'ao-chou.[179]

Han Yü also promoted Confucian education in the area. Noting that Ch'ao-chou had never produced a candidate for the metropolitan examinations, Han Yü opened a school in the district and appointed a local scholar named Chao Te, then chief of employees at Hai-yang, to full-time teaching duties. The prefect himself contributed 100,000 cash toward maintenance of the school and its students. Su Shih (1037–1101) later traced the beginnings of Confucian learning in Ch'ao-chou to Chao Te and this school.[180]

12 Han Yü and Ta-tien

Han Yü also furthered his own education during his stay at Ch'ao-chou. His encounters with the Ch'an monk Ta-tien Pao-t'ung (732-824) testify to his interest in Ch'an and provide the most extensive evidence for judging his understanding of the movement. Ta-tien was a disciple of the famous Shih-t'ou Hsi-ch'ien (700-790), who had established himself on Heng Mountain during the *t'ien pao* period (742-756). He and Chiang-hsi Tao-i (709-788), otherwise known as Ma-tsu, were reputed to be the two most influential teachers of late eighth-century Ch'an. Ta-tien had established himself on Ling Mountain, about fifteen miles west of Ch'ao-yang, itself thirty-five miles south of Ch'ao-chou and across the mouth of the Kiyang River from modern Swatow.

There exists among Han Yü's works three letters inviting Ta-tien to visit him in Ch'ao-chou.[181] The first is dated early summer and mentions he has only recently arrived. He has long heard of Ta-tien's virtue (*tao-te*) and wished to meet him. He has instructed the county magistrate to deliver his calling card and arrange for water transport for Ta-tien to come to Ch'ao-chou. The second letter restates the invitation, adding that in distant Ch'ao-chou there is no one to converse with. If Ta-tien would only deign to come, he could return home after a day or two. The third letter acknowledges a reply from Ta-tien that apparently answered some questions Han Yü had put to the monk. He confesses the explanations are too abstruse. The "Great Treatise to the *Changes* says, 'Writing cannot express words completely. Words cannot express thought completely.' Does this mean that ultimately we cannot comprehend the thought of the Sages? If this is so, then even to read something a hundred times is not as good as seeing someone face to face, where the answers to one's questions can be readily understood." Han Yü once again urges the monk to come to Ch'ao-chou. "I have heard that when one's *tao* is unimpeded by doubt, one is entangled [neither] in action [nor] in repose. If one is attached to nothing, then the peace and serenity of mountains and forests is no different from the city."

Han Yü himself described his relations with Ta-tien in a letter to Meng Chien (d. 824) written the following year from Yüan-chou.[182]

The rumors now circulating that I have recently begun to believe and to practice Buddhism are untrue. When I was in Ch'ao-chou, there was an old monk named Ta-tien who was intelligent and understood the *tao*. Since in that distant place I had no one to converse with, I invited him to come from the mountains into the town. He stayed for a week or so. He was actually able to transcend his physical body and to conquer his desires through intellect so that the material world neither intruded upon him nor troubled him. I conversed with him and, although I could not understand everything, most important was to eradicate impediments and obstacles from one's thoughts. I consider this difficult to achieve, so I associated with him.

When I went to the seacoast to sacrifice to the spirits, I visited his lodge. And when I departed for Yüan-chou, I left him some clothes as a parting gift. But this was done because of my feelings for him as a person, not because I believe in his faith, nor because I want blessings or merit.[183]

By far the most detailed account of the relationship between Han Yü and Ta-tien is contained in the *Collection from the Hall of the Patriarchs (Tsu-t'ang chi)* completed in 952 at Ch'üan-chou in modern Fukien.[184]

[1]

The monk Ta-tien was the successor of Shih-t'ou Hsi-ch'ien in Ch'ao-chou. In 818 the true body [of the Buddha] was welcomed into the capital. At the An-yüan Gate, the Yüan-ho emperor personally burned incense, waited to receive it, and then prostrated himself before it. The emperor and his entourage saw a multicolored light, and all said it was the Buddha-light.[185] His entourage extended their congratulations for his sagacious influence.[186] Only one man, the Vice-Minister Han Yü, said it was not the Buddha-light and was unwilling to congratulate the emperor on his sagacious virtue.

The emperor asked,

"If it's not the Buddha-light, then what light is it?"

The vice-minister could not answer and was exiled to

Ch'ao-chou. When he arrived there, he asked his subordinates if there were any lofty practitioners of Ch'an in the area, and they replied there was the monk Ta-tien.

[2]

Although the vice-minister sent messengers and requested three times, he did not come. Later, when the monk heard about the Buddha-light, he came on his own accord. But the vice-minister would not agree to see him and sent someone to ask him,

"I invited you three times and you did not come. Why is it that you have come now by yourself?"

The master answered,

"That I did not come when thrice invited was not because of you. That I have come now by myself is only because of the Buddha-light."

When the vice-minister heard this, he was delighted and stated what had formerly been on his mind.

"When your disciple said previously that it was not the Buddha-light, was I correct or not?"

The master replied,

"You were correct."

"But if it was not the Buddha-light, then what light was it?"

"It was simply the light of the eight classes of superhuman beings or of Indra or Brahmā assisting the spread of the faith."

"Had there only been a man such as the master in the capital then, your disciple would not be here today!"

[3]

Another time, the vice-minister asked,

"I do not know if the Buddha really has a light or not. Does he?"

"He does."

"Then what is this Buddha-light like?"

The master called to him,

"Vice-minister!"

He replied,

"Yes?"

"Have you not seen it yet?"

Then the vice-minister said,

"This your disciple does not understand."

And the master answered,

"If you do understand this, then that's the real Buddha-light. For the way of the Buddha is a single way. Its light is neither blue, yellow, red, nor white. It penetrates Mount Sumeru and illumines all mountains and rivers of the great earth; yet no eye sees it, no ear hears it. The five sorts of vision cannot see its form; the two sorts of hearing cannot hear its sound.[187] If you comprehend this Buddha-light, then everything sacred and mundane is illusion and cannot delude you."

When the master was about to return to the mountain, he left a gāthā:

I leave you now
    but wonder not, I return
        to the mountain so soon

for I recall the pine
    creepers—my
        palace under the moon,

I locked not
    with golden chains
        its spires and halls

and while I've come
    the white clouds
        have closed them in.[188]

[4]

Later the vice-minister went to the mountain especially to return the monk's visit. He asked,

"Your disciple is much occupied with military and civil affairs; could the master point out what he considers the fundamentals of the law of the Buddha?"

The master was silent for a long time, and the vice-

minister was at a loss what to do. Suddenly the attendant
San-p'ing knocked on the meditation bench behind the
master, who turned around and said,

"What is it?"

He answered,

"First one loosens through meditation, then one roots
up through wisdom."[189]

The vice-minister turned to San-p'ing and said,

"The personality of the master is very lofty, and this
disciple was at a loss. But now from his attendant I have
obtained a point of entry." He thanked San-p'ing and
returned to Ch'ao-chou.

[5]

At a later time, he ascended the mountain to pay homage to the master, who was sleeping at the time. When
he saw [Han Yü] had come, he did not get up but rather
asked at once,

"Did you come mountain climbing or did you come
to pay homage to this old monk?"

And he answered,

"I came to pay homage to the master."

The master said,

"Well, you haven't so far; what are you waiting for?"

The vice-minister at once paid homage.[190]

Later he ascended the mountain again, and again the
master asked,

"Did you come mountain climbing or did you come
to pay homage to this old monk?"

The vice-minister replied,

"I came mountain climbing."

The master asked,

"Did you come bringing your mountain-climbing
staff?"

"I came without it."

"If you did not bring it, then you came empty, and
there's nothing to be done."[191]

Although the above passage presents serious problems of
interpretation, several general observations seem possible.

There is no mention of his memorial, yet Han Yü's exile is clearly attributed, as in the historical sources, to *lèse-majesté*. His refusal to acknowledge the Buddha-light has affronted both the authenticity of the relic and the reputed virtue of the emperor. The second section is independent confirmation that Han Yü did indeed thrice invite Ta-tien to Ch'ao-chou and argues for the ultimate genuineness of the three letters to the monk. The dialogue, or *mondo*, begins in earnest in the third section. A general spiritual progression is present as Han Yü learns through his Ch'an encounters. After initial bafflement ("This your disciple does not understand"), he receives a verbal explanation of the "real Buddha-light" from Ta-tien. In section four he fails to comprehend the meaning of the master's silence and receives an "entry point" from San-p'ing. In the last section he learns the value of nonreflective, spontaneous action. The master's words, "then you came empty, and there's nothing to be done" (*k'ung lai ho i*), seem to imply that Han Yü no longer needs the intellectual crutch (the staff) of the master's instruction. He has "come empty."

On August 7, 819 the submission of the emperor's posthumous name occasioned a general amnesty. The minister Huang-fu Po blocked a full recall to Ch'ang-an for Han Yü, and so on November 12 he was notified to assume duty as prefect of Yüan-chou in modern Kiangsi. He proceeded to his new post at a leisurely pace, pausing at Shao-chou where he had spent time as a child when his brother was prefect there over forty years ago. He asked the local officials to provide maps for better sight-seeing in the area. And his encounters with Ta-tien seem to have made a lasting impression:

On the House of the Ch'an Master Hsiu

A bridge flanked
    by water pines
        a hundred paces

reaching the bonze's lodge
    with bamboo bed
        and bulrush mat

> a fist cupped
>> beneath my chin
>> I doze awhile
>
> then pole in hand
>> I descend
>>> to fishing sand.[192]

Fishing is a common metaphor in Ch'an poetry for the pursuit of enlightenment.[193]

When Han Yü arrived in Yüan-chou on February 25, 820, he probably already knew of the death nine days earlier of Emperor Hsien-tsung and the ascension of his twenty-four-year-old son to the throne as Emperor Mu-tsung. Although the transition brought the demise of Han Yü's current political enemies—Huang-fu Po was exiled to Yai-chou on Hainan Island on February 21—he must surely have lamented the passing of the strong-willed monarch whom he had tried hard to serve and to whom he had addressed some of his greatest writing. On March 18 a general amnesty was proclaimed from the Vermilion Phoenix Tower at the entrance of the palace of Great Brilliance in Ch'ang-an, and Han Yü knew he would be going home. The call finally came on November 1, 820. He was to return to the capital to serve as rector of the Imperial University, his fourth tour of duty with the institution he was now to head.[194]

The road back to Ch'ang-an took Han Yü past the make-shift grave of his daughter outside Shang-chou. Confronted with the physical reality of the consequences of his impetuosity, Han Yü composed one of the most remarkable poems of his life. There are no images or symbols and only one analogy, and that used with exquisite precision.[195] This direct expression of genuine feeling gives the poem an emotive force proportional to the author's sense of grief and guilt.

> Last Year I was Exiled from the Ministry of Justice to Be Prefect of Ch'ao-chou and Set Off on the Post Road to Assume my Position; Later My Family Was Also Banished. My Daughter Died on the Road and Was Buried

in the Mountains by the Ts'eng-feng Post Station. Now
I Have Been Pardoned and on My Return to the Capital,
I Pass By Her Grave and Inscribe This On the Beam of
the Post Station.

Strands of vine bound
    round the tree-bark coffin
rudely interred in desolate hills,
    your white bones cold.
Panic pierced your heart, your
    body already in pain
palanquin-carried down the road
    whose hardships were known to all.

No time was there to circle the mound
    thrice with lamentation,
a single plate of rice, I heard,
    was your only oblation.
Thus did my crimes bring you
    guiltless to this,
and for me a hundred years
    of shame, remorse, and tears.[196]

A variety of documents written in the spring of 821 testify
to Han Yü's participation in national policy debate and to his
efforts to improve the Imperial University, of which he was
now director. He set out first to reorganize and enlarge the
student body. During the latter half of the eighth century
attendance had fallen off and the class distinctions that determined in which college a student could enroll were no longer
strictly observed. Han Yü noted that children of the upper
classes were ashamed to attend the College of Superior Studies
because many of the students were sons of artisans and merchants. He proposed that the old class distinctions be maintained but relaxed and that the number of students in each
college be brought up to the levels mandated in the statutes
of 739.[197]

Next he turned his attention to the faculty, which presented
a perennial problem:

A Memorandum from the Imperial University to the Ministry of Personnel Concerning Recent Faculty Appointments

This year's Act of Grace commissioned the rector of the Imperial University to fill faculty positions by selecting persons possessing a knowledge of the Classics and an ability to instruct and guide students. But in recent years the Ministry of Personnel has assigned posts largely in accordance with service records and without examinations for actual ability. As a result, the students have not been encouraged to exert themselves. It is therefore requested that only persons with detailed knowledge of the Classics and the commentaries, adequately versed in literature and history, or persons having sat for the *chin-shih* or Five Classics examinations be assigned faculty posts. Persons having already received such posts will be required on the first of the month to submit to an examination before beginning their duties, the intention being to assist our Sagacious Dynasty to uphold Confucian teachings and promote learning.[198]

Li Ao's "Life of Han Yü" has a fascinating anecdote about Han Yü's term as university rector:

There was a lecturer who could explicate the *Record of Rites* but who had an ugly appearance. Most of the faculty were from noble families, so they ostracized him and would not allow him to dine with them. Han Yü told his orderly, "Invite the lecturer to come and dine with the rector." And from then on the faculty did not dare to mistreat this lecturer.

He petitioned the throne that Confucian scholars be appointed to the faculty and had them meet together every day for lectures. The students rushed to hear them, saying with delight, "With Master Han as rector, the university is no longer quiet."

As soon as he arrived back in the capital he petitioned the new emperor to enforce the statutes against bond slavery of the children of freemen. During his short term as prefect of the small district of Yüan-chou he had freed 731 children. One can only imagine how many children are thus enslaved nationwide. "They are no different from slaves, being whipped and flogged and finding no rest until death." Such actions are not compatible with the newly inaugurated age of "Grand Felicity" (ta-ch'ing).[199]

Han Yü also submitted a long memorial on the colonization and conquest of aboriginal populations in the south.[200] The native inhabitants of the T'ang protectorates of Jung and Yung in modern Kuangsi belonged to the Liao culture, which even in much more recent times practiced headhunting and cannibalism. Late in the eighth century, the Huang tribe, also called the Man of the Western Plain, attacked the Yung protectorate and overran thirteen counties. The warfare continued sporadically for over two decades. In 816 P'ei Hsing-li (774-820), the Kuei protectorate commander, and Yang Min (d.820), the Jung protectorate commander, undertook a two-year campaign that resulted in the slaughter of 20,000 Huangs. An estimated eighty percent of the population of Jung and Yung died from warfare or disease. In January 821 a new commander proposed further punitive measures against the Huang.[201]

Han Yü's memorial first describes the primitive culture of the aborigines. Human in neither dress nor language, they have no towns or fixed dwellings but rather live in caves in the hills and crags; they assemble together only for defense and once disturbed are hard to pacify. Minor incidents, therefore, should be glossed over. P'ei Hsing-li and Yang Min started the recent troubles. Their campaigns were undertaken only to obtain personal wealth and advancement; they had no long-range strategy. Over 20,000 people have been killed, and ninety percent of the households are empty, but the bandits are even angrier and more resentful than before. The present commander is no better than P'ei and Yang and should not be allowed to wage further warfare. Han Yü also notes the enormous loss of government troops in these wars. Soldiers sent south are unfamiliar with the climate or the terrain.

Only a quarter of the soldiers sent from the Yangtse provinces to the deep south survive a year. It would be much better to recruit and provision forces from areas adjacent to Jung and Yung. "The cost will be no greater, but the soldiers will grow accustomed to the area. . . . They will not be an occupation army." Finally, the recent southern campaigns have greatly reduced the Huang population. The south is a huge area with a small population at best. To exterminate the Huang and take over their lands will not profit the T'ang. "If we rather relax our control, then we can treat them as we would a wild animal: if it approaches, we defend ourselves; if it departs, we do not give chase and in doing so deplete the power of the court." He suggests His Majesty send a censor to proclaim this policy to the Huang, and they will surely submit. This, and the appointment of qualified and trustworthy commanders, will end the rebellion of the Huang. Han Yü's advice was ignored.

13 The Last Adventure

In 819, while Han Yü was in Ch'ao-chou, Emperor Hsientsung secured from the major separatist governors in the northeast acknowledgment of the crown's authority to appoint their successors. Thus was the theoretical subjugation of the separatists completed and the "restoration" of the T'ang empire achieved. The new agreement was soon put to the test. When the governor of Ch'eng-te district died in the winter of 820, the court exercised its newly won prerogative and appointed T'ien Hung-cheng (764-821) from the neighboring province of Wei-po to succeed him.[202] The appointment was a grave miscalculation. Local military rivalries and feuding were common in the northeast, and T'ien took two thousand of his own troops from Wei-po as a personal guard when he assumed his position as governor of Ch'eng-te at Chen-chou. A narrow-minded bureaucrat in the Ministry of Finance refused four requests from T'ien to fund these troops and held up a million cash to pay the Ch'eng-te troops. As a result, T'ien was forced to send his own guard back to Wei-po. Wang T'ing-ts'ou (d.834), a Ch'eng-te officer angered by his district's loss of its autonomy, stirred up local resentment against T'ien and on August 29, 821 massacred him and three hundred of his family and retainers.[203] Wang appropriated the title of viceroy and requested the court to confirm him as governor of Ch'eng-te. The court, however, decided to fight. Niu Yüan-i (d.823?), prefect of Shen-chou in Ch'eng-te territory, was named governor; T'ien P'u (785-822), son of the slain ex-governor, was named governor of Wei-po; and the venerable P'ei Tu was named field commander of government forces set in motion against Wang T'ing-ts'ou. When Wang threw a siege around Niu Yüan-i at Shen-chou, the pieces were in place for a replay of many a battle already fought by Hsien-tsung.[204]

All the ills of the earlier government operations against Huai-hsi plagued the campaign against Ch'eng-te: lack of coordination, eunuch interference at the front, determined resistance, and bureaucratic indecision in Ch'ang-an. By February 822, shortage of rations had all but immobilized the imperial forces. Starvation was weakening the fortitude of the defenders of Shen-chou. On February 27, the court capitulated, named Wang T'ing-ts'ou governor, and ceased all military action against him. Wang, however, much to the court's embarrassment refused to release Niu Yüan-i, who had been named to another post, or to lift the siege of Shen-chou.

Han Yü, who at this time was vice-president of the Ministry of War, drew the unenviable assignment as special "commissioner for the propagation of assuagement" in Ch'eng-te, or, in simple words, he was to go to Chen-chou and persuade Wang T'ing-ts'ou to release Niu Yüan-i. When Yüan Chen heard the news of the commission, he is reported to have remarked, "What a pity for Han Yü!" His Majesty himself had second thoughts and emended the order so that Han Yü was required to proceed only to the edge of Ch'eng-te, survey the situation, and then decide whether to enter Chen-chou. He traveled northeast to the "northern capital" at T'ai-yüan where his old patron P'ei Tu was now military governor.

This was their first meeting since Han Yü's exile to Ch'ao-chou. On the road, he exchanged poetry with his assistant Wu Tan. One product was the beautifully crafted lyric, whose contrast between the lush spring already in progress in the capital and the harsh realities of the northeast frontier betrays the author's carefully controlled anxieties about his mission.

IN THE EVENING, STOPPING AT THE SHOU-YANG
POST STATION, WRITTEN AFTER A POEM BY
BUREAU PRESIDENT WU

The face of things
        about to change
                I left Ch'ang-an

yet half through spring
        this border town
                still bitter cold

I see
        no garden flowers
                no lane willows

from horseback
        only the moon
                round and cold.[205]

He stayed several weeks at T'ai-yüan while P'ei Tu coordinated political pressure against Wang. In April, he proceeded to Chen-chou. What ensued marks the climax of Li Ao's "Life of Han Yü":

Wang T'ing-ts'ou put his troops on alert, and they confronted Han Yü with swords bared and bows drawn. When he reached headquarters, armored soldiers were arranged in the courtyard. Han Yü, Wang T'ing-ts'ou, and the eunuch army supervisor each took their places, and when they were seated, Wang T'ing-ts'ou said,

"These disorders were the soldiers' doing. It was not my idea."

Han Yü replied in a loud voice,

"Because of your ability as a general, the Son of Heaven has bestowed upon you the insignia of office. But in truth he knew not that you feared to speak openly with your troops. There's been a mistake."

The soldiers pressed forward and said,

"The former grand preceptor attacked Chu T'ao on behalf of the state, and Chu T'ao was defeated; his bloody clothes are still here. This army has submitted to the court. How can you consider us rebels?"[206]

And Han Yü replied,

"Don't speak—any of you! Listen to me! I thought none of you would remember the merits and loyalty of the former grand preceptor. But since you do remember, so much the better. I need make no appeals to ancient history to illustrate the consequences of rebellion. Look only since the *t'ien-pao* period (742-755): An Lu-shan, Shih Szu-ming, Li Hsi-lieh, Liang Ch'ung-i, Chu T'ao, Chu Tz'u, Wu Yüan-chi, Li Shih-tao—do any of them have sons or grandsons alive today? Do any of them hold office?"

All answered,

"None of them."

And he continued,

"T'ien Hung-cheng returned the six prefectures of Wei-po to the court, was named governor, and eventually became president of the secretariat. His insignia of office passed to his sons; his sons and grandsons, even as small children, received good posts. They are extremely wealthy and honored, and their glory radiates through the empire.[207]

"Wang Ch'eng-yüan (grandson of Wang Wu-chün) was only sixteen when he first held the insignia of office. You all know this!"

But they responded,

"T'ien Hung-cheng oppressed this army, so we were discontent."

Han Yü replied,

"Correct! So you violated his person and killed his family. What more is there to say?"

Then they all clamored,

"What he says is so."

Wang T'ing-ts'ou, fearing his troops were changing their minds, ordered the guard to disperse and withdrew. Then weeping, he addressed Han Yü,

"What is it you wish me to do?"

He replied,

"The Six Armies of the Divine Plan have many generals like Niu Yüan-i. But the court is concerned with the larger principles involved and cannot simply abandon him. Why have you besieged him so long?"

Wang T'ing-ts'ou said,

"I'll release him at once."

"If you do so, then there's no problem."

So they feasted together, and Han Yü returned. Niu Yüan-i was released.

When he was back in the capital, Han Yü reported in detail his conversations with Wang T'ing-ts'ou and the soldiers to His Majesty, who was very pleased and wanted to employ him in a major position.[208]

This is the closest Han Yü ever came to serving in the state's highest office. It is not likely, however, that Mu-tsung would actually have appointed Han Yü to the prime ministership or that Han Yü would have long survived in that post. For instance, the emperor on March 16, 822 did indeed appoint the fiery and impulsive Yüan Chen (779-831) minister. "The appointment was made solely at the insistence of the Emperor and met with a very hostile reception."[209] Yüan's tenure as minister lasted only two months and was marred by political and personal feuding remarkable even for that time. The episode taught Mu-tsung the perils of appointing brilliant and engaging but inexperienced and unsupported men of letters to run his government.[210]

Han Yü was back in Ch'ang-an by the end of April, where a disappointment of a different sort awaited him

JUST BACK FROM CHEN-CHOU

When I left
>the willows
>>by the wayside

flirting
>with the spring breeze
>>tried to fly

But the garden
>still has plum
>>and peach buds

flowers as yet
>unopened
>>they await my return.[211]

A Northern Sung collection of T'ang lore records that Han Yü had two concubines named Crimson Peach and Willow Branch. The poem written at Shou-yang station contrasts his enjoyment of these ladies' company with the loneliness of the frontier. Back from Chen-chou, however, he learned that Willow Branch had tried to flee (fly) the household but had been caught and returned. Thereafter he favored Crimson Peach as explained in "Just Back from Chen-chou."[212]

In early May the court received a proposal to reform the salt monopoly by requiring government officials to market salt directly to the consumer without the merchants as intermediaries. The court solicited opinion from various scholars. Han Yü replied in a long memorial that reveals both detailed knowledge of the nation's finances and a keen understanding of the lifestyle and psychological motivation of the nation's poor. He argued against the new proposal, which was not adopted.[213]

On September 21, 822 Han Yü was transferred to be vice-president of the Ministry of Personnel, which regulated the selection, assignment, and promotion of government officials. Because of the sensitive nature of their work, clerks were not permitted to leave the personnel ministry offices during their tours of duty and were locked within the premises at night. Han Yü abandoned this custom and when challenged replied, "People fear ghosts because they cannot see them. If ghosts could be seen, they would no longer be feared. Likewise if the applicants for office cannot see the clerks, their influence increases. If I allow them to come and go as they please, their influence will diminish."[214]

On July 19, 823 Han Yü was transferred from the Ministry of Personnel to serve as metropolitan prefect of Ch'ang-an.[215] Personal jealousies and factional strife, however, marred his last year in office. The new appointment brought him into conflict with Li Shen (775-846), an aristocrat whom he had once recommended for the *chin-shih* examination of 802. Emperor Mu-tsung appointed Li to the Han-lin Academy where he formed a clique with Li Te-yü and Yüan Chen. When Li Feng-chi (758-835) became prime minister in June 822, he was able to take advantage of the quarrel between P'ei Tu and Yüan Chen to oust both from the ministership. Li Feng-chi then turned his attention to ridding the Han-lin of potential rivals. He had Li Te-yü sent to the provinces and Li Shen posted to the vice-presidency of the Censorate. Han Yü's appointment as prefect of Ch'ang-an required a courtesy call at the Censorate, but he requested and was granted by Mu-tsung a dispensation from performing this ritual.[216]

The haughty Li Shen interpreted Han Yü's request as a slight, and friction between the two offices ensued. Han Yü detained and disciplined unscrupulous and unruly elements in the "Army for Defense of the Emperor," whose regulation was the statutory responsibility of the Censorate. The eunuch generals feared to protest, murmuring to one another, "he's the one who wanted to burn the bones of the Buddha. How can we oppose *him*!" When Li Shen sent hoards of petty offenders in shackles to the prefect's office to receive their bastinadoes, Han Yü released them unpunished.[217] The Censorate memorialized on these incidents, and Li Feng-chi took advantage of the discord to have Li Shen sent to the provinces and Han Yü returned to his former position at the Ministry of War. Both scholars, however, realized that Li Feng-chi had misrepresented their disagreement to the emperor and managed to explain matters to Emperor Mu-tsung. A week later on November 25, 823 Han Yü was returned to his post at the Ministry of Personnel.[218]

14   Last Days

On February 25, 824 the Emperor Mu-tsung died as a result of a fall from his horse during a polo match the previous year. The eunuchs engineered the accession of a fifteen-year-old wastrel as the future Emperor Ching-tsung (809-827), and there was no longer any doubt that the spirit of the age of Primal Harmony (*yüan-ho*) had passed. By midsummer Han Yü was too ill to attend his office and requested sick leave. He returned to a villa south of the city between the tomb of the First Emperor of Ch'in and the Southern Mountains. Chang Chi, who was between positions at the time, stayed with him through the summer. Once they were joined by Chia Tao, and the trio undertook a boating excursion on South Stream in the vicinity of Han Yü's estate. His verse account of this outing is his last great poem.

FIRST TRIP TO SOUTH STREAM, THREE POEMS

I
Poling a boat by the foot of Southern Mountains
up and up and no way to return,
quiet diversions follow us by, so many
who counts the distance?

Plunged into shadows past twining trees
skirting a sloping shore hidden then high,
over stones once rough now sharpened to nothing
worn out pulling through wicked currents,
we dock awhile against leaning palisades and fish
then reach at last a flat island and eat.
Drop after drop an evening rain falls,
sliver-like and fine the new moon reclines.

I fear the years that remain will be few,
my days for rest have come too late;
but only illness makes me live like this,
I have no wish to disdain the world.

II

South Stream runs clear and fast
but seldom sees scull and sail,
so the mountain farmers look on in surprise
following us with unstopping gaze—
and not just crowds of children,
some with canes and grey hair
offer me melons in a basket
and urge me to stay on a while.

I tell them an illness brought me here
but already I feel more at ease.
Luckily I have some extra salary
to buy a place in the western fields
with silos full of rice and grain
and never a care from morning till night.
Rising to the top was never a joy,
so coming down's been easy to take.
I'm only afraid I may trouble you villagers
with a call for help from time to time,
so I'd like to join the local shrine
and with fowl and pork feast the springs and falls.

III

With weakened legs unable to walk
so best I halted my tracks at Court,
but this thin frame can move by palanquin
so never could I leave these fine vistas.

Here now, up under the southern slopes
long famous for waters and rocks,
the boat's been pulled in, right
to where current is clear and fast.

I lack courage to trust the waves
so rather pole the boat through swift rapids,
an egret rises as if to show me the way,
flying twenty to thirty feet ahead.

Upright willows belt the sands,
clustered pines cap the bluffs.
Back home, already the night is over,
so who says it's not as hard as the service![219]

This series is remarkable for its subtle transitions between radically different narrative and descriptive voices and styles. The dense, almost Swinburnian, description in the first poem leads easily into the relaxed conversational tone of the second, and the two voices mesh together harmoniously in the final poem of the group. This *tour de force* prompted the Ch'ing critic Chu I-tsun to remark that the series "is not Ancient and not T'ang, it's Han Yü's own" (*pu ku pu T'ang, Ch'ang-li pense*).

By the autumn the sick leave had elapsed, and Han Yü resigned as vice-president of the Ministry of Personnel.[220] When Chang Chi received a new appointment, they moved back to the city, Han Yü to his mansion in the Ching-an Ward and Chang Chi to quarters in an adjoining ward. Chang Chi's "Elegy for T'ui-chih" contains a minute description of Han Yü's last days:

At mid-autumn, the night of the sixteenth,
the sky shone with the moon's light;
he urged me to stay, and we sat
talking on the front steps of the hall.
He brought out two servant girls
who played for us guitar and zither.
Facing the breeze, listening to strings resound,
in no time, the evening was over.
He urged me to come again—
that evening I shall never forget.[221]

It was during this celebration of the Mid-Autumn Festival, September 12, 824, that Han Yü wrote his last surviving poem.

ENJOYING THE MOON, I REJOICE AT THE ARRIVAL OF AUXILIARY SECRETARY CHANG AND LIBRARIAN WANG

Although last night was the fifteenth,
and the moon not quite a full circle,
when you came to visit,
soft winds and light dew were everywhere.
Clouds adrift scattered like white boulders,
the heavens opened to a blue pool,
solitary and unafraid, the moon
at the sky's zenith arrayed itself for you,
a pleasure to watch through the long night
till far distant dawn began to break.
More perfect will tonight's roundness be
with fine friends again to accompany me.
My regrets I may not enjoy more food and drink,
from me there will be only poetry and laughter.[222]

Chang Chi's elegy continues:

But his illness worsened by the day,
though his wife tended him with medicine-broth.
I could never stay over when I came to visit,
and each time I left with greater worry.
When the illness became critical,
callers' carriages filled the street,
but the gatekeeper turned them all away,
and only I was allowed in the sickroom.
He was wide awake, his mind clear,
he said life and death were one.
When the morning of the last day came
his mind, his manner were unperturbed;
as he delivered to me his parting words,
he haughtily pushed off the shroud

and said he wanted to write; his will
had some sections he wanted to change.
He asked me to witness the text
and see to its provisions after his death.
But the family was wailing all around,
and we could not finish the document,
so his son Tzu-fu took down his words
and sent his orders to the other relatives.
His *Analects* commentary was left unfinished,
the handwriting already fading away.
Neither was his new pavilion completed
but was closed off in the villa's western wing.
Letters and papers and drafts of poems
were piled in heaps and filled the chests.

Han Yü died on December 25, 824 and was buried April 21, 825 in the ancestral cemetery at Ho-yang.[223]

Before concluding this chapter it may be useful to review several larger patterns in Han Yü's life, specifically his economic situation and his personality. Han Yü's writings occasionally refer to the poverty of his youth.[224] Although a standard topos of T'ang literati biographies, it is probable that Han Yü did suffer from relative poverty in comparison with other members of his class. Although the family owned land on both sides of the Yellow River around Lo-yang, this wealth was essentially not portable.[225] Unless some members of the family received a salary from holding office, the family seems to have been physically tied to its landholdings. Thus when Han Hui died in Shao-chou, his wife took the family back to Lo-yang and when the rebellions made life there impossible, she moved once again to family lands in the southeast. Once on such land, however, there seem to have been few financial worries. Han Yü spent these years studying and learning the ways of the literati, not tilling fields.

As suggested above, the patronage of Ma Sui seems to have eased Han Yü's early "student" days in Ch'ang-an. The frustrations, inherent in the famous 795 letters to the prime ministers, however, were certainly motivated by considerations that were other than moral. He probably had married by this time and felt an urgency to secure the financial security that only office could provide. After Han Yü assumed his first post in Pien-chou in 796, he was in continuous government service until his death in 824. It is thus possible to calculate his official salary for any given year. The following table summarizes this information for years that marked significant advances in his career.[226]

Although such hypothetical economic reconstructions should be used with caution, these statistics do tally with Han Yü's own statements about his economic situation. Already in the Pien-chou years, his household numbered over thirty individuals since he took responsibility for the household of his brother Han Hui after the latter's wife, nee Cheng, died in 794. His salary was probably just adequate to provide for his household. By 807, Han Yü was the sole "working" member of his clan and had assumed responsibility for over ten more of the offspring of his deceased brothers and cousins. Moreover, his biography in the *Old T'ang History* states that he "guided and encouraged younger students and housed sixteen or seventeen of them. Although there was often not enough breakfast to go around, he was cheerful and unconcerned."[227] As we have seen above, economic considerations probably influenced the move to Lo-yang in 807.

A major improvement in Han Yü's financial situation seems to have occurred about 815-816. His "mansion" in the Ching-an Ward of Ch'ang-an as well as his villa south of the city were probably purchased during these years.[228] The T'ang economy experienced a protracted period of deflation during all of Han Yü's adult life, and the general shortage of money in circulation increased the value of the cash salaries paid to officials. The increasing affluence of the official class during the early ninth century was cause for much soul-searching among its more ethically minded members. It is possible Han Yü's sizable real estate investments during 815-816 represented an effort to divest himself of excess cash; for, in 817 the government forbade cash hoarding, and this injunction was much in the spirit of the times.[229]

		Salary Sources for T'ang Officials					Number of persons who could be supported for 1 year[4]
Year of appointment	Office	Cash[1] (yearly)	Grain[2] (yearly)	Lands pertaining to office[3] (chih-fen-t'ien)	Lands held in perpetuity[3] (yung-yeh-t'ien)	Total cash value	
799	Collator of Texts in the Imperial Library	300,000	40 hu. (20,000)	2 ch'ing (20,000)	2 ch'ing (20,000)	360,000	36
801	Professor in the College of the Four Gates	300,000	80 hu (40,000)	3.5 ch'ing (35,000)	2.5 ch'ing (25,000)	400,000	40
806	Professor in the Imperial University	480,000	200 hu (100,000)	6 ch'ing (60,000)	8 ch'ing (80,000)	720,000	72
816	Imperial Palace Secretary	960,000	200 hu (100,000)	6 ch'ing (60,000)	8 ch'ing (80,000)	1,300,000	130
823	Metropolitan Prefect	1,080,000	360 hu (180,000)	9 ch'ing (90,000)	12 ch'ing (120,000)	1,470,000	147

[1] Figures represent yearly totals and are based on *T'ang hui-yao* 91/1661–63 and *HTS* 55/1402–05.

[2] Grain allotment measured in *hu* (approximately 1 3/4 bushels) as recorded in *T'ang hui-yao* 90/1648 and *HTS* 55/1393. Figures in parentheses represent the cash value of these allotments based on the rate of 500 cash per *hu*, the prevailing rate from about 800 until well past Han Yü's death (see Twitchett, *Financial Administration*, p. 78).

[3] Figures represent the number of *ch'ing* (13.3 acres) under cultivation (*HTS* 55/1393–94). Officials were paid at the rate of 20 *hu* per *ch'ing*, thus 1 *ch'ing* equaled 10,000 cash per year at current exchange rates.

[4] This assumes the cost to support one person to be 10,000 cash per year, derived as follows: *HTS* 55/1387–88 records a discussion from about 763 on economics, in which it is stated that the average person consumed 7.2 *hu* of grain per year, that this represented one-third his total living costs (or 21.6 *hu* per year), and that 1 *ch'ing* of land could produce about 50 *hu* of grain (cf. William Hung, *A Supplementary Volume of Notes for Tu Fu*, pp. 26–27, where the same figures are used to calculate the relative wealth of Tu Fu's family). Rounding off 21.6 to 20, and using the *yüan-ho* period exchange rate of 500 cash per *hu*, the annual cost of one person was about 10,000 cash.

All the major accounts of Han Yü's life (Li Ao's "Life," Huang-fu Shih's "Epitaph," and the biographies in the *Old* and *New T'ang Histories*) agree that he had an open and forthright character, which manifested itself in his unswerving loyalty to his friends. Huang-fu Shih writes that "in his relations with others he was totally open and without guile." Li Ao adds that his expansive personality also extended to his intellectual outlook, such that "in discussion he was always concerned with the larger principles involved." He was a great conversationalist and an inspired teacher: "his teaching and his efforts to mold his students were unrelenting, fearing they would not be perfect. Yet he amused them with jokes and with the chanting of poems, so that they were enraptured with his teaching and forgot about returning home." The sense of humor that is so obvious in his writing was also important in his life. Li Ao writes that "although he himself was retired and in ill health, when I lay sick in bed he came three times to visit me, and we passed the days talking and laughing."[230] And the *Old T'ang History* relates that Chang Chi "even after he became well established would retire together with Han Yü, and they would talk and feast together, discussing literature and composing poetry as they had in earlier days." The same text continues in a different vein: "he looked upon those from wealthy and influential families as his menials and steadfastly ignored them." And finally, Huang-fu Shih records that sure trait of the great scholar and man of letters: "ordinarily, even when relaxing or eating, he was never without a book. When he was tired, they were his pillows; and when he ate, they were like sweets to his mouth."

CHAPTER TWO

The Politics
of Empire

The Master said, "Kuan Chung
served as minister to Duke
Huan, made him hegemon over
the feudal lords, and brought
unity and order to the empire.
To this day, the people still enjoy these benefits from him:
without Kuan Chung, we would
all be wearing our hair unbound
and fastening our clothes on the
left."
—*Analects* XIV. 17

In 647, two years before his death, Emperor T'ai-tsung, first
architect of the T'ang state, put the following question to his
assembled courtiers: "Since Antiquity, many emperors have
brought peace to the Chinese lands but were unable to bring
the Jung and the Ti into submission. My abilities do not reach
to those of the Ancients, yet my achievements have surpassed
theirs. I do not understand the reasons for this." When his
courtiers replied in unison with their usual flatteries, the great
monarch, as was no doubt his intention, answered his own
question: there were five reasons for his unique accomplishments, and the last was that "since Antiquity all have honored

the Hua and despised the I and the Ti; only I have loved them both as one, with the result that the nomad tribes have all held to me as to father and mother."[1] A modern scholar has noted that this concept—equality of "Hua" ("Chinese") and "I and Ti" ("non-Chinese," "barbarian") was more than a theoretical innovation of the T'ang founder; it was a concrete policy he consistently maintained, often over the opposition of his advisers. For example, in 630 T'ai-tsung settled 100,000 Eastern Turks on "Chinese" territory within the bend of the Yellow River and granted court positions of the fifth rank and above to their leaders who moved permanently to Ch'ang-an with almost 10,000 retainers.[2]

The T'ang house, perhaps as a result of its own "mixed" racial origins, was careful to exclude the issue of race from the governance of its multiracial empire; and this principle was often reaffirmed throughout the course of the dynasty. For example, Li Hua wrote that "the dynasty unites the empire in a single house, where Hua and I are as one."[3] Statistics will support this principle: of the 369 prime ministers during the course of the T'ang, 32, or one in twelve, were of non-Chinese origin. Only the lack of literacy in Chinese, for instance, prevented Li Lin-fu from conferring the post on An Lu-shan.[4]

T'ai-tsung's own origins among the military aristocracy of the sinicized Altaic tribes that had ruled northwest China since the fourth century certainly nourished this cultural broadmindedness of the T'ang founder.[5] In 636 he organized these hereditary military families into the *fu-ping* or "militia troops," the basic military units that made possible the consolidation of T'ang power in China proper and its projection into Central Asia. These militia units were heavily concentrated in the Ch'ang-an area, thus constituting an essential component of the "Kuan-lung aristocracy" of early T'ang.[6] Although this society exalted military values, it could also produce "scholars" in the bold northern tradition, of which T'ai-tsung's own literary productions are probably representative.[7] Thus, the same class of people in the early T'ang held both civil and military power, and this class naturally looked to its most illustrious member for leadership. The importance of the person of the emperor throughout the T'ang, at least through the middle of the ninth century, cannot be overestimated. Wei Cheng (580–643), advisor to T'ai-tsung, was not exaggerating when he admonished: "The security of the state, the stability of the country depend entirely on the One Man."[8]

When the one man was gone, the fragility of his achievement soon became apparent. Whether the Empress Wu (627?–705) used the examination system to recruit a new class of bureaucracy to oppose the old aristocracy is still a matter of some dispute. But writing from the much closer vantage point of the late eighth century, the T'ang historian Shen Chi-chi (c.740–c.805) attributed the fashion of choosing officials by examining their literary ability to Empress Wu's tastes in literature.[9] "The Empress was tolerably versed in literature and history and enjoyed poetizing (lit. 'worm-carving'), so beginning in 680 one began to use literary composition to select officials. During the next twenty years in which she controlled the empire, the ministers and high officials all achieved their success through literature, and as time continued this fashion became a fixed custom." During the peaceful years before 755 the practice of obtaining office through literary expertise became hereditary: "Fathers taught their sons, older brothers taught their younger brothers and none changed from this course. The great rose in the ministries and bureaus, and the lesser ones found work in the prefectures and counties, bringing a sufficiency of wealth to themselves and their families. Even small boys were ashamed not to talk of literature and composition. They held that the *chin-shih* was the most refined of the official examinations, and the successful candidates each year were known within a fortnight throughout the empire. Most of these were honorable, talented, and intelligent men, but there were also rogues and scoundrels among them who confounded right and wrong to create factions and private alliances in order to pass the examinations and make their names known to the world."

Whatever social class, if any, these new officials may have represented and for whatever specific political purposes, if any, they may have been recruited, the advent of an ethic that defined suitability for office in almost exclusively literary terms was new to the T'ang and probably to all of the Chinese experience up to that time.[10] The almost universal acclaim for the examination system as a major stimulus to the growth of T'ang literature should not becloud the fact that this growth came at the expense of those martial qualities that had been so important to the early T'ang spirit. There was throughout the course of the dynasty a steady shift in emphasis among officials of the central government from martial (*wu*) to literary (*wen*) values. By the early eighth century this shift had already resulted in the sort of literary dilettantism that Shen Chi-chi associated with the examination process and that the real intellectuals and writers of the age held in contempt. It was against this *wen*—the hereditary practice of literary "worm-carving" solely for the purpose of passing the examinations and obtaining office—that Han Yü fought throughout his life. For him, this Six Dynasties literary style, codified in the *Literary Anthology* (*Wen hsüan*) and encouraged through its use as an examination standard, constituted "contemporary literature" (*shih-wen*).

A much more important consequence of the growth of this official-literary ethic among the T'ang ruling class was the concomitant decline in the complementary military ethic that the T'ang founders had manifested. It is certainly no coincidence that the *fu-ping* military system declined at precisely the same time the examination system prospered. The *fu-ping* system declined when the honors and rewards to be obtained through conscription into it no longer compensated the value of the time thereby lost to preparation for examinations: as the examination system grew, preparation for it became a full-time occupation that left no time for military conscription and training.

As is well known, the professional soldiers and mercenaries that replaced the conscripts of early T'ang were largely of non-Chinese origin. As a result, the early T'ang equilibrium between literary and military values dissolved into a dichotomy that came to be defined largely along cultural lines: to be literary was to be Hua, to be military was to be Hu.[11] As the old literary-military coalition disappeared, the polarization of Hua and Hu intensified; the ruling class at court no longer represented the country as a whole. These cultural differences eventually escalated into the political, economic, and social conflicts behind the An Lu-shan rebellion, a military action that effectively split the T'ang into two socially and culturally distinct states: (1) a loyalist, imperial, heavily Hua culture centered around the T'ang capital in Ch'ang-an, and (2) an independent, separatist, largely Hu culture centered in the northeast.[12]

Although the Ch'ang-an society of the post An Lu-shan rebellion years was heir to the heritage of the T'ang founders, its real power structure had fundamentally changed. The fragmentation of the old ruling coalition resulted in the diffusion of government powers among at least five distinct groups. (1) The imperial T'ang house of Li continued at each succession through the course of the eighth century to produce basically competent rulers capable of generating support from the other groups. (2) The old aristocracy of early T'ang times continued to live on, even to prosper, in its new mainly literary guise. (3) A newly emerging class of "literati," officials from less than aristocratic backgrounds that prospered along with the examination system, grew during the first half of the eighth century. The introduction of this third group into the political scene fundamentally altered the relations between the first two, for the aristocrats and literati often shared common concerns, and these common concerns as well as conflicts destroyed the homogeneity of the nobility and made it an uncertain ally of the crown. As a result, the crown turned increasingly throughout the eighth century to the eunuchs as personal retainers and servants. (4) Eunuchs, often with the support of the throne, moved quickly to assume power vacuums created by feuding bureaucratic factions. By the late eighth century, they controlled all functions of the imperial palace, most of the imperial military forces around Ch'ang-an, and through their control of Buddhist and Taoist monasteries, much of the metropolitan economy. (5) Finally, the military outside the capital area was controlled by career military officers whose loyalty to the crown was always suspect.[13]

The first three of these groups were largely Hua or sinicized Hu: the imperial family and aristocracy were keenly aware of their ethnic origins, and this awareness certainly accounts for the continued T'ang receptivity at the highest levels of society to Central Asian music, literature, religion, and material culture. The literati, presumably the most Hua among the ruling class by virtue of their training in the Chinese written tradition, seem to have been little troubled by the threat that the steady absorption of foreign influences posed to the continued viability of that tradition. Yet despite these disclaimers, there is little doubt these first three segments of the mid-T'ang ruling class represented its more sinicized components, as compared with the last two groups. The eunuchs were certainly of non-Chinese origin; most came from the aboriginal populations of modern Fukien. The chief eunuch under Emperor Hsien-tsung, for instance, T'u-t'u Ch'eng-ts'ui (d. 820), was a Fukien aborigine, although the official T'ang histories attempt to conceal this origin.[14] The provincial T'ang military after the demise of the *fu-ping* system was the most strongly Hu element in the power structure. The rank-and-file troops, certainly those of mercenary forces like the Uighurs, spoke no Chinese. The increasingly frequent use by literati through the eighth century of epithets such as "crude military" (*ts'u-wu*) to refer even to important provincial officers testifies to the increasing cultural gap between the two groups.

Nowhere was the gap greater than between Ch'ang-an and the provinces of the northeast—the modern Hopei. This area, site of the ancient Warring Kingdoms states of Ch'i, Yen, and Chao, had long been an integral part of the Chinese lands and a center of Hua civilization. Yet throughout the course of the seventh century this area received successive migrations of Hu from Central Asia, who intermingled there with elements of the Eastern Turks and with the Khitan of modern Manchuria.[15] Accordingly, this area became culturally more distant from the increasingly dilettantic court at Ch'ang-an, and these differences eventually fostered the separatist rebellion of An

Lu-shan. During the early 770s, the leaders of these provinces actually achieved many of the goals of the earlier rebellion; they revered An Lu-shan as a sage (*sheng*).[16] So strong was separatist sentiment in Hopei that the natives there considered it normal. So Tu Mu (803-852) wrote that "the people east of the mountains (i.e. Hopei) revolted almost five generations ago; and their descendants today, in their speech and actions, are so thoroughly seditious that they believe this to be the natural state of affairs; so deeply imbued in them is this sedition that they do not even consider they have done wrong."[17]

The cultural differences between Ch'ang-an and the separatist provinces are highlighted in another text of Tu Mu, his "Epitaph for Master Lu P'ei of Fan-yang":

> The ancestors of Master Lu P'ei for three generations after the An Lu-shan rebellion served either in Yen or in Chao. These two places have good pastures for grazing horses, and for the first twenty years of his life Master Lu never heard that in Antiquity there existed the Duke of Chou or Confucius. He played polo, drank wine, and hunted hares from horseback. In speech and action all was fighting and warfare.
>
> In Chen-chou there was a Confucian scholar named Huang Chien whom the people revered and called their teacher. He spoke to Master Lu about Confucian studies and the way of the former kings. He often told him how south of the River there were broad lands ten times greater than Yen and Chao, how there was an eastern and a western capital, how in the western capital there was a Son of Heaven with great lords and nobles who dwelt about him, how the two capitals had millions of people, and how the neighboring states paid court each year bearing the products and treasures of their lands, how by mastering Confucian studies and the way of the former kings he could attain a position among these lords, and so gain glory and wealth to pass on to his children and how he could live till the end of his days without fighting or killing.[18]

This contrast between the Spartan, military existence in the northeast and the more "refined" lifestyle of the capital is even clearer in the following passage from the *Old T'ang History* biography of Chang Hung-ching (760-824), who was appointed military governor of Yu-chou when the court finally regained a measure of control over that district in 821:

> When Chang Hung-ching entered the district of Yu-chou as military governor, the people of the town of Chi, young and old, men and women, flanked the road to see him. Now the officers of the northeast armies braved heat and cold together with their troops and did not ride in fine carriages with spread awnings. Hung-ching had been wealthy for a long time and moreover did not understand the customs of the country. When he entered Yen, he traveled in a sedan-chair among the troops. The people of Chi marveled mightily at him.
>
> Because the An Lu-shan rebellion had begun in Yu-chou, Hung-ching began with this issue in his effort to reform their ways: he opened the tomb of An Lu-shan and defiled the casket. And the people became even more disaffected.
>
> A group of his subordinates, Wei Yung and Chang Ts'ung-hou and the like, were repeatedly dissolute and given to drink, often returning late in the night, their blazing torches and their cursing and swearing filling the streets. The people of Chi were not used to such behavior.
>
> Moreover, Wei Yung and the others ridiculed the soldiers, often calling them "rebel barbarians"; and they said to the troops, "now the empire has no wars, so even if you can draw a 200-pound bow, it's not worth being able to read even the simplest character." The troops kept in their anger yet hated them deeply.
>
> When ex-military governor Liu Tsung returned to the Court, he left a million strings of cash for the troops. But Hung-ching retained 200,000 and gave this to his own troops. The people of Chi could endure their anger

no more, and their leaders rebelled *en masse*, and imprisoned Hung-ching in the Chi *yamen*.[19]

With this fiasco ended the central government's long campaign to regain control over the northeast, which remained independent through the end of the dynasty.

The events in Yu-chou soon took on special significance for Han Yü. His friend of many years, Chang Ch'e (d.821) was a subordinate to Chang Hung-ching. A passage in Han Yü's epitaph for Chang Ch'e picks up the story:

> Several days later the troops revolted and, killing those on the governor's staff against whom they had grievances, imprisoned the governor. They then agreed:
> "Chang Ch'e is the best among them; he has never insulted or mistreated us. There is no need to kill him." And they placed him in prison with the governor.
> Several months later, when it was learned that a eunuch envoy was arriving from the capital, Chang said to the governor, "You have done no injustice against the local people here; when the messenger from His Majesty arrives, you could request that he arbitrate this matter, and with luck you may obtain release and return to Court." So he pushed on the door and tied to escape.
> When the guards reported this to their leader, he was surprised and said to his retainers, "It must be Chang Ch'e. He is a loyal man. He has certainly put this idea in the governor's head. It's better we move him to another location." Yet as soon as Chang was outside, he cursed the soldiers, saying,
> "How could you dare to rebel? Wu Yüan-chi was beheaded in the eastern market in 817 and Li Shih-tao has just been beheaded by his own troops. Their cohorts, their parents, wives, and children were all executed, and their flesh made food for dogs and rats. How could you dare to rebel?"
> And he continued to curse them as he went, until they could bear it no longer and beat him to death. And since, up till the moment of his death, he ceased not to curse

them, they all acknowledged he was a patriot, and someone among them took his corpse for burial.[20]

Those few northeasterners who supported rapprochement
with the T'ang court, apparently because of a fascination with
literati-scholarly traditions, felt most acutely this cultural and
political estrangement between the court and their homeland.
One such person was the unfortunate Lu P'ei; another was
Shih Hsiao-chang (800–838), the son of a military family in
Wei-po. During the early 820s when the court briefly regained
control over the province, Li Su, the hero of Ts'ai-chou,
served as military governor and, surprised to find a local youth
with literary ability, employed Shih Hsiao-chang in his headquarters. In 822 his father, Shih Hsien-ch'eng (d. 829), with
the support of local troops, declared himself military governor
and reassumed local control of the province. Shih Hsiao-chang
pleaded with his father not to renounce allegiance to the T'ang
court:

> "Here north of the great River our lands are rich and
> our weapons true, yet the world ridicules us in their
> hearts and looks upon us as barbarians (*i-ti*). This is be-
> cause we rely too much on force of arms rather than on
> a sense of justice to settle affairs. . . . If we do not purge
> ourselves of these coarse ways and profess our allegiance
> to the court, there will be no way to stop this ridicule
> or to awake to the designs of our enlightened sov-
> ereign."[21]

Likewise, the intellectuals of the late eighth and early ninth
centuries tended to view the struggle to unify the T'ang state
as a struggle between civilization and barbarism. For instance,
Li Ao commended Lu Ch'ang-yüan for engineering the defeat
and arrest of Teng Wei-kung, the leader of the rebellious
military element at Pien-chou in 796, by comparing this ac-
complishment to that of persuading the barbarians to "bind
up their hair and adopt Chinese writing and customs."[22]

But without a clear definition and consensus of what was
to constitute civilization, subduing the recalcitrant military

was only a short-term solution. The T'ang founders had looked to Buddhism as the creed most suited to serve as a unifying force for the empire's different races and cultures; and this tendency certainly continued under the Empress Wu.[23] Yet the growing social fragmentation, plus the increasing fossilization of the Buddhist schools themselves, slowly eroded the ability of the faith to provide the intellectual underpinnings of empire. The synthesizing and syncretist tendencies in the post – An Lu-shan revivals of the T'ien-t'ai and Hua-yen doctrines are probably best understood as responses to this lack of a unifying intellectual basis upon which to redefine civilization and barbarism. Yet these syncretist movements touched only the higher levels of philosophical discourse; and although they intrigued such intellectuals as Liang Su and Li Ao and generated popularizations such as the *Treatise on the Origins of Humanity (Yüan jen lun)* of Tsung-mi, their popular appeal and thus their political utility were limited. The facile conclusions of popular syncretism such as the famous court debates between the "Three Religions" were little more than light court entertainment.[24] These Buddhist syncretistic movements also failed because they could not provide a framework for resolving the Hua-Hu dichotomy among the groups that held power in the late eighth and early ninth centuries. The Buddha was, after all, himself a Hu; and it is hardly surprising that Buddhism was most firmly entrenched among the old aristocracy, the eunuchs, and the military, the most distinctly Hu of these groups.[25]

In the end Han Yü, Li Ao, and like-minded colleagues rejected the facile syncretism of their age in favor of a rigorous delineation of the boundaries between Hua and Hu culture. In so doing, they cast a wide survey over all that remained of earlier Chinese traditions in order to isolate whatever might be useful in helping them form a clearer definition of what it meant to be Hua. Their method was not a facile syncretism but rather a focused eclecticism; and much of what they found useful will perhaps surprise those scholars accustomed to thinking of their achievements in terms of the narrower Confucianism of later times.

An essential part of this process was the identification of "culture heroes," men of Antiquity whose names evoked specific achievements of the past that the authors believed needed to be duplicated in their own time: emblems for necessary action. One such emblem was Kuan Chung (d.645 B.C.), the famous minister of Duke Huan of Ch'i (r.685-643 B.C.). Li Ao repeatedly refers to Kuan Chung as one who served his lord well, first by making him hegemon of the feudal lords, and then by using this strength to repulse the incursions of the Jung and the Ti, thus bringing order and unity to the crumbling Chou empire.[26] Han Yü also realized the aptness of Kuan Chung as an emblem for his political program. One of the questions he posed as an examiner, probably for the Pien-chou provincial examinations in the late 790s, reads:

> Are not those honored for their Way who bring benefit to others and success to themselves? When the Chou dynasty was in decline, Kuan Chung made his sovereign hegemon, assembled the feudal lords, and brought unity and order to the empire. He moderated the Jung and the Ti barbarians and brought honor to the capital. All within the four seas benefited from his acts; the feudal lords of the empire rushed to accept his command, and none opposed him. Was this not bringing benefit to others and success to oneself?
>
> The Ch'in used the methods of Shang Yang to enrich and strengthen their state. The feudal lords dared not resist and after seven rulers, the empire belonged to Ch'in. This was due to Shang Yang. Yet those who spoke of the Way in later ages were all ashamed to mention Kuan Chung and Shang Yang. Why? Did they not merely accept their reputation without investigating the facts?
>
> It is desired that you discuss this with fellow students, and do not be misled by the old explanations.[27]

Although Han Yü's rhetoric is based on *Analects* XIV.17, he cites the achievements attributed there to Kuan Chung and Shang Yang in order to underline their relevance as an agenda for contemporary political action: restoration from decline of the central power through ordering of the feudal lords (i.e. provincial military powers) to suppress non-Hua elements—actions that will bring about political order and above all unity.

There runs throughout Han Yü's political thought a latent admiration for the Ch'in Dynasty achievement in forging the first unified empire in Chinese history. So strong was Han Yü's urge for political unity that his thinking shows affinities to that of contemporary intellectuals routinely identified as "Neo-Legalist." Pulleyblank describes Tu Yu and his opinion of the *Kuan-tzu* in terms that Han Yü could easily have agreed with:

> He [Tu Yu] admired Legalist statesmen for the way they developed institutions suited to the conditions of their own days, untrammeled by the imitation of past models; ancient books should be consulted for the basic principles they propounded rather than for ideal patterns. He himself valued the economic ideas of *Kuan-tzu*, but speaking of that work, he remarked: "Whenever one consults the books of the ancients, it is because one wishes to reveal new meanings and form institutions in accordance with present circumstances. Their Way is inexhaustible. How much more are plans for contrivances and expedients subject to a thousand changes and ten thousand alterations. If one imitates in detail, it is like notching a boat to mark a spot. . . ."[28]

Han Yü's basic program for political restoration called for a simplification of the existing pentarchical division of power outlined above. The result was to be a sharing of power between only two elements, the monarchy and the bureaucracy; these, however, were each to be transformed considerably in the process. Han Yü posited a return to the multiracial empire of the T'ang founders, but it was not to be multicultural. All was to be Hua, a new definition of which he provided. At the same time, the eunuchs and the military were to disappear as independent actors in the political arena, and their powers and functions delegated to the bureaucracy. The bureaucracy, in turn, was to divest itself of the dilettantish and literary trappings acquired over the last century and recultivate that earlier T'ang union of civil and military virtues. Participation in this bureaucracy was to be open to aristocrat and literati alike but only after an individual's ability had been demonstrated through an unbiased examination and promotion system, itself revised to test real understanding and administrative talent. The ubiquity of this model in later times should not overshadow the fact that in the early ninth century it was a novel and dramatic agenda, the result of a typically innovative Han Yü blend of "antique" ideals selected as emblems to guide the development of contemporary trends in what he considered the morally correct direction. The program was to resolve the existing dichotomy between Hua and Hu by reasserting the power of a rejuvenated Hua monarchy against recalcitrant Hu forces in the provinces; it was also to bridge the gulf between civil (*wen*) and military (*wu*) values in government service by redefining the standards for the newly emerging bureaucracy. The order and unity of the early T'ang were to be restored, not as a scholastic anachronism but as a living creation formulated to solve the pressing political and cultural problems of the age.

It is quite easy to trace the specific details of this program through Han Yü's writings and by examining his own political actions and affiliations. Central to this program was Han Yü's strong support for the institution of the T'ang monarchy and for the persons of its rulers. Han Yü served four T'ang emperors and maintained toward them an attitude of reverence and respect. His early criticisms of administration policy, the 795 letters to the prime ministers, and the 803 memorial on the drought, specifically exclude Emperor Te-tsung from personal responsibility. The opening passages of the *Veritable Record of Shun-tsung* present a glowing portrait of the heir apparent's virtues, both literary and military. Even if this text is no reliable guide to Han Yü's opinions on Shun-tsung, his poetry on the Wang Shu-wen affair confirms the *Veritable Record*'s image of Shun-tsung as an able and virtuous ruler.

Han Yü's congratulatory text to Emperor Mu-tsung on the ascension to the throne and his services to that monarch in Chen-chou in 822 have been noted above. And both Hsien-tsung and Mu-tsung are on record as having personally commended Han Yü for his services to the dynasty.

But the T'ang monarch with whom Han Yü had the longest working relationship and with whom his career and outlook were most closely intertwined was Emperor Hsien-tsung (r. 806-820), the architect of the T'ang "restoration." As seen in the preceding chapter, Han Yü had high expectations for this monarch and his reign. In the poetry on the Wang Shu-wen affair, Hsien-tsung is the sun rising in the east, and Han Yü developed this standard metaphor to almost religious intensity in the great poem on the royal temple on Heng Mountain written in 805. Similarly, the extensive elaboration of the mountain as imperium metaphor, which is central to the famous "Poem on the Southern Mountains," is an affirmation of Hsien-tsung and the policies Han Yü associated with him.

The most powerful encomium to Hsien-tsung, however, is the "Poem on the Sagacious Virtue of Primal Harmony." Han Yü placed this work first among the verse compositions in his collected works, an indication of the significance he attached to it. The poem, as Han Yü states in the preface, "constitutes a true factual record that illumines in detail the Son of Heaven's divine sagacity in civil and military matters." This balance and interdependence between civil and military prowess are maintained throughout the narrative: by first suppressing the military challenges to his authority, Hsien-tsung is able to institute a "period of Great Tranquillity" (t'ai-p'ing) for the empire. The poem opens with an episode (ll. 5-20) that reveals Hsien-tsung's resolve to suppress separatist military power. Yet when Liu P'i usurps power in Szechwan, the monarch is willing to yield for the sake of the common people (ll. 32-36). The lines "But mind you restrain their ferocity, / do not lay waste my land and my people" (ll. 59-60) again emphasize Hsien-tsung's compassion as a ruler. The grisly passage describing the execution of Liu P'i (ll. 93-118), to which some later critics objected on grounds of taste, is best read as complementary to the following passages on the largess awarded to the heroes of the war and the leniency shown to the populace (ll. 119-130). Both are appropriately commensurate manifestations of the sovereign's sense of justice (*i*). As a result,

> In the whole world between Heaven and Earth
> there was nothing not disposed to order:
> from the districts of Wei, Yu, Heng, and Ch'ing
> (so eastward down to the edge of the sea)
> southward to the districts of Hsü and Ts'ai
> and even till the rude races beyond
> all feared his awesome might; and shamed by his
> *virtus*, they danced for joy in reverence
> and cast off armor and weapons of war
> to practice with basins of ritual grain.
> They came to audience at autumn Court,
> over a thousand together there were.
> The August Thearch addressed them thus: "Lo,
> my uncles, brothers of both my parents,
> each of you be content with your station
> and look well to your lands and your people."
> (ll. 131-146)

If this first section is a paean to Hsien-tsung's martial (*wu*) *virtus*, the next section (ll. 147-202), which describes his performance of the suburban ancestral rites with the same degree of detail as the earlier section described the defeat of Liu P'i, is a paean to his civil (*wen*) *virtus*. The four matching segments that conclude the poem each praise a specific virtue of Hsien-tsung: he is intelligent (ll. 203-214), frugal (ll. 215-226), just (ll. 227-238), and filial (ll. 239-250). The poem's technical brilliance, the artistic virtuosity with which Han Yü molds the ancient four-character line of the *Book of Poetry* into a vigorous narrative of contemporary events, lends scope and grandeur to the poem's theme: "a period of Great Tranquillity has come to pass in this age"; Hsien-tsung has "restored Antiquity."[29]

As the details of his career reveal, Han Yü continued to support the monarch until the end of his life. His "summon-

ing" of the recluse Li P'o in 809, his actions against the separatist underground in Lo-yang in 811, his formal affiliation
with the prowar faction of Wu Yüan-heng in 813, and his
participation in the Huai-hsi campaigns during 815-817 all
indicate a personal commitment to Hsien-tsung and his policies. Yet not all his colleagues shared or even sympathized
with this commitment. It has been maintained elsewhere that
Hsien-tsung's "restoration" was achieved at enormous cost
to the empire and was viewed in some quarters as simply a
drive to aggrandize his personal fortune.[30] A majority of the
bureaucracy seems to have held to the middle-of-the-road
position that recovery of the separatist provinces was not
worth the financial cost and the disruption of the status quo
involved. Han Yü thus consistently maintained a minority
opinion and suffered both professionally and emotionally for
it. This perhaps explains his one disrespectful act against
Hsien-tsung, the infamous "Memorial on the Buddha Relic."
Central to Han Yü's support for the monarchy was his conviction that the ruler must lead in establishing those new Hua
cultural standards he had outlined in "Essentials of the Moral
Way." Hsien-tsung had been eager and diligent in taking the
difficult action necessary to affect a military union of the empire, which was basically achieved by 819. Yet he seems to
have been much less eager to pursue with equal diligence the
cultural orthodoxy that was even more essential to Han Yü's
long-term vision of a politically and culturally united T'ang
empire. The "Memorial on the Buddha Relic" exudes a sense
of betrayal, anger, and personal disappointment. Hsien-
tsung's active participation in the Buddha relic ceremony
probably sparked in Han Yü the long-suppressed realization
that Hsien-tsung was not the model monarch of "Primal Harmony," that personal vanity and the spoils of military victory
had perhaps been his prime concerns after all. This realization
and the ultimate conclusion that Hsien-tsung did not share
nor was he any longer interested in the larger vision for which
Han Yü had already sacrificed so much produced the emotional outburst in the "Memorial on the Buddha Relic."[31]

Han Yü's espousal of a vigorous monarchy was matched by his equally strong advocacy of the career bureaucracy. Upper echelon positions were to be filled from a pool of professionally trained talent, which in turn was to serve as a check on the authoritarian inclinations of the monarchy. Han Yü thus envisioned the ideal government as a bipartite sharing of power between monarchy and bureaucracy. His own writings and actions reveal him as steadfastly opposed to any faction, grouping, or interest that acted to weaken either half of this idealized union or to interfere with its standard organization and functioning. He opposed the aristocratic claim to office by virtue of birth, a legacy of the Six Dynasties system for recommending officials known as "the nine categories and the impartial and just" (*chiu-p'in chung-cheng*).[32] On the other hand, he resisted both the proliferation of narrowly focused "experts" who seldom obtained office through the *chin-shih* examination system and the influence of their extraordinary commissions and agencies that circumvented the jurisdiction of the orthodox bureaucratic establishment.

This establishment, often called the "outer court" (*wai-t'ing*), steadily lost ground throughout the reign of Emperor Te-tsung (r.779-805) to the "inner court" (*nei-t'ing*), which comprised the Han-lin Academy, the eunuchs, and the imperial relations.[33] The "outer court" supported a conception of government that derived ultimately from the Han Confucian vision of the Chou state as represented in the *Rituals of Chou (Chou li)*, which delineated the jurisdictions of each ministry and the number and duties of each functionary. The *Administrative Regulations for the Six Ministries during the T'ang (T'ang liu tien)*, completed in 739, codified T'ang practice along the lines of this earlier Han Confucian model. The "inner court" supported an antithetical conception of government that derived from the Buddhist-Taoist image of the saint-ruler surrounded by a small group of advisors, all equal in rank and chosen for specific talents and assignments. Han Yü, of course, advocated the former conception, and his efforts to redefine the career bureaucracy are best seen as attempts to halt the pervasive influence of "inner court" elements on the political life of his age.

Han Yü's biography in the *Old T'ang History* clearly records that "he looked upon those from wealthy and influential families as his menials and steadfastly ignored them."[34] Several incidents reveal Han Yü's impatience with aristocratic presumption of superior status and with condescension toward their perceived social inferiors. His rectification of their ostracism of the ungainly *Record of Rites* lecturer has already been noted, and class antagonisms may also have contributed to his bureaucratic feud with the aristocrat Li Shen in 823. A recent discussion of the seemingly innocuous, "An Excursion to the Mountain Villa of the T'ai-p'ing Princess," written in 813, emphasizes the antiaristocratic sentiment of the poem:

> Her Highness
> > in those days, wanted
> > > to usurp spring
> so she pressed
> > her towers and turms
> > > hard by the city gate,
> and would you know
> > how far before us
> > > stretched her flowers?
> all the way, straight
> > to the Southern Mountains
> > > belonged to no man.[35]

The Princess of Great Tranquillity (d. 713) was the third daughter of Empress Wu and one of the principal actors on the early eighth-century political scene. The suppression of her and her faction in 713 consolidated power in the hands of Emperor Hsüan-tsung. "The confiscation of the immense wealth and property she had accumulated during her years of influence took years to complete."[36] Her "mountain villa" was located less than three miles south of the city and was called the Plain of Joy and Pleasure. Yet as stated in Han Yü's poem, its lands stretched to the Southern Mountains almost twenty miles away. The diction of the poem—"usurp spring," "pressed . . . hard by the city gate (i.e. the legitimate imperium)," "belonged to no man"—all contribute to the message: the accumulation of political power and wealth in the hands of imperial relatives and an untrained aristocracy is a danger to the state (i.e. the Southern Mountains).[37]

Many passages in Han Yü's works laud officials who refused to be cowed by aristocratic pretension in the discharge of their duty. The "Epitaph For the Former Prime Minister Ch'üan Te-yü" records that when Ch'üan (759-818) directed the Ministry of Personnel in 802 "if those that were recommended to him were men of their word, he excluded no one just because he was a commoner. But if they were untrustworthy, he paid them no heed whatever, even though they be high officials and influential people."[38] Similarly, in the "Spirit Inscription For the Former Military Governor and Inspector-General of Ho-tung, Master Cheng Tan of Yingyang," Han Yü writes that when Cheng Tan (741-801) assumed his post in Ho-tung in 800 "there were some military officers who, because of their aristocratic status, demanded important positions. But he would not employ them, using instead experienced people of proven ability and those without local influence." The move reduced bribery and ostentation and increased efficiency.[39]

Although certain of these texts can perhaps be read as examples of "class conflict" between the old aristocracy and Han Yü's own emerging class of literati, the real focus of his concern was the conflict between those who were trained for office and those who were not. Presence of social pedigree was not as important as the broad humanistic training and moral foundation the examination system supposedly provided. The leaders of his own political coalition, Wu Yüanheng and later P'ei Tu, both came from great aristocratic lineages, yet both had also passed the *chin-shih* examination and risen through the bureaucracy by virtue of their training and talent. If Han Yü unalterably opposed the aristocratic claim to office by virtue of birth, he unalterably supported the bureaucratic claim to office by examination.[40] His conduct, in both word and deed, in response to the Wang Shu-wen government reveals most clearly his attitude toward this question of suitability for office. I have elsewhere suggested that the Wang Shu-wen affair is best understood as an attempt, using the basically pro-Buddhist inclinations of its members as cohesion, to forge a heterogeneous collection of minor Han-lin academicians and young career bureaucrats into a ruling coalition under the political umbrella of the heir apparent Li Sung (760-806).[41] Although this novel coalition shared many of Han Yü's political goals—elimination of eunuch influence, a strong antiseparatist stance, and a heightened concern for the welfare of the populace—his refusal to participate was unequivocal and the price he paid, the 803 exile to Yang-shan, was immediate.[42] As the poem "Inscribed on the Temple at Coal Valley Tarn" shows, this refusal was rooted in Han Yü's distrust of the coalition's heterogeneity, of its ad hoc and extraordinary unorthodox character. Despite the noble aims of the Wang Shu-wen government, its alignment of political power was essentially Buddhist and "inner court." Han Yü was opposed, on moral grounds, to government at the hands of chess players like Wang Shu-wen and calligraphers like Wang P'ei, even though such persons may have possessed genuine talent in specific areas of administration.

The issues involved in the 818 conflict between P'ei Tu and Hsien-tsung over the latter's nomination of Huang-fu Po and Ch'eng I to the office of prime minister further clarify Han Yü's attitudes toward suitability for high office.[43] P'ei Tu objected that Huang-fu and Ch'eng were mere "finance clerks, fawning and opportunistic petty men," lacking the moral qualities necessary for the state's highest office. As we have seen above, Han Yü's "Memorial on the Buddha Relic" is probably to be construed as an attack on Huang-fu Po's ministry and its associations with the Buddhist-eunuch establishment.[44] On the other hand, Han Yü's cautious yet steady support for Liu Tsung-yüan and Liu Yü-hsi, the only career bureaucrats in the inner circle of the Wang Shu-wen government, can be plausibly interpreted as loyalty to that class of civil servants he identified as his own.

Many scholars have focused on the rise of the Han-lin Academy in the latter eighth century as indicative of the growing influence of the "inner court," the Buddhist conception of government, and the increasingly "dilettantish" nature of T'ang official mentality.[45] It is significant that Han Yü had little contact with the Han-lin. Neither of his major political mentors—Wu Yüan-heng or P'ei Tu—ever served as Han-lin scholars, and both are on record as having opposed members of the academy or their policies.[46]

Han Yü's actions against the eunuchs in Lo-yang in 809-810 demonstrate how his concern for bureaucratic exactitude could outweigh his proroyalist attachment to Emperor Hsien-tsung. His efforts to regulate the Buddhist community in Lo-yang and separate its financial links to the eunuchs were a direct violation of Hsien-tsung's order of 807 assigning supervision of the monasteries to the eunuch "commissioner of merit and virtue." Likewise, his actions in 811 against eunuch financial exploitation of the Palace Armies and the 819 "Memorial on the Buddha Relic" touched on the sensitive issue of monarch-eunuch relations. These actions, along with many passages in Han Yü's writings, demonstrate that the ultimate aim of the antieunuch element of his political program was to dissuade the crown from diminishing its own authority through continued delegation of ad hoc powers to the eunuchs. As Han Yü professed in the famous poem written while crossing the Lan-t'ien Pass on the journey to exile in 819, he wished only "to save His Sagacious Brilliance from treacherous evils." He was of course unsuccessful; Hsien-tsung was murdered by the eunuch Ch'en Hung-chih in 820.[47]

But the mainstay and most visible element of Han Yü's program to restore T'ang unity was his consistent participation in the military and political struggle to eliminate separatism. Although Han Yü's support for the antiseparatist policy certainly coincided with his larger intellectual and philosophical outlook, purely personal reasons may also have heightened these sentiments. The Han family homestead in Ho-yang was in the direct path of invading forces from Ho-pei. The area had been devastated in the An Lu-shan rebellion, and the rebellions of the early 780s prevented the Han family from returning there after the death of Han Hui. Similarly, it is probable that Han Yü's four years of service on the "front lines" at Pien-chou and the tragic events there in 799 further convinced him of the need to purge the military of separatist elements.

It must be emphasized that Han Yü's antiseparatism was quite different from the antimilitarism of "pacifist" literati like Li Chiang or Po Chü-i. There is no trace in Han Yü's writings of the overbearing condescension of the military as seen among literati figures such as Lu Ch'ang-yüan and Chang Hung-ching. On the contrary, Han Yü's origins in the military aristocracy of the Northern Wei and, more directly, the influence of his first patron, Ma Sui, seem to have instilled in him a respect for military virtues. His concern for the quality of the military has already been noted ("If anyone who sits in the market selling griddle cakes can call himself a soldier, then who is *not* a soldier?"). This protest against eunuch impairment of military effectiveness was translated into concrete action when P'ei Tu's removal of the eunuch military supervisors in the Huai-hsi campaign prepared the way for government victory. Han Yü himself probably saw action in this campaign during the various raids on P'ei Tu's party. His 821 memorial on the Huang aborigines of modern Kuangsi reveals a man at home with military strategy and logistical problems. Finally, Han Yü's 817 mission to Han Hung and the 822 mission to Wang T'ing-ts'ou demonstrate that the court had considerable confidence in his ability to handle sensitive politico-military situations.

Among Han Yü's many writings that espouse his proroyalist, antiseparatist sentiments are two texts that laud the past exploits of earlier fighters for T'ang unity. First and most important is the "Postface to the Biography of the Vice-President of the Censorate Chang Hsün."[48] Composed in 807, this text purports to add information omitted from a biography of Chang Hsün (709-757) written by Li Han, one of the sons of Li Hua. Chang Hsün was martyred to the T'ang cause at the hands of the An Lu-shan separatists in 757 at the conclusion of the siege of the strategic city of Sung-chou, whose heroic and prolonged defense had denied the rebels access to the Huai River valley. Li Han's biography and a memorial he submitted to Emperor Su-tsung calling his attention to Chang's deeds on behalf of the dynasty had secured the latter's reputation. Han Yü's postface underscores these deeds and adds to them an account of one Hsü Yüan (709-757) who had died along with Chang at Sung-chou. The "Postface" is a paean to the two men's loyalty to the T'ang, to their learning and their fortitude, and an attack on those who because of jealousy had refused to help them.[49]

Another text, the "Epitaph for Prince Ch'eng of Ts'ao," also attempts to set the historical record straight by chronicling the unsung praises of an earlier defender of the dynasty, in this case, Li Kao (733-792), who had been instrumental in defeating Li Hsi-lieh and ending the separatist uprisings of the 780s.[50]

Han Yü's greatest literary contribution to the antiseparatist cause was the monumental "Inscription on the Pacification of Huai-hsi." Other less ambitious tracts treat the problem of separatism in a subtle and private way. Two prefaces in particular reveal Han Yü working on a personal level to advance the interests of the crown. The first of these is the "Preface Seeing Off the Master-in-Charge Li I of Yu-chou," composed at Lo-yang in 810. In 785, during the military disorders in the northeast, one Liu P'eng (727-785) had assumed control over the military district of Yu-chou, the old headquarters of An Lu-shan. When he died three months later, the soldiers selected his son Liu Chi (757-810) to assume command. This latter had spent time as a youth in Ch'ang-an and had even sat for the *chin-shih*. The court therefore confirmed his status as military governor at Yu-chou, and although he maintained the province's autonomy from Ch'ang-an, he never rose in open defiance. Accordingly, successive courts showered him with honors: in 796 he was made honorary prime minister and in 805 honorary lord chief instructor (*szu-t'u*), one of the Three Lords (*san-kung*) or highest posts in the state. Li I (d. 827) was a poet of considerable talent and reputation whose court

career had suffered because of public ridicule at his patholog-
ical jealousy. As a result he had taken service with Liu Chi
in Yu-chou. The text is as follows:

In 806 the present prime minister Li Fan was auxiliary
secretary in the Ministry of Personnel. I was once together with him at court and the talk turned to the virtues
of the Lord Chief Instructor at Yu-chou. Li said,

"Last year I was ordered to proceed on a protocol
mission to Yu-chou. As soon as I entered the territory,
messengers with greetings and solicitudes arrived at
every mile. The further I went, the more deferential they
became. When I reached the outskirts of the city, the
Lord Chief Instructor himself—a red turban round his
head, in black boots and pantaloons, a sword to his left
and a bow and quiver of arrows hung to the right from
the belt—bowed low by the side of the road to welcome
me. I declined on the grounds of protocol, saying,

'Your Lordship is minister to the Son of Heaven, the
proper protocol need not be like this.'

"When I reached his office, he again conducted affairs
in his uniform, and I again said,

'Your Lordship is one of the Three Lords, you need
not accept a station based on your military uniform.'

"But finally I could not refuse him, and when we entered his hall, he assumed the visitor's position and sat
facing east."

To his account, I replied,

"It has been almost sixty years since our state lost its
great tranquillity. Based on the combination of the ten
stems and the twelve branches, a sexagenary cycle will
soon be completed and peace will return (fu). This peace
will surely begin in Yu-chou, the source of the rebellion.

"There is now a great sage as Son of Heaven and a
Lord Chief Instructor attentive to protocol. Will he perhaps be first among the generals of Honan and Hopei to
come to Court and receive his charge as in the days of
the k'ai-yüan period [713-741]?"

And Li answered,

"I think he will be."

Now, Li Fan is prime minister and will certainly repeat this story to His Majesty, so my words of 806 may perhaps come true.

The Master-in-Charge has come for the new year to visit his parents in Lo-yang, and the scholars of the city have all paid respects at his gate. As a man, he is a loyal retainer and would wish to pass on to all the future the works and good name of the Lord Chief Instructor. Please accept these words of mine as a parting gift for your return.[51]

The suggestion of course is that Li I should use his influence to persuade Liu Chi to submit to the full authority of the crown. It is interesting that Han Yü makes reference to the completion of the sexagenary cycle that began with the An Lu-shan rebellion in 755 and would end several years hence in 814. He uses the world *fu* "to return" to refer to this completion. The argument that 815 would mark the sexagenary anniversary of the loss of T'ang political unity and that the decade was the natural time for a renewal (*fu*) of that unity seems to have been a powerful psychological force in support of Hsien-tsung's "restoration."[52]

Much more subtle than the preface for Li I is the "Preface Seeing Off Tung Shao-nan" of 803. The latter was a recluse who lived in the Shou-chou area of the Huai River valley and was renowned for his filial piety.[53] He was unsuccessful at the *chin-shih* examinations and decided to try his fortune in the northeast, the ancient provinces of Yen and Chao. Han Yü's preface turns on the contrast, implied but not stated, between the qualities of the heroes of these provinces as manifested in Antiquity and in the present.

In Antiquity, the states of Yen and Chao boasted many fine men who were moved to indignation and sad song.[54]

Master Tung was a candidate for the *chin-shih* examination, but time and again he found no success with those in charge. So he now clasps his fine talent to his bosom and with pent up anger will move to those lands. I know there will certainly be something suitable for him there. Take courage Master Tung!

Although you have not yet met your time, any who love justice and practice humanity will cherish you; so even more will the fine men of Yen and Chao whose natures engendered these virtues cherish you.

Yet I have heard that customs and cultures change; and I do not know if their present is the same as what has been said of them in Antiquity. But we shall know from your travels there. Take courage Master Tung!

You have stirred my emotions. Make lamentation for me at the tomb of Yüeh I.[55] And have a look in the marketplace, if again a butcher of dogs is there as in days of old.[56] Offer my respects and tell him for me that a bright Son of Heaven now sits on high, and so he should come and take office.[57]

The reference to Yüeh I and allusions to Ching K'o underscore the virtues of integrity and loyalty to state and sovereign under difficult political and personal circumstances. Since Tung Shao-nan is a virtuous man, he could expect the men of Yen and Chao to receive him well, *if* there are any such men left in the region. Since it is well known that this is not the case, it is thus incumbent upon Tung Shao-nan to persuade those presently there to rekindle these qualities by returning their allegiance to the T'ang. If Tung Shao-nan is *not* prepared to do this, then the text implies he should not go, thus the repeated warning "take courage Master Tung." The text is both a lamentation for the cultural and spiritual decline of Yen and Chao and an admonition to Tung Shao-nan to maintain in himself and rekindle in others the old virtues traditionally associated with that area.

The "Essentials of the Moral Way" is the major statement of Han Yü's social and political thought. If the text was written (as seems most probable) in the summer of 805, then its relation to the contemporary political scene is obvious: the future Emperor Hsien-tsung had been named heir apparent on April 27, 805, and the Wang Shu-wen government was unraveling. One could clearly sense the direction of the new winds of political change. Between the lines of the text one can feel Han Yü's disgust with the ad hoc novelty of the Wang Shu-wen coalition's conception of government and with the administrative chaos that resulted from it. Overtly, the text reads well as a theoretical "position paper," expressing Han Yü's hopes for what the new government would be and what it would do. Yet these aspirations contained the conceptual framework for nothing less that a wholesale reordering of T'ang culture in accordance with what Han Yü had at that point in his life determined to be eternal verities. "Essentials of the Moral Way" is thus much more than an agenda for immediate political action; it is a summation and distillation of Han Yü's entire life as a thinker and man of action.

The main goal of the text is to define the contours of the Chinese body politic—to demarcate the cultural boundaries between Hua and Hu. As the end result of this process, Han Yü envisions a simpler culture, less diverse, but therefore more homogeneous and stronger. His passionate call for social and cultural strengthening through simplification echoes back to the post - An Lu-shan writings of Li Hua and harks forward to the similar call of Lin-chi for spiritual strengthening through simplification. Han Yü introduces this theme at the beginning of section III, his famous appeal for the simplification of the contemporary sixfold stratification of society into the orthodox fourfold stratification by the elimination of the Buddhist and Taoist clergy. The appeal is based, however, on the grounds of economic necessity: "under such conditions, is it any wonder the people are impoverished and driven to brigandage?" The reference is certainly to the growth of the so-called monastic estates and the wealth of the eunuch-aristocratic Buddhist economic establishment. The paragraph is thus an oblique attack on aristocratic exploitation of the peasantry, and its intent has much in common with the poem "An Excursion to the Mountain Villa of the Princess of Great Tranquillity," which warns against the political dangers of useless and ostentatious opulence. In contrast, the way of the Sage is "easy to explain; its teachings are easy to execute."

"Essentials of the Moral Way" also shares the Ch'an concern for unity of theory and action. Han Yü takes pains to explain in section II that centuries of Taoist and Buddhist speculation have diluted the original teachings of the Sages to the point where even self-styled Confucians no longer understood these teachings: "they do not inquire into fundamentals or essentials, but wish only to hear of the fantastic." Han Yü returns to this theme at the end of his tract (section VII), where he posits an orthodox lineage of the "moral way," which he terminates with Mencius. As we shall see momentarily, direct, personal action is at the core of this moral way, and the favor shown to theory over action that began after the Duke of Chou signaled the demise of the old tradition. Han Yü emphasizes this point in the final verse recapitulation of the text:

Before the Duke of Chou
our sages were kings
and things got done.
After the Duke of Chou
our sages were subjects
and long theory won.

Han Yü sets forth the basic elements of his reconstituted "moral way" in sections II through VI. A shorter text that stresses many of the same points as "Essentials of the Moral Way" is the "Preface Seeing Off the Buddhist Master Wen-ch'ang," composed in Ch'ang-an in 803. Han Yü scholars have long recognized that this preface constitutes an earlier yet more distilled version of the larger and more famous treatise.[58]

Some men are Confucian in name and Mohist in deed: the name is right, the deeds wrong. Should one associate with such men? Then there is the Mohist in name but Confucian in deed: the name is wrong, but the deeds right. Should one associate with these men? Yang Hsiung maintained that he would bar one who stood by the gate but admit one who stood among the barbarians. I take my standards from him.[59]

The Buddhist Master Wen-ch'ang enjoys literature. Wherever he travels in the empire he asks the officials and scholars to record in verse what is on their minds. Now, in the spring of 803, he is about to travel to the southeast. Liu Tsung-yüan asked me to write something for him, and when he opened his bags, we found he had over a hundred poems and prefaces. If he were not an extremely good man, he could hardly have attracted so many.

Yet I regretted that not one of these works told him of the moral way of the Sages; they only presented him with Buddhist teachings. Now Wen-ch'ang is a Buddhist, and if he wishes to hear Buddhist teachings, then he can go himself to his own teachers and ask them. So why does he visit and request works from us? He has seen the virtues of the social relations between ruler and servitor, between father and son, and the richness of our cultural activities. His mind yearns for them, yet he is bound by his doctrine and cannot join us, so he likes to hear our teachings and request writings from us.

Were he one of ours, I would tell him of the moral way of Yao and Shun and of the Hsia, Shang, and Chou kings, of the movements of the sun, the moon, and the planets, of the manifestations of Heaven and Earth, of the secrets of the spirits, of the increase of our human kind, and of the flow of rivers—of all these would I speak to him. There would be no need to sully him once again with Buddhist teachings.

When people first came forth, they were like birds and wild beasts or like the I and Ti barbarians. Then the Sages arose, and the people learned to dwell in buildings and to eat grains, to draw near to kin and to honor the honorable, to nourish the living, and to bury the dead.

For this reason, no way is greater than that of humanity and justice, no teachings straighter than those on ritual, music, chastisement, and government. Spread these over the empire, and all creatures will obtain what is right for them; apply them to your own self, and your body will find rest and your spirit peace. Yao passed them on to Shun, Shun to Yü, Yü to T'ang, T'ang to Wen and Wu, and Wen and Wu to the Duke of Chou and Confucius. These wrote them in books, and the people of the central lands have preserved them for generations. Yet among today's Buddhists, who will practice them and who pass them on?

Birds look down to eat, then look up to the four directions; wild beasts live hidden away and seldom come out because they fear other creatures will harm them. Yet still they cannot escape danger: the flesh of the weak is food for the strong.

Now Wen-ch'ang and I dwell in peace, eat at leisure, and enjoy our lives. We cannot ignore that which makes us different from birds and beasts. To be unaware is no crime, yet to know and not to act is a mistake. To delight in the old and yet be unable to advance to the new is weakness. To know and not to tell others is inhumane. To tell and not to practice is untruthful.

I value Liu Tsung-yüan's request, and I admire this Buddhist who enjoys literature; so I have written this.

This text, as does section III of the "Essentials of the Moral Way," stresses the humanitarian character of the early Sages' contributions to the formation of human civilization: their teachings comprise the essential difference between "birds and beasts or the I and Ti barbarians" on the one hand and civilized humanity on the other. The proper practice of the Sages' teachings, especially observance of the social relations between ruler and servitor and between father and son, ensures the security and prosperity of every individual. Both texts stress the importance of these two relationships, which constitute the outer, public, and governmental versus the inner, private, and familial halves of the Confucian social order. Buddhist and Taoist asceticism, advocating *śuddha* (purity) and "nonaction," by refusing to sanction the practice of these social relationships has resulted in a society in which "the flesh of the weak is food for the strong"—a society more resembling that of "birds, beasts, and barbarians" than of civilized humans.

Yet the masterstroke of Han Yü's proposal in "Essentials of the Moral Way" is not his condemnation of the Buddhist and Taoist cultivation of an inner spiritual life but rather his insistence that the cultivation of spirituality serve as a connecting link to integrate the private and public halves of Confucian life into a unified and holistic social order. Han Yü's vehicle for this proposal is the lengthy quotation (the only one in "Essentials of the Moral Way") from the beginning of the *Great Learning*. The full passage in the latter text is as follows:

> In Antiquity those who wished to radiate their bright inner strength through the empire first put their states in good order. To put their states in good order they first regulated their families. To regulate their families, they first cultivated their individual persons. To cultivate their individual persons, they first set their minds right. To set their minds right, they first made their thoughts true. To make their thoughts true, they first called forth their knowledge. The calling forth of knowledge consisted in attracting objects.[60]
>
> As things were attracted, their knowledge became perfect. Their knowledge perfect, their thoughts became true. Their thoughts true, their minds were set right. Their minds set right, their persons were cultivated. Their persons cultivated, their homes were regulated. Their home regulated, their states were put in good order. Their states in good order, the empire was made tranquil.
>
> From the Son of Heaven down to the common people, all were united in this: that they took the cultivation of their individual persons as basic.

These rhetorical catenations are central to the "Essentials of the Moral Way," to Han Yü's thought in general, and indeed to all that was later to pass for Neo-Confucianism. Once again, care must be taken not to allow the ubiquity of these concepts in post-T'ang China to overshadow recognition of the brilliance that led Han Yü to isolate and focus on this passage, which in his day was only a fragment from a minor chapter toward the end of the *Record of Rites*.

Han Yü opens section V of the "Essentials of the Moral Way," the section that contains the central message of his treatise, by citing the beginning of this catenation from the *Great Learning*. The text emphasizes the interrelated, holistic nature of all human activity and posits a direct link between personal moral and spiritual cultivation and the political health of the state. Lest his reader miss this point, Han Yü reminds him that "what the Ancients called setting the mind right and making the thoughts true were things they actually put into practice." There was thus in Antiquity a personal unity of thought and action that made possible in turn the political and social unity of the state. Yet today this unity is gone because too many have "abrogated the natural principles of human relations." The practice of Buddhist and Taoist monasticism has undermined family and private life by destroying the proper relations between father and son; it has also undermined governmental and public life by destroying the proper relations between ruler and minister. Han Yü no doubt had in mind here the Buddhist-Taoist-eunuch-Han-lin complex, all of which served to decrease the influence of the prime minister and his position as head of the regular bureaucracy. Han Yü then draws attention to the cultural criteria Confucius used in compiling the *Spring and Autumn Annals*: he treated as "central states" (*chung-kuo*) all those who adopted their culture; and "if the feudal lords followed the usages of the barbarians, he treated them as barbarians." Thus Confucius established a cultural orthodoxy to underlie the political unity he desired for his own day. Han Yü's text would do the same for his age: it lays down a cultural orthodoxy upon which to craft the restored political unity of the future, otherwise "how

long will it be before we ourselves have all become barbarians?"

Section VI defines this cultural orthodoxy. The reintro-
duction of the definitions of "humanity," "justice," "the
moral way," and "inner strength," with which the text
opened, emphasizes the new meanings these terms are to assume when understood in their proper context of the *Great
Learning* catenation. The cultivation of one's "sense of humanity" (*jen*) is no longer a purely private endeavor; rather
the extension of the benefits of *jen* to as many people as possible becomes the moral imperative of the "superior man"
(*chün-tzu*). The unity of the state becomes the measure of the
success of this extension of *jen* into the wider political sphere.
Such is the real significance of Han Yü's definition of *jen* as
po-ai "to love widely": the "superior man" who has perfected
his own sense of humanity in his immediate surroundings has
directly contributed to the health of the state and thus enhanced the possibilities for a wider diffusion of such love.
There is no distinction between private moral and public political action.

Failure to understand *po-ai* in the context of the *Great Learning* catenation has led to charges against Han Yü of apostasy
to Mohism, to the charge that this extension of *jen* implied
in *po-ai* is synonymous with the Mohist doctrine of "universal
love" (*chien-ai*).[61] Yet Han Yü's short tract "On Reading Mo-
tzu" delineates quite clearly his thoughts on the subject.

> Those in the Confucian tradition criticize Mo-tzu for
> his "unity with the superior," his "universal love," his
> "elevation of the worthy," and his "explanation of
> ghosts."
> And yet Confucius himself "stood in awe of great
> men" (*Analects* xvi.8) and when he resided in a certain
> state he would not castigate its great lords (*Hsün-tzu* 20/
> 7b). Furthermore, the *Spring and Autumn Annals* criticize
> ministers who usurp royal authority. Was this not unity
> with the superior?
> Confucius "broadly loved [the multitude yet] drew

near to the humane" (*Analects* I.6); he considered the Sage one who "brought wide benefits [to the people] and helped the multitude" (*Analects* VI.30). Was this not universal love?

Confucius "admired the virtuous" (*Analects* I.7) and used the four classes of excellence to advance and praise his disciples (*Analects* XI.3). He "was distressed if they parted this world without achieving a good reputation" (*Analects* XV.20). Was this not elevation of the worthy?

Confucius "sacrificed as if [the gods were] present" and criticized those who sacrificed "as if there were no sacrifice" (*Analects* III.12). He said, "When I sacrifice, I receive blessings" (*Li chi chu-shu* 23/11a; trans. Legge, *Book of Rites*, 1:403). Was this not an explanation of ghosts?

Those in the Confucian tradition and Mo-tzu alike endorse Yao and Shun, alike condemn Chieh and Chou. We alike cultivate our individual persons and set our minds right for the purpose of regulating empire and state. Should we both not delight in what we have in common? I believe these discords have arisen through pedantry and through each side striving to sell its master's doctrines, not through anything essentially inherent in the Ways of the two masters.

Confucians should make use of Mo-tzu, and Mohists should make use of Confucius; otherwise they are not worthy of these names.[62]

Han Yü's third paragraph explication of "universal love" by reference to two *Analects* quotations reveals how he understood the term. The more important quotation is the second, *Analects* VI.30:

Tzu-kung asked, "If there was one who could bring wide (*po*) benefits to the people and could thus help the multitude, what would you say of him? Could he be called humane (*jen*)?"

The Master replied, "Much more than humane—he

would certainly be a Sage. Even Yao and Shun sorrowed that they did not attain this.

"A man who has a sense of the humane strengthens others through his wish to strengthen himself and perfects others through his wish to perfect himself. The ability to draw analogies from what is close can be said to constitute the way of the humane."[63]

Whether one translates this passage in moral or political terms, Han Yü states unambiguously in paragraph six of "On Reading Mo-tzu" that both schools of thought agree on the ultimate identity of private moral and public political action. Alluding to the *Great Learning* catenation, he writes "we alike cultivate our individual persons and set our minds right for the purpose of regulating empire and state." Han Yü is thus not advocating the Mohist love without distinctions but rather pointing out the common practical effect of both "universal love" and his own extension of *jen*: the creation of widespread prosperity and political order, the "Grand Unity" (*ta t'ung*). This is the point of the verse summation in section VI:

take it unto yourself,
find ease and happiness

use it with others
be loving and fair

take it to your own mind,
find peace, quietness

use it for empire and state
find it works everywhere.

It is interesting to note that the four key terms of Han Yü's "Essentials of the Moral Way" occur together and with similar implications in a much earlier and dissimilar text. This is the preface to the "Eulogy on an Image of the Buddha Śākyamuni" by the famous fourth-century Buddhist scholar Chih Tun (314-366). The opening sentence of this preface reads, "The way that 'strengthens others' (*li jen*) is called humanity (*jen*) and justice (*i*); and the foundation of humanity and justice is what is called the moral way (*tao*) and inner strength (*te*)."[64] This allusion to the same *Analects* VI. 30 is, as Zürcher correctly maintains, "here ingeniously applied to the idea of Bodhisattvahood." Since the introduction of Buddhism into China, its apologists had often linked the old concept of *jen* with the Buddhist idea of *karuṇā* or "compassion," "mercy," that quality of the Bodhisattva synonymous with his vow to bring salvation to all sentient creatures.[65]

Han Yü's extension of *jen* made it possible for him to claim for his own image of the Sage similar qualities of universal benefactor and savior of mankind. Yet this was a radically new and innovative conception of the Sage because, although it was produced through an eclectic reordering of Confucian, Mohist, Buddhist, and Taoist elements, it united both private and public spheres of action. This innovation made Sagehood accessible to all practitioners of the way ("Shun was a man; I also am a man"), yet at the same its ultimate realization was the person of the emperor himself—the Sage-King under whose rule "things got done." The pursuit of personal spiritual goals was now no longer incompatible with a public career in government service. On the contrary, even the lowest ranking "servitor" shared in the spiritual aura that radiated down from his "ruler," the Sage-King, and the higher he ascended the official ladder (or to use the Chinese metaphor, the official "mountain") the closer he himself approached to Sagehood. Such a conception possessed definite ideological advantages over the Buddhist and Taoist conceptions of the emperor as bodhisattva or as transcendent, since these systems never posited that key link between private devotion and public service; rather, the holier the monk, the more secluded his retreat. This new conception of Sagehood as spiritual wisdom expressed through political action was to form the intellectual basis for the spiritual and political world of Neo-Confucianism.

Like any piece of good literature, the style of "Essentials of the Moral Way" reflects and reinforces its content. Ch'en Yin-k'o has pointed out that Han Yü's use of the *Great Learning* catenation can be viewed as an example of Confucian "*ko-*

i," an early Chinese Buddhist method of explicating Indian texts by "matching the idea" with native Chinese expressions.[66] Han Yü has here adapted this instructional and rhetorical technique by pinpointing a passage from the traditional Chinese canon that also emphasized the Indian concern with "mind" (*hsin*) and "nature" (*hsing*) and at the same time linked these concerns to indigenous social and political traditions. Again, rather than constituting evidence of a supposed apostasy, Han Yü's use of this technique placed him in that venerable tradition of those who opposed Buddhism by highlighting its affinities to the Confucian tradition. Gernet observes that "one notices even among its most courageous opponents a concurrence in principle to the doctrines of the new religion: they found in it an echo of the moral rules with which they had been inculcated." He cites as the first of several examples the following sentiments attributed to Emperor Wen of the Ch'en Dynasty (r. 560–566): "I have observed that the most profound meaning of the *Documents* is that the august kings furthered the idea of depending only on themselves, and that the best statute of the *Rites* is that the Sages promoted the concept of taking blame into themselves. Therefore the constant thought of the humane man (*jen*) is to give of himself in order to save the world, the constant virtue (*te*) of the superior man (*chün-tzu*) is to overcome himself in order to benefit others. Even more are these the essential path of the bodhisattvas."[67] Han Yü was thus adopting a technique of argumentation that both proponents and opponents of Buddhism had long practiced: consciously anachronistic interpretation of Chinese canonical texts in order to make the weight of their authority relevant to the discussion of contemporary issues. The institutionalization of this practice, which is already well developed in Han Yü's own canonical exegesis, was to have a major impact on Neo-Confucian textual scholarship and commentary.

Yet Han Yü's "Essentials of the Moral Way" combines this technique of "matching the idea" with the very traditional Confucian practice of the "rectification of names" (*cheng ming*). The traditional doctrine of *cheng ming* held that the "name" of any object is "rectified" when its behavior accords with its essential nature. As Hsün-tzu maintained in his classic exposition of the concept, "names have no intrinsic appropriateness."[68] And since appropriateness is revealed through an object's actions, a moral injunction to right (appropriate) action lies at the center of the *cheng ming* concept.[69] The first two sections of "Essentials of the Moral Way" are basically an attempt to "rectify" the sense in which Han Yü intends his four basic terms—*jen, i, tao, te*—to be understood. The emphasis is on definition, not through scholasticism but through action: "the ruler is the one who issues commands. . . . If the ruler issues no commands, then he loses his reason for being a ruler." The force of these arguments culminates in the important fifth section: "although ministers, they do not regard their ruler as a ruler." When compiling the *Spring and Autumn Annals*, Confucius used "rectification of names" to distinguish Chinese and barbarian; "if the feudal lords followed the usages of the barbarians, he treated them as barbarians." The logic that concludes the section is inescapable: those who "today elevate barbarian practices" *are essentially* barbarians.[70]

Another seldom-noted stylistic feature of the text is its admixture of prose and verse. As we shall see in a later chapter, a softening of the rigid early T'ang boundaries between prose and verse is central to Han Yü's literary theory and practice. There are two rhymed passages in "Essentials of the Moral Way": the citations from *Chuang-tzu* in section III and the longer series of original verses at the conclusion of the tract. The rhyme scheme in the latter passage is very broad, employing rhymes from three traditional rhyming categories.[71] Such verse insertions in prose texts can be traced to the pre-Ch'in philosophers, notably Taoist and Legalist authors.[72] Han Yü uses verse in "Essentials of the Moral Way" to recapitulate and emphasize his main points. Such use recalls the alternating prose-verse narratives of the Buddhist tradition, for instance, Kumārajīva's translation of the *Saddharmapuṇḍarīkasūtra* or perhaps even popular prosimetric styles such as the "transformation texts" (*pien-wen*). Certain, however, is that the verse recapitulations in "Essentials of the Moral Way" are yet another example of Han Yü's appropriation of his opposition's own stylistic devices to argue against them. Indeed, the entire concluding paragraph is almost Ch'an-like in its use of pseudo paradox, iconoclasm, and violent hyperbole.[73]

Several final points must be made concerning the general tone of Han Yü's most famous text. Han Yü's cultural attitude has often been labeled xenophobic, largely on the basis of "Essentials of the Moral Way" and "Memorial on the Buddha Relic." The latter text, because it focuses solely on Buddhism and labels the person of the Buddha an "I-Ti barbarian," can certainly be read as xenophobic; yet again, its main arguments are cultural, not racial. "Essentials of the Moral Way" is clearly not xenophobic: Lao-tzu and his followers come under more sustained attack from Han Yü than do the Buddhists. As has already been stated above, Han Yü's basic solution to the T'ang dichotomy between Hua and Hu is articulated in "Essentials" section V: to behave like a Hua is to be a Hua, to behave like a barbarian is to be a barbarian. The exact same sentiment, illustrated and elaborated, is found in a remarkable treatise called "The Heart of Being Hua" (*Hua hsin*) by Ch'en An, a little-known literatus of the generation immediately following Han Yü's.

> In 847, the military governor of Ta-liang, the Duke of Fan-yang,[74] discovered one Li Yen-sheng, a native of the Arabian empire, and recommended him to the throne. The Son of Heaven ordered the Ministry of Rites to examine his abilities, and the next year he did well at the *chin-shih* examinations. But those who had sponsored other candidates were not content with the results.
>
> Someone asked me,
>
> "Liang is a great city, and its governor a worthy man. He has received his charge from a Hua sovereign and his salary from Hua people; yet when he recommends candidates, he takes them from among the barbarians. Are there none praiseworthy among the Hua that this bar-

barian is the only one who could be employed? I am afraid I have misgivings about our governor."

I answered,

"The governor in truth recommended this man for his ability, without regard to his origins. If one speaks in terms of geography, then there are Hua and barbarians. But if one speaks in terms of education, then there can be no such difference. For the distinction between Hua and barbarian rests in the heart and is determined by their different inclinations.

"If one is born in the central provinces and yet acts contrary to ritual and propriety, then this is to have the look of a Hua but the heart of a barbarian. If one is born in the barbarian lands and yet acts in accordance with ritual and propriety, then this is to have the look of a barbarian but the heart of a Hua.

"There was, for instance, the rebellion of Lu Wan. Was he a barbarian?[75] And there was the loyalty of Chin Jih-ti. Was he a Hua?[76] From this we can see that all depends on inclination."

Now Li Yen-sheng came from beyond the sea yet was able to make his virtues known to the governor, who singled him out for recommendation so as to encourage the Jung and Ti and to cause all the world to submit to the influence of our bright culture. For one is Hua by heart and not by geography. And since there are still barbarians among us, I have composed "The Heart of Being Hua."[77]

The spirit of this text, its confident and constructive tone, seems rooted in a confidence similar to Han Yü's that the traditional Hua virtues, properly practiced, can once again be the foundation for political and cultural unity.

Another important achievement of "Essentials of the Moral Way" was to introduce the notion of an orthodox Confucian "succession of the Way" (*tao-t'ung*) and to lay out Han Yü's version of that succession. A necessary first step toward the establishment of cultural unity was to establish the parameters of orthodoxy within the Confucian tradition itself. Han Yü's ultimate decision to route this succession through Mencius rather than through Hsün-tzu and Yang Hsiung, even though he admired and learned much from these two thinkers, had, as is well known, monumental consequences for the history of Neo-Confucianism. Although there can be no doubt that the idea of transmission lineages in the Chinese scholarly tradition dates from at least the Han Dynasty and probably before, Ch'en Yin-k'o has suggested that Han Yü derived his concept of the *tao-t'ung* from the more immediate example of the Ch'an practice of the "transmission of the dharma" (*ch'uan-fa*).[78] The key point of similarity between the two concepts, despite contemporary claims or later definitions, was that in both cases the positing of a lineage based on intuitive understanding of an ancient master's teaching was used to circumvent the perceived decay of that teaching through doctrinal fragmentation and proliferation of commentary. In conjunction with this antipathy to commentarial tradition was the appeal to the direct, verbal transmission of this intuitive understanding. The emphasis in both cases was on education and transmission through action rather than through study, on actualization of moral principles rather than on exegesis of texts that explicated these principles.

Much has been made of the fact that Han Yü permitted long gaps in his *tao-t'ung*, whereas the Ch'an *ch'uan-fa* postulated an unbroken chain of personal transmission from the disciples of Buddha Śākyamuni to Bodhidharma—the so-called twenty-eight Indian patriarchs.[79] Although this is certainly a valid observation and represents one real difference between the two concepts of transmission, it is not likely to have been a source of concern to Han Yü. Since both transmissions depended on intuitive understanding obtained through the disciple's own efforts, the absence or presence of temporal gaps in the transmission was irrelevant. Han Yü often implies, and sometimes states, that "on my own I attained the Way of the Sages and discoursed on it."[80] The Ch'an concept of face-to-face master-to-disciple transmission arose during the course of the eighth century as a consequence of the struggle between the Northern and Southern schools over doctrinal orthodoxy; it may also owe something to the esoteric transmission of the Taoist alchemical schools. It is clear, however, that there was no need for Han Yü to postulate a series of Confucian worthies to rival the "twenty-eight Indian patriarchs" of Ch'an. He was confronted not with a schism within a thriving tradition but rather with a tradition so moribund that few even had an interest in resuscitating it. To postulate an unbroken series of "transmissions" back to Yao and Shun within the historical-minded acuity of the Confucian tradition would have been a much more complicated task than it was within the ahistorical haze of the Indian world and, for Han Yü, an essentially needless one.

Although Han Yü did not share the Ch'an school's need for an historical face-to-face transmission lineage, he did share their partiality for face-to-face oral transmission of a teaching method. This preference for the spoken over the written word as a vehicle for instruction is clearest in Han Yü's famous exchange of letters with Chang Chi written in Pien-chou in 798.[81] In reply to Chang Chi's suggestion that he should commit his anti-Buddhist and anti-Taoist sentiments to writing, Han Yü answered:

> When you commit something to writing, your ideas are limited by the written word. How then should you choose between proclaiming your ideas through word of mouth and committing them to writing? Mencius did not write the book called *Mencius*. After he died, his disciples Wan Chang and Kung-sun Ch'ou simply recorded what Mencius had said. Now, on my own I have attained the Way of the Sages and discoursed on it, objecting to Buddhism and Taoism for many years. Those who do not know me think I like to argue. A few are persuaded but twice as many still harbor doubts. These I press even harder, but if in the end my verbal arguments cannot convince them, any writings I might have would certainly not sway them. This is why I have refrained from writing; it is not because I begrudge the effort in-

volved. And then there is the saying, "For educating the
present age, use the spoken word; for transmitting to
later ages, write books."

In his second letter, Han Yü acknowledges his fear of political
repression, should he too publicly oppose Buddhism and
Taoism:

> In ancient times, the Sage wrote the *Spring and Autumn
> Annals*, but its words were so deep, he dared not publicly
> transmit it, and so he passed it on verbally to his disciples
> who only in later ages committed it to writing. He was
> concerned about the fragility of the way.
>
> Those who now honor Buddhism and Taoism are, at
> the very lowest, lords and ministers (i.e. the emperor is
> the highest). I cannot attack them in a direct voice. I can,
> however, persuade those that can be spoken to. Yet
> sometimes I encounter those who oppose me, and they
> sound the voice of alarm. If I were then to write a book,
> I would anger even more people, and they would con-
> sider me crazy and deluded. My life would be in danger,
> and what then would become of my "writings"?

He notes that Confucius suffered political persecution for his
teachings but that he was able to preserve them for posterity
by confiding them to his disciples. Confucius and his disciples
confronted a gap of only several hundred years between the
early Chou paragons and their own time. Buddhism and
Taoism have dominated the "middle land," however, for over
six hundred years. Their extirpation will be no easy task. Yet
the quiet propagation of oral teachings will be the essential
base. "If one observes those ancients who were successful in
their own time and whose teachings were put into practice,
none of them wrote books. What is written down is always
something that found no acceptance in its own age but only
in later ages."

Han Yü's clearest exposition of his opinion on teachers is
the famous "Discourse on Teachers" written in 802 during
his first year of service at the Imperial University.

Students of Antiquity must have teachers to pass on the tradition, give instruction, and resolve doubts. Since men are not born with knowledge,[82] all have doubts; and if they do not seek out a teacher, then their doubts will never be resolved.

One born before me has naturally learned the tradition before I have, so I follow him as my teacher. Yet if one born after me has also learned the tradition before I have, then I follow him as my teacher; for, my teacher is the tradition. It makes no difference if someone was born before or after me. And so for this reason there is neither rich nor poor, old nor young; where the tradition is, there the teacher is.

It is said that for a long time now the tradition of teachers has not been passed on; and it is difficult to loosen people from their mistakes.

The Sages of Antiquity far surpassed other men, yet they followed teachers and learned from them. The ordinary man of today is far inferior to the Sages, yet he is ashamed to study with a teacher. So the Sage grows sager, and the fool more foolish, because what separates Sage and fool is their different attitudes toward teachers.

A man who loves his child selects a teacher to instruct him. But the same man is ashamed to take a teacher for himself, and this is an error. The teacher of this child assigns him books and rehearses his memorizations. This is not what I would call passing on the tradition or resolving doubts. To take a teacher when one cannot memorize and yet to reject the same when one cannot resolve doubts is to study what is of minor significance and neglect what is major. I do not see the wisdom of this.

Shamans, musicians, and craftsmen are not ashamed to teach each other. Yet should anyone among the literati class call himself "teacher" or "disciple," all ridicule him. If one asks why, the answer is that the two parties are about the same age, or that their understanding is about the same, or that if the teacher's official position is lower than the disciple so it's too demeaning, or higher so it verges on flattery. Unfortunately, it is clear the tradition of the teacher cannot be brought back (*fu*). The superior man shuns shamans, musicians, and craftsmen; yet in these days his wisdom does not measure up to theirs. This is most strange.

A Sage has no constant teacher.[83] Confucius took as teachers T'an-tzu, Ch'ang Hung, Master Hsiang, and Lao-tan, yet they were less worthy than he.[84] And so he said, "When three people walk together, there will certainly be one who can be my teacher."[85] So disciples are not necessarily better than their teachers, nor are teachers necessarily worthier than their disciples. One has simply learned the tradition earlier than the other or is more specialized in his scholarship and learning.

Li P'an, who is seventeen, likes the writings of the Ancients (*ku-wen*) and has memorized the six classics and their commentaries. Unfettered by the conventions of the times, he now studies with me. I applaud his ability to practice the tradition of the Ancients and have composed this "Discourse on Teachers" to give to him.[86]

This famous tract, when read in the context of Han Yü's letters to Chang Chi, makes clear that Han Yü's insistence on the necessity of "teachers" is an insistence on the primacy of oral instruction. More than anything else, this insistence links his concept of the "lineage of the way" and the Ch'an "transmission of the dharma." We have seen in chapter one above that he instituted the practice of daily lectures when he became rector of the Imperial University in 820. There is unfortunately no direct evidence that the model of the Ch'an lecture hall was behind Han Yü's innovation.[87] In the next generation, however, P'i Jih-hsiu (c.834-c.883) made the analogy:

Yet our present efforts at instruction and explication are not half of what they once were. Our texts have become corrupted and our commentaries trivial. Now the masters of the Western regions, when they teach their disciples, make it their practice to instruct and explicate their doctrines every day. When we look at our own Imperial

University, we should really feel shame before the masters of the Western regions.[88]

A somewhat more extended reference to the superiority of Buddhist over Confucian teaching methods occurs in the "Preface Seeing Off the Master Hung Sun" of Shen Ya-chih (782?-831?), who lauds the Buddhist technique of varying their teaching method to accord with the capability of each disciple.

> Since Buddhism has come to the central states, the number of our people who have taken up its study has greatly surpassed those who study Confucianism and the other schools. This is because the institution of teacher and disciple and its transmission among them have been specific and strict; and so today the Confucian path has fallen into decline and cannot compare with Buddhism, which has even divided into schools and subschools. Their teachers gauge the level of their disciples' individual natures and provide them with the appropriate instruction. It is for this reason they employ such divergent methods as meditation and deficient conduct, physical austerities and discussion meetings.[89]

This emphasis on the primacy of face-to-face encounters continued to play an important role in Sung Neo-Confucianism. One of the two Ch'eng brothers wrote, "There is indeed no conflict between transmitting the way through writing and through oral transmission. When we speak face-to-face we use actions to illustrate our meaning and our thoughts come together. But when writings are transmitted over time, although there are many words, they are not really complete."[90]

The "Discourse on Teachers" also emphasizes the egalitarian nature of the *tao-t'ung*: "my teacher is the tradition . . . neither rich nor poor, old nor young; where the tradition is, there the teacher is." Han Yü seems clearly to realize the difficulty of achieving such a goal in the highly stratified society of his time and therefore remarks that "the tradition of the teacher cannot be brought back" (*fu*) under these circumstances. A letter of Liu Tsung-yüan testifies to the pressure Han Yü's concept of teachers generated from his contemporaries. According to Liu, Han Yü's open acceptance of "disciples" and his advocacy of this practice in the "Discourse on Teachers" earned him the reputation of being too forward and aggressive, a charge not without political overtones and one that forced his withdrawal to Lo-yang in 807.[91] It is not difficult to sense from this account that Han Yü's egalitarian concept of the *tao-t'ung* threatened the socially stratified political configurations among the literati of his age. To the extent that the Ch'an monk had withdrawn from the world of politics, his egalitarian ways posed no immediate threat. But the introduction of such ways among the literati, proposing as it did a totally new relationship between education and power, directly challenged the existing social and political structure.

A natural corollary of this proposed egalitarianism is the emphasis on *Analects* XIX.22 and its conclusion that the Master had no "constant teacher." There is, as Han Yü states, something of the way (*tao*) to be learned everywhere, a notion that coincides with the Ch'an practice of "traveling by foot" (*hsing chiao*) to different teachers in search of the way and enlightenment. The equation of "traveling by foot" and "having no constant teacher" is common in Ch'an texts.[92] Han Yü's appropriation of this equation for the Confucian tradition foreshadowed the Neo-Confucian conception of the physical world as the repository of Principle (*li*), the understanding of which by the Sage constituted knowledge.[93]

There are several texts that articulate Han Yü's ideas for concrete political reform. One of the most revealing, yet seldom cited, is the "Preface Seeing Off Ch'i Hao After His Failure at the Examinations," written in 794. Ch'i Hao's eldest brother was Ch'i Yang (748-795) who had been a protégé of Ma Sui and had served as prime minister in 786-787 when Han Yü had first come to Ch'ang-an. After his dismissal from his post in 787, Ch'i Yang served in a number of southern inspectorships until his death in 795.[94]

When the Ancients spoke of being "disinterested and not selfish" they meant that the selection and promotion of officials was to depend not on personal relations but only on an individual's suitability for the position. When inferiors looked to their superiors they saw only those who had been justly promoted and did not suspect them of having personal connections. And so superiors effected their policies with a preference for what was just; in this they were easy and caused no distress to their inferiors. Inferiors controlled themselves and acted with caution; in this they were firm and caused no misgivings among their superiors. For these reasons, being a ruler was not hard, and it was easy to be a minister: if one saw a good person, one could publicly promote him; if one saw a bad person, one could openly dismiss him.

But when the Way fell into decline, superiors and inferiors began to distrust one another. And so the case where one man employed his enemy and then employed his son was recorded in the *Commentary of Tso*, where he was praised and called impartial.[95] When one saw a good man, if he were a relative or friend, one dared not employ him. When one saw an evil man, if he were a stranger, one dare not dismiss him. So now only those whom all like can be chastized and demoted—and this is "disinterested"; only those whom all dislike can be encouraged and promoted—and this is "impartial." Thus one who acts contrary to his own heart, speaks against his own will, and has a reputation he himself is ashamed of—such a person is commonly called a "good functionary." When denunciations that build up like dirt on the skin move not the ruler, false accusations will not arise among the people.[96] But to rule the empire today takes effort, to serve as an official is difficult, and to guide the people in the right way takes exhausting diligence.

If one calmly reflects on this situation, one will see it is the fault neither of the ruler, nor of the officials, nor of the people of the empire. Yet there is a root and a cause: it is born in partiality (*szu*) toward relatives and matures in partiality toward oneself. It is to be dishonest with oneself and then to maintain that all others are the same. The longer it grows, the more difficult to root it out. To effect a change would take a hundred years and one who knew the will of Heaven and was free from doubt.[97] In the end, could even one such as this renew Antiquity (*fu-ku*)?

The case of Master Ch'i of Kao-yang has moved me. His older brother was a sometime minister, now demoted to military duty in the South. So the great officers of the court have all known him for a long time. When Master Ch'i sat for the *chin-shih* examinations, those in charge failed him because of this relationship. Yet he said simply, "My lack of success is only because those in charge treated me unjustly. I will sharpen my talents and wait for my time." So shouldering this task, he will return now to his home in the East.

I have seen many who failing to attain success blamed their superiors without taking stock of their own short-comings. Yet one such as Master Ch'i, who has already succeeded but protests he has not yet done so and is not at all concerned with those in charge, is rare. I know from this that Master Ch'i will later be a truly good official who will be able to renew Antiquity (*fu-ku*), be disinterested and not selfish, know the will of Heaven, and be free from doubt.[98]

Although this preface concerns a specific case of bureau-cratic injustice, the larger issues involved are both that conflict inherent in Confucian polity between duty to family and duty to state and the ensuing despoliation of the state at the hands of private interests.[99] Han Yü expresses his clear preference for the primacy of the state by formulating this problem in terms of the ancient contrast between *kung* ("disinterested-ness, impartiality, public-mindedness") versus *szu* ("selfish-ness, partiality, private-mindedness").[100] Yet his solution, rather than advocating an arbitrary increase in the power of the state to combat private interests, calls for moral renewal at the level of the individual functionary: the cause of political decay is personal moral decay. "It is born in partiality toward relatives and matures in partiality toward oneself. It is to be dishonest with oneself and then to maintain that all others are the same." This expressed interrelationship of personal values and public goals is identical to the concept of the political extension of *jen* as envisioned in the *Great Learning* catenation and articulated in the "Essentials of the Moral Way." So important was this identification that the definition of *jen*, "sense of humanity," as *kung*, "disinterestedness," later became a cardinal tenet of Neo-Confucianism.[101] "Antiquity" is thus a condition in which each individual by perfecting his own sense of personal integrity (*ch'eng*) helps to order the state. The "renewal of Antiquity" (*fu-ku*) then becomes a moral injunction to political action that begins with the individual's private struggle to "make true his intentions" (*ch'eng*).[102]

The opposite of this condition is slander: lack of integrity (*ch'eng*) causes laziness toward the cultivation of one's own person and jealousy toward others who have already achieved it. "On the Origins of Slander" (*Yüan hui*) is Han Yü's major treatise on this problem, and this text links the theoretical framework outlined in the "Essentials of the Moral Way" with the practical example adduced in the "Preface Seeing Off Ch'i Hao." The Sages of Antiquity expected more of themselves than they did of others, thus they avoided sloth and the people enjoyed doing good. Shun was "humane and just" (*jen i*), so they strove to emulate these qualities. The Duke of Chou was talented and able, so they strove to emulate these qualities. "Shun and the Duke of Chou were both great Sages, and in later times none equaled them. Yet these men said, 'I sorrow that I am not like Shun, that I am not like the Duke of Chou.' " Although they thus constantly strove for perfection in themselves, they were less exacting toward others, content if others practiced only a single beneficial quality: "a single good is easy to practice, a single virtue easy to attain."

The "Sages" of today are the opposite. They are exacting toward others but easy on themselves, considering themselves perfect upon the attainment of only a single virtue, criticizing others if they lack even the slightest virtue. "Thus outwardly do they deceive others and inwardly deceive themselves . . . failing to apply to themselves the standards of even ordinary men, yet expecting of others the behavior of Sages. . . . And thus does an accomplished good provoke slander, a virtue perfected attract calumny. . . . It is difficult under these circumstances for a man to achieve both a good name and morally correct behavior. Yet if those who are to work in high places would accept these ideas, then our state could still approach to good order."[103]

Han Yü's own experiences certainly contributed to the intensity of feelings apparent in this analysis of the personal and political effects of slander. We have seen that Liu Tsung-yüan believed slander against Han Yü forced him from the capital in 807, a belief that coincides with Han Yü's own account of these events.[104] A poem written at that time also reveals Han Yü believed himself fated to suffer from slander and calumny.[105] Yet "On the Origins of Slander" is much more than a private attack on its author's detractors. For Han Yü, slander is the antithesis of "humanity and justice" (jen i) and an evil that leads to the corruption of the state precisely because it breaks apart those links in the *Great Learning* catenation that unite personal integrity and political order. It prevents the extension of *jen* and the practice of "disinterestedness." Han Yü's emphatic denunciation of slander places him squarely in line with earlier paragons in the Confucian tradition such as Confucius, Mencius, and Ch'ü Yüan, all of whom warned against the political danger of the slanderer and the flatterer; for, calumny destroys that trust necessary for the proper practice of the relationship between ruler and servitor. The discernment to resist slander and flattery accordingly became a hallmark of the Confucian Sage and a moral injunction, as in Han Yü, to all in office.

This moral injunction was heaviest on the most exalted in the bureaucratic structure. Throughout the T'ang, the office of prime minister (*tsai-hsiang*) was the pinnacle of the civil service system. As the *New T'ang History* writes without exaggeration, "The duties of the prime ministers are to assist the Son of Heaven, to oversee all government functionaries, and to direct all affairs. Their charge is the heaviest."[106] That Han Yü shared his age's conception of the prime ministership as the state's highest charge is clear from his three 795 letters, in which he held the ministers accountable for the welfare of each individual in the state. Most important among these responsibilities was "to oversee the functionaries," that is, to ensure the fair and impartial administration of the civil service system itself, including the recruitment of talented individuals into its ranks. This ability to locate and foster "talent" was among the essential qualities of the Confucian Sage-Kings, and the return of this quality was high on Han Yü's program for practical political reform. Perhaps the most famous affirmation of the value of this ancient attribute is the last of the four "Miscellaneous Discourses," the celebrated allegory of Po-lo. The name Po-lo seems originally to have referred to a star in the constellation of Ts'ao-fu, a legendary official in charge of horses.[107] It was then applied as a sobriquet of one Sun Yang, a connoisseur of horses who lived during the reign of Duke Mu of Ch'in (r.659-621 B.C.). The analogy that Po-lo recognizes and trains fine horses as a ruler recognizes and trains fine officials occurs often in pre-Ch'in literature and was a favorite metaphor of Han Yü.[108]

> If the age possesses a Po-lo, it will have horses that can run a hundred leagues.
>
> There are always hundred-league horses, but not always a Po-lo. So even fine horses suffer at the hands of servants and die yoked together in their stable, their hundred-league quality unknown.
>
> A hundred-league horse will consume two bushels of grain at a single feed. But in these days the one who feeds horses does not recognize those with the hundred-league potential. And these horses, although they have the potential, cannot eat their fill, cannot develop their strength, so their fine talents go unnoticed, and they cannot rank equal even with ordinary horses. How can they reach their potential for a hundred leagues?

They are whipped, but not in the right way; fed, but cannot perfect their talents; they call out, but cannot make their meaning understood. So with whip in hand he approaches near to them and says, "In all the empire there is no decent horse."

Is it that there are truly no horses or truly no one who recognizes horses?[109]

Most commentators have read this text as self-allegory: Han Yü is the "hundred-league horse." Although this intention is certainly present, this seemingly self-pitying lament reads much better as a harsh condemnation of the political inertia and stagnation that characterized the last decade of Te-tsung's reign: the incompetent in high office complain of the lack of talent among their subordinates, yet that very complaint betrays their own ignorance and inability, for "there are always hundred-league horses, but not always a Po-lo" to recognize them.

It is true that most of these writings on the theory of political reform date from Han Yü's early years of frustration with the examination system. Yet they are not merely private laments but rather visions of a very different polity—one that is "ancient" and Confucian. It is vital to note that Han Yü took these visions as practical goals for himself and for the state, that he never deviated from their pursuit, and that his was the difficult choice among the many easier options chosen by his contemporaries—capitulation to corruption, abandonment of political goals, retreat into pedantry, or solace in Buddhist or Taoist escapism—all options that for Han Yü constituted a loss of "integrity" (ch'eng). If these politically visionary writings tapered off during his later years, this was because from about 814 on Han Yü saw himself as personally participating in the actual creation of his visions. And the real Confucian is, in his integral soul, always happier with action than with theory.

The Oneness of
the Sage

"All movement under Heaven is
regulated by unity."
—*Book of Changes*

In recent times it has been usual to disparage Han Yü's status
as a creative thinker and to negate his contributions to the
realm of purely speculative thought. This development arose
from the attempt by some early twentieth-century Chinese
intellectuals to isolate from the holistic world views of premodern Chinese thinkers only those elements that could contribute to a history of the evolution of a "Chinese philosophy"
(*che-hsüeh*) conceived along Western lines. Thinkers, especially
Confucian thinkers like Han Yü, whose contributions *appeared*
to be simple reorderings of earlier elements and ideas, fared
badly in this process. There was the additional problem that
Han Yü's best known writings, famous primarily because of
their literary style, were basically political rather than philosophical tracts. Certainly, the historians of Chinese "philosophy" saw in Han Yü's writings adumbrations of things to
come, but the Sung Neo-Confucians were clearly of greater
interest to them, and so Han Yü became a "forerunner of the
Neo-Confucianism that developed in the eleventh century."[1]
I hope to demonstrate in this chapter that, far from being a
forerunner or precursor of Neo-Confucianism, Han Yü to-

gether with Li Ao had in fact already worked out many of the major "philosophical" premises that underlie the "Neo-Confucian synthesis."

A proper understanding of these accomplishments first requires a proper appreciation of the depth and quality of Han Yü's scholarship. Many of Han Yü's own attestations to wide learning occur in obviously self-serving contexts such as letters to potential employers and patrons, and they have therefore been dismissed as self-aggrandizement. Yet the standard biographical sources are quite insistent on the breadth of Han Yü's learning, a learning demonstrated by the depth and appropriateness of the many allusions in his poetry.[2] There is also considerable incidental and anecdotal evidence. Thus Chang Chi wrote in his "Elegy for T'ui-chih" that "We searched to the end through books ancient and modern, / discussing and considering with each other every detail."[3] Han Yü's expertise in paleography is also well documented.[4] As we shall see momentarily, recently focused attention on Han Yü's long-neglected "Disquisition on the Preface to the *Book of Poetry*" has underlined his position among the scholastic vanguard of his time.

Han Yü had strong sympathies and sometimes direct contacts with the new innovative school of classical scholarship that began with the Tan Chu (725-770) exegesis on the *Spring and Autumn Annals*.[5] In a sense, however, Han Yü's scholarship moved a step beyond this school. Although their approach was a radical departure from the existing tradition of writing subcommentaries on existing commentaries, they still adhered to tradition by limiting their attention to one text. This tradition probably derived from the Han Dynasty establishment of "chairs" for specific classics at the state university; it was reinforced by the Chinese Buddhist habit of identifying specific schools with specific texts and by the importance of textual preparation in the T'ang examination format. Thus, for Han Yü's contemporaries, learning essentially meant learning a text.

But for Han Yü, and for Liu Tsung-yüan whose links to the Tan Chu group were much closer, scholarship was an attempt to preserve all that could be known of "Antiquity," that is, of the "state of unity and harmony which had existed in the beginning."[6] This much more eclectic approach gave rise to new genres of scholarly inquiry, one of which was titled "On Reading . . ." (*Tu* . . .). Han Yü's "On Reading *Mo-tzu*" is a good example.[7] The prime purpose of this and similar genres was to redefine Antiquity through a reexamination of *all* existing records from that time. Han Yü's "Song of the Stone Drums" illustrates his passion for "antiquities" and is a harbinger of that Neo-Confucian infatuation with physical relics of the past, an infatuation that became so prominent a part of the mentality of Ming-Ch'ing literati. Yet an equally passionate selectivity tempered Han Yü's eclecticism, a selectivity rooted in the need to redefine an image of Antiquity that could serve as a model for changing the present. For the real antiquity had held as many heterodox notions as did the present. Han Yü's efforts to formulate new cultural standards for his own age thus entailed a thorough reexamination and reevaluation of the past, the results of which were codified in the "succession of the Way," an orthodox chronological lineage of those who, in Han Yü's view, had maintained similar cultural standards in their age.[8]

But, as we have also seen above, Han Yü's cultural standards were social goals that resulted naturally from his adherence to Confucian moral injunctions. Scholarship thus became an attempt to isolate those texts and passages that, among all the existing traces of ancient times, best conformed to a view of Antiquity formulated as a moral imperative for the present. Writings that conformed to this view were "authentic" (*cheng*); those that did not were "false" (*wei*).[9] "Authenticity" in this sense has no relation to its modern meaning but rather reflects the degree to which an ancient work manifests "the Way of Antiquity" (*ku tao*). Liu Tsung-yüan's "Judgement on the Granting of a Fief by Means of a Paulownia Leaf" will illustrate this principle. The question concerns the credibility of the tradition that when the young King Ch'eng of the Chou Dynasty playfully enfeoffed his baby brother Yü, his regent and advisor the Duke of Chou insisted on the act being taken for real.

> There is a tradition concerning Antiquity that once when King Ch'eng was playing with his little brother he bestowed on him a paulownia leaf and said, "I hereby enfeoff you." When the Duke of Chou entered to congratulate him, the King replied he had only been jesting. But the Duke of Chou answered, "The Son of Heaven cannot jest." And so the little brother was enfeoffed in T'ang.

Liu Tsung-yüan questions the "authenticity" of this fragment of antique lore, which is preserved in the *Spring and Autumn Annals of Master Lü* (*Lü-shih ch'un-ch'iu*) and in the *Garden of Persuasions* (*Shui yüan*). Liu's conclusion is that "this was not something the Duke of Chou would have done, and therefore it is not credible."[10] Liu's arguments are "rational," yet they are rooted in the moral assumption that the Duke of Chou, the sage-advisor par excellence of Antiquity, could not have acted contrary to the King's, and to his own, best interests *as Liu saw them.* Han Yü's "On Reading *Mo-tzu*" follows the same basic intellectual procedure: Mo-tzu is "authentic" when his ideas, *as Han sees them,* coincide with those of Confucius.

Sakata Shin describes this process as follows: "During the *ku-wen* renaissance movement, the orthodox Way of Antiquity (*ku tao*) that was supposedly present in *ku-wen* was to be revealed through an examination of the old texts. More exactly, using the movement's own ideology as a standard for determining this Way of Antiquity, they either judged the authenticity of the old texts or singled out those portions of these texts that contradicted this Way of Antiquity."[11] The field of textual analysis affected this examination through recourse to that method of exegesis known as "overall meaning." Such analysis made the bold assumption that the raw text of the classics could be understood without reference to existing exegesis. Li Ao's "Writings on Returning to One's True Nature" (*Fu-hsing shu*), which, as Ou-yang Hsiu pointed out, are essentially a commentary on the *Doctrine of the Mean,* well illustrate the principles of "overall meaning" exegesis. In reply to a question why his explication of the *Doctrine of the Mean* was different from others, Li Ao replied, "Others explain it in accordance with individual facts; I penetrate it with my mind."[12]

Han Yü's forays into textual exegesis are all based on the "overall meaning" method. When considered together with the methodologically similar *Fu-hsing shu* of Li Ao, one can isolate characteristics of this approach:

1. The assumption that all texts from Antiquity contained something of the *ku-tao* justified the eclectic search of uncanonical works, such as *Mencius*, for "Antique" expositions of modern problems.

2. Touchstone passages were isolated and interpreted as highly condensed, almost mystical encodings of the works as a whole and then used as keys to interpret the main body of the text.

3. Rather than adduce scholarship from outside the text, this exegesis explicated the text from the inside out. Frequent juxtaposition and comparison of passages, and the use of one passage to explain another, served to spread the "overall meaning" of the key passages throughout the text.

4. Contradictions were often eliminated by appeal to a concept of "layering" or "stratification," according to which the Sages of Antiquity supposedly adapted or layered the same teaching to fit the mental capacities of specific disciples. This practice, most common in *Analects* exegesis, certainly derived from similar T'ien-t'ai and Hua-yen tenets that the teachings of different Buddhist schools were all reflections of the same doctrine, differently formulated by the Buddha for different audiences.

5. Simple and blatant alteration of the text was often used to resolve contradictions arising from textual problems.

The end result of this exegesis was a radical shift in the perception of the nature of the classical canon: the view of the classics as monolithic and unchanging compilations of sacred texts, with fixed interpretations and all parts of essentially equal value, declined. There arose a new conception of the classics as anthologies of touchstone passages, some more important than others, repositories of living spiritual wisdom to be meditated upon again and again during the course of the scholar's lifetime. The large amounts of dialogue in the *Analects* and in *Mencius* furthered the image of them as works of action rather than theory, and this image helped to make them cornerstones of the new canon. This transition parallels the demise of the scholastic Buddhist "doctors of scripture" and the increasing popularity of the Ch'an monks with their *logia* (*yü-lu*), their own anthologies of living spiritual wisdom.

Concentration on those texts later to be known as the *Four Books* (*Szu shu*)—the *Great Learning*, the *Doctrine of the Mean*, the *Analects*, and *Mencius*—is already well advanced in Han Yü's writings. The "Essentials of the Moral Way," especially, established the opening catena from the *Great Learning* as the beginning (and end), the ultimate touchstone, of the entire corpus. Moreover, the relative frequency with which Han Yü cites these works leads to the supposition that he had already conceived their orthodox Sung sequence: a gradual unfolding of Confucian wisdom from its concentrated nucleus in the *Great Learning* to the developed meditations of *Mencius*. The *Great Learning* postulated the relation between inner wisdom and political order. The *Doctrine of the Mean* then proceeded to define the qualities of the Sage and outline the foundation and initial steps toward achieving that state of "integrity, sincerity" (*ch'eng*) that the text makes synonymous with Sage-hood. It was certainly no accident that Han Yü and Li Ao adopted the *Mean*'s definition of Sagehood, for its image of the Sage as metaphysical Absolute, as a spiritual hero at one with the universe, was unique in the traditional Confucian canon yet had much in common with Buddhist and Taoist views of Sagehood.[13] Liang Su had quoted from the *Doctrine of the Mean* to support T'ien-t'ai precepts, and Ou-yang Chan had written an "Essay on 'Integrity from Brightness,'" which was essentially a commentary on *Doctrine of the Mean* section 21.[14] Although it is thus obvious that Han Yü was hardly the first to note the *Mean*'s metaphysical vision of the Confucian (or Buddhist) Sage, he was probably the first to join together the *Mean* and the *Great Learning* to form an organic conception of the inner spiritual and outer public life of the new Confucian Sage.[15] That Han Yü should have recognized the natural affiliation of these two *Record of Rites* chapters is not surprising. His writings show an intimate knowlege of the entire *Record of Rites*, and I suspect it was the "big classic" he prepared for the *chin-shih* examination.[16]

Han Yü's attention to the *Mencius* has been noted above and is well known. Fung Yu-lan has observed, no doubt correctly, that the "mystical tendency apparent in Mencius's philosophy . . . provided answers to the same problems that were debated in Han Yü's age by Buddhism, and that men of his time regarded as being significant."[17] Specifically, the focus of attention was the seventh and final book of the *Mencius* with its touchstone passage that "the ten thousand things are all complete in ourselves; and through self-examination they are made true (*ch'eng*)." Similarly, the Mencian discussions of "mind" (*hsin*) and "human nature" (*hsing*) provided a ready Confucian context for subjects that had hitherto been the sole domain of Buddhist or Ch'an teachers. Furthermore, the short exchanges and maxims of the seventh chapter were much closer to the Ch'an *logia* that the longer disquisitions and set speeches of the earlier chapters. One of Han Yü's clearest discussions of Mencius is the "Preface Seeing Off Master Wang Hsün," undated, but probably written in the early 800s.

I have always felt that the Way of Confucius was so vast and comprehensive that no one of his disciples was able to obtain a total view and a complete understanding of it; and so when they studied it, each took what was closest to his own nature. Afterwards, when they dispersed to the various feudal states, each passed on what he could to his own disciples: the more distant the source, the more divided will be its flows.

The learning of Tzu-hsia was passed on to T'ien Tzu-fang, and from him to Chaung-tzu. Therefore, the *Chaung-tzu* praises the kind of man T'ien Tzu-fang was.[18]

When the *Hsün-tzu* talks about the Sage, it usually mentions Confucius or Tzu-kung. But the works of Tzu-kung have not been passed on; Szu-ma Ch'ien's "Biographies of the Disciples of Confucius" says only that his name was Han Pi and that he received training in the *Changes* from Shang Chü.[19]

Mencius took Tzu-szu as his teacher, and the learning of Tzu-szu came from Tseng-tzu.[20]

So after Confucius died, his disciples all produced some writings, but only the traditions of Mencius attained to the mainstream; and so I have enjoyed reading him since I was young.

Wang Hsün of T'ai-yüan has shown me some compositions he has done, in which he often quotes Mencius. In my conversations with him he expressed his delight in the *Mencius* and praised its writing.

If one follows unchecked the downward flow of a river, one will arrive at the sea, no matter what the speed. But if one does not attain its proper course (*tao*), there is no hope of arriving, no matter how fast one travels. Likewise, in learning one must be attentive to the proper course. To follow the learning of Yang Chu, Mo-tzu, Lao-tzu, Chuang-tzu, or Buddha, and so hope to travel the proper course (*tao*) to Sagehood can be compared to a boat, cut off in a side channel or bottled up in a harbor, that yet hopes to reach the sea. And so one must begin with Mencius in the search for the proper course to Sagehood.

What Wang Hsün has now produced shows that he already understands this course. When he finally obtains his boat and his oars, he shall know how to follow its way unchecked. Such is his capacity.[21]

It is important to note here Han Yü's concern with establishing the proper lineage (*tao-t'ung*) for early Confucian teachings. This preface attempts to fix this lineage from Confucius through Tzu-szu to Mencius. Li Ao adhered to the same lineage and stressed Tzu-szu's role as the supposed author of the

Doctrine of the Mean and the transmitter of this text to Mencius.[22]

Han Yü's opinion of Mencius as the "purest of the pure" is also the major conclusion of his "On Reading Hsün-tzu," a text that both shows the history of Han Yü's personal experience with these then-unread survivals of Antiquity and reveals much about his scholarly attitude toward them.

> When I read the writings of Mencius, I realized for the first time how worthy of respect was the Way of Confucius, how easy to practice was the Way of the Sage, and how easy to effect was the Way of good government through king and feudal lord. I considered Mencius as the only disciple of Confucius who honored the Sages.
>
> Later I obtained the writings of Yang Hsiung and came to respect and trust Mencius even more. And because of this I also considered Yang Hsiung a disciple of the Sages.
>
> But the Way of the Sages was not passed on to later ages. During the decline of the Chou Dynasty, each mischief-maker used his own theories to beseech the lords of the age; and in the confusion and disorder the Six Classics became intermingled with the theories of the hundred philosophers. But great teachers and Confucian scholars still existed. Then there was the burning of the books in Ch'in and Taoism in the Han. The only pure writings to survive were Mencius and Yang Hsiung.
>
> When I obtained the writings of Hsün-tzu, I learned for the first time of his existence. I examined the text and, although in places it seems somewhat adulterated, it differed little in essentials from the teachings of Confucius. He was perhaps somewhere between Mencius and Yang Hsiung.
>
> When Confucius edited the *Poetry* and *Documents* and compiled the *Spring and Autumn Annals*, he retained all that conformed to the Way and omitted all that departed from it. So these works are without defect. I would like to excise all that does not conform to the Way in the *Hsün-tzu* and add it to the writings of the Sages. Such

was the intention of Confucius. Mencius is the purest of the pure; Hsün-tzu and Yang Hsiung are pure but with minor defects.[23]

This text confirms Han Yü's interest in all writings from Antiquity. Furthermore, his determination to excise the existing text of "nonauthentic" elements reveals quite clearly his view of the responsibility of the Confucian editor. He may actually have begun this work, for the first commentary to *Hsün-tzu*, completed by Yang Liang in 818, often quotes Han Yü's opinions on the text.[24] Most commentators agree that the blemish Han Yü wished to excise from Hsün-tzu was his teaching on the ultimately evil character of human nature. This conflicted not only with the *Mencius* but, more important, with the Ch'an spirit of the age that stressed the metaphysical, universal, and salubrious aspects of that nature.

The most extensive source for observing directly both Han Yü's attitude toward textual scholarship and his position on various issues is the *Random Notes on the Analects (Lun yü pi-chieh)*. This book, which survives in a Southern Sung edition now in the Palace Museum Library in Taipei, contains passages from the *Analects* followed by comments attributed to Han Yü and to Li Ao. There seems to be no criteria for the selection of passages: some discussions confine themselves to textual matters, others are broader treatments of "overall meaning."[25] Many make a specific point of countering the opinions of the Han commentators, especially K'ung An-kuo and Ma Jung, that were known in the T'ang through their incorporation into the *Lun yü chi-chieh* compiled by Ho Yen (A.D. 190-249). Often Han Yü's explanations attempt to link two contiguous passages that the Han commentators treat as unconnected.[26] Several examples will perhaps best give the flavor of the text. Concerning the famous and enigmatic *Analects* II.11 "The Master said, 'He who recalls the old and so knows the new can be a teacher,' " Han Yü took exception to the narrow explication of K'ung An-kuo, according to which a teacher by constant repetition keeps the texts he has previously learned fresh in his mind.

Han Yü: Earlier scholars all maintain this means pe-
riodically to repeat a written text so as to turn it from
something old to something new. But this would be
"study by rote memory does not qualify one to be a
teacher" (*Li chi chu-shu* 36/9b; Legge, *Rites*, 2: 89-90). I
maintain "the old" here means the Way of Antiquity;
"the new" means one's own ideas, something that can
become new teachings.

Li Ao: Confucius praised Tzu-kung as one who "when
told of something past he knew what was to come" (*Analects* 1.15). This is the same meaning as "to recall the old
and know the new." K'ung An-kuo's explanation that it
means to repeat a written text is wrong.[27]

Han Yü thus interprets the passage to mean that a teacher is
one who forms his own ideas in accordance with the Way of
Antiquity. The point of reference is not only the *Rites* passage
Han Yü quotes but, also by implication, *Doctrine of the Mean*
XXVII.6, in which the phrase "Recall the old and so know the
new" also occurs in a context that is obviously broader than
K'ung An-kuo's "to repeat written tests."[28] It is interesting
to note that Han Yü's broadening of *Analects* II.11 formed the
basis of the Neo-Confucian understanding of the passage.[29]

The above is an example of Han Yü, rightly or wrongly,
enlarging the mundane interpretations of the Han commentators so as to cast the *Analects* in a metaphysical light more
in keeping with his own views. In addition to renouncing the
traditional commentaries, Han Yü was not above altering the
text itself if this were the only way to bring it into accord
with his own view of the Way of Antiquity. A good example
is the puzzling *Analects* XIV.6 "The Master said, 'There have
been superior men (*chün-tzu*) who have not had a sense of
humanity (*jen*); but there has never been a petty man (*hsiao-
jen*) who had a sense of humanity.' "

Han Yü: *Jen* (a sense of humanity) must be a mistake
for *pei* (perfect). How could there be a superior man who
had no *jen*? As for the petty man, how could he seek out
jen? I maintain that there might sometimes be a superior

183

man whose talents and character are not perfect (*pei*). But there has never been a petty man who sought out this perfection.[30]

Han Yü thus understands the text: "There may be a superior man who is not perfect, but a small man is never perfect." This alteration avoids what for Han Yü is the impossible statement that there can be a superior man with no sense of humanity.

We have noted above Shen Ya-chih's reference to the superiority of the Buddhist pedagogical technique of "gauging the level of their disciples' individual natures and providing them with the appropriate instruction."[31] The *Lun yü pi-chieh* turns this teaching technique into a principle of textual exegesis. It is probable that this attempt to apply "situational" exegesis to the *Analects* marked the beginning of the reading and new appreciation of the text as a sort of proto-Ch'an Confucian *logia*. By maintaining that a certain saying of the Master was meant to apply only to the specific intellectual needs of a particular disciple at a particular time, many seeming contradictions could be resolved. The text was "layered." That many of Confucius's utterances in the *Analects* are addressed to specific disciples and that little is known of these disciples naturally facilitated use of this method. An example will illustrate this technique. In *Analects* VII.15 Jan Yu has Tzu-kung ask Confucius his opinion of the struggle for control of the state of Wei between Che, the ruling Lord of Wei, and his exiled father Prince K'uai K'ui. Tzu-kung asked the question indirectly by asking Confucius his opinion of the legendary brothers Po I and Shu Ch'i. Confucius replied with praise for this pair who had renounced the throne and pursued their humanity (*jen*) without remorse as hermits. This opinion about the brothers, however, seemingly conflicts with *Analects* XVIII.8 in which Confucius maintains he is different from these hermits because "I have nothing preconceived about what I can or cannot do." Han Yü resolves the contradiction by writing that "the idea of this passage is simply to praise Sagehood and humanity and so to dissuade Jan Yu from being for the Lord of Wei."[32] In other words, in *Analects* VII.15 Confucius is merely offering Po I and Shu Ch'i as contrasts to the Lord of Wei and his father for the specific purpose of dissuading Jan Yu from involving himself in the latter's dispute over the throne of Wei; he is not making a categorical statement about Po I and Shu Ch'i.[33]

It is quite clear that the *Lun yü pi-chieh*, when considered along with and in light of Han Yü's other surviving examples of classical exegesis, constitutes strong evidence that Han Yü shared with the Tan Chu *Spring and Autumn* exegetes the same impatience with the restraints of traditional commentary and the same desire to make the classics and their study relevant to contemporary issues.[34] Recent research on the Tan Chu school has stressed these goals as common concerns of this group of scholars and of Han Yü and Li Ao, and it has emphasized the contributions of both groups to the formation of the new critical attitude of the Sung Neo-Confucians toward the classics.[35] Further evidence for the authenticity and the influence of the *Lun yü pi-chieh* on the Sung scholars are the numerous, and violent, textual emendations Ch'eng I adopted from it.[36] An example is *Analects* XI.21: "When the Master was in danger in K'uang, Yen Hui fell behind. The Master said, 'I thought you were dead,' Hui replied, 'So long as you are alive, how could I dare to die?' "

> Han Yü: *Szu* (to die) is a scribal error for *hsein* (before). The first phrase means that Yen Hui had dropped behind, and the next phrase means he would not presume to go ahead of the Master. The meaning is obvious and has nothing to do with death.[37]

Han Yü thus understands the passage as follows: "When the Master was in danger in K'uang, Yen Hui fell behind. The Master said, 'I thought you were ahead of me.' Hui replied, 'How could I presume to go ahead of where you are?' "

The centerpiece of Han Yü's efforts in the domain of pure thought is his conception of the Confucian Sage. Han Yü achieved this first, and remarkably distinct, image of the Neo-

Confucian Sage by fusing the old Buddhist concept of the Sage as *bodhisattva* who progressed through ten stages to spiritual and inner perfection with the old Confucian concept of the Sage as teacher, as administrator, and ultimately as sovereign. He applied the Buddhist definition of the Sage as metaphysical Absolute to the old Confucian definition of the Sage as the worldly and practical man of action. The catalyst in this fusion was of course Ch'an, which in the generation before Han Yü had also produced a new vision of the Sage. In this vision the Sage was still Buddhist, but one who dwelled simultaneously in the realms of the sacred (*sheng*) and the profane (*fan*) by pursuing an existence that merged the theory of the Absolute with the practice of normal daily life.

Han Yü's most concrete portrayal of Sagehood as a spiritual journey toward inner and outer perfection is the description of the early Sages in his essay "On the Origins of Slander."

> They heard that in Antiquity there had been a man called Shun who was humane and just (*jen i*), so they sought these qualities that had made Shun what he was and required the same of themselves, saying, "He was a man. I am a man. What he could do, I should be able to do also." So from morning to night they struggled to remove from themselves qualities that were unlike Shun's and to acquire those that were like his.

> They heard that in Antiquity there had been a man called the Duke of Chou who was talented and able, so they sought those qualities that had made the Duke of Chou what he was and required the same of themselves, saying, "He was a man. I am a man. What he could do, I should be able to do also." So from morning to night they struggled to remove from themselves qualities that were unlike the Duke of Chou's and to acquire those that were like his.

> Shun was a great Sage, and in later ages none equaled him. The Duke of Chou was a great Sage, and in later ages none equaled him. Yet these men said, "I sorrow that I am not like Shun, that I am not like the Duke of

Chou." This shows that what they required of themselves was heavy and comprehensive.[38]

The Buddhist element of progress toward a spiritual and metaphysical Absolute in this view of the Sage's struggle is apparent in the *General Principles of Cessation and Contemplation* (*Chih-kuan t'ung-li*), a major tract by Liang Su that summarizes these two cornerstones of T'ien-t'ai doctrine.

> Cessation (*chih*) and contemplation (*kuan*) occur when one leads the principles (*li*) of all the dharmas (*fa*) and rejuvenates (*fu*) them again in reality, reality being the base of human nature (*hsing*).
> Yet all things can seldom be rejuvenated; this is because of darkness and motion. To illuminate what is dark is enlightenment (*ming*), and to halt what is moving is quiescence (*ching*). Enlightenment and quiescence are the embodiments of cessation and contemplation.

Liang Su next proceeds to introduce and define the Three Truths (*san ti*), which are *k'ung*, the essentially unreal universe; *chia*, its derived, illusory form; and *chung*, the "mean," the unity and ultimate identity of the two.[39]

> The cultivation of these is called the Three Insights. Their essence is the saying that the Sage "reaches all depths and grasps the seeds [of all things]" (*Chou i chu-shu* 7/15a; trans. Richard Wilhelm, *The I Ching, or Book of Changes*, p. 315) and that he "develops his nature to perfection through the understanding of Principle" (*ch'iung-li chin-hsing* in *Chou i chu-shu* 9/2a; trans. Wilhelm, *Changes*, p. 262). He enlightens the obscure and penetrates the obstructed. He penetrates and is aware (*wu*), is aware and is perfected, is perfected and is made constant, is constant and is so made complete. His own understanding (*ming*) clarifies, and this then teaches, and his teaching brings things to perfection and to unity in the One.[40]

The essay goes on to identify this unity with Buddhahood and "enlightenment" (chüeh).

Liang Su's catenation describing the Sage's role in bringing "unity in the One" to all things is mirrored in the famous description of the Sage from *Doctrine of the Mean* section 22 in which the Sage's perfection is achieved through his understanding of the world and the world's salvation achieved in turn through his understanding.

> Only he possessed of the most complete integrity (chih ch'eng) under Heaven can develop his nature to perfection (chin ch'i hsing). He who can develop his nature to perfection can perfect the natures of other men. He who can perfect the natures of other men can perfect the natures of all things. He who can perfect the nature of all things can assist Heaven and Earth in their transforming and nourishing. And he who can assist Heaven and Earth in their transforming and nourishing forms then with Heaven and Earth a triad.[41]

This definition of the Sage from the *Doctrine of the Mean* expresses in spiritual and metaphysical terms that same hierarchical progression from the individual self to world order and unity that the *Great Learning* expresses in social and political terms. In both cases the results are the same: the ultimate identity of the private and public spheres of human endeavor, the ultimate unity of theory and action.

Han Yü's explication of *Analects* XI.3 offers another fascinating glimpse of how profoundly this concept of a stratified progress toward Sagehood affected him. The passage in question is Confucius's famous fourfold classification of his disciples:

> The practice of moral strength: Yen Yüan, Min Tzu-ch'ien, Jan Po-niu, and Chung-kung.
> Theory and language: Tsai Wo and Tzu-kung.
> Government and administration: Jan Yu and Chi-lu.
> Culture and learning: Tzu-yu and Tzu-hsia.

Li Ao offers a highly creative interpretation of this text, which is then elaborated by Han Yü with a concluding summary by Li Ao.

Li Ao: Confucius laid out these four categories to make clear to his students that, no matter at what stage they are, it is necessary to proceed from the lower toward the higher, from the outer door to the inner hall, if they are through study to attain Sagehood. The meaning is quite profound. Common pedants will never be able to follow the order of these categories and so peer into the depths of Sagehood.

Han Yü: The highest stage is the practice of moral strength. The *Changes* say, "In silence, to understand . . . depends on the practice of moral strength."[42] This means there is no need for words.

The stage below is language. The *Changes* say, "consider and then speak; deliberate and then act. Through consideration and deliberation they perfected the changes and transformations."[43] "But these cannot be confined within a rule."[44] This means they are not something that can be restrained by government and by laws.

The stage below is government administration. So it is said, "Although there are no old and perfected men, there are the statutes and the laws."[45] This means that the laws are not a function of the words alone.

The lowest stage is culture and learning. The *Rites* say, "They read the classics and determined the meaning . . . then discussed the subjects of their studies and selected their friends . . . small attainments . . . then great attainments."[46] Thus one rose from the lower to the higher.

Li Ao: All who study the Way of the Sages begin with literature (*wen*). When literature is mastered, then one brings order to human affairs. When one understands human affairs, then one attains to good speech. When speech is forgotten, then one understands in silence his own actions. This is called the practice of moral strength, and it is to enter into the profound depths of the Sages.

These four stages are thus in this order, but no commentator has explained why.[47]

Again, the interpretation of this passage to accord with the catenations from the *Great Learning* and the *Doctrine of the Mean* is too obvious to require elaboration. The implications of this passage on Han Yü's conception of literature, however, will be considered in the next chapter.

Another passage from the *Random Notes on the Analects* confirms, although in an oblique way, Han Yü's conception of the Absolute nature of Sagehood. Han Yü refutes the K'ung An-kuo interpretation of the enigmatic *Analects* XIX.11, "Tzu-hsia said, 'Great moral strength does not transgress barriers; but it is permissible for small moral strength to come in and go out.'" According to K'ung An-kuo's interpretation, "barriers" means "laws," and the passage means that in matters of great moral import one may not transgress the laws, but latitude is permitted with regard to lesser matters.[48]

> Han Yü: The interpretation of K'ung An-kuo that in matters of great moral importance one cannot transgress the law is wrong. I maintain "great moral strength" indicates the Sage. The passage means that, as far as the student is concerned, Sagehood is a threshold he cannot pass beyond. "Small moral strength" indicates the Worthy Man (*hsien jen*). The student can still "come in and go out" to peer into his depths.[49]

According to Han Yü, because Sagehood is the ultimate Absolute, the student can attain to this state but not surpass it. The condition of the Worthy Man, however, being just short of Sagehood, is more approachable and easier to attain.

A fundamental axiom of this new composite image of the Sage is the ultimate identity of the Sage and the common man, a notion Han Yü states most forcefully in his trenchant "Shun was a man; I am a man." The idea is stated with equal clarity in Liang Su's *General Principles of Cessation and Contemplation*:

Can the state of supreme Sagehood (*sheng*) be separated and far distant, cut off from the realm of ordinary men (*fan*)? Both have but a single nature. Those who attain it become enlightened (*wu*), those who lose it become deluded. There is only one Principle (*li*), but delusion makes ordinary men, and enlightenment makes Sages. The deluded distance themselves, Principle is not distant. The lost lose themselves, their natures are not lost.[50]

The same notion is basic to Ch'an. Thus the *Platform Sutra of the Sixth Patriarch* maintains:

Among men there are the stupid and the wise. The stupid are insignificant, the wise, great men. Should deluded people ask the wise, the wise will expound the Dharma for the stupid and enable them to understand and gain a deep awakening. If the deluded person understands and his mind is awakened, then there is no difference between him and the man of wisdom. Therefore we know that, unawakened, even a Buddha is a sentient being, and that even a sentient being, if he is awakened in an instant of thought, is a Buddha. And thus we know that the ten thousand dharmas are all within our own minds. Why not from your own natures make the original nature of True Reality suddenly appear? The *P'u-sa-chieh ching* says: "From the outset our own nature is pure." If we perceive the minds and see our own natures, then of ourselves we have achieved the Buddha Way. "At once, suddenly, we regain our original mind."[51]

The expression Han Yü and his generation adopted from their native tradition to articulate this new concept of the Absolute was the four-character phrase from the *Changes*, already encountered in the above quotation from Liang Su: "to develop one's nature to perfection through the understanding of Principle" (*ch'iung-li chin-hsing*). This phrase occurs at the conclusion of the first section of the "Discussion of the Trigrams" (*Shuo kua*) chapter of the *Changes*. The section begins with an account of the creation of the *Changes* by the Sages of

Antiquity. Beginning with the milfoil stalks and the proper numbers attached to Heaven and Earth, they proceeded to observe the alternation of *yin* and *yang* and so created the hexagrams and the individual lines. "Through harmony they followed the Way and ordered what was right. They developed their natures to perfection through the understanding of Principle and thereby attained to the will of Heaven."[52] K'ung Ying-ta interprets this passage as follows:

> When the milfoil and the numbers arose and the lines and the hexagrams were established, the way of the *Changes* was comprehensive and complete, and it encompassed all Principles (*li*).
>
> The Sages used the *Changes*, first, through harmony with them to follow to completion the moral strength of Sagehood, and next, through government in accord with them to determine the right course for human relationships. They were also able to understand fully the deepest and most mysterious Principle of all things and to develop to perfection that nature given to them as human beings. And when they had understood this Principle of things, their natures were also developed to perfection. When these two were achieved simultaneously, then they understood perfectly their allotted destiny (*ming*) and were certain about their fortunes.

Several points in this explication warrant emphasis. First, K'ung Ying-ta equates *ch'iung-li* with the outer, public endeavors of the Sage and *chin-hsing* with his inner, private life. Second, the former element is accomplished first and is the mechanism through which the latter is attained. Third, simultaneous attainment of both affords the Sage perfect knowledge of the world and of himself. He thereby "attains to the Will of Heaven."[53]

It is easy to see why Han Yü found much of interest in K'ung Ying-ta's interpretation, for here again was another restatement of the basic ideas of the *Great Learning* and *Doctrine of the Mean* catenations. Yet K'ung Ying-ta's reading still fell far short of positing *ch'iung-li chin-hsing* as a metaphysical Absolute, though it tended in that direction. The disciples of the great Kumārajīva (344-409) had in fact already made this equation two centuries earlier. These Buddhist scholars, who were eager for pedagogical purposes to find correspondences between Chinese and Indian concepts, had already identified *ch'iung-li chin-hsing* as an equivalent for the *prajñāpāramitā*, the Perfection of Wisdom, for enlightenment, and for Buddhahood itself. Thus Seng-jui (352-436) opened his "Preface to the Smaller *Prajñāpāramitā-sūtra*": "The *Prajñāpāramitā-sūtra* is the precept of 'developing one's nature to perfection through the understanding of Principle,' it is the great path through which the bodhisattva becomes Buddha."[54] And Seng-chao (384-414) wrote in his commentary to the *Vimalakīrtinirdeśa*, "What is Buddhahood? It is a term for one who has 'developed his nature to perfection through the understanding of Principle,' a term for the grand enlightenment (*ta chüeh*). . . ."[55]

This Buddhist interpretation of the phrase seems to have been normal in Han Yü's time. In addition to the passage already quoted from Liang Su, the phrase also occurs in the *logia* of the Ch'an Master Nan-ch'üan P'u-yüan (748-834).[56] Especially interesting is its use by Tsung-mi (780-841) in the preface to his *Treatise on the Origins of Humans (Yüan jen lun)* in which he states—in the context of a discussion of features common to Confucianism, Taoism, and Buddhism—that *ch'iung-li chin-hsing* is possible *only* through the practice of Buddhism.[57] Since Tsung-mi was well educated in the Chinese classics and advocated a form of Confucian-Buddhist syncretism based on filial piety, his insistence on reserving this phrase for the highest expression of the Buddhist faith may testify to the strength of its Buddhist connotation during this period.[58] So pervasive was this association that *ch'iung-li chin-hsing* even occurs in popular contexts as an epithet for enlightenment. Li Chao's *Supplement to the State History of the T'ang (T'ang kuo-shih pu)*, completed about 825, records the following anecdote:

In Hang-chou there was a woman called Third Aunt Huang who had "developed her nature to perfection through the understanding of Principle."

At that time, Fa-ch'in of Ching-shan (714-792) was at the height of his fame; grown weary with the constant stream of visitors, he complained to Third Aunt. But she replied,

"It's all your own doing. If you want to chew on a mass of fish roe, you'd better be prepared for big trouble!" And Ching-shan acknowledged she was right. Some say this woman was called Third Aunt Hsia.[59]

Ch'iung-li chin-hsing occurs twice in the *Random Notes on the Analects*, once in the beginning to explicate *Analects* II.4 and again in the last entry of the work to explicate *Analects* XX.3. The first use explicates the famous statement of Confucius that "at fifty I understood the will of Heaven."

Han Yü: The will of Heaven (*t'ien-ming*) is the deepest mystery, the profoundest subtlety; it is not simply "what begins with the first line and is summed up in the last."[60] Confucius "at fifty studied the *Changes*" (*Analects* VII.17) and so "he developed his nature to perfection through the understanding of Principle and attained to the will of Heaven." So it is said that he "understood the will of Heaven."

Li Ao: "The will of Heaven is called nature."[61] The *Changes* is a book about Principle and nature. But the earlier scholars lost its proper transmission and only Mencius obtained the essence of Confucius. Therefore his chapter on "Developing the Mind" says: "Developing the mind to perfection is that by which we know our own nature. Cultivating this nature is that by which we know Heaven."[62] This is the pinnacle of the teachings on the will of Heaven. None of the others approaches its subtlety.[63]

Han Yü's remarks equate *ch'iung-li chin-hsing* with the highest attainment of the Sage by rejecting the inference of the Han commentators that Confucius's mastery of the "will of Heaven" was a simple understanding of the mechanics of the *Book of Changes*. It was rather the principles, or Principle, of the book that Confucius mastered, not its simple use.[64] Li Ao's remarks are a logical elaboration of Han Yü's: after Confucius, only Mencius understood the real esssence of the *Changes* as the ultimate expression of the unity of ontological Principle and human nature. Li Ao's paraphrase of Mencius, which links the function of mind, the cultivation of human nature, and the understanding of the physical universe, must have seemed to his contemporaries more like Ch'an *logia* than Confucian exegesis.

The last entry in the *Analects* begins, "The Master said, 'He who does not understand the will [of Heaven] has no way to become a *chün-tzu*.' " Against K'ung An-kuo's interpretation that *ming* means simply "the fate of either success or failure," Han Yü writes that

> *ming* means "to develop one's nature to perfection through the understanding of Principle and thereby to attain to the will of Heaven." It is not simply "success or failure."[65]

It is clear that Han Yü's use of *ch'iung-li chin-hsing* merges K'ung Ying-ta's scholastic exegesis of the phrase with its popular connotation as an epithet for the ontological Absolute of Perfect Wisdom (*prajñāpāramitā*). It is also clear that although Liang Su had earlier used the term in much the same way, Han Yü was probably the first to apply this meaning to a strictly Confucian image of Sagehood. The later history of the phrase supports such an inference. In the developed Neo-Confucianism of Chu Hsi, the *Great Learning* expression "the extension of knowledge consists in the investigation of things" (*chih-chih tsai ko-wu*) became the ultimate goal of human endeavor. It was the final link in the *Great Learning* catenation, the Absolute to which all tended and from which all flowed. Yet this development was not achieved without considerable philological contortions. The basic problem was that although the phrase occurred at the right place in the catenation, the following passages made it clear that *chih-chih tsai ko-wu* was not the ultimate link in the catenation but simply a turnaround mechanism to reverse the chain of argument from the ascending to the descending order. The ultimate link in the chain was to "make true one's thought" (*ch'eng ch'i i*). Such was the usual interpretation as K'ung Ying-ta understood it. The problem was solved by rearranging the order of the later sections and by glossing *ko-wu* (the investigation of things) with *ch'iung-li* (the understanding of Principle). This solution, which was canonized by Chu Hsi, seems to have been first proposed by the Ch'eng brothers, whose rearranged versions of the text still exist.[66] The basic equation of *ko-wu* and *ch'iung-li* occurs often in their writings. For example:

> As for the "investigation of things" (*ko-wu*), *ko* means "arrive at"; *wu* means "anything one encounters." One desires to understand and thus arrives at the Principles of things (*ch'iung chih wu li*).[67]

Neo-Confucian discussions of the entire phrase *ch'iung-li chin-hsing* also suggest that the eleventh-century thinkers received this phrase replete with connotations of the Buddhist Absolute. Shao Yung (1011-1077) defined the three basic terms involved—*li* (Principle), *hsing* (nature), and *ming* (will [of Heaven] or decree)—and their relations to each other. All entities (*wu*) possess each of these three. The Sage was one who had attained knowledge of all three, for "these three are the True Knowledge of the world" (*t'ien-hsia chih chen-chih*).[68] Chang Tsai (1020-1077) developed this position by insisting on the distinctness of each of the terms and the necessity of attaining Sagehood through a gradual and progressive mastering of each process in the stated order of the original *Changes* expression. Thus one begins by observing the Principles in all entities (*li*); once these have been observed and understood, one comprehends the natures of other men (*hsing*); and by comprehending the former two, one finally attains to an understanding of one's own destiny or what Heaven has willed for him (*ming*). Because this is a gradual and protracted sequence, Chang Tsai insists on the difference between "knowledge" (*chih*) and "attainment" or "perfection" (*chih*), maintaining that they are not identical.[69]

Ch'eng Hao (1032-1085) on the other hand advocated both the identity of all three terms and the immediacy of their interaction. There was neither a proper sequence nor an effort involved in attaining one of the triad. Although not specifically stated, for Ch'eng Hao, "knowledge" and "attainment" were obviously identical.[70] Ch'eng I seems to have held to an intermediate position, maintaining the ultimate identity of the three terms yet insisting on adhering to the stated sequence in the pursuit of Sagehood.[71] Su Chi-ming, a disciple first of Chang Tsai and then of the two Ch'engs, attempted a synthesis of the two opinions based on the intermediate compromise of Ch'eng I.

> The two Ch'engs' explanations of this phrase was that simply to understand Principle (*ch'iung-li*) was then to attain to the will of Heaven (*chih yü ming*). Chang Tsai also maintained this but faulted their explanation as being [something that happened] too quickly.
>
> Yet there is an order to this interpretation. One must understand Principle and then one can comprehend his own nature, and after that, by inference, one can comprehend the natures of other men. After this, one must unite the natures of all things and comprehend them together. When one has accomplished this, one has attained to the Way of Heaven (*t'ien tao*). Yet during all this time there are many things happening and one cannot immediately understand everything. The student must first understand Principle and he will then have a method of study.
>
> So we now maintain that to understand the will of Heaven (*chih ming*) and to attain to the will of Heaven (*chih yü ming*) are not at all the same. Just because one knows something (*chih*) does not mean one has attained it (*chih*).[72]

As is well known to historians of Chinese philosophy, this difference of opinion regarding the nature of the progress to

Sagehood later became a central issue for Neo-Confucian thinkers. The Ch'eng-Chu school, advocating gradual progress through study of Principle, has been traced to Ch'eng I; the Lu-Wang school, advocating sudden perception through cultivating of the mind, has been traced to Ch'eng Hao. It is also well known that this dichotomy mirrors the division that arose among eighth-century Ch'an thinkers between gradual and sudden enlightenment, the Northern versus the Southern schools of Ch'an. Less often observed is that the entire context of these discussions presupposes a prescribed regimen of progress through progressive stages toward "attainment" of Absolute wisdom or Sagehood. It is probable that this idea of progression toward Sagehood derived from the Mahayana notion of the *daśabhūmi* or "ten stages" through which the bodhisattva progressed to Buddhahood.[73] This association was probably reinforced by K'ung Ying-ta's commentary to the *Doctrine of the Mean*, which sharply distinguished between the "worthy man" (*hsien-jen*) and the Sage (*sheng-jen*), a distinction corresponding to that between bodhisattva and Buddha in the Buddhist tradition.[74]

With this background in mind, and considering the later Sung elaborations on the question, a review of Han Yü's use of *ch'iung-li chin-hsing i chih yü ming* in the *Random Notes on the Analects* shows that in both cases he used the phrase as a gloss for *chih ming* "to understand the will of Heaven," thus equating *chih ming* with *chih yü ming*. This suggests that Han Yü would have sanctioned the position of Ch'eng Hao, which posited the ultimate identity of the three terms and the quick leap from "knowledge" to "attainment." Such a conception of the Absolute would coincide with his manifest interest in contemporary Ch'an.

Such an explanation also helps to explain why in the "Essentials of the Moral Way" quotation from the *Great Learning* catenation Han Yü did not continue and include the famous Neo-Confucian expression of their Absolute in *chih-chih tsai ko-wu*, "the extension of knowledge consists in the investigation of things."[75] As we have seen above, this phrase contained no such notions for the T'ang reader who knew the text from K'ung Ying-ta's interpretation. The transference of the T'ang phrase for this Absolute, *ch'iung-li chin-hsing*, onto the Sung phrase *chih-chih ko-wu* was essentially a product of the eleventh century. For Han Yü, the ultimate was to make true the intentions (*ch'eng ch'i i*).

Two other texts afford more direct insight into Han Yü's conception of the Sage. The first is "A Reply to Student Hou's Inquiry Concerning the *Analects*," written to Hou Hsi probably about 801. The letter contains an explication of the ambiguous term "to fulfill the body" (*chien-hsing*) that occurs in *Mencius* VII.A.38: "Mencius said, 'The body and its functions have the nature of Heaven. Only the Sage can fulfill his body.' "

The questions you have presented me regarding the *Analects* are very good. Concerning the theory that "the Sage fulfills his body," the writings of Mencius discuss it in detail, but I shall examine it more thoroughly here.

The idea is that "the myriad things are all complete in ourselves; and through self-examination we are made true (*ch'eng*)" (*Mencius* VII.A.4). If, however, there is something false in us, then the myriad things will not be complete. So the idea of "fulfilling the body" is simply integrity (*ch'eng*).

You are wrong when you maintain that the worthy man (*hsien-jen*) cannot "fulfill his body." Rather, the worthy man *must* "fulfill his body"; it is simply that his capacity to do so is not yet complete. "Body" expresses "completeness." The idea is that "he has all the parts, though in lesser degree."[76] Also, "fully to realize [goodness and reliability] is called beautiful; fully to realize these and to blaze them forth is called greatness" (*Mencius* VII.B.25.5,6). This "fully to realize" corresponds to "to have all the parts." And what is not yet great is "in lesser degree."

Therefore, those who depart even slightly from the goal of Sagehood or those who obtain but a single part of it are all ones who have not completely "fulfilled their bodies." Only he who "through self-examination is made true" can complete the "fulfillment of his body."

Some time ago I annotated these texts but did not dare go too far in searching out their meaning. I tried only to take the intentions of the Sages and reconcile them so they could inspire the confidence of later generations. But the explication of this passage is quite secure, and you should consider it carefully.[77]

This letter is important for the following reasons. By reference to *Mencius* VII. A. 4 Han Yü posits the concept of *ch'eng*, "integrity, sincerity, the true," as the principal quality of the Sage and affirms that this quality entails knowledge of the "myriad things" obtained through "self-examination."[78] By emphasizing the necessity of completeness and perfection, he reinforces the unity of the individual and the world. Developing the metaphor of the Sage as one who is complete in all his parts as the human body is complete in all its members, Han Yü considers the distinction between the "worthy man" and the Sage to be one of degree: the Sage has completed the realization of all things in himself, the worthy man has not yet done so.[79] The letter is also important because it demonstrates the technique of explication by cross-referential analysis within the same text, the same basic method used in the *Random Notes on the Analects*. Finally, the concluding paragraph lends strong support to the contention that Han Yü did indeed produce a commentary on *Mencius*.

The next text is more extensive and more formal, being Han Yü's response to the Placing Examination (*po-hsüeh hung-tz'u*) of 794. The subject in question was *Analects* VI. 3, which contained Confucius's statement that his disciple Yen Hui "did not repeat his errors."

> *Question*: Confucius had over 3,000 disciples in four classes. Did they not all follow the Way of the Sage and practice the life of the superior man? Errors in behavior or in speech were rare. And yet Confucius mentioned

only Yen-tzu as one who "did not repeat his errors." What is the reason for this?

Answer: The Sage embraces integrity (*ch'eng*) and enlightenment (*ming*) as his true nature (*cheng hsing*); he takes as his base the perfect virtue that is equilibrium and harmony (*chung yung*). He generates (*fa*) these inside and gives them form outside; they do not proceed from thought, yet all is in order. Thus a mind set on evil has no way to develop within him, and preferable behavior cannot be applied to him; so only the Sage commits no errors.

What is meant here by "error" is not an act or speech acknowledged as an error only because others have so termed it. When something is engendered in the mind (*Mencius* II.A.2.17), it is already an error, and Yen-tzu's error was of this kind. That he "did not repeat it" means that he was able to halt it at inception and cut it off before it had taken form: he "did not repeat it" in word or deed.

The *Doctrine of the Mean* says "Enlightenment that proceeds from integrity is ascribed to nature. Integrity that proceeds from enlightenment is ascribed to education."[80] One who has the former "without effort hits upon what is good and without thought perceives it; naturally and easily he embodies the Way: he is the Sage" (*Li chi chu-shu* 53/1a). Such is one without error. One who has the latter "chooses what is good and holds it firmly."[81] Without effort he does not hit upon it, without thought he does not attain. Such is one who "does not repeat his errors."

Therefore the Master said, "As for the kind of man Yen Hui was, having chosen equilibrium and harmony, when he had attained to one thing that was good, he clasped it fast to his bosom with both hands and would not let it go" (*Li chi chu-shu* 52/3a-b).

And he also said, "Yen Hui has almost achieved it."[82] This means he had not yet achieved perfection (*chih*). And so Mencius also said that Yen-tzu had all the parts of the Sage though in lesser proportions (paraphrased from *Mencius* II.A.2.20).

All of these citations indicate that Yen Hui could not help engendering things in his mind (*Mencius* II.A.2.17) that he could not manifest to the outside. When one compares this to the Way of the Sage, then there is a great difference.

Yen-tzu himself acknowledged he was like this and so lived in a mean street in order to perfect his integrity and drank only one gourd-full of water in order to obtain his resolve (paraphrase of *Mencius* IV.B.29). He did not impede his Way with riches; he did not trouble his mind with subtleties. Verily, he cannot be uprooted; greatly, he maintains his own (paraphrase of *Chou-i chu-shu* 1/8a; trans. Wilhelm, *Changes*, p. 379). He knew what was worthy in the "high and the hard," yet forgot the toil of "looking up and boring into" (*Analects* IX.10). But "the burden is heavy and the Way is far" (*Analects* VIII.7), and in the end he did not reach it.

This is why the Master sighed that "unfortunately his allotted span of life was short. Now there is no one" (*Analects* VI.3). This means that he could not stand together with Confucius in the realm of the Perfect Sage.

Yet when we look at the great undertaking of rule through moral instruction, then actions, although they originate with individuals, extend to other men. Words originate close at hand, but their effects are seen far away (paraphrase of *Chou-i chu-shu* 7/10b; trans. Wilhelm, *Changes*, p. 305). If we are not cautious, defeat and disgrace will ensue upon us. And after this, to desire "not to repeat our efforts" is far indeed from the Way of the Sage.

But the Master still said of Yen-tzu that he "has almost achieved it" and Mencius still said of him that he "had all the parts of the Sage though in lesser proportions." Therefore, as to the passage "Yen-tzu did not repeat errors," its explanation must be as I have outlined.[83]

Despite its formal, academic tone, this discourse bears a striking affinity in both form and content to the "Letter to Hou Hsi," to the *Random Notes on the Analects*, and to certain sections of Li Ao's *Fu-hsing shu*.[84] Han Yü, drawing on the K'ung Ying-ta commentary to the *Doctrine of the Mean*, accepts two paths to Sagehood: (1) through inner integrity that enables one to understand by effortless intuition the outside world (enlightenment); this is the nature (*hsing*) of the Sage; and (2) through study of the outside world that enables one to perceive by thought and effort the integrity that is within him; such is the education of the worthy man. Han Yü's clear preference is for the former; Yen Hui was an example of the latter who, because of his early death, had not been able to attain Sagehood through the latter, slower method. Once again, when one views this text from the twin vantage points of the contemporary Ch'an dispute over gradual and sudden enlightenment and of the later Neo-Confucian division over the approach to Sagehood through the cumulative accretion of knowledge about the outside world (School of Principle) or through the direct examination of the mind (School of Mind), Han Yü's preferences are clear. This is not to say that Han Yü was a practitioner of Ch'an or a predecessor of Wang Yang-ming. It is only to emphasize that his approach to philosophical questions often has elements in common with groups and attitudes with which his name is not commonly associated.[85]

It may be useful at this point to summarize Han Yü's statements on important philosophical terms. Beginning with mind (*hsin*), the essay on Yen Hui makes clear that the qualities of the Sage do not "proceed from throught." The mind of the Sage is passive: without thought the Sage perceives what is right. In the case of the worthy man, the mind is active; for the worthy man progresses to Sagehood through the exercise of mind in the investigation of things. Han Yü's reference to the mind of the Sage being "without thought" (*wu szu*) is developed at length in the second of Li Ao's "Writings on Returning to One's True Nature":

When one is tranquil, one knows that the mind is without thought, and this is "fasting." But to know that the mind is in essence without thought, that it is separated from both movement and tranquillity, that it is absolutely still and unmoving—this is Perfect Integrity (*chih ch'eng*). The *Mean* says, "From integrity there is enlightenment." The *Changes* say, "All movement under Heaven is regulated by unity."[86]

Han Yü also stresses the primacy of the mind in the attainment of Sagehood in his *Random Notes on the Analects. Analects* XI.19 reads: "Tzu-chang asked about the way of the good man. The Master answered, 'Such a man does not tread the old tracks, but neither can he enter the inner room.' "[87]

> Han Yü: K'ung's explanation is wrong. I maintain the "good man" is another term for the Sage. How could it be possible for one who does not follow in old tracks likewise neither to enter the inner room of the Sages? Confucius is instructing Tzu-chang that the good man cannot attain the mind's inner room by following in the tracks of others. For the inner room, the mind of the Sage, is profound and is subtle. It has no form that can be observed and no track that can be followed. It is not something Tzu-chang could attain.
>
> Li Ao: Confucius said, "As for Yu [i.e. Tzu-lu], he has ascended the hall but not yet entered the inner room" (*Analects* XI.15). This inner room is the "mind-ground."[88] The Sage has both mind and its traces. He has created form and is without form. Grand indeed was Tzu-chang! But in truth he could not attain to this.[89]

Han Yü thus interprets Confucius's remark as a warning to Tzu-chang: "Do not follow in the tracks of others or you will not enter into the inner room [of Sagehood]."[90] This is a good example of the spirit of the *Random Notes* and strong evidence for the Ch'an influence on Han Yü's concept of mind.

Han Yü's ideas on human nature (*hsing*) and the emotions (*ch'ing*) are best known from his often-quoted "On the Origins of Human Nature" (*Yüan hsing*).[91] Unfortunately, this piece is not one of Han Yü's better efforts. The text is unclear on a number of important points and is usually understood according to the reading of Chu Hsi. According to this common interpretation, human nature is inborn at birth. It has five constituent parts: a sense of humanity (*jen*), propriety (*li*), trustworthiness (*hsin*), justice (*i*), and wisdom (*chih*)—the so-called Five Norms (*wu ch'ang*). Human nature is divided into three grades (*p'in*) depending on how these five norms function within the individual. The highest grade is good, the lowest evil, and the middle can become either better or worse. Emotions (*ch'ing*) are not inborn but rather arise in response to contact with the external world. There are seven emotions: joy (*hsi*), anger (*nu*), sorrow (*ai*), fear (*chü*), love (*ai*), hate (*wu*), and desire (*yü*). There are likewise grades of emotion depending on the degree to which these emotions when stirred "abide in the Mean" (*chung*). Thus when Mencius and Hsün-tzu spoke of human nature as good or as evil, they spoke only of the medium grade. The higher and lower grades, however, can be improved through education and controlled through government respectively.

This text presents a number of problems. Most significant is the apparent contradiction between (1) Han Yü's supposed belief in the goodness of human nature and in the ultimate identity of the Sage and the common man and (2) the text's stated theory of the three grades, the higher and lower of which are immutable. This seeming contradiction, however, probably results from the missing contemporary context of the text. The "Essay on the Origins of Human Nature" can be understood only when viewed in light of other contemporary discourses on the subject.[92] Apparently no contradiction was assumed to exist between these two concepts, for the theory of the three grades of human nature was a commonplace in the Buddhist schools, who likewise preached the Buddha nature inherent in all things.[93] A resolution to the problem is suggested by the fifth chapter of the *Lotus Sutra*, which develops the metaphor that each creature hears and responds to the preachings of the Buddha according to his own capacity just as the different grasses and trees of the forest respond and grow each in a different way to rain from the same cloud. The Buddha by virtue of his omniscience knows beforehand the capacity of each creature to respond to the teaching.[94] In a Confucian context, Huang-fu Shih takes a similar line in his "Essay on the Mencius and Hsün-tzu Explanations of Nature," which affirms the theory of the three grades of human nature and maintains that the Mencian theory of the goodness of human nature and the Hsün-tzu theory of the evil of human nature were not ultimate opinions on the subject but simply different methods to guide their students along "the Way of the Sages." "The idea of Mencius that the natures of all men are like Yao and Shun was to encourage those who had not yet perfected themselves. The theory of Hsün-tzu that the natures of all men are like Chieh and Chou was to retard those who had not yet sunk to that level. The streams were different, but they came from the same source."[95]

Fortunately, the *Random Notes on the Analects* contains several entries that clarify Han Yü's conception of human nature. The first of these is a short note on *Analects* v.13: "Tzu-kung said . . . one cannot learn what the Master said about human nature (*hsing*) and the Way of Heaven (*t'ien tao*)." The Han exegesis maintained that "human nature is what men receive at birth. The Way of Heaven is what is supreme, all-pervasive, and daily-renewing. These are deeply profound, and therefore one could not learn about them." Han Yü replies,

> K'ung's explanation is crude and misses the essence of the passage. I maintain that human nature and the Way of Heaven are one and the same idea. If one explains them as two separate ideas, then what is there about "something that men receive at birth" that one cannot learn about?[96]

The implications of this exegesis are clear: the nature that is "something men receive at birth" is different from the nature that is identical to the Way of Heaven. Li Ao's comment emphasizes this difference.

A much longer passage, this time a dialogue between Han Yü and Li Ao, further clarifies Han Yü's ideas on *hsing*. The subject is the famous and enigmatic *Analects* XVII.2:

The Master said, "By nature, men are close; by practice, they grow distant." The Master said, "Only the very wisest and the very stupidest do not change."[97]

Han Yü: The first text "by nature men are close . . ." means that men through practice can either improve themselves or make themselves worse. The following text that "the very wisest and the very stupidest do not change" means that men cannot through practice change. The two ideas are contradictory and earlier scholars have not understood the meaning. I maintain that these two ideas should be explained together with the earlier passage: "Highest are those wise at birth; next are those grown wise through study; next are those who are troubled and so study: those who are troubled yet do not study are the lowest of the common people" (*Analects* XVI.9).

Li Ao: "To develop one's nature to perfection through the understanding of Principle and thereby to attain to the will of Heaven" is the ultimate expression of human nature and decree (*hsing ming*). Yet scholars have seldom elucidated these basic concepts.

Now the two ideas in the passage in question seem contradictory, yet they can be explained through the Principles of the *Changes*: "It is the Way of the Creative [power of Heaven] to change and to transform so that everything has its correct nature and decree."[98] And also "the furtherance and perseverance [of the Creative] constitute the nature and emotions."[99] And also "a unity of *yin* and a unity of *yang* is called the Way. That which makes it continue is goodness. That which brings it to completion is the nature."[100]

This means that in quietude men's natures are close to each other; but when they are moved in response to outside objects, this can be either to correctness (*cheng*) or to perversity (*hsieh*). When they are moved to correctness, then they become the very wise. When they are moved to perversity, then they become the very stupid. "Absolutely still and unmoving," then the emotions and natures are both left behind.[101] So it is difficult even for the Sages to tell [the difference between the wise and the stupid]. And therefore Confucius said of Yen Hui that he does not speak "as if he were stupid. But when he retires and I examine his conduct in private, I find it well expresses my ideas. Hui is not stupid" (*Analects* II.9).

And so in the states of "sitting in forgetfulness" and "passing on the image"[102] one does not practice, as if stupid. Among the hexagrams this is *Fu* ("The Return"), "the mind of Heaven and Earth," and is profound.[103] Yet after Mencius, nature and practice drew farther apart and the wise and the stupid grew far distant from each other. So when Confucius spoke of those who "are troubled yet do not study" and said "the very stupidest do not change," these were simply words to incite and encourage students. As for "developing one's nature to perfection through the understanding of Principle," one cannot understand it without the *Changes*.

Han Yü: With your explanation, although the texts appear contradictory, there is no conflict in meaning. Indeed, "it is the Way of the Creative [power of Heaven] to change and to transform so that everything has its correct nature and decree." And "it is the Way of the Receptive [power of Earth] to conform unto the receiving of Heaven," so that "without practice all is furthered."[104] This is the ultimate. Indeed, "the mind of Heaven and Earth" is profound![105]

This somewhat intricate passage can be summarized as follows. Han Yü's opening statement acknowledges the seeming contradiction between the two halves of the passage in question. The first sentence implies men's natures can change, the second states certain men's natures do not change. This is the essential contradiction in "On the Origins of Human Nature."

Han Yü's introduction of *Analects* XVI.9, which ranks four classes of men from those with inborn wisdom to those with no education at all, suggests he is positing a distinction between the specific nature "conferred" on each individual at birth and a higher form of nature, which his commentary to *Analects* V.13 has already stated is equivalent to the "Way of Heaven." Li Ao begins by invoking once again the ubiquitous *Changes* expression of the Absolute to equate "nature" (*hsing*) and "decree" (*ming*). His quotations from the *Changes* demonstrate that the "Way (of Heaven)" functions such that each person receives nature and decree proper (*cheng*) to him. There is thus no essential difference between an ultimate nature (the "Way of Heaven") and the natures of specific individuals. All men receive the nature and decree proper to them, and thus goodness should ensue. But this identity between one's own nature and the Way of Heaven can be realized only in a state of quietude described as "absolutely still and unmoving." This is the state of the nature of the Sage, and in this state all distinctions between wisdom and stupidity disappear. Thus even Confucius first mistook Yen Hui's silence for stupidity. The recovery of this original nature is to "return," to realize the identity of one's own nature and decree with the "mind of Heaven and Earth." This is the real definition of Sagehood and the real meaning of the *Changes*. Han Yü's summation is largely a rhetorical affirmation of Li Ao's position, but he does add the *Changes* phrase that "without practice all is furthered," which emphasizes the need for the recovery of the true nature through attainment of that state where one is "absolutely still and unmoving." This process seems identical to the main point of Li Ao's *Fu-hsing shu*, which is defined as "a process of spiritual or mental self-discipline aimed at the recovery or realization of an innate state of perfection."[106]

Han Yü's emphasis on the phrase *ch'iung-li chin-hsing i chih t'ien-ming*, which was discussed in detail above, foreshadows the Sung Neo-Confucian definitions of *li*, *hsing*, and *ming* and their relations to each other; for, the use of this term as a gloss for the metaphysical Absolute implies (1) the unity of Principle (*li*), (2) its ultimate identity with the will of Heaven (*t'ien-*

ming), and (3) the possibility of its attainment through the cultivation of one's own nature (*hsing*). Han Yü's understanding of these terms and their relation is thus a crucial link between the early medieval Buddhist conception of *li* as Absolute and the Sung Neo-Confucian conception of *li* as Principle.[107]

If this *Changes* phrase detailed a paradigm to reach this highest state to which a man could attain, the term *ch'eng*, for Han Yü, described both this state and the man who had attained it, the Sage. The "Letter to Hou Hsi" and the "Examination Response" on Yen Hui both identify *ch'eng* as the most important quality of the Sage. *Ch'eng*, usually translated "sincerity," also has overtones of "absence of fault, seriousness, being true to one's real self, being true to the nature of things, actuality, and realness."[108] *Ch'eng* describes for Han Yü the ultimate goal of the path to Sagehood, the final achievement of the Sage: a perfect integration of his inner spiritual and outer public life. Han Yü fused the *Doctrine of the Mean*'s description of *ch'eng* as a cosmic principle and the *Great Learning*'s definition of *ch'eng* as the unity of inner and outer wisdom into a single, unified goal of Confucian life: public order through inner tranquillity. *Ch'eng* is to attain and to actualize this unity of inner and outer being through realization of the unity of theory and action. In this sense, perhaps the best single-word translation of *ch'eng* is Graf's *Wesenstreue*; for by understanding the true nature of the world, the Sage discovers that same true nature in himself.[109] He realizes the ultimate identity and unity of himself and the world, and knowledge gained through active participation in the world enlightens his own private search for spiritual understanding. He becomes "true to his own being."[110]

CHAPTER FOUR

The Unity
of Style

"Every object rightly seen un-
locks a quality of the soul."
—Emerson

Han Yü was often somewhat
facetious. Once he said to Li
Ch'eng, "The Chief Minister
Ts'ui Ch'ün and I passed our
chin-shih examinations in the
same year and have been friends
ever since. I find him really intelligent, an outstanding man."
Li asked, "How is he
outstanding?"
And Han Yü answered, "Well,
I have known him now for over
twenty years, and he's never
once discussed literature with
me. That shows he's a really
smart man."[1]

Han Yü's sheer prowess and stature as a man of letters have
often daunted later scholars who, like the prudent Ts'ui
Ch'ün, shrank before the prospect of engaging Han Yü on

the subject of literature. As a result, the "writings that lifted the decadence of eight dynasties" have seldom drawn critical analyses equal to the task of explaining their literary success.[2] The discomfort of the Sung Neo-Confucians with imaginary literature and their corollary emphasis on Han Yü as moralist and Confucian spokesman further impeded dispassionate contemplation of his literary accomplishments. Scholars of this persuasion, and they live on in a variety of modern guises, have, by maintaining that Han Yü's major goal as a writer was to "make literature a vehicle for the Way," insisted on reading his works as a repository of Confucian doctrine.[3] Such insistence not only makes Han Yü's writings the servant of a later, more narrowly defined sense of Confucian morality; it also makes Han Yü the man a rather poor precursor of later, more Neo-Confucian paragons. This attitude, by reading the man through his works, finds the man wanting and the works ultimately inexplicable as literary creations. My method in this chapter will be to reverse this procedure in the hope of demonstrating that Han Yü's literary theory and practice, indeed, his whole life as a man of letters, grew from his fundamental Confucian concern with political and social questions. Rather than a mysterious literary genius trapped in the body of a morally feeble Confucian, Han Yü was a quintessentially Confucian author whose compulsion to forge a new literary style sprang from his vision of a radically new Confucian order, a vision that contained in turn a basic rethinking of the role of literature in a Confucian society.

Han Yü directed his efforts as a writer, both as a theoretician of literature and as the first practitioner of a new literary style, toward the creation of a suitable medium to express his concept of a unified social and intellectual order. His commitment to political unity through the elimination of T'ang separatism and his struggle to define a new concept of Confucian sagehood mandated the creation of a unified literary style appropriate to the articulation of these new unities. There are several aspects to this unity of style. On the theoretical plane, Han Yü posited the mutual identity of literature (*wen*) and the Way (*tao*), thus creating a secure and respectable place for literature among the activities of the new Confucian intellectual. On

the practical plane, he forged a unified literary style by blurring the artificial distinctions between the various genres that
were a legacy of Six Dynasties and early T'ang literary
practice.

Of course, both these goals are related. Although poetry
was a vital presence in the public life of early China, by the
Later Han it had already begun to recede from public use to
become the normal medium for the expression of private
emotional, religious, and psychological states. The prose genres in turn assumed wider use at public and ceremonial functions. This dichotomy between the versified and nonversified
genres thus reflected and reinforced the dichotomy between
the inner, private and outer, public aspects of intellectual existence that Han Yü found so socially debilitating. A unified
style that could be adopted for use in any genre was thus not
only a literary reform but also an active moral agent for the
ultimate unity of *wen* and *tao* This explains Han Yü's insistence
that his "antique prose" (*ku-wen*) must be *used* by others; the
personal aesthetic satisfaction derived from its creation was
not a satisfactory literary goal. It must find *public* acceptance
before Han Yü could claim for his new style complete literary
(*wen*) and moral (*tao*) success.[4]

This unity of *wen* and *tao* is implied in almost all of Han
Yü's statements about literature. It is formulated most clearly
in his "Postface to a Lament for Ou-yang Chan":

> When I write *ku-wen*, I do not merely adopt a rhythm
> different from that in use today. Although I may ponder
> the Ancients, I will never actually meet them, so in order
> to study the Ancient Way (*ku-tao*), I must at the same
> time master their style. Mastery of their style is basic for
> those whose goal is the Ancient Way.[5]

The dialectic posited here between *ku-wen* and *ku-tao*, a dialectic that culminates in their mutual identity, is developed
at greater length in the following passage by Li Ao:

> You must not believe those who maintain that litera-
> ture is merely a skill. What they call a "skill" is only
> writing which our modern age enjoys and which has

become popular in recent times. Any work that can attain to the Ancients has perforce a style of humanity and justice (*jen i*), and it is hardly proper to call this a "skill."

Confucius and Mencius died over a thousand years ago, so I shall never see them. But I can understand their wisdom and goodness by reading their words. I will never meet those who are to come after me, but I know they will read my words and so understand what was on my mind. And neither will they be able to give a false picture of me.[6]

I have never met a man by nature (*hsing*) humane and just (*jen i*) who did not write literature. And of those authors whose writings were able to attain to [the Ancients] I have never met one who did not strive toward humanity and justice. For it is by nature (*hsing*) that one proceeds from these to the creation of literature, and by practice (*hsi*) that one proceeds from literature to humanity and justice. This is like the mutual dependence of integrity (*ch'eng*) and enlightenment (*ming*).[7]

Li Ao states explicitly what Han Yü's shorter formulation only implies: the relation between literature and the moral Way is such that the quality of each is enhanced by the degree to which the practitioner is able to realize and effect its identity with the other. They are distinct entities in practice but ultimately identical in the perfected, that is, "natural," state. Li Ao's comparison of *wen* and *tao* to "the mutual dependence of integrity and enlightenment" makes this dialectic explicit and recalls Han Yü's quotation of these terms from the *Doctrine of the Mean* in his response to the examination question on "Yen Hui did not repeat his errors."[8]

Han Yü's efforts to minimize the stylistic distinctions between genres flew directly in the face of contemporary literary education and practice, which were heavily dependent on the generic distinctions established in the *Wen hsüan*.[9] And this explains the strong opposition among his contemporaries to Han Yü's unified style. In later times discussion of these issues was largely subsumed within the controversy over whether

Han Yü "made poetry from prose" (*i wen wei shih*). The following conversation from the mid-eleventh century records the inception of the confusion:

> Shen Kua (1030-1094), Lü Hui-ch'ing, Wang Ts'un, and Li Ch'ang (1027-1090) were discussing poetry together at an inn during the *chih-p'ing* period (1064-1067). Shen Kua said,
> "The poetry of Han Yü is merely rhymed prose. Although it is strong in beauty and rich in its learning, its structure is not that of poetry."
> Lü Hui-ch'ing replied,
> "But that's exactly what poetry should be. I think there has never been a poet as great as Han Yü."
> Wang Ts'un agreed with Shen Kua, and Li Ch'ang agreed with Lü Hui-ch'ing. The four argued for a long time but were unable to come to a decision. Suddenly Li Ch'ang assumed a grave expression and said to Wang Ts'un,
> "A gentleman 'comes together with other gentlemen without forming cliques' (*Analects* IV.22). Why are you forming a clique with Shen Kua?"
> Wang Ts'un replied angrily,
> "But that's really the way I see the question! I am not forming a clique. You call us a clique just because I happen to agree with Shen Kua. But aren't you forming a clique with Lü Hui-ch'ing?"
> At which they all laughed heartily.[10]

That this discussion actually involved two separate issues certainly contributed to the inability of the "cliques" to resolve their differences. Shen Kua's remark is a critical statement about Han Yü's poetry. Lü Hui-ch'ing's remark, on the other hand, addresses the general appropriateness of using the technique of one genre to revitalize another—genre cross-fertilization—a practice that ultimately results in the blurring of generic distinctions.[11]

This discussion thus reveals the basic problem that impeded later appreciation of Han Yü's unified style: although his prose works became universal and canonical models for emulation in the Sung, his poetry, even though it exerted a major influence on some Sung authors, eventually became the domain of a rather parochial "school" of post-Sung poetry. *Ku-wen* thus came solely to refer to prose, and Han Yü's poetry became a rather quixotic byproduct, unrelated to his *"ku-wen."* A typical expression of this dichotomy is the puzzled comment by the Yüan scholar Wu-ch'iu Yen (d.1311):

> The prose of Han Yü is on par with the *Analects* and *Mencius*. And yet he enjoyed the poetry of such as Lu T'ung, Liu Ch'a, and Meng Chiao; and in his own works he imitated their diction. How could his poetry and his prose be so different![12]

Obviously this approach could not lead to an integrated evaluation of Han Yü as a complete man of letters.

Yet some perspicacious scholars recognized that the enormous influence of Han Yü's prose could not be explained without reference to the catholicity of his style. So Liu Hsi-tsai (1813-1881) observed:

> That Han Yü's writings "lifted the decadence of eight dynasties" was actually because they brought together the accomplishments of those same dynasties. For only one who excels at using Antiquity can change Antiquity (*pien ku*); and only one whose embrace is complete can so completely cleanse away.[13]

Liu's point is that the power of Han Yü's style to "cleanse away the decadence of eight dynasties" derived from his unique ability to forge a style catholic and unified enough to absorb all that was best from that same "Antiquity."

Han Yü himself traced the origins of his *"ku-wen"* not to prose but to the poetry of Ch'en Tzu-ang (661-701), whose long series of poems, "Moved by What Has Happened," was thought to begin the T'ang tradition of "allegorical lodging" (*hsing-chi*) that passed to Li Po and Tu Fu and from them to Han Yü and Liu Tsung-yüan.[14] The contemporary scholar

The Unity of Style

Ch'ien Mu has in fact turned around the old saw that Han Yü "made poetry from prose" (*i wen wei shih*) into a newer saw that Han Yü "made prose from poetry" (*i shih wei wen*). This formulation would underscore Ch'ien's contention that Han Yü's most important contribution to Chinese letters was to fashion essentially new prose genres such as the allegorical biography, the preface, and the letter by introducing into these then quotidian and moribund genres a concept of "pure literature" that hitherto had existed only in poetry.[15]

Clearly, the older attempt to explain Han Yü's versified work in terms of his prose (*i wen wei shih*) and the newer attempt to explain his prose by reference to verse (*i shih wei wen*) are, taken together, a critical reflection of the underlying stylistic and conceptual unity inherent in his entire literary corpus.[16]

I have elsewhere suggested the prudence of questioning the received wisdom concerning the evolutionary pedigree of the "*ku-wen* movement." The often-used term "to return to Antiquity" (*fu-ku*) requires a similar prudence. "To return to Antiquity" is commonly conceived as the goal of the *ku-wen* author. Yet not surprisingly this *fu-ku* goal has proved as difficult to define and as chimerical as the hypothetical string of *ku-wen* authors who supposedly aspired toward it. Thus a leading proponent of *fu-ku* as a major theoretical force in T'ang literature is forced to admit that although "*fu-ku* theory is found throughout the T'ang, what it means is so vague and flexible that in itself it can hardly define a literary movement."[17] Yet the term may nevertheless serve as a useful starting point for a discussion of Han Yü's ideas on literature; for although he used the expression *fu-ku* only once (and in a context largely unrelated to literature), its two elements, "to return" (*fu*) and "Antiquity" (*ku*), are central to his literary theory and practice. And this theory and practice manifest a radical departure from those of earlier authors commonly associated with *fu-ku*.

We have already seen that Han Yü conceived of "Antiquity" (*ku*) as an almost spiritual state, yet a state that stood in di-

217

alectical complementarity to "modernity" (*chin*); the two states, although distinct, are ultimately identical, and when each is perfected, "Antiquity is now." *Fu* "to return" is the twenty-fourth hexagram in the *Book of Changes*. Because the Chinese conception of time is cyclical, not linear, "return" is the coming back again of something that once existed before, not a going back to something that will never exist again. Thus Wilhelm glosses "Return" as the "Turning Point" to emphasize this concept of cyclical return.[18] Of course, each entity or concept in nature has its own cycle of return. We have seen above that Han Yü himself used the contemporary notion that the completion of a sexagenary cycle in 814, sixty years after the An Lu-shan rebellion in 755, signaled the return of political unity.[19] Li Ao in his "Writings on Returning to One's True Nature" (*Fu-hsing shu*) states, "But when the Way reaches its nadir in being overthrown (*po*), it will then certainly return (*fu*). Am I not at a time when it is about to return?"[20] If *fu-hsing* is then, as was explained above, "the recovery or realization of an innate state of perfection," then *fu-ku* should mean the realization of the state of perfection represented by "Antiquity."

And this is precisely what Han Yü's sole use of the term implies. In the "Preface Seeing Off Ch'i Hao After His Failure at the Examinations," Han Yü used *fu-ku* "renewal of Antiquity" to refer to the realization of the perfect political state conceived as "Antiquity."[21] At the core of this state is the concept of *ch'eng*, seen morally as "personal integrity" and philosophically as *Wesenstreue*, the perfect integration of the Sage. Since Han Yü viewed the writing of literature as a natural outgrowth of moral action, it is thus hardly surprising that he also postulated *ch'eng* as a fundamental characteristic of good writing, of *ku-wen*, the literature of "Antiquity."[22] His fullest exposition of this thesis is in the "Letter to Li I" to be discussed below. Another, less detailed statement is the "Letter in Reply to Master Yü-ch'ih Fen" written in 801:

> What I call literature must have integrity at its core, and for this reason the superior man is attentive to ac-

tualities (*shih*) and expresses these, concealing nothing, whether it be good or evil.

When roots are deep, the branches flourish; when the instrument is large, its sound is ample. When a man's conduct is strict, his language is stern; when his mind is pure, the style is soft; clear and sharp with no uncertainties, or large and free with something left over. If the body is not whole, one cannot become a complete man (cf. *Analects* XIV.12); if diction is not sufficient, one cannot complete a piece of literature. Such is my understanding and my reply to those who question me.

Now all you have written is excellent, and you have modestly put your works before me for my opinion, which I certainly do not begrudge you. Yet all that I am able to say concerns the Way of Antiquity. And the Way of Antiquity will not find you acceptance among the man of today. But do you really want something different?

Worthy lords and ministers crowd each other at the top. Worthy scholars, just entering the service, crowd each other below. They have all obtained a position and must have some method for doing so. If you seek government employment, then go and inquire of them. They are all people you can study with. If, on the other hand, you are attracted to the Way of Antiquity and not to employment, then you can study with me, in which case I look forward to further discussions with you.[23]

As the "Way of Antiquity" differs from seeking employment, so the literature of Antiquity differs from literature written to pass the *chin-shih* examinations and obtain government employment. Real literature has *shih* "truth, integrity," an honest reflection of the world's realities, both good and bad. "Integrity" is thus a characteristic both of the personality of the author and of the literature he writes. Both are based on minute observation of the real world and on honest depiction of that observation in the literary work. When this integrity is achieved, the literary work becomes "full," meaning artistically sound.

This letter shows that, for Han Yü, an author's own private actualization of the moral and spiritual Absolute inherent in Antiquity (*ch'eng*) afforded his literary style the force necessary to "return Antiquity" (*fu-ku*), thus unifying form and content, literature (*wen*) and morality (*tao*), private and public, ancient and modern.[24] Although Han Yü does not use the term *fu-ku* to express this idea, his conception of the literature of Antiquity exactly parallels his political use of the term *fu-ku* in the "Preface Seeing Off Ch'i Hao." This conception is radically different from contemporary T'ang usages of *fu-ku*. One such literary usage of *fu-ku* is in the *Models for Poetry (Shih shih)*, completed about 785 by Chiao-jan (734?–799?), where it refers to stylistic archaism.[25] Chiao-jan contrasts *fu-ku* with *pien* "change, innovation," and this was certainly its contemporary meaning: *fu-ku* was imitation. For Chiao-jan, good poetry consists of a mixture of imitation and innovation; an excess of the latter is permissible, but an excess of the former is harmful. This passage constitutes strong evidence that Han Yü inherited little from *fu-ku* adherents of the generations immediately preceding him. As we shall see momentarily, his literary work is characterized by radical "innovation" rather than imitation and shocked the more conservative writers of his age.[26]

Unlike the expression *fu-ku*, *ku-wen* was a term Han Yü used often and with a precise meaning that differed from those in contemporary use. Prior to Han Yü, *ku-wen* designated primarily two things: (1) the "old script" in use prior to the Ch'in language reforms, and by extension (2) "old texts" written in that script. Hsü Shen, compiler of the *Shuo-wen chieh-tzu* completed about A.D. 100, used the term in both these meanings, and both meanings were current in eighth-century T'ang usage.[27] Han Yü uses the term in two senses, both of them different from this contemporary usage. For him, *ku-wen* is first that style opposed to *shih-wen* "contemporary writing," by which he meant writing with required parallelism and thus a fixed number of graphs per phrase. *Ku-wen* is, on the contrary, writing with no restrictions on the length of periods.[28]

Hints of a much deeper meaning, however, can be found in many passages. Thus, for instance, Li Ao wrote that "my friend Han Yü—his is not the literature of this age, it is the literature of Antiquity; he is not a man of this age, he is a man of Antiquity."[29] This passage implies what has already been stated above: "literature of Antiqity" (*ku-wen*) possesses a moral and spiritual power that derives from its ultimate identity with the "Way of Antiquity" (*ku-tao*). This identity occurs when the practitioner has through his own attainment of "integrity" (*ch'eng*) perfected and thus united his spiritual (*tao*) and literary (*wen*) life.

Han Yü is often on record as advocating this union of *tao* and *wen*. In 802 he wrote to one Li Shih-hsi, a friend of his old acquaintance Li Kuan (766-794), who had asked to study with him:

> You say that what I am doing does not differ from what Confucius did, that I do not indulge in literary carving and polishing (i.e. writing parallel prose), and that you would like to follow me. Indeed, I could not presume to treasure this Way and refuse your request. But understand that what I aim at from the Ancients is not only the excellence of their language, but also the excellence of their Way.[30]

In addition to the "Postface to a Lament for Ou-yang Chan" cited above, there is also the often-quoted yet enigmatic opening to the "Preface Seeing Off Master Ch'en T'ung" written in 804:

> One reads books in order to study and one joins together words in order to write, not to flaunt erudition or contend for quantity. One studies in order to pursue the Way and one writes (*wen*) in order to pursue principles (*li*).
>
> If a man's actions attain to what is right and his words match what is essential, then even though I have never met him, I can be certain he is versed in literature and scholarship.[31]

Principles (*li*) are best understood here in the Neo-Confucian sense of the specific natural and ethical realities that taken together constitute the Way (*tao*).[32] Han Yü sees the exercise of literature as an exploration and mastery of the principles and workings of the real world. Thus as more *li* are understood, an author's style becomes more capable of expressing the nuances of these realities, until "his words match what is essential," which is the state of "integrity" (*ch'eng*). The general meaning of this preface is similar to the "Letter in Reply to Master Yü-ch'ih Fen."[33]

Han Yü's fullest and most profound exposition of the unity of *tao* and *wen* is the "Preface Seeing Off the Monk Kaohsien," probably written toward the end of Han Yü's life. The monk Kao-hsien was famous for his cursive or "grass" style calligraphy and later received imperial patronage under Emperor Hsüan-tsung (r. 846-859).

> If a man have somewhere to lodge his skill and intelligence so as to keep his own mind responsive to the power of invention and his creative energy unbroken by vicissitude, then his spirit will be whole and his resolve will be firm. Though external matters may reach him, they will not cling to his mind.
>
> So the Emperors Yao, Shun, Yü, and T'ang perfected ruling the world; Yang Shu perfected archery; Cook Ting was perfect at slaughtering oxen; Master K'uang at music, Pien Ch'üeh at medicine, Hsiung I-liao at juggling, I-ch'iu at chess, and Liu Ling at drinking.[34] They all loved these activities to the end of their days without fail and had no time for external interests; for, no one swayed by external interests to change his field of endeavor can enter the hall or savor the finest morsels (*Analects* XI.15).
>
> In former times, Chang Hsü excelled at calligraphy in the grass style and perfected no other art.[35] Whenever his mind was moved by joy or anger, by despair, by sorrow or delight, was resentful or lustful, full of wine or of ennui or of injustice, he would always express these in his calligraphy. Whatever he saw in the world—moun-

tains and streams, peaks and valleys, birds, animals, insects, and fish, flowers and fruits, the sun, the moon, or
the stars, the wind, the rain, flood and fire, thunder and
lightning, song and dance or warfare and contention, all
the transformations of heaven and earth joyous or trou-
bling—all these he lodged in his calligraphy. Therefore,
the permutations of his writings are like those of ghosts
and spirits and cannot be fathomed. He practiced in this
way to the end of his life and so became famous in later
ages.

Now when Kao Hsien writes grass calligraphy does
he have the same mind (*hsin*) as Chang Hsü? If he cannot
attain to this mind and only follows Chang's outer traces,
he will never be able to equal him. The way to become
like Chang Hsü is to know clearly what is in your interest
and what not and to let nothing escape your attention.
Then when an emotion burns within, the desire for that
interest will fight its way forth and whether you succeed
or fail, you will be uplifted and held fast. After that, let
everything flow forth through your calligraphy, and you
will be close to Chang Hsü.

Now Master Kao Hsien is a Buddhist. He considers
life and death as one and is free from outside attachments.
His mind must be still so nothing will arise. Toward the
world he must be impassive so he will desire nothing.
Yet when stillness and impassivity occur together one is
fallen and exhausted, defeated and without hope of recovery. And his calligraphy will be an expression of this
also.

But I have heard that Buddhists are good at magical
illusion and so have many talents. Perhaps Kao Hsien has
mastered these arts, but I am unable to tell.[36]

Although the last paragraph of this text presents a difficult
problem of interpretation concerning Han Yü's ultimate attitude toward the monk, the general outlines of the text are
clear enough. The great Ch'ing critic Yao Nai (1730-1815)
rightly observed that Han Yü's thoughts on the relation of

calligraphy as an art form to the spiritual life of the calligrapher are certainly based on his own experience of literature as an art form. Han Yü begins by emphasizing the function of the mind (*hsin*) as the crucible where life (*tao*) and art (*wen*) are forged together. This comes about first as a result of total concentration and devotion to one's particular art. Artistic perfection is possible when the artist can express his experience of the world ("mountains and streams . . .") and the emotions generated by those experiences ("joy or anger . . .") without the dissipation of his creative energy. This goal can be actively pursued only if the artist remains fully involved with the real world. He must struggle for the expression of each emotion as others struggle for self-interest. In the Neo-Confucian terms of the "Preface Seeing Off Master Ch'en T'ung," art is the expression of the realization of the identity of the Principle (*li*) of mind with the principles (i.e. entities) of the outside world. An artist who is detached and withdrawn from the world will be unable to create artistic works of the first rank, for his mind is "still and impassive."[37]

Before leaving the subject, it may be helpful to clarify several misconceptions about Han Yü's concept of *ku-wen*. It is usual to disparage Han Yü's contribution to "*ku-wen* theory" and to stress his indebtedness to his eighth-century predecessors. Although it is true that most Confucian-minded literati of the mid-T'ang advocated the need for *tao* in the context of literary reform, none posited a *union* of *tao* and *wen* or had thought out the stylistic consequences of such a union. Much more typical of the age is Liu Tsung-yüan's formulation that "literature illumines the *tao*" (*wen i ming tao*), which quite clearly conceives of *wen* and *tao* as separate entities.[38] Similarly, Liu Mien insists on the need for an author to cultivate his *tao*, but the relation is simplistic compared with Han Yü's insight.[39]

Another common misconception is that *ku-wen* refers only to prose.[40] Han Yü's "Letter to Yü Ti" clearly shows that he considered verse a part of *ku-wen*.[41] Early Sung anthologies such as the *Wen-ts'ui* completed by Yao Hsüan (968-1020) in 1011, which admit a bias for *ku-wen*, also include poetry. It was not until after the revival of interest in Han Yü's prose in the eleventh century that *ku-wen* came to refer exclusively to prose.[42]

The lack of an extended, sympathetic study of the tradition of Confucian didacticism in Chinese literature hinders discussion of Han Yü's contributions to that tradition. We have seen that his theory of the union of *tao* and *wen* is too sophisticated and subtle to be subsumed under the later Neo-Confucian rubric that "literature is a vehicle for the Way" (*wen i tsai tao*). Nor has the general assumption that Chinese didacticism was confined to the Confucian tradition proved helpful for a fuller understanding of either phenomena. Most early and mid-T'ang advocates of a renewal of didacticism (from Ch'en Tzu-ang through Liang Su) were more Buddhist than Confucian in their philosophical and political orientation.[43] Po Chü-i for instance refers specifically to a didactic ethic among contemporary Buddhist poet-monks. His preface to a collection of poems by the Buddhist monk Tao-tsung relates that the monk "composed out of a sense of justice (*i*), for the sake of the *dharma*, for *upāyajñāna*, and to liberate his own nature—not for the sake of poetry."[44] In short, "literature is a vehicle for the Way" is too simplistic a formulation either to summarize the entire range of Chinese didacticism or to explain Han Yü's contribution to the theory of literature in a Confucian context.

Ch'ien Mu has provided a much more useful framework for discussing these questions, a framework he has adapted from Liu Tsung-yüan's "Postface to the Collected Works of the Judicial Inquirer Yang Ling."[45] According to Liu's conception, there are only two justifiable uses for literature: (1) to record praise and blame, and (2) to proclaim indirect criticism. This first purpose he associated with a narrative or expository mode (*chu-su*) and the second with an analogical or allegorical mode (*pi-hsing*). The first derives from the proclamations of the *Book of Documents*, the images and "Great Treatise" of the *Changes*, and the *Spring and Autumn Annals*; the second derives from the *Book of Poetry*. According to Liu, the best contemporary literature should represent a combination of these two modes, a combination that has resulted in the creation of new literary forms: prose that is analogical and poetry that is expository.

Liu Tsung-yüan's paradigm is another way of saying that all literature should possess analogical (*pi-hsing*) value—the "allegorical lodging" (*hsing-chi*) associated with earlier reform advocates such as Ch'en Tzu-ang and Li Po. This proposition, along with the new literary genres it spawned, gave a new focus and sophistication to the didactic tradition. Simplistic views of Chinese didactic theory usually assume the author's emotional detachment from his subject: that subject, being naturally in the public and governmental domain, would seem not to touch his private, thus emotional, life. And it would indeed seem that during the Six Dynasties and early T'ang, the production of emotionally sterile court didacticism did trouble at least a small portion of writers. But the realization of "integrity" (*ch'eng*) through the union of theory and practice and the identity of public and private life laid a different foundation and thus created the potential for a new, more personal form of didactic literature. Now even private meditations could serve the public function of indirect criticism (*feng*). A good example is Han Yü's poem "Craven," discussed above, in which the poet's personal anxieties and desire to serve are developed into a criticism of the ministerial function of the contemporary government. Of course, Tu Fu was the immediate source of this voice in poetry, but Han Yü was the first to effect its successful transition into prose genres. One of the best examples is his "Preface Seeing Off Tung Shao-nan." In this short piece, Han Yü fuses both Tung Shao-nan's distress at not being able to find a government position and his resultant decision to seek employment in the separatist provinces together with his own distress at this decision. The result is a skillful blend of sympathy for Tung, disdain for the separatists, and implied criticism of the central power. The force and beauty of the piece arise from this fusion of private emotional anxiety and comment on public policy. It is prose with poetic, analogical value.

Two elements were crucial to this new sense of didacticism that arose in the eighth century. "Allegorical lodging" presumes a moral stance on contemporary issues; and this moral stance presumes a cultivated sense of humanity and justice—the Way. Thus although literature and the Way are ultimately identical, the creation of good literature presumes its author has first cultivated the Way.[46] Second, the new didacticism demanded that literature be "used" in society: on the personal level, it demanded that an author's works be circulated and read by others, an author's private enjoyment derived from the process of artistic creation was not sufficient justification for literary activity; and on a grander level, it demanded that these works achieve real influence on others—if not on contemporaries, then on posterity. Han Yü's comments on *Analects* XI.3, the fourfold classification of Confucius's disciples, in the *Random Notes on the Analects* envisions the four classifications as four stages in the process toward Sagehood: through literature, administration, and thought, toward moral action. Although this scenario definitely entails the primacy of the Way (*tao*—moral action) over literature (*wen*), the series is progressive, and literature is viewed as the base upon which all other attainments rest. Nevertheless, there is the clear implication that advancement to a higher stage increases and enhances understanding of the lower stages; all stages attain perfection in Sagehood.[47]

This new view of literary didacticism, as the *Analects* exegesis makes clear, integrates literary creation as a moral activity into all aspects of the author's life; and this integration is doubtless one reason for the considerable expansion of subject matters in the Neo-Confucian literary world. At the same time, literature and personal action became synonymous with moral involvement and comment (*feng*) because everything an author "lodged" entailed a value judgment based on his moral sense. Of course, this theory of literary worth naturally generated a corresponding view of literary history: the history of the literature that mattered became a history of works whose "lodgings" revealed the moral stance of their authors.

Han Yü inherited an incipient and narrowly conceived version of such a literary history from the reform-minded authors of the eighth century and from his immediate family. The "Balance of Literature" (*Wen-heng*) attributed to Han Hui, Han Yü's older brother and first literary mentor, contains a typical expression of this history.

When emotions avail themselves of our natures, the myriad transformations (*pien*) arise. The Sages knew that if these transformations were not regulated there would be disorder, so following the natural hierarchies they brought order to the world, acting as sovereigns and as ministers, as fathers and as sons so that all would have constant standards. They discoursed on the Way and its power, on humanity and justice, on the rites, on wisdom, and on truthfulness in order to regulate the emotions and to bring back our original natures (*fu ch'i hsing*). This was the origin of literature.

And so the major functions of literature are to bring together Heaven, Earth, and man and to bring order (*li*) to the myriad things; then to set forth what is advantageous and disadvantageous and to assist in civilizing through education; and finally to expose what is good and what is bad and to provide exhortation and admonition. Beginning with Fu Hsi through the disciples of Confucius, all followed this Way.

Yet later students daily departed from these fundamentals. Some were frivolous and exaggerated, immoderate and unrestrained. The worst were gaudy and excessive, disordered and profligate. Their diction was suave and seductive, their music superficial and insistent. The worst instigated turmoil and led the way toward depravity, corrupting popular custom and slighting justice. And since the Han and Wei Dynasties, sovereigns have used such writing to instruct their subjects and fathers to instruct their sons. This situation began when Lao-tzu and Chuang-tzu departed from the principles of governing the state, when Ch'ü Yüan and Sung Yü departed from the literature of criticism by analogy, and when Szu-ma Ch'ien and Pan Ku departed from the format of chronological narration.

The learned know that if literature is to consist of the Way and its power and of the five constancies (i.e. humanity, justice, the rites, wisdom, and truthfulness), if the writing of literature is to be of use to sovereign and subject, father and son, then it must be simple and unadorned, supple and effortless (*wu wei*). If one's writing is like this, one can gradually approach the spirit of the Sages.[48]

This tract contains several assumptions basic to eighth-century reform theory: (1) the purpose of literature is to further political and social order, (2) there is a direct correspondence between literary style and the health of this order, and (3) an "unadorned, supple, and effortless" style characterized the order of Antiquity; "gaudy and excessive" style characterized the disorder of the ensuing periods. Untypical, however, is the emphasis at the beginning of the tract on the role of literature in regulating the relation between the emotions and human nature. Use of the term *fu-hsing* in this connection is important and presages of Li Ao's later development of these ideas.

It is useful to compare Han Hui's view of this myth of literary decline with another slightly older, yet by the ninth century still popular, account. The *Bunkyō hifuron* completed by the Japanese monk Kūkai (774-835) in 819 contains a "Discussion on Literature and Meaning" taken from the *Standards of Poetry (Shih-ko)* by Wang Ch'ang-ling (698-756). This treatise begins with a discourse on the origins of literature in high antiquity and its progressive decline to the point where "by the Chin, Sung, Ch'i, and Liang Dynasties all had fallen to ruin."[49] Wang Ch'ang-ling's version of literary history has many of the same motifs as Han Hui's. Literature arose in connection with the Grand Way (*huang-tao*), the political way of the legendary sovereigns of antiquity. Its style was simple and easy, devoid of ornamentation, and did not rely on earlier texts for diction. Each line was a self-contained semantic unit, an obvious reference to the relative scarcity of parallelism in this early style. The major difference between the two accounts is that Wang conceives his political and literary utopia as Taoist, whereas Han Hui conceives his as Confucian. For Wang, Confucianism represents a decline from the pristine Taoist antiquity of the Grand Way. The similarities and dissimilarities between these two texts underscore the many non-Confucian elements that went into Han Yü's view of literary history. And his ultimately fully Confucian version of this history represents a more significant effort at synthesis than is usually recognized.

One of Han Yü's most important statements on literature, its origins, purpose, and history, is his "Preface Seeing Off Meng Chiao" written in Ch'ang-an in 803. Meng Chiao at this time was fifty-two years old; his position was still only chief of employees at Li-yang county in modern Kiangsu, an extremely low post for a man of his age. He was obviously in low spirits at the prospect of returning there, and it was in this context than Han Yü wrote his preface.

Whatever does not attain a state of equilibrium will sound forth. Trees have no sound but will cry forth when the wind stirs them; water has no sound but will sound forth when the wind roils it, leaping out if blocked, speeding along if constrained, bubbling up if heated. Metal and stone have no sound, yet if struck will sound forth.

Man with his gift of speech is the same. When there is no other recourse, then he speaks out, singing songs if moved, wailing if deeply touched. Every sound that comes from his mouth shows a lack of some inner equilibrium. Through music we vent forth what wells up inside. We choose objects that make the best sounds and use them to sound forth. These are metal, stone, silk, bamboo, gourd, earth, skin, and wood.[50]

Now Heaven with its seasons of the year is the same, choosing what sings best and using it to sound forth. So birds sing in spring, thunder in summer, insects sing in autumn, and winds in winter. The push and pull of the four seasons shows indeed their lack of equilibrium.[51]

Heaven is also the same with men. The essence of human sound is language, and literature is the essence of language. It chooses the best of those who sing well and uses them to sound forth. Thus in the times of Yao and Shun, Kao Yao and Yü sang best and were used to sound forth.[52] K'uei was unable to sound forth through the written word, so he sounded forth through the *shao* music.[53] During the Hsia Dynasty, the five sons sounded forth through their song. Yi Yin sang during the Shang; the Duke of Chou during the Chou.[54] Everything in the Six Classics is by those who were good at sounding forth. During the decline of Chou, the disciplines of Confucius sounded forth, their voices large and far-reaching. So it was said, "Heaven is about to use your master as the wooden tongue for a bell."[55] How true this was!

Toward the end of the Chou, Chuang Chou sounded forth in vast and unbounded words; and during the fall of the great state of Ch'u, Ch'ü Yüan sounded forth. Tsang-sun Ch'en, Mencius, and Hsün-tzu sounded forth with their understanding of the Way.[56] Those like Yang Chu, Mo Ti, Kuan Chung, Yen Ying, Lao Tan, Shen Pu-hai, Han Fei, Shen Tao, T'ien P'ien, Tsou Yen, Shih Chiao, Sun Wu, Chang I, and Su Ch'in all sounded forth with their various arts.[57] During the ascendancy of Ch'in, Li Szu sounded forth. In the Han, Szu-ma Ch'ien, Szu-ma Hsiang-ju, and Yang Hsiung were the best of those who sang well.

During the Wei and Chin Dynasties, those who sounded forth did not reach the Ancients, yet the tradition was still not broken. But of those who did sing well, their tone was serene and light, their rhythms over-measured and strict, their diction fulsome and sentimental, their purpose loose and unfocused. Their language was confused and unstructured. Perhaps Heaven thought vile the virtues of these times and so did not regard them.

Why otherwise would it not cause to sound forth those who could sing well?

Since our T'ang has held the empire, Ch'en Tzu-ang, Su Yüan-ming, Yüan Chieh, Li Po, Tu Fu, and Li Kuan have all sounded forth as best they could.[58] Of those in lesser stations among our contemporaries, Meng Chiao was the first to sound forth in poetry. His loftiness surpasses the Wei and Chin and with unrelenting energy reaches the Ancients, while others have immersed themselves only in the Han.[59] Among my followers, Li Ao and Chang Chi are the best. The sounding forth of these three is truly excellent. Yet I know not whether Heaven will soften their sound and cause them to sing the fullness of our State or whether it will starve their bodies, trouble their spirits, and so cause them to sing their own misfortune. Their fate hangs with Heaven. If they are among the upper stations—what cause for joy? If they are among the lower stations—what cause for grief?

Meng Chiao goes now to assume duty south of the River, and since he has these misgivings I have explained that his fate rests with Heaven in order to dispel them.[60]

A casual and unfortunately too common reading of this famous text attributes "lack of equilibrium" (*pu p'ing*) solely to an author's pent up anger and despair over his own political frustrations. Marxist critics, pushing this reading a step further, cite the text as evidence that Han Yü believed literature arose from "social oppression."[61] A more careful reading, however, reveals that "lack of equilibrium" results not only from despair but also from joy. Literature is the product of the entire range of emotions (*ch'ing*), themselves seen as disequilibriums, both joyful and sorrowful, of man's pristinely tranquil nature (*hsing*).[62] The individual author has little or no choice in which voice he will sing, for the choice rests with Heaven who uses authors to "sound forth" as men use musical instruments to express their emotions. It is Heaven that causes authors to lodge their emotions in their work. This admittedly deterministic concept opens the way for a much broader sense of literary history. Although Han Yü's debt to earlier literary histories is evident, the doctrine of lodged emotions as a standard of literary quality enables him both to broaden the base of his literary tradition by including Taoist and Legalist writers and to extend that tradition to his own contemporaries. The conclusion of the text is particularly important: Han Yü maintains there is no difference between singing the joyous emotions of a successful political career ("the fullness of our State") and the mournful emotions of failure ("their own misfortunes"). Both public success and private failure are emotions lodged by the poet and determined by Heaven. And Han Yü's litany of literary greats has numerous examples of each, although the careful reader will notice that a majority of the voices of affirmation lived in Antiquity.[63]

Another related text is the "Preface to Poems and Replies Between Ching and T'an" written at Chiang-ling in 805. Han Yü's superior at this time was P'ei Chün (750-811), military governor of Ching-nan from 803-808. T'an is T'an-chou, modern Ch'ang-sha, seat of the regional inspector for Hunan, who from 802 to 805 was Yang P'ing.

> A colleague showed me the *Poems and Their Replies Between Ching and T'an*, which I took and read through to the end. Then I looked up and said to him:
>
> "The tone of the contented is weak and thin; but the sound of the troubled is subtle and to the point. Words of joy are hard to fashion; but the language of suffering is easy to enjoy.
>
> "And so for this reason the making of literature has always begun among travelers and the out of favor. Princes and nobles are full and satisfied and, unless they have a natural ability and liking for literature, they will not find the time to write.
>
> "The Vice-President Lord P'ei defends Man and Ching, a total of nine prefectures. The Officer-in-Attendance Lord Yang governs south of the lake, an area of two thousand *li*. Their administrations of virtue and

justice go forward together; with title and emolument both are honored.

"And yet, still able to devote attention to *Poetry* and *History*, they have lodged their words in songs and poems that have gone and returned round in a circle of chant and reply. They seek the new (*ch'i*), pick out the unusual (*kuai*), carving and inlaying their words; yet their works are scarcely different from those of commoners in village and lane or of our ashen-hued, full-time poets. Their clear sonorities rise like bell and chime; their profound subtleties stir even ghosts and spirits. Truly can it be said that their talents are perfected, their abilities supreme.

"Our colleagues in the two offices and the clerks under them should write harmonizing poems. If these were first put together in a book, then all could read them and it will be easier to have them performed to music and written into the historical record."

My colleague replied,

"What you have said is so. I shall inform the Lord P'ei, and use your words as a "Preface to Poems and Replies Between Ching and T'an.""[64]

Although the transparent purpose of this preface is to flatter his present administrative superior P'ei Chün and perhaps influence Yang P'ing, who was at this time blocking Han Yü's return to Ch'ang-an, its unstated assumptions about the provenance of literary works are revealing. Having stated that poetry expressing sorrowful emotion is more aesthetically pleasing and thus easier to enjoy, he posits the poetry of the "commoners in village and lane and our ashen-hued, full-time poets" as the aesthetic standard against which all other poetry, even that of the highly placed, must be measured. Poetry is still the voice of emotion, but "our sweetest songs are those that tell of saddest thoughts."[65] This preface is actually the logical extension of the "Preface Seeing Off Meng Chiao"; for Han Yü's implied intention in that work is to demonstrate to Meng Chiao that the suffering he has endured "among the lower stations" will secure for him an important position among "those who have sounded forth."

Before proceeding to an analysis of Han Yü's actual literary practice, it will be necessary to recall the distinctive features of composition in literary Chinese. Unlike the "written word" in purely alphabetic systems of writing, monosyllabic Chinese characters or graphs do not stand in any simple one to one relation to words in any spoken Chinese language. Through their continued use over the centuries, Chinese graphs accrued meanings and connotations in such a way that they became not words in a Western sense but symbols or emblems whose implications and associations reverberate back over the centuries and provide a sense of continuity that simple "words" do not possess. Chinese graphs are *not* words but focal magnets that can gather anything from the most precise unit of lexical meaning to such metaphysical abstractions as the *tao*. Their range of semantic meaning is much larger than words, and unlike words, whose morphological form and semantic meaning mutate and change over time, Chinese graphs are relatively fixed in both form and meaning.[66] But because Chinese graphs are not words, which are learned as a child learns to speak, they must be memorized as the first stage of the educational process. In traditional China this process began when the child of six or seven copied out and memorized selected passages of text, even though these passages made little or no sense to him when read aloud. This process continued until the age of eleven or twelve, at which time a teacher began to explain the meanings of individual graphs and specific phrases. But because the student had by this time memorized a considerable body of material and was thus able to make immediate conceptual links between similar passages and usages, these explanations in a short time opened for him the meaning of the entire memorized corpus.[67] During this last stage the student began in earnest to compose on his own, using an ever greater number of graphs and syntactic constructions as the meaning of these became known to him. This entire process is roughly comparable to that by which seventeenth-century European schoolboys learned Latin composition. After having memorized sufficient portions of the Roman authors and having had the meanings of these explained by the teacher, the boys then patched together snippets of memorized Virgil and Horace into Latin verses of their own.

The implications of such a writing and educational system on the world of serious letters are manifold. First, it is apparent that the body of memorized texts rather than any individual talent will determine style; and conversely, an institutional change in this memorization corpus will result in a change of style for all writers. Accordingly, a unique, individual style is very difficult to achieve and will necessarily involve some private deviation or expansion in this institutionalized memorization corpus. Second, there is a greater cohesion between the author and his audience, a cohesion based on a more intimately shared common lexicon. Since the meanings of the graphs are learned from a designated corpus of texts, there is little room for the variations in meaning that arise when an author confronts words as they relate in a living language to the real world. The diction of the Chinese literati comes not from the real world but from texts. Thus in theory every graph constitutes an allusion to the memorization corpus, and such "allusion" will be neither vague nor recondite but rather precise and quite normal. Third, creativity under these circumstances assumes a very different connotation than is now usual. In contrast to "allusion," usually two-graph compounds taken from the memorization corpus, "created expressions" (*tsao-yü*) are compounds formed by the author himself. This practice increases ambiguity and makes his style more difficult for his contemporaries yet also more individualistic. The great Sung poet Huang T'ing-chien (1045-1105) was speaking to this issue when he wrote to his nephew:

> To create your own diction is extremely difficult. In the poetry of Tu Fu and the prose of Han Yü there is not one graph that does not have some point of origin.

But the men of later ages read too little, so they believe
Han and Tu created these expressions themselves.

The old authors who wrote well were in truth able to
mold and smelt the myriad things. Although they used
the clichéd expressions of the ancients, when these entered the ink of their brushes, it was like when a single
drop of the philosophers stone is applied to iron and
produces gold.[68]

Huang T'ing-chien is here addressing the difficult question of
originality in a system where the acceptable diction is not, as
in modern poetry, based on the practically infinite reserves
of the spoken language but rather is confined within artificial
parameters well known to author and reader alike. Originality
does not consist of devising new formulations but rather of
displaying virtuosity at juxtaposing old formulas. So strong
was the hold of the memorization corpus on the traditional
method of composition that when a commentator discovers
Tu Fu creating "new expressions" he labels the passage an
example of Tu Fu's "wild and unrestrained" style (k'uang-
fang).[69] Finally, it should be stated that an author was always
free to introduce "words" from the living language into his
writing, although such diction was always outside the memorization corpus and would probably be viewed as "vulgar"
(su) by the orthodox. The relation between the spoken and
the literary languages in China was, and still is, complicated
and ever-shifting; for what may have been an obvious and
forceful colloquialism for the T'ang poet probably passed
unobserved as such into the memorization corpus of the Sung
student. It became "literary Chinese." And as long as memorization remained the basis of literary composition, there was
always a line, although a fluid one, between the literati and
"popular literature" (su wen-hsüeh).

I have undertaken to explain, at grave risk of oversimpli-
fication and generalization, the process of composition in literary Chinese because without this background in mind it is
impossible to understand how Han Yü "reformed Chinese
prose" or to appreciate the magnitude of his achievement.

During the eighth century, serious secular education aimed at preparing the student to pass the "presented scholar" (*chin-shih*) examination, the importance of which has been mentioned above. The memorization corpus for the literary portions of this examination was based largely on the *Anthology of Literature (Wen hsüan)* compiled by Hsiao T'ung (501-531), a prince of the southern Liang Dynasty (502-556), and promulgated with an official commentary by Li Shan (d.689) in 658. The accepted style was "parallel prose" (*p'ien-wen*) whose two main distinguishing features were fixed periods of either four or six characters in length and rigid syntactic parallelism between periods.[70] The following passage from a memorial submitted by Yang Wan (d. 777) in 763 demonstrates the pernicious effect of these requirements on education and literary style:

> When Emperor Yang of the Sui Dynasty established the *chin-shih* examination, one was tested only by dissertations written in response to questions (*ts'e*). But during the time of Emperor Kao-tsung, when Liu Szu-li was auxiliary secretary in the Bureau of Scrutiny [A.D. 681], compositions in various genres were added to the program of the *chin-shih* examination and interrogation by means of citations was added to the program of the examination "elucidating the classics" (*ming-ching*). Unhealthy effects ensued and became widespread. When children first began their studies, they all memorized recent poetry; when they grew older and their style had supposedly matured, it did not encompass more than the collections of these few authors. Generations succeeded one another in this way, and literary cliques formed; yet none achieved anything except empty repetition. No one ever opens the Six Classics or takes the Three Histories from their shelves. How could anyone in this way summon up the Way of Confucius and live the life of a superior man?[71]

Yang Wan's concerns are clear: the memorization corpus required for the examinations is too small and morally inconsequential. It excludes the classics, emphasizing instead "recent poetry."

It should be stated in passing that the link between the *Wen hsüan* and parallel prose was not absolute. The *Wen hsüan* was a repository of examples of parallelism in both prose and poetry from the Han through the early sixth century. Yet a T'ang author who had memorized the *Wen hsüan* was always free to use its diction for his own purpose in nonparallel ways. Han Yü's "Autumn Sentiments," for instance, draws so heavily from *Wen hsüan* texts that it was criticized as "*Wen hsüan* style" by a Sung scholar. But the great Ch'ing commentator Fang Shih-chü (1675-1759) saw the situation more clearly:

> One can study the *Wen hsüan* and still maintain individuality. The study of the *Wen hsüan* went on unabated throughout the T'ang, but famous authors all maintained their own individuality. Li Po and Tu Fu, for instance, took much in the way of materials and techniques from the *Wen hsüan*, yet the robust and unrestrained nature of their poetry did not suffer. How could it not be likewise with Han Yü?[72]

The popularity of the *Wen hsüan* and of parallel prose, however, affected all levels of literary style in the T'ang. Wang Yün-hsi, a leading scholar of T'ang literature, has recently emphasized the ubiquity of the parallel prose influence, equating it quite rightly with the "contemporary writing" (*shih-wen*) that Han Yü opposed.[73] He cautions that although many of the *Wen hsüan* texts were written in a highly refined and elegant parallel prose style, T'ang continuations and modifications of that style often tended toward the plebian and quotidian. Wang provides an instructive and representative list of such "contemporary writing": (1) the chancery pieces of Lu Chih (754-805) whose edicts written during the imperial flight to Feng-t'ien in 783 "moved even the most violent soldiers to tears";[74] (2) examination papers; (3) the "Dwelling of the Playful Goddesses" (*Yu-hsien k'u*), an erotic *ch'uan-ch'i* story by Chang Tsu (657-730);[75] (4) popular poetry by Po Chü-i such as the "Song of Everlasting Lament"; (5) "regulated *fu*" (*lü-fu*) especially as practiced by such late T'ang authors as Hsü Yin and Huang T'ao; and finally (6) popular literature from Tun-huang.[76] These extremely diverse works all demonstrate fairly rigid six/four periods and a limited memorization corpus that largely excludes the classics. It was precisely these stylistic characteristics to which Yang Wan objected.

Stylistically, Han Yü's *ku-wen* is a direct attack on these features of "contemporary writing." By adopting the flexible periods of pre-Ch'in prose, *ku-wen* opened the possibility for an infinitely greater variety of prose rhythms than was possible within the rigid six/four "harness" of parallel prose. This in turn required greater use of "empty graphs" (*hsü-tzu*), particles indicating grammatical function, to control the increased variety of syntactical constructions. This rhythmic flexibility also allowed for the subtle introduction of contemporary speech rhythms into this "ancient prose" without the danger of exposure to a charge of "vulgarity" to which Po Chü-i's efforts at "popular literature" were often subjected. *Ku-wen*, as the name implies, is also based on a much older and more varied memorization corpus than contemporary writing. Even a cursory glance at the textual references for such *ku-wen* masterpieces as the "Poem on the Sagacious Virtue of Primal Harmony" or the "Inscription on the Pacification of Huai-hsi" will reveal their relation to the Six Classics, especially the *Book of Poetry, Book of Documents*, and *Commentary of Tso*. This broadening of the memorization corpus for *ku-wen* enlarged in turn the allusive possibilities of the style and so acted further to expand the range of themes and emotions the style could articulate. As Han Yü himself put into the mouth of his student interlocutor in "An Explication of 'Progress in Learning,' "

> Truly, Sir, it can be said,
>   your labors at literature
> have enlarged its core,
>   its form set free.

But most of the contemporary readers and writers were concerned not with the increased expressive possibilities of the new style but only with the increased erudition and time needed to master it. This explains the considerable opposition to *ku-wen* in Han Yü's own lifetime and after. Only in the eleventh century did Ou-yang Hsiu's *ku-wen* revival finally overcome this opposition to make *ku-wen* the accepted examination style. The following anecdote affords a fascinating glimpse of the difficulty *ku-wen* presented to the traditionally educated scholar of the time:

> Mu Hsiu (979-1032) was among the first scholars in the Sung to study *ku-wen*. When he first obtained good editions of Han Yü and Liu Tsung-yüan he was very pleased and wanted to circulate these two collections further, so he had the blocks carved and sold them himself at the Hsiang-kuo Temple in K'ai-feng. But Mu Hsiu was by nature straightforward and intolerant. There was one scholar who did not wish to pay the price asked, so Mu Hsiu snapped back at him,
>
> "If you can even punctuate the phrases properly, I'll give you the whole set!"
>
> When some bystanders rebuked Mu, he assumed a grave face and said,
>
> "But I really meant what I said; I presume to cheat no one!"[77]

So great thus was the difficulty of *ku-wen* for a normal "scholar" of the early eleventh century that he could not even punctuate and construe its phrases correctly.

Han Yü's longest exposition on the theory and practice of literature is the "Letter in Reply to Li I," dated August 9, 801. Li I was apparently at this time a student of Han Yü, for he recommended Li the next year to Lu Ts'an, who was to assist at the administration of the 802 *chin-shih* examinations, and Li I indeed passed the examinations in that year.[78] Although this letter contains a remarkably detailed account of Han Yü's ideas on composition, two points should be kept in mind before an exegesis is attempted. First, the letter is largely an autobiographical record of Han Yü's own experience as a writer during the twenty-year period from about 780 when he was twelve years old until 801. It thus predates all his major creative works. Second, it was written for the benefit of a student whose intentions Han Yü obviously considered somewhat circumspect. His letters to students written during this period repeatedly emphasize that those who struggle to attain real excellence in literature must separate that struggle from the rush to obtain office through the pseudo-literary success that passage of the *chin-shih* confers. In short, this letter is a work about apprenticeship for an apprentice still unsure of his true goal.

> Your letter is so well written and your questions so deferentially put that no one could refuse to relate to you his ideas. That morality and virtue (*tao te*) toward which you aim will soon be yours, not to mention literature which is but the outward expression of these. Now I am like one who has seen the gate and the walls of Confucius's house but not yet entered his hall (*Analects* XIX.23), so although I cannot be sure I am right, nevertheless I feel compelled to address you on these subjects.
>
> What you say about "establishing one's words" is correct. And what you have written is very close to what you set out to do. Yet I am not sure whether your intention is to surpass your contemporaries and so find employment or to attain to those who "established their words" in Antiquity. If it is the former, you can certainly surpass them and find employment. But if you would attain the latter, then do not expect a quick success and do not be enticed by power and profit. You must nourish its roots and wait for the fruit, add oil in expectation of the flame; for when the roots flourish, then the fruit ripens, and only with surfeit of oil will the flame blaze. Just so are the words of the humane and just man (*jen i*) beautiful and prolific.
>
> Yet there are difficulties, and I do not know if my own writing has attained their goal or not. Nevertheless, I have been working toward it for over twenty years. In

the beginning, I read only works from the Hsia, Shang, Chou, and the two Han; I retained only that which contained the intentions of the Sages. When at home, it was as if I had forgotten everything; when outside, as if I had left something behind. I was grave like one lost in thought; dazed like one who had lost his way. Yet when I took something from my mind and put it to paper, I worked only to remove the old clichés, and the result was cacophonous and difficult. Yet I did not acknowledge the criticism of others to whom I showed these works [stage one].

I continued like this for many years without change and then began to discern what was true and what was false in the ancient writings and what, although it may have been genuine, was imperfect; thus I could clearly separate white from black. I worked to remove the latter and slowly made progress. When I took something from my mind and put it to paper, it came in fast torrents. When I showed these works to others, I was happy if they criticized them and troubled if they praised them, because that meant there was still something in them that people liked [stage two].

I went on like this for a number of years, and then my writing began to flow like a great current [stage three].

Yet I was afraid it might still be mixed, so I confronted and restrained it, then examined it with a calm mind and only when all was pure did I let it flow forth [stage four].

Nevertheless I must continue to nourish my writing: I move it along the paths of humanity and justice (*jen i*), send it to the sources in the *Poetry* and *History*; and to the end of my life I may never lose sight of these paths nor be cut off from the sources [stage five].

Vitality of style is water; the language is a floating object. If the water is vast enough, it will float any object large or small. And such is the relation between style and language: if there is an amplitude of vitality, then all will be as it should, regardless of the length of the periods or the pattern of the tones.

Although my writing is now like this, I do not claim to have approached perfection. And even if I were to do so, its acceptance by others would not benefit my writing. To wait to be employed by others is to be like a vessel: its use or rejection depends on another person. The superior man (*chün-tzu*) is not like this. He puts his mind toward the moral way (*tao*) and conducts himself according to these principles. If employed, he spreads these to others; if not, he passes them on to his disciples and hands them down in writings that serve as models for future ages. And this is truly something one can rejoice about.

There are few who aspire to Antiquity, for those who aspire to Antiquity are left behind by the present. In truth, I rejoice in the former as I lament the latter. I often praise such people in order to encourage them, presuming not to laud what might be lauded or to fault what might be faulted.

There are many who ask me questions, but I recall you said you did not intend toward profit, so I have addressed you on these subjects.[79]

The ultimate and most basic meaning of this letter is that good writing through vitality of style (*ch'i*) attains to a unity of form (*wen*) and content (*tao*). The end of the second paragraph posits a series of metaphors that establish the relation between *tao* and *wen*: as are the roots to the fruit and the oil to the flame so are the actions of the humane and just man (*jen i*) the base of "beautiful and prolific words." Both these metaphors well express those fundamental features of the *tao/wen* dialectic outlined earlier: although the two are mutually dependent and ultimately identical in their perfected state, the root, the oil, and the *tao* are primary. This perfected state is of course *ch'eng* "integral," or as Han Yü says in paragraph eight "when all is as it should be." Paragraphs three through seven outline the process by which Han Yü has sought to attain this perfection. The Ming commentator Mao K'un (1512-1601) divided Han Yü's account of this process into five stages as indicated in the translation. These divisions, although tenuous, do serve to underscore the slow and cumulative nature of Han Yü's progress as a writer.

It is important to note that at all stages, but especially during the first two stages, learning the craft of composition is intimately linked to the reading and evaluation of earlier literature. Paragraph three describes the initial difficulty of creating a new memorization corpus based solely on Han and pre-Han works that "contained the intentions of the Sages." This phrase is synonymous with the Way of Antiquity: *in the beginning* the memorization corpus must contain only works that manifest acceptable moral and social values. This is the foundation, at the most basic level, for the union of *tao* and *wen*. "Old clichés" (*ch'en-yen*) were fossilized expressions from this corpus that "contemporary writing" continued to use in hackneyed and stereotyped ways. Thus when Han Yü refused to use such expressions, he at once removed from his writing the only element his contemporaries would have recognized. It is hardly surprising that this removal made Han Yü's early writing "cacophonous and difficult."[80] In the second state of the process, continued practice at composition refines the author's awareness of the relative "perfection" of "ancient writings." He can distinguish "white from black," what is important from what is trivial. As the author gains a deeper understanding of Antiquity, he composes more fluently; for his focus on the "true" (*cheng*) writings of Antiquity increases the "integrity" (*ch'eng*) of his own writings. The author continues to refine this procedure until at stage four all "mixed" elements have been removed and his writings are "pure." There is now a perfect integration between the *tao*, meaning the author's own understanding of Antiquity as expressed through his own moral actions, and *wen*, the articulation of this understanding through his writing. The final stage involves nourishing or maintaining this purity and unity by constantly renewing in one's own life the moral standards of humanity and justice and rejuvenating one's writings through constant return to the literary sources of these virtues in the *Poetry* and *History*. These latter stages contain a strong echo of the Ch'an adept's efforts to "maintain" (*pao-jen*) the enlightenment he has labored so hard to attain.[81] Indeed, it should be hardly surprising that Han Yü's account of his progress toward the goal of literary perfection has strong spiritual overtones; for if *tao* and *wen* are ultimately one, then the actualization of their union will obviously be a spiritual experience. *Ch'i*, here understood as "style" or "vitality of style," is both a means to this union and a result of it. Han Yü's conception of *ch'i* relates to Mencius's "nourishing the flood-like *ch'i*," although the relation is by no means direct.[82] In the context of the dialectic between *tao* and *wen*, *ch'i* is both the author's vital force or vitality of spirit that results from his cultivation of moral values (*tao*) and the force of his literary style that results from the honest expression of these values (*wen*). Good writing can thus have no fixed style, for the vitality that results from the union of *tao* and *wen* will ensure that "all will be as it should, regardless of the length of the periods or the pattern of the tones."

The phrase to "remove old clichés" that Han Yü characterized as a goal of the initial phase of his literary training has become itself a cliché to describe an important principle of his literary practice. Yet scholars differ on exactly what constituted for Han Yü an "old cliché."[83] Fortunately, Li Ao's "Letter to Chu Tsai-yen" quotes Han Yü's phrase and gives five unambiguous examples of "old clichés":

> Han Yü said one must "work to remove old clichés." If I wish, for example, to describe laughter, and write "with a grin" (*huan-erh*), then the *Analects* has already said that.[84] If I write "ha-ha" (*e-e*), that is the *Changes*.[85] If I write "guffawed" (*ts'an-jan*), that is the *Ku-liang Commentary*.[86] If I write "chortled" (*yu-erh*), that is Pan Ku.[87] If I write "heartily" (*ch'an-jan*), that is Tso Szu.[88] If I were to repeat these expressions, then there would be no difference between mine and these former writings. This is the principle of creating your own expressions.[89]

Thus for Li Ao "old clichés" seem to have meant descriptive binomes that bear no real semantic connection to the object or action described. With the exception of the character *e*, which is obviously onomatopoetic, no character in Li Ao's list has a primary semantic meaning related to laughing. Rather, these expressions, because of their *loci classici* in the passages Li Ao indicates, became traditionally descriptive of laughter. *Huan-erh*, for instance, occurs twice in the *Wen hsüan*, *ts'an-jan* three times—all without reference to their *locus classicus*. In short, these expressions had become through the widespread use of the *Wen hsüan* as a repository of "poetic diction" stereotypically associated with laughter.[90]

Other aspects of Han Yü's literary practice are outlined in his "Epitaph for Fan Tsung-shih of Nan-yang," written in 824 shortly before his own death. We have already seen that Fan Tsung-shih's "literary style was different from that of normal men." Li Chao in his *Supplement to the State History of the T'ang* wrote that his contemporaries "in order to write prose studied unconventionality (*ch'i*) with Han Yü and asperity (*se*) with Fan Tsung-shih."[91] This characterization of Fan Tsung-shih's prose style as "harsh, rough" (the graph *se* designates "water flowing over rocky terrain"), the remarks in Han Ch'ang's funeral inscription, and an examination of Fan Tsung-shih's two surviving works all indicate that a rugged independence of diction was the hallmark of his style.[92] Han Yü's inscription begins by relating the vast number of writings found in Fan Tsung-shih's lodgings after his death: two collections of thirty *chüan* each, a fifteen-*chüan* commentary on the *Spring and Autumn Annals*, 290 miscellaneous prose texts, 220 lesser inscriptions, ten *fu*, and 719 poems.

> From Antiquity till now there has never been a writer as prolific as Fan Tsung-shih. And it all came from Fan himself: not one word or phrase did he parrot or imitate from earlier authors. Truly a difficult feat!
>
> And all was filled with a sense of humanity and justice (*jen i*). The wealth of his art, as if he had stored it up since birth, like the sea's reach and the earth's support, encompassed all the universe. Unrestrained and free, without master plan, and with no troubling over plum

line or saw, yet he brought all together. Such was the perfection of his art. . . .

There was nothing he had not studied. His gift for language and for music was Heaven-sent. . . . His epitaph is as follows:

In Antiquity all phrases
    came from the men themselves
but later on the unskilled
    stole and robbed
and still later, looking to their
    elders, they plundered openly
so from Han till now
    is a single voice,
empty and desolate with no one
    who knew how to write:
the Sage spirits had fallen low,
    the Way was broken and blocked,
then with things at their worst
    came Fan Tsung-shih;
the diction of his writing was fluid and apt
    each graph fulfilling its duty,
for those who seek this goal
    here is your model.[93]

This text shares with the "Letter in Reply to Li I" a similar emphasis on originality of diction, a conviction that "all phrases must come from the men themselves" (*tz'u pi chi ch'u*). This latter concern is a natural result of the earlier injunction to the beginning student to "remove old clichés." Li Ao's "Life of Han Yü" refers unambiguously to Han Yü's avoidance of imitation: "Those who know literature all agree there have been no great writers since Yang Hsiung. What Han Yü wrote never imitated the expressions of earlier men, and is certainly on par with Yang Hsiung."[94] Li Ao's own list of clichés descriptive of laughter contrasts such usage with "creating your own expressions" (*tsao-yen*). Later critics called such phrases *tsao-yü* "created expressions," which usually comprised two characters, to distinguish them from expressions the author took ready-made from his memorization corpus. Han Yü's works abound in "created expressions." A good example is the phrase "to draw up Antiquity" (*chi ku*) in ll. 7-8 of the fifth poem in the "Autumn Sentiments" series:

Return to the simple and know the tranquil road:
to draw up Antiquity takes a long rope.

Literally these lines are

kuei	*yü*	*shih*	*i*	*t'u*
return	simplicity	know	level	road
chi	*ku*	*te*	*hsiu*	*keng*
draw up	Antiquity	takes	long	well rope

This couplet relies on two earlier passages. The primary meaning of *chi* is "to draw up water from a well" as in *Chuang-tzu* 47/18/31 (Watson trans., p. 194): "Small bags won't hold big things; short well ropes (*keng*) won't draw up (*chi*) deep water." When Han Yü changes this negative image to a positive one, his line requires a "long" rope. His choice of the graph *hsiu* over several other possibilities affords a glimpse of something very close to the heart of the creative process itself. "Level road" (*i t'u*) is a phrase direct from the memorization corpus, in this case Chang Heng's "*Fu* on the Western Capital": "with high banks, level roads (*i t'u*), / Long (*hsiu*) avenues, climbing sheer and precipitously" (*WH* 2/6a; trans. Knechtges, *Wen Xuan*, p. 189 ll. 116-117). Han Yü has taken from this passage not only "level roads" but also the adjective "long" for his well rope. These two passages, *Chuang-tzu* and Chang Heng, thus contain five of the ten graphs in Han Yü's couplet: "level" (*i*), "road" (*t'u*), "draw up" (*chi*), "long" (*hsiu*), and "well rope" (*keng*). The couplet is a good example of the intimate connection between quotation from the memorization corpus and the making of "created expressions." "Return to the simple" (*kuei yü*) and "to draw up Antiquity" (*chi ku*) are both created expressions and are balanced by the more easily understandable "level roads." But this quotation, far from being a cliché, acts as a catalyst to fuse *hsiu* and *keng*, linking the two quoted passages and providing background and context for the "created expressions." This couplet well illustrates both Han Yü's precept that "phrases must come from the men themselves" and the seemingly contrary observation of Huang T'ing-chien that every character in Han Yü's writing has a "point of origin."[95]

The eighteenth-century critic Ma Wei appreciated the artistic effect of Han Yü's practice of creating expressions based on the classics:

> In Han Yü's old style poetry, the created expressions (*tsao-yü*) are all based on the classics and their commentaries. Therefore, reading them is like a display of Shang and Chou bronzes: their ancient mottled crenelations inspire our reverence; sometimes precious stones or pearls blind our eyes in bright confusion. We should take them up but often have no time; for, they are not simply obscure and jagged expressions or outlandish monstrosities.[96]

Chu Hsi singled out "remove old clichés" and "diction that is fluid and apt" (*wen ts'ung tzu shun*) as the two most important compositional principles of Han Yü's style.[97] The latter idea begins with the notion that each graph should be used with lexical precision so that "each fulfills its duty" and contributes something essential to the total meaning of its period. This demands in turn a detailed knowledge of etymology and lexicography. Tseng Kuo-fan has noticed that Han Yü gained his formidable knowledge in these areas from his intimate familiarity with scholia (*hsün-ku*) to the classic texts.[98] Han Yü himself remarks in his "Postface to Some Tadpole Script Calligraphy" that "for anyone to create good literary diction he must have a fair knowledge of the graphs."[99] This knowledge enabled the author, when creating his own expressions, to confine his use of each graph to pristine and basic meanings sanctioned by classic usage and to avoid such stereotyped misusages as those in Li Ao's list of clichés for laughter. This careful usage of each individual graph is an important feature of Han Yü's literary classicism and an important reason why his writings attained a preeminent position in the Sung Dynasty and after as models for training in the literary language. It was this aspect of Han Yü's style that prompted Ma Wei to remark that his diction was based on "the classics and their commentaries," so reading Han Yü was "like a display of Shang and Chou bronzes."

Several recent studies have increasaed awareness of the relation between the contemporary colloquial language and Han Yü's style.[100] There is little doubt that the increasing use of the colloquial in post - An Lu-shan times betrays an urge among literati to articulate the new social values of the age in a language that was itself the product of that age.[101] The new emphasis on oral teaching in both Ch'an and Neo-Confucian circles manifests a related desire to bring language into closer accord with reality. Han Yü's natural gifts once again prepared him to appreciate the significance of a contemporary trend and to make use of it for his own purposes. As the correspondence with Chang Chi attests, Han Yü was by nature a skilled conversationalist and a determined debater, a man whose spoken word possessed real power. Li Ao's "Life of Han Yü," for instance, culminates in his encounter with Wang T'ing-ts'ou at Chen-chou, which well illustrates his skill as an orator and persuader.[102]

Han Yü's frequent use of colloquial elements accounts for much of the vivaciousness of his style. Fundamental was his abandonment of the artificial six/four periods of parallel prose for the irregular periods of *ku-wen*. This move freed him to mold his periods and his rhythms more closely to the patterns of spoken speech. Typically, Han Yü's freest and most widely varying periods often occur in his most serious texts, such as the "Essentials of the Moral Way," the "Memorial on the Buddha Relic," and the "Lament for my Nephew." Frequent dialogue is another result of colloquial influence on Han Yü's style. Many of his prefaces seeing off individuals use dialogue with great effect to increase the full dramatic possibilities present in the tension of the approaching parting and separation. Likewise, the imperial monologues in the "Poem on the Sagacious Virtue of Primal Harmony" and the "Inscription on the Pacification of Huai-hsi" contribute toward the vivid characterization of the emperor and the high drama of the occasions.

By far the most important effect of the colloquial language on Han Yü, however, is something much more subtle and difficult to perceive than the above features. No matter how much colloquial vocabulary and rhythm Han Yü's style absorbed, his is still a literary Chinese style based mainly on memorized texts, not on spoken speech. Yet Han Yü has so well mastered his chosen memorization corpus of "the classics and their commentaries" that he is able to manipulate their vocabulary and syntax as fluently and as easily as he could manipulate his own speech. In short, the memorization corpus became for him a spoken language. So well has he assimilated through texts the written graphs and their meanings that he could fuse them together in his writing so that "one sees no seams," as later critics would say. This verbal dexterity is most apparent in the "Explication of 'Progress in Learning.' " Although Han Yü uses few quotations or allusions in this piece, its pronounced classic flavor as *ku-wen* arises from the careful juxtaposition of individual graphs so as to highlight the precise meanings of each graph. A good example is the four-graph expression *t'ou t'ung ch'ih huo* "your head's gone bald, your teeth are gapped," which describes Han Yü's age and physical deterioration. *T'ung* means principally "a young boy" but also "a calf without horns," thus a "denuded mountain; terrain without vegetation." *Huo* is "a passage between two mountains; a large opening." All these meanings reverberate through the clause. The semantic parallelism of mountain and valley demands we understand that Han Yü's head is a "denuded mountain," and his teeth contain "passages between two mountains." But his "denuded mountain" derives ultimately from "a young boy"; and this precise etymology sparks the irony and humor of the phrase. Far from simply patching together snippets of memorized text, Han Yü is here using the Chinese graph with the ease and force of the spoken word.

This successful union of high moral content with "colloquial" form, as witnessed for instance in "Essentials of the

Moral Way," was Han Yü's unique contribution to the literature of his age. Rather than subject its author to charges of "vulgarity" as did similar efforts by Po Chü-i, Han Yü used contemporary rhythm and flavor to enhance the moral integrity and seriousness of his subject matter. T. S. Eliot has a paragraph in his obituary for Charles Whibley that may serve to conclude this discussion of the relation between Han Yü's spoken and written language:

> Now, one could not say of Whibley, any more than of any one else, that he wrote as he talked, or that he talked as he wrote. Nevertheless, his writings have a quality which relates them more closely to his speech than to the writing of any one else. I know the word "sincerity" sounds very vague; yet it represents that moral integrity which unites the prose styles of speech and writing of any good writer: however the rhythm, the syntax, the vocabulary may differ. One cannot, obviously, produce negative instances; I can only repeat that whenever I have known both the man and the work of any writer of what seemed to me good prose, the printed word has always reminded me of the man speaking.[103]

Eliot's use of "sincerity" and "moral integrity" as attributes of good prose recalls Han Yü's conception of *ch'eng* "when everything is as it should be" as the highest state to which literature can attain. His fullest exposition of this idea is the "Letter to Liu Cheng-fu."

> All those who sit for the *chin-shih* examination come naturally to the gates of those who have gone before them, who, when they see them arrive, cannot but respond to their call. So these callers are received when they arrive, and all the scholars of the city do this. Unfortunately, only I have the *reputation* of so receiving my juniors. And where reputation exists there also slander disposes.
> So I answer with the truth those who come to question. If someone should ask,

"Whom is it best to take as a model for writing?"

I would have to answer respectfully,

"It is best to take the Sages and worthies of Antiquity as a model."

"But in those writings of the Sages and worthies of Antiquity that survive the diction is not uniform. Whom is it best to take as a model?"

I would answer respectfully,

"Take their ideas as your model, not their diction."

And if again someone asked,

"Should literature be easy or difficult?"

I would answer respectfully,

"Neither hard nor easy, only appropriate."

And so it should be. I do not firmly advocate one nor prohibit the other.

No one pays attention to the hundreds of objects they see all day long. But when they see something unusual they all stare at it together and talk about it. It is the same with literature. Everyone could write at the Han court, yet Szu-ma Hsiang-ju, Szu-ma Ch'ien, Liu Hsiang, and Yang Hsiung stand out. Because they applied themselves intensely, the reputations they acquired were far-reaching. If they had followed the fashions of their age, they would not have established themselves, their contemporaries would not have marveled at them, and there would have been nothing passed on to later ages. There are hundreds of things in your house that you use; yet you treasure that thing which is not ordinary. The superior man's attitude toward literature is no different from this.

Now if my juniors who write literature can explore and attain this principle by taking the Sages and worthies of Antiquity as their standard, although all may not succeed, the important thing will be that if followers of Szu-ma Hsiang-ju, Szu-ma Ch'ien, Liu Hsiang, and Yang Hsiung do emerge, they certainly will be from this group and not from among the followers of those who pursue the ordinary.

If the Way of the Sages does not make use of literature, then literature will cease; but if it is to use literature, then we must honor those who do it well. And these are none other than those who can establish themselves and do not follow others. There have been writers ever since the beginning of writing, but those who have endured to our day are those who were able to do this. Such has always been my opinion.[104]

This letter contains two separate but related ideas: (1) there can be no established style, only individual styles that are "appropriate" to their subjects; (2) writers can achieve this goal only by going against the established standards of their time and creating works that are "unusual." These works in turn establish literary tradition and preserve the Way of the Sages.

The first idea is another articulation of the definition of good writing as ch'eng. Since literature (wen) is an expression of the Way (tao), and this latter is both ubiquitous and multifarious, there can never be one correct literary style. Rather many styles are possible as long as each is an "appropriate" expression of the work's unity of language and reality. This work then possesses "integrity" (ch'eng). Han Yü often mentions this principle. In 806 he wrote to Yü Ti:

You are the assistant to the Son of Heaven, the teacher of the feudal lords because the language of your compositions is in accord with reality. Rich and yet without one superfluous word; compact and yet not omitting one phrase—faithful to reality and logically tight.[105]

Han Yü himself wrote effectively and with ease in many styles, from four-character epics like the "Poem on the Sagacious Virtue of Primal Harmony" to short "modern style" lyrics, from syntactically diverse tracts like the "Discourse on Teachers" or "Essentials of the Moral Way" to masterpieces of parallel prose like the "Explication of 'Progress in Learning.' " All are ch'eng; and a style that manifests ch'eng is but a natural literary reflection of the Sage's mind, which is also *ch'eng*.[106]

The practice of *ch'eng* as a literary principle resulted in writings that were *ch'i*, a term often mistranslated as "weird" or "bizarre." Fortunately, precise, contemporary definitions allow us to interpret more correctly. Thus Huang-fu Shih wrote in his letters to Li Ao:

> When an idea is new, then the work is different from the ordinary; different from the ordinary is *kuai* (unprecedented). Diction that is lofty and departs from what is common is *ch'i* (unconventional).

And again:

> *Ch'i* is something that is not standard (*cheng*), and yet does not harm what is standard. *Ch'i* is something out of the ordinary—that means it is not like the ordinary: it departs from the ordinary. And it is permissible to revere something that does not harm the standard and that is out of the ordinary.[107]

The best translation for *ch'i* would seem to be "unconventional," which well expresses the ambiguity of the term. As used by Huang-fu Shih, Han Yü, Liu Tsung-yüan, and other *ku-wen* authors, *ch'i* was a positive term that expressed the "difference" between their writing and "contemporary writing" (*shih-wen*). *Ch'i* in this sense does not mean "weird"; it is merely the opposite of parallel prose. Since the latter was common and ordinary at the time, *ku-wen* was thus "unconventional."[108] For those opposed to *ku-wen*, however, this same *ch'i* described all that was novel and heterodox in the new style, all that was "unconventional" in the worst sense.[109]

There is considerable critical consensus that although *ch'i* may refer to individual graphs and phrases, its use as a positive approbation of *ku-wen* was applied primarily to longer formal and conceptual elements.[110] Such is certainly the meaning of Liu Tsung-Yüan's statement that Han Yü's writings possessed "prodigious *ch'i*."[111] *Ch'i* does not refer to any simple or single stylistic feature such as the use of "bizarre" graphs but rather to the sum total of all contextual and formal features that set a work apart from other contemporary works as unconventional.

This concept of *ch'i* also contributed to Han Yü's definition of value in literary history. The "Letter to Liu Cheng-fu" singled out Szu-ma Ch'ien, Szu-ma Hsiang-ju, and Yang Hsiung as Han exemplars of the unconventional. Yang Hsiung was probably Han Yü's most important literary hero. He drew constant inspiration from Yang's works, both adapting their diction and taking them as larger structural models for his own writings.[112] Yang Hsiung's literary principles have been summarized as "directness, plain diction, personal statement, and didacticism," all clear characteristics of Han Yü's own corpus.[113] The "Preface Seeing Off Meng Chiao" praises Ch'en Tzu-ang, Yüan Chieh, Li Po, and Tu Fu—all authors who achieved an immediate reputation for the unconventional—yet pointedly does *not* mention Hsiao Ying-shih, Li Hua, and Tu-ku Chi. Among his contemporaries, Han Yü's highest praise was reserved for Meng Chiao and Fan Tsung-shih, both masters of *ch'i*. If good literature is an expression of the moral values of the Sage and so possesses "integrity" in his own eyes, then his contemporaries will see his writings as "unconventional" and laud them or oppose them according to their own light.

A number of scholars have suggested various divisions of Han Yü's prose corpus into generic classifications. The following scheme is both traditional and representative:

1. Disquisitions (*lun-shuo*): for example, "Essentials of the Moral Way" and "Discourse on Teachers";

2. Dialogues (*wen-tui*): "Explication of 'Progress in Learning' " and "Explanatory Words";

3. Occasional Accounts (*tsa-chi*), with many subdivisions: (a) miscellaneous accounts such as the "Account of the Pavilion of Feasting and Joy" and the "Account of the I-ch'eng Post Station," (b) postfaces like the "Postface on Some Tadpole Script Calligraphy," (c) allegorical biographies like the "Biography of Fur Point," (d) scholarly notes like "On Read-

ing Mo-tzu," and finally (e) the famous "Miscellanea" (*tsa-shuo*);

4. Encomiums (*tsan-ming*): for instance, the "Eulogy for Po-i";

5. Letters and Reports (*shu-chi*), with two subdivisions: (a) letters, of which there are fifty-seven in Han Yü's corpus, and (b) memorials such as "A Memorial from the Censorate on the Subject of the Drought and Famine" and the "Memorial on the Buddha Relic";

6. Prefaces (*hsü*), with two subdivisions: (a) prefaces seeing someone off, of which there are thirty-four in Han Yü's corpus, and (b) prefaces to collections of poetry like the "Preface to Poems and Replies Between Ching and T'an";

7. Stele Inscriptions (*pei-chih*) with several subdivisions: (a) commemorative pieces like the "Inscription on the Pacification of Huai-hsi," (b) temple stele like the "Inscription at the Temple of the God of the South Sea," and (c) epitaphs, of which Han Yü's works contain fifty-two examples, like the "Epitaph for Fan Tsung-shih of Nan-yang" and the "Epitaph for Liu Tsung-yüan";

8. Laments and Offerings (*ai-chi*): for example, the "Lament for My Nephew" and the "Address to the Crocodiles";

9. *fu*, of which there are four examples of "old-style *fu*" such as the "*Fu* on Renewing my Purpose" and one "regulated *fu*," Han Yü's examination piece, the "*Fu* on the Clear Waters."[114]

Although Han Yü produced works of significant literary merit in all these generic classifications, his most consistent efforts, and thus his major influence on the development of Chinese prose, centered on the genres of preface, letter, and stele inscription, three genres that account for almost half his prose corpus. If, as Ch'ien Mu has suggested, Han Yü effected the transformation of Chinese prose by infusing it with the poetic qualities of "pure literature," then it is easy to see why Han Yü concentrated his efforts on these three genres. The social contexts from which these three genres arose afforded the author the greatest number of opportunities for the expression of the fullest range of possible human emotions. Circumstances and tradition had fixed the content of chancery documents like memorials and of scholarly notes like the disquisitions. These were not proper genres for the display of emotion. And we should remember that for Han Yü emotion was the basis of good literature: "whatever does not attain a state of equilibrium will sound forth."

Writings classified as stele inscriptions were thought to have descended from ancient monuments erected at sacred mountains. The major subgenre of epitaphs erected at burial sites, however, originated with Ts'ai Yung (132-192).[115] Because they could enhance the prestige of the newly emerging literati clans, epitaphs enjoyed great popularity in the mid-T'ang. Li Hua is reputed to have subsisted during certain periods of his life entirely from epitaph commissions. These epitaphs consisted of a prose introduction that recounted highlights of the subject's career and concluded with a verse eulogy. The form quickly atrophied, however, into stale recitations of the subjects' official positions connected by stereotyped formulas.[116] Han Yü used possibilities latent in the dual format of prose narration and verse recapitulation to explore important aspects of the deceased's emotional and psychological life. He wrote about the actual lives of his subjects, and about his own interaction with them, rather than about superficial details of their official careers. In short, he revived the genre by bringing its deceased subjects to life again as real individuals with real passions and concerns.

Although Han Yü wrote epitaphs on commission, his best works in the genre were written for those he knew—for his relatives and colleagues, for Li Kuan, Chang Ch'e, Meng Chiao, Fan Tsung-shih, and Liu Tsung-yüan. His "Epitaph for Ma Chi-tsu, Assistant Director of the Imperial Household Service" is an excellent example. Ma Chi-tsu (785-821) was the grandson of Ma Sui, first patron of Han Yü. In his epitaph, Han Yü passes quickly over the details of Ma Chi-tsu's official life to recall the largess of Ma Sui, the grandeur of his household, and his magnanimous treatment of the young Han Yü. Thus, although Han Yü seems not to have known the subject well, he used the occasion of his death to record the depth of his own gratitude to the Ma family.[117] Likewise, the epitaph for Chang Ch'e dwells on the years of Han Yü's exile to Yang-shan and on the friendship with Chang Ch'e that obviously did much to sustain him during those years. In the epitaph for Fan Tsung-shih, Han Yü admires Fan's prowess as a man of letters and uses the genre to expound their common ideas on literary theory. The "Epitaph for Liu Tsungyüan" is probably Han Yü's most psychologically penetrating and emotionally intense work in this genre. The tension arises from Han Yü's own emotional effort to reconcile his admiration for Liu's literary work with his distaste for Liu's politics. Han Yü solves this dilemma with the psychologically true observation that it was only Liu's political defeat and exile that turned him into a great writer.[118]

Several of Han Yü's greatest works are in the subgenre of stele inscriptions that commemorate significant places or events. Prominent among these is the "Inscription on the Lo Pool Temple in Liu-chou," composed in 823 for a temple to the spirit of Liu Tsung-yüan. This text opens with a narration of Liu Tsung-yüan's virtues and achievements during his tenure as prefect of Liu-chou and concludes with a hymn in the *sao* style for ritual use at the temple by the residents of Liuchou. Between these segments, however, is a section that relates Liu Tsung-yüan's prophecy of his impending death, his wish to have a temple constructed to house his spirit, the return of that spirit, and its retribution on an impious attendant. This section is written in a style reminiscent of the *chih-kuai* fiction of the Six Dynasties, a mode seemingly incongruous with the usual formality of the genre and with this text's serious beginning and conclusion. Yet Han Yü's skill as a master of many styles enabled him to merge the three segments into a harmonious whole.[119] A related text is the "Inscription on the Temple to the God of the South Sea," which relates the restoration of this temple at Kuang-chou, modern Canton, by K'ung K'uei (752-824), who served as governor there from 817 to 819. If the previous text attained its unconventionality by encompassing a section of *chih-kuai* fiction, this text achieves the same result by modeling itself on the florid descriptions characteristic of the Han dynasty *fu*. The following passage describing K'ung's return by river to Canton after sacrificing at the temple is representative:

> Then he closed the temple and turned round his prow,
> and a fortunate gale sped the sails along,
> while banners and pennants, yak-tails and standards
> flew high to darken the sun.
> Bell-drums sounded and rumbled,
> tall pipes wailed and clamored
> as soldiers strained at their oars,
> and master craftsmen sang in harmony.
> Vaulted turtles and long fishes
> leaped and jumped before and aft
> and from Heaven's zenith to Earth's nadir
> all showed forth high and open.[120]

This dazzling word magic, a technique borrowed from the Han *fu*, is fully appropriate to describe the pomp and triumph of K'ung K'uei's return from the sacrifice: the language of the style matches the content of the occasion.

Han Yü's most formidable achievement in the genre of stele inscriptions, and one of the best known works in his entire collection, is the "Inscription on the Pacification of Huai-hsi," composed to commemorate the victory of government armies over the separatist province of Huai-hsi in 817. Han Yü received this imperial commission on 22 February 818 and completed the work on 3 May 818, which he apparently considered a long time.[121] The work was unlike other commissions not only because the emperor himself requested it but also because Han Yü had long been personally and emotionally involved in the political and military struggles that culminated in the government victory. Han Yü's text makes full use of the combined prose/verse format of the inscription by twice narrating the details of the government victory, each time emphasizing different aspects of the story. The technique is reminiscent of the prosimetric formats common in Buddhist literature, canonical like the *Saddharmapuṇḍarīka* or popular like the *pien-wen*.[122] The preface or prose introduction to Han

Yü's inscription concentrates on the emperor's personal resolve to suppress the separatists and on the factual details of the military operation. The poetic text, however, is more expansive, concentrating on the psychological state of the various parties involved. Small details such as the laughter of the women of Ts'ai-chou as they greet the returning soldiers or the city gates left open at night underscore the emotional release among the population after the suppression of the rebels. These details culminate in the conclusion of the text, which returns to the theme of imperial resolve:

> That he gave no pardon and had no doubts
> sprang from the Son of Heaven's bright wisdom,
> and all efforts in this matter of Ts'ai
> were through his decision brought to this end.

Critics as early as Li Shang-yin recognized that Han Yü's work shattered contemporary notions of style by creating a "T'ang classic" that combined the expository tradition of the *Book of Documents* and the lyrical tradition of the *Book of Poetry*.[123]

Han Yü also revolutionized the genre of letters by broadening the social uses of the genre and enlarging its range of subject matter. Early examples of the letter such as Szu-ma Ch'ien's "Letter in Reply to Jen Shao-ch'ing" confined themselves to important moments in the lives of their authors; and although the *Wen hsüan* contained examples from the Wei Dynasty of letters on lighter topics, no author before Han Yü succeeded in combining the possibilities of these earlier prototypes into a cohesive genre capable of expressing the full range of human emotions.[124] In this respect, Han Yü's letters, read as a collection, seem almost modern in their scope. The famous three letters to the prime ministers of 795 are a public outcry of frustration; and the "Letter in Reply to Ts'ui Li-chih" is a private expression of the same frustration. Han Yü also took full advantage of the genre's potential to convey advice, as can be seen in his many letters to students about both specific and general literary questions. Other letters convey personal solace and encouragement such as the "Letter to Meng Chiao" and the "Letter to Ts'ui Ch'ün."[125] Finally, many letters such as those to Cheng Yü-ch'ing and Yü Ti concern details of Han Yü's bureaucratic life and his search for a patron. This variety established the parameters of the classical Chinese letter until the introduction of Western models in the twentieth century.

Han Yü's greatest contributions to Chinese prose occurred in the genre of preface. The pre-T'ang preface was an ill-defined category of works, consisting mostly of introductions to longer verse writings or to scholarly works.[126] The preface as a lyrical prose text composed to "see off" (*sung*) an individual on a journey is basically an innovation of the T'ang. Sometimes these works were actual prefaces to collections of poems composed at a party to see someone off, but often they stood alone as independent works. The many poems of parting and farewell banquets in the *Wen hsüan* confirm that in the Six Dynasties period verse compositions were usual on such occasions. It is thus hardly surprising that Han Yü's prefaces are the most lyrical in his prose corpus. Han Yü seems to have taken his lead for this development of the genre from Li Po, whose works contain two *chüan* of such prefaces. Again, it was the potential of the social occasion that afforded Han Yü the range of emotional expression found in the totality of his prefaces. Partings were a painful but necessary reality in the closely knit T'ang literati society. Friendships were intense and distances were long, so the parting was always fraught with hightened emotion. Han Yü's lesser efforts in this genre, such as the "Preface Seeing Off Ou Ts'e," are lyrical narrations of his relationship with the departing person. His better prefaces, however, maintain the lyrical intensity particular to the genre but shift the focus of the subject matter to concerns that the impending departure of the individual evokes. Han Yü uses the specific reality of the departure and the causes behind it to discourse on questions of larger, more general interest. Thus the preface for Ch'i Hao is a discourse on political ideology; the prefaces for Li I and Tung Shao-nan are exhortations to political and personal courage; the preface for Ch'en T'ung is literary criticism, and the preface for Kao Hsien treats of aesthetics. Ou-yang Hsiu thought that Han

Yü's "Preface Seeing Off Li Yüan on His Return to Winding Valley," a paean to the virtues of rustic life that enlarges into a meditation on the meaning of life itself, was the best single prose work of the T'ang dynasty.

Later critics often resorted to the vocabulary of poetry criticism to describe Han Yü's prefaces. Thus Liu Ta-k'uei (1698–1779) wrote that the preface for Tung Shao-nan is "profound and subtle: the reader feels its high passion and elevated tone but knows he can never attain them."[127] Ch'ien Mu even goes so far as to associate these prefaces with modern Chinese unrhymed "prose-poetry" written in imitation of Western models.[128] Indeed, if one disregards the often arbitrary assignment of individual works to specific genres by recourse to their titles or placement in a literary collection, many of Han Yü's works could pass as either prose or verse. A good example is the poem "How Abject." Another is "Alas for Master Tung: A Ballad," also written during the late 790s when Han Yü seemed to be trying consciously to blur the distinctions between prose and verse. Master Tung is the Tung Shao-nan of the 803 preface.

> The Huai River rises in the T'ung-po Mountains
> and rushes far to the east for a thousand leagues without
>   cease.
> The Fei River rises by its side
> and after a hundred leagues
> (not a thousand leagues) enters the Huai's currents.
>
> Among the counties of Shou-chou is An-feng
> and in the *chen-yüan* period of the T'ang
> Master Tung Shao-nan
> lived in retirement there and practiced what is right.
> The prefect could not recommend him,
> the Son of Heaven never heard his name.
> Neither rank nor salary reached his gate,
> beyond which were only bailiffs
> come daily to collect taxes and press for money.
>
> Alas for Master Tung!
> Mornings he went out to plough,

evenings he returned to read the books of the Ancients
(no rest the whole day long),
or he gathered firewood in the mountains
or he fished in the river.
He entered the kitchen to fix his parents the finest
    morsels
and rose in the hall to ask their health;
so his father and mother did not worry,
his wife and children did not grieve.
Master Tung was filial and kind;
yet no one knew him,
only the Old Man of Heaven knew
and sent good fortune and happy signs:
their house once had a nursing hound that went out to
    forage for food;
so the hens came to feed her young,
pecking in the courtyard for worms and ants
to feed the pups; and when these would not eat but
    whined sadly,
the hens lingered long about and would not leave,
spreading their wings to cover them and await the
    hound's return.

Alas for Master Tung!
What man is your equal?
The people of our time
(husbands and wives are cruel, brothers feud)
feed on the salary of their Lord
and bring sorrow to their parents.
What mind is this?
Alas Master Tung you have no equal.[129]

Line length in this poem varies from three to nine characters; there is a loose rhyme structure but no tonal patterning. The syntax is that of prose, with generous use of connective particles. Furthermore, the overall rhythm of the text, its leisurely, relaxed pace that generously admits the story of the hound and her pups, is more like prose than verse.

    Related to these issues is the question of Han Yü's role in

the development of Chinese fiction. Ch'en Yin-k'o first posited a relation between *ku-wen* and that genre of writings known as *ch'uan-ch'i* fiction in 1936, and the subject has drawn wide attention since that time.¹³⁰ Some scholars have argued that the looser syntax of *ku-wen* provided a more supple medium for the fictional dialogues and narration of *ch'uan-ch'i*; others have argued the opposite—that *ch'uan-ch'i* provided a popular example for the *ku-wen* style of Han Yü and Liu Tsung-yüan.¹³¹ A major complication is the as yet unresolved question of exactly what constitutes a *ch'uan-ch'i*. Recent scholarship has emphasized the fluid contours of the genre and suggested its strong affinities to obviously related genres such as the *chuan* "biography."¹³² Indeed, it is easier to link Han Yü's "fictional" works to the "biography" of traditional Chinese history writing than to contemporary *ch'uan-ch'i* like Yüan Chen's "Story of Ying-ying."¹³³ The intention of these *ch'uan-ch'i* pieces is to narrate a story that will arouse pleasurable emotions and so excite the reader. The narratives are often romantic, the language suggestive with no attempt to avoid the parallelism associated with the erotic literature of the late Six Dynasties. These qualities made the *ch'uan-ch'i* important sources for later drama and fiction, whereas *ku-wen* works in the *chuan* genre enjoyed no such influence.

Han Yü's major works in the *chuan* category are the "Biography of Fur Point," the "Biography of Wang Ch'eng-fu, the Mason," and the "Preface to the Linked Verses on the Stone Tripod."¹³⁴ These three texts exhibit a common *ku-wen* style, and all express the author's opinion on political realities through allegory and satire. Even though specific details of these topical allegories are no longer certain, their general character as didactic moralities is clear. They are not *ch'uan-ch'i* fiction. Nienhauser has deftly demonstrated the underlying analogy between Fur Point and the chief minister; the analogy between the mason and the minister is explicitly stated in the "Biography of Wang Ch'eng-fu." Stone tripods have been since ancient times an emblem of the state, and most critics also understand them as a figure for the minister.¹³⁵

Han Yü's efforts in the genre of allegorical biography, a genre related to but nevertheless distinct from the *ch'uan-ch'i*, are best understood as manifestations of his "ability to attain perfection in all styles" (*neng pei chung t'i*).[136] This was an acknowledged goal of *ku-wen* authors and seems to have reflected not only their ability to manipulate language through a variety of different styles but also their search for an underlying theory of style that would make possible the creation of a unified language appropriate for all genres. If Han Yü's *ku-wen* style was catholic enough to allow him to incorporate popular and fictional elements into his writings, his sense of Confucian didacticism prevented him from composing pure *ch'uan-ch'i* as did Yüan Chen and others.[137]

> Han Yü strove his whole life to emulate and to trace the works of Li Po and Tu Fu. But prior to Li Po and Tu Fu there was no one of their stature, so their brilliance was domineering and knew no restraint; each opened new vistas in his poetry and has remained unique for a thousand years.
>
> But for Han Yü's generation Li Po and Tu Fu already existed, so although he worked hard at innovation and change, in the end he could not open yet another path. Only among Tu Fu's unconventional and unprecedented (*ch'i hsien*) passages was there still some possibility for further development. So Han Yü fixed on these with a steady gaze, intending from them to open up new territory and form his own style. And it was here he focused his attention.
>
> But such passages have both good and bad aspects. Han Yü worked singlemindedly to perfect what Tu Fu had achieved through an occasional brilliant insight, and therefore one sometimes sees the scars of ax and chisel in Han Yü's poetry. It is the difference between being intentional and being unintentional.
>
> Yet Han Yü's poetry actually possesses its own distinctive flavor, which resides in the principle of diction that is fluid and apt—a flavor naturally powerful, intense,

267

expansive, and unpredictable. One cannot through unconventionality alone realize its merits. I am afraid even
Han Yü himself may not have realized this point, but if
you read him with an unbiased mind, you will realize it
for yourself. To seek Han Yü only in his unconventionality is to miss his essence.[138]

These remarks by Chao I (1727-1814) are among the keenest
observations ever made on the poetry of Han Yü. The great
Ch'ing critic correctly perceived that historical circumstances—in this case the existence of Li Po and Tu Fu in the
generation immediately preceding Han Yü's—created a literary background for Han Yü's experiences in poetry fully
opposite to that for his experiments in prose. As we have seen
above, there were no T'ang prototypes or exemplars for Han
Yü's innovations in prose; on the contrary, Yang Hsiung
seems to have been the last author whose prose style Han Yü
emulated. The towering genius of Li Po and Tu Fu, however,
had so fulfilled the potential of the traditional verse genres
that further innovation was possible only in a limited number
of already defined directions. One of these directions was
toward the "unconventional," as illustrated in the later poetry
of Tu Fu, a quality we have also seen as vital to Han Yü's
prose. But Chao I was careful to caution that although the
"unconventionality" of Tu Fu's later poetry was an important
point of departure for Han Yü's verse experimentations, it
cannot define the totality of his poetic work. Han Yü did
actually achieve his own individual style as a poet, a style
based on the same principle that infuses his prose work ("diction that is fluid and apt"), and a style Chao I finds "powerful,
intense, expansive, and unpredictable."[139]

We have encountered above the critical suggestion that the
distinctive power of Han Yü's poetry derives from his practice
of "making poetry from prose" (*i wen wei shih*). Several scholars have seen adumbrations of this theme in the comment of
Ou-yang Hsiu that "there was no turn the power of Han Yü's
pen could not accomplish, yet he often took poetry as a lesser
aspect of prose."[140] Ch'en Shih-tao's attribution of the fol-

lowing remarks to Huang T'ing-chien would seem to be the earliest use of the phrase *i wen wei shih*:

> Prose and poetry each have their own style; so when Han Yü makes poetry out of prose and when Tu Fu makes prose out of poetry, neither can achieve complete perfection.[141]

We have also seen above that this critique, although it makes a valid observation on the practical relation between Han Yü's poetry and his prose, is grounded in the assumption that there exists a finite line of demarcation between prose and verse and that to blur this line is to violate generally valid literary principles. This latter was a Sung concern, witnessed in the development of this theme from Ou-yang Hsiu through Ch'en Shih-tao; but these scholars projected their concern back to the T'ang, fusing it with their critique of Han Yü as poet.[142] Yet at the same time the Sung scholars questioned the theoretical foundations of Han Yü's poetry, they admired and imitated his exuberance and technical virtuosity as a poet. Even such avowedly anti - Han Yü authors as Wang An-shih looked to him as a major source of their own poetry.[143] The great Ch'ing critic Yeh Hsieh (1627-1703) rightly stressed Han Yü's role as the forebear of much Sung poetry:

> Han Yü was among the greatest innovators in T'ang poetry. He had great energy, a vigorous intellect, and so arose to become an originator. It can be said that in the Sung, Su Shun-ch'in, Mei Yao-ch'en, Ou-yang Hsiu, Su Shih, Wang An-shih, and Huang T'ing-chien were the culmination of what Han Yü first brought forth.[144]

One possible explanation for this Sung schizophrenia toward Han Yü as a poet may be related to the already noted Sung attitude toward him as a philosopher: because many of the theoretical and practical precedents for Han Yü's poetry were in Buddhist and/or Ch'an literature, the Sung Neo-Confucians, although they recognized the literary and aesthetic power of this literature, were embarrassed by the poverty of the Six Dynasties and T'ang Confucian literary

tradition that the existence of these precedents implied and
by the visibility of their own sizable debt to the Buddhist
literary tradition. Hu Shih called attention some time ago to
the popular nature of the prosaic verse used in such medieval
Chinese translations as the *Buddhacarita* of Aśvaghoṣa.[145] And
Ch'en Yin-k'o and others have suggested the existence of a
conscious *i wen wei shih* tradition extending from the early
Buddhist translators through Han Yü to the Sung poets.[146]
Another scholar has observed that the open, prosaic structure
of the poetic line used in Han Yü's verse narratives is stylistically similar to that used in popular *pien-wen* narratives: fluid
rhythms achieved through relaxation of the rigid patterns for
caesura deployment usual in literati verse, free use of particles,
a loose colloquial rhyme scheme, avoidance of allusion, and
little fear of repetition—all these features characterize both
bodies of verse.[147] The sum total of this evidence suggests
that the same drive for innovation that shaped Han Yü's prose
and created *ku-wen* also shaped his verse. In response to the
new social and intellectual priorities of his age, Han Yü undertook eclectically to reorder existing literary priorities so as
to expand the technical parameters and the thematic content
of Chinese verse.

There is considerable evidence that the same eclectic spirit
that formed Han Yü's concept of prose style also formed his
concept of style in poetry. Just as *ku-wen* prose could accom-
modate a wide spectrum of features from earlier styles so Han
Yü's *ku-wen* poetry could encompass a wide range of seemingly incompatible stylistic phenomena. Han Yü seems to
have envisioned these phenomena as congregating around two
poles, each representing a contrasting tendency of poetic diction. In "Drunk: For Secretary Chang," he described these
two poles, one as

> rough words that terrify even ghosts,
> exalted diction that matches the Three Emperors

and the other as

> the best treasures need no refining,
> inspired results without tilling.[148]

A later critic defined this first pole as "difficult, full of the unusual and innovative" (*chien ch'iung kuai pien*) and the second as "even and light" (*p'ing tan*).[149] Another passage from "Seeing Off the Master Wu-pen on his Return to Fan-yang" proves that Han Yü conceived these two poles not as opposites but rather as two extremes along a continuum of stylistic possibilities:

> As his mad diction, a free torrent of blooms,
> ebbs and flows, we see his joys and his woes;
> and when his unusual innovations are over,
> he has often created the even and light.[150]

The implication of this passage is that an "even and light" quality is an end result of the search for "unusual innovation" (*kuai pien*). "Even and light" is the result of earlier attempts at innovation; it is the final amalgamation of disparate stylistic features into a satisfying artistic whole.[151] Han Yü's last great poem, "First Trip to South Stream," with its many turns and transitions is often cited as a mature expression of "even and light," a harmonious blend that "is not Ancient and not T'ang, it's Han Yü's own."[152]

There is little doubt that Han Yü's expansive view of earlier literature, as reflected in the "Preface Seeing Off Meng Chiao," affected this conscious enlargement of the techniques and subject matters proper to verse. Thus Han Yü's early experimental poem "How Abject," an extreme example of "making poetry from prose," is modeled on *Chuang-tzu*.[153] But the experiment is based on the critical insight that much of the *Chuang-tzu* is indeed a kind of free verse that often afforded an indigenous model for later Chinese philosophical verse. Han Yü's critical realization that the rigid generic distinctions of "contemporary writing" possessed no historical validity beyond the Six Dynasties period supported and, in his own mind, no doubt justified his own literary practice, which strove to blur these artificial distinctions.

Prominent among Han Yü's methods to expand the parameters of verse composition was the cannibalization of techniques from other genres, especially from the *fu*.[154] We have

seen above an example of how Han Yü adapted the narrative
and descriptive qualities of this genre to a prose stele inscription. Two features common to *fu* and employed by Han Yü
to great effect in his poetry were the use of repeated, multiple
metaphor and careful choice of representative detail. The first
feature, a conspicuous accumulation of metaphors all describing the same—or different aspects of the same—reality, is well
illustrated by the four lines that immediately follow the above
quotation from "Seeing Off the Master Wu-pen on his Return
to Fan-yang." Each line is a metaphor both describing and
illustrating "even and light";

> flying cicadas gossamer on silk brocade,
> a green pool covered in water lilies,
> iris flowers peaking over wild shrubs,
> lone wings rising from strands of rush.[155]

The four metaphors, taken collectively, describe the delicately
crafted and unique "even and light" quality of Chia Tao's
verse. The most obvious example of this technique in Han
Yü's poetry in his "Poem on the Southern Mountains," long
sections of which are litanies of similes and metaphors describing various mountain configurations:

> some joined together
>   like followers
> or pressed
>   like in combat . . .
>
> some stacked up
>   like pots and pans
> or erect
>   like sacrificial urns
>
> or upturned
>   like terrapins sunning themselves
> or collapsed
>   like sleeping quadrupeds
>
> or undulating
>   like hidden dragons

or wings flapping
    like a captured condor.

These metaphors, along with other features of the poem, prompted the Sung scholar Hung Hsing-tsu (1090-1155) to liken this "Poem on the Southern Mountains" to the *fu* of Szu-ma Hsiang-ju.[156]

Another feature Han Yü borrowed from the *fu* is the careful concentration on narrative details that contributed to the overall meaning of the poem: minuteness of detail serves not only to enhance the visual reality of the scene but also to imbue that scene with its symbolic and representational value. A good example is the poem "The Pheasant Shot With an Arrow," written in Hsü-chou in 799 as a mild satire against Han Yü's then superior Chang Chien-feng.

Fires burn on the prairie
    quiet and relentless;
a wild pheasant fearing the hawk
    rises and drops again.
The general will awe
    his troops with skill,
circles his horse, draws his bow,
    but careful, not shooting;
space gets smaller,
    onlookers increase,
the pheasant startles, the bow is full,
    a strong arrow is off.
Pressed by people, then straight up
    a hundred feet
red feathers and white barb
    collide at angle.
Soliders congratulate; the general
    looks up and laughs,
as bright colors scattered and broken
    fall before the horse.[157]

Chu I-tsun has aptly remarked that in this poem "each line depicts a real scene." Indeed, although the poem is composed of a staccato repetition of assorted visual detail, many of these details contribute to a mood of subtle tension that in turn conveys the satirical message of the poem. This satire derives from the Han dynasty *fu* on hunts, where the detailed descriptions of opulent hunts were traditionally read as remonstrations against imperial extravagance. In this poem, Han Yü expresses his displeasure with Chang Chien-feng's ostentation through a similar use of detail—the circling horse, the drawn bow, the excited spectators, the laughing general, the cheering troops, the multicolored pheasant dropping in front of the general's horse.

The prosaic structure of Han Yü's verse line, his attention to concrete detail, and his obvious delight in the use and invention of metaphor have prompted some scholars to categorize Han Yü as a "baroque" poet.[158] Although there is good reason to caution against facile comparisons, recent work has done much to define the nature of a Chinese "baroque" style.[159] And the question would benefit by expanding the discussion to include the similarities between *ku-wen* and seventeenth-century European prose.[160] No one has yet noted, however, that the very features of both prose and verse that have been labeled "baroque" are often the same features that the formal literature of this period shared with the literary and aesthetic expression of Ch'an Buddhism. Again, this statement is not meant to imply a cause and effect relationship between the literary practice of the Ch'an school and of Han Yü, only to stress the existence of similarities between them and to suggest that these are parallel reactions to the realities of mid-T'ang intellectual and literary life. The minute attention to details of the physical world that characterizes the *yüan-ho* style in poetry—either as "baroque" in Han Yü or as "earthy" in Po Chü-i—is obviously paralleled in the Ch'an attention to the *realia* of the mundane world, in the insistence of the Ma-tsu school that "the ordinary mind is the Way." In short, I believe the "sense of the human delight in little things" that a critic has noticed in Han Yü's poetry is related to the Ch'an "emphasis on the particular . . . an unlimited acceptance of innumerable individual, particular events as representative of something inexpressable in abstract terms."[161] Han Yü shared with the Ch'an adepts a like desire to bring the language of written discourse into as close an accord as possible with the workings of the human mind, to make literature a clear reflection of the author thinking.[162]

ABBREVIATIONS

AM	*Asia Major*
BIHP	*Bulletin of the Institute of History and Philology, Academia Sinica*
BMFEA	*Bulletin of the Museum of Far Eastern Antiquities*
BSOAS	*Bulletin of the School of Oriental and African Studies*
Cam. Hist.	*The Cambridge History of China.* Vol. 3: *Sui and T'ang China*
Changes	Richard Wilhelm, trans., *The I Ching, or Book of Changes*
CLEAR	*Chinese Literature: Essays, Articles, Reviews*
CTS	*Chiu T'ang shu*
HJAS	*Harvard Journal of Asiatic Studies*
HS	*Han shu*
HTS	*Hsin T'ang shu*
JAOS	*Journal of the American Oriental Society*
JAS	*Journal of Asian Studies*
JRAS	*Journal of the Royal Asiatic Society*
PEW	*Philosophy East and West*
Poetry	*Han Ch'ang-li shih hsi-nien chi-shih*
Prose	*Han Ch'ang-li wen chi chiao-chu*
Rites	James Legge, trans., *Li Chi: Book of Rites*
SC	*Shih chi*
SPPY	*Ssu-pu pei-yao*
SPTK	*Ssu-pu ts'ung-k'an*
Taishō	*Taishō shinshu daizōkyo*
TCTC	*Tzu-chih t'ung-chien*
TP	*T'oung Pao*
TSCC	*T'u-shu chi-ch'eng*
WH	*Wen hsüan*
ZDMG	*Zeitschrift der Deutschen Morgenländischen Gesellschaft*

NOTES

Orientations

1. For these statistics see Hanabusa Hideki, *Kan Yu kashi sakuin* [A concordance to the poems of Han Yü], introduction pp. 67-69. The most detailed biographical study of Han Yü is Lo Lien-t'ien, *Han Yü yen-chiu* [Han Yü studies], pp. 1-136. This study carefully summarizes prior scholarship and contributes much that is new to the chronological arrangement of Han Yü's works.
2. See Ch'en Yin-k'o, "Lun Han Yü," pp. 105-114, reprinted in his *Ch'en Yin-k'o hsien-sheng lun-wen chi*, 2:589-600, and in Chou K'ang-hsieh, ed., *Han Yü yen-chiu lun-ts'ung* [Collected studies on Han Yü], pp. 1-10. On Ch'en Yin-ko's contribution to T'ang studies see Denis Twitchett, eds., *The Cambridge History of China*, vol. 3: *Sui and T'ang China, 589-906, Part 1* [hereafter cited as *Cam. Hist.*], pp. 10-11, and Paul Demiéville, "Nécrologie," pp. 136-143.
3. "Letter to Meng Chien," in Ma Ch'i-ch'ang, ed., *Han Ch'ang-li wen chi chiao-chu* [Han Yü's prose, collated and annotated; hereafter cited as *Prose*], p. 126.
4. "Preface to the Collection of the Master from Ch'ang-li," *Prose*, p. 3. For biographical details on Li Han and a complete translation of this preface see Charles Hartman, "Preliminary Bibliographical Notes on the Sung Editions of Han Yü's *Collected Works*," pp. 89-91.
5. For the attack on Ch'en see Huang Yün-mei, "Tu Ch'en Yin-k'o hsien-sheng 'Lun Han Yü' " [Reading Ch'en Yin-k'o's "On Han Yü"], pp. 23-35. For Ch'an-Confucian parallels see Yanagida Seizan, *Rinzai roku* [Dialogues of Lin-chi], pp. 285-291.
6. Edwin G. Pulleyblank, "Neo-Confucianism and Neo-Legalism in T'ang Intellectual Life, 755-805," p. 84.
7. Philip B. Yampolsky, trans., *The Platform Sutra of the Sixth Patriarch*, p. 139.
8. *Mencius* III.A.1; D. C. Lau trans., p. 94.

9. Thomas Cleary, trans., *Sayings and Doings of Pai-chang* (Los Angeles: Center Publications, 1978), p. 26.

10. Chang Chung-yuan, trans., *Original Teachings of Ch'an Buddhism*, p. 149.

11. This précis is based on Tu Sung-po, *Ch'an-hsüeh yü T'ang-Sung shih-hsüeh* [Ch'an and T'ang-Sung poetics], pp. 88-93.

12. Demiéville, "Les entretiens de Lin-tsi," p. 2. Although this notion is certainly not new with Ch'an—it has precedents in early Taoism and Indian *mādhyamika*—it seems to have enjoyed new popularity as a dialectic tool in the eighth century.

13. Ch'ien Chung-lien, ed., *Han Ch'ang-li shih hsi-nien chi-shih* [The poetry of Han Yü arranged chronologically with collected annotations; hereafter cited as *Poetry*], p. 7; Erwin von Zach, trans., *Han Yü's poetische Werke*, p. 152. The quotation "Antiquity is now" is from *Chuang-tzu* (Harvard-Yenching ed.) 60/22/70,71; Burton Watson, trans., *The Complete Works of Chuang-tzu*, pp. 245-246.

14. The foregoing is not meant to suggest the identity of Ch'an and the Confucian revival of the T'ang but rather to emphasize that because both movements arose at the same time and in response to the same social, political, and intellectual circumstances, so both often manifest similar concerns and methodologies. There were of course also profound differences. Ch'an, for all its violent antischolastic temper, remained essentially a Buddhist school, rejecting the philosophical reality of the visible world and of social obligations, in contrast to the Confucian embrace of both. A ramification important for the history of Chinese literature was that whereas Confucians maintained that *wen* "literature" was perfectly adequate to express the spiritual perfection of the *tao* "moral Way," the Ch'an adepts held that language could never adequately express enlightenment.

15. Cf. Thomas A. Metzger, *Escape from Predicament* (New York: Columbia University Press, 1977), p. 74: ". . . even if one can refute the thesis that Buddhism positively supplied the main metaphysical formulae of Neo-Confucianism, the effects of Buddhism can be seen in the agenda of issues and criteria of validity shaping Neo-Confucian thought."

16. *T'ang-tai cheng-chih shih shu-lun kao* [A draft political history of the T'ang] in Ch'en Yin-k'o, *Ch'en Yin-k'o hsien-sheng lun-wen chi*, 1:174-179.

17. Cf. the fine summation in Timothy Hugh Barrett, "Buddhism,

Taoism and Confucianism in the Thought of Li Ao," p. 213: "The foregoing examination of the circumstances of composition of the *Fu hsing-shu* suggests that its author was, under the influence of Han Yü, attempting to write as a Confucian to friends more favorably inclined to Buddhism and Taoism."

18. Quoted by Han Yü in "Essentials of the Moral Way" (*Prose*, pp. 9-10) from *Li chi chu-shu* (*SPPY* ed.) [*Great Learning*] 60/1a-2b. Throughout this book, I refer to this passage as the "*Great Learning* catenation" after its rhetorical form—a chain of phrases constructed such that a prominent word in the latter half of one clause is repeated at the beginning of the next clause. One such link constitutes anadiplosis; extended repetition of the pattern is *gradatio* in Latin and in English is sometimes also referred to as "climax." See Heinrich Lausberg, *Elemente der literarischen Rhetorik* (Munich: Hueber, 1967), pp. 84-85.

19. It is possible than Han Yü's focus on the *Great Learning* catenation and its ultimate equation of thought and action may derive from the Ch'an Buddhist equivalence of mind and action. For perceptive remarks on Han Yü and other contemporary thinkers as important forerunners of Sung Neo-Confucianism see Ch'ien Mu, "Tsa-lun T'ang-tai ku-wen yün-tung" [Notes on the *ku-wen* movement of the T'ang], pp. 156-166.

20. From Han Yü's "Poem on the Sagacious Virtue of Primal Harmony," written as a paean to Emperor Hsien-tsung. See *Poetry*, p. 281.

21. *Li chi chu-shu* (*SPPY* ed.) [*Doctrine of the Mean*] 53/1a-2a. Cf. James Legge, trans., *Li Chi: Book of Rites* [hereafter cited as *Rites*], 2:317-319.

22. *Mencius* VII.A.4: Lau trans., p. 182.

23. Many of these same motifs are contained in a long and perceptive paragraph on Han Yü in Georges Margouliès, *Histoire de la littérature chinoise: Prose*, pp. 169-171:

> The genesis of Han Yü's work is clear: ever since his youth, he lived near the disciples of Li Hua and his contemporaries and received their teaching. All preparatory labors having been finished, in his work he had only to realize the acquired outcome: to produce finally a *ku-wen* model embracing all genres, a unique style that could render the ideas of all branches of literature. Yet it would be unjust to reduce his role to a simple promulgation of something already created and ready for use. He had to join solidly the diverse parts

from which the new manner was composed—the attainments of many generations and schools—and to form from these a coherent whole; and above all he had to render this style alive, to find for it a soul in harmony with its means of expression. The great, the immense merit of Han Yü—that which makes it impossible for him, even though he was above all a man of his own time, ever to forfeit the unique place the literary history of China assigns to him—is precisely to have learned how to discover this soul of the *ku-wen* style, a soul that corresponds to its own universal character. The impersonal method to which Chinese authors readily took recourse necessitated continual changes in style; objectivity obliged the author to change his style when he changed his subject. Consequently, Han Yü chose the opposite point of view and judged things not outside of himself but always in relation to his own personality, and this permitted him to maintain a great unity throughout all subjects and genres. *Ku-wen* was a style destined for all uses; from lamentations and petitions to private letters and stories. Under the pen of Han Yü the spirit that animated this style was the tableau of the life of an everyday man, his hopes and disappointments, his everyday feelings and sufferings—a spirit of universality equal at least to that of the style. Among all Chinese authors, Han Yü is indisputably the one who speaks the most about himself, about his personal and private affairs. One could say that he is so filled with these feelings and with his own life that he can hardly ever think of anything else and that he constantly comes back to his own life no matter what the subject of his composition may be. However, the imprint of his talent makes this life—itself without remarkable events, woven of petty hopes and humiliations, of minor daily vexations—through its very down to earth character extend its importance from a particular case to the general. Never has an author been so intimate, had so few hidden feelings; and yet because of the sincerity of his emotion and the breath of life that one can feel vibrating in his writings with an intensity unequaled in Chinese literature, instead of displaying only the life of Han Yü, his work displays life itself, the human soul.

24. See Wing-tsit Chan, trans., *Reflections on Things at Hand*, pp.

64-65, and Olaf Graf, *Tao und Jen*, p. 111. For Chu Hsi's thoughts on *tao* and *wen* see Ch'ien Mu, ed., *Chu-tzu hsin hsüeh-an* [A new casebook for Chu Hsi], 5:158-162.

Chapter One

1. The *Yüan-ho hsing tsuan* [A compendium of surnames from the *yüan-ho* period] completed by Lin Pao in 812 lists four Han clans in the T'ang, all descended from Han Hsin. See Ts'en Chung-mien, ed., *Yüan-ho hsing tsuan ssu-chiao chi*, 1:357-369. The information on the Han clans in this work basically tallies with the genealogical tables in Ou-yang Hsiu and Sung Ch'i, *Hsin T'ang shu* [New T'ang history; hereafter cited as *HTS*] 73A/2854-2873. For the pre-Ch'in principality of Han, see Szu-ma Ch'ien, *Shih chi* [Records of the historian; hereafter cited as *SC*] 54/1865-1878, trans. Édouard Chavannes, *Les mémoires historiques de Se-ma Ts'ien*, 1:197-223; H. G. Creel, *Shen Pu-hai*, pp. 15-20; and Henri Maspero, *China in Antiquity*, pp. 229-230. Szu-ma Ch'ien's account of Han Hsin is in *SC* 93/2631-2636, trans. Burton Watson, *Records of the Grand Historian of China*, 1:233-238.

2. Biographies of Han Yü's sixth-century ancestors are included in *Wei shu* [History of the Wei dynasty] (Peking: Chung-hua, 1974), 51/1127-29. See also Wolfram Eberhard, *Das Toba-Reich Nordchinas*, p. 38, family number 26. For Han Yü's own account of his ancestry see "Epitaph for Han Chi (750-806), Kuo-chou Bureau of Finance," *Prose*, pp. 320-321.

3. Li Po's inscription for Han Chung-ch'ing (see note 4 below) records Han Jui-su's honorific title as *ch'ao-san tai-fu* (fifth degree fourth class), which corresponds exactly to the statutory rank of a chief administrator at Kuei-chou (*HTS* 43A/1105; Robert des Rotours, trans., *Traité des fonctionnaires et traité de l'armée*, 2:705). Such rank would have entitled one of his sons to a position requiring rank of the eighth degree fourth class (Robert des Rotours, trans., *Le Traité des examens*, p. 225). On the governments-general during the early T'ang see Twitchett, *Cam. Hist.*, pp. 203-205. On Han Yü's ancestry see Lo Lien-t'ien, *Han Yü yen-chiu*, pp. 5-8; and Maeno Naoaki, *Kan Yu no shōgai* [The life of Han Yü], pp. 3-13.

4. *Fen-lei pien-tz'u Li T'ai-po wen* (*SPTK* ed.) 30/384-385. Li Po was commissioned to write this text by Han Chung-ch'ing's successor

as Magistrate of Wu-ch'ang, one Wang T'ing-lin. For dating the composition of the text to 759-760, see Yen Keng-wang, *T'ang p'u shang ch'eng lang piao* [Tables of high officials in the Department of Affairs of State during the T'ang], 2:468-469.

5. Denis Twitchett, *Financial Administration under the T'ang Dynasty*, pp. 67, 91-92, 180-181, and *Cam. Hist.*, p. 478; *HTS* 41/1068-69.

6. This anecdote is recorded in the *Lung-ch'eng lu*, attributed to Liu Tsung-yüan, but shown by Hans Frankel to date from the eleventh century (see Frankel, "The Date and Authorship of the *Lung-ch'eng lu*," pp. 129-149). The text of this anecdote is cited after Ch'ien Chi-po, *Han Yü chih* [Monograph on Han Yü], p. 29. On Han Chung-ch'ing's last post see Li Ao, "The Life of the Lord Han Yü, Late Vice-President of the Ministry of Personnel, Grand Pillar of State, and Posthumous President of the Ministry of Rites," in Kao Pu-ying, ed., *T'ang-Sung wen chü-yao* [Essential T'ang and Sung prose], 2:555, and Huang-fu Shih, "Epitaph for Han Yü," *Huang-fu chih-cheng wen-chi* (*SPTK* ed.) 6/4b, reprinted in Liang Jung-jo, *Wen-hsüeh shih-chia chuan* [Biographies of ten Chinese authors], p. 117.

7. Denis Twitchett, "The Composition of the T'ang Ruling Class," p. 82. See also Twitchett, "Chinese Social History from the Seventh to the Tenth Centuries," pp. 47-49.

8. See Liu Hsü, *Chiu T'ang shu* [Old T'ang history; hereafter cited as *CTS*] 38/1425-26, *HTS* 39/1009-10. Confusion from the mistaken attribution of Han Yü as a "native of Teng-chou" in *HTS* 176/5255 has generated an enormous literature on Han Yü's "native place." Although this was known to be Meng-hsien as early as the Ming dynasty, one still finds careless references to Han Yü as a native of Teng-chou. The literatus Keng Yü (1430-1496) (L. Carrington Goodrich, ed., *Dictionary of Ming Biography* [New York: Columbia University Press, 1976], 1:713) determined in 1485 that the old "Han family manor" was located 3.3 miles west of Meng-hsien and that Han Yü's tomb was also located there (Cheng Chih-chou, *Huai-ch'ing fu chih* [1518 ed.] 2/18a, 10/12b, 10/22a, 12/40b-41b). The great Ming Confucian Ho T'ang (1474-1543) (Goodrich, *Ming Biography*, 1:518-520), who was a native of the area, did much to further the memory of Han Yü by participating in the refurbishing of a temple to Han Yü in Meng-hsien in 1517 (Ho T'ang, *Ho Wen-ting kung wen-chi* [1576 ed.] 7/13b-19a). The *Huai-ch'ing fu chih* of 1789 reports (5/18a) that a local official in the early fifteenth century appropriated an "unholy

temple" near the Han ancestral tombs for another "Han Yü temple" and that this structure was turned into a "Ch'ang-li Academy" by Li Hua-lung (1554-1611) in 1589 during his service as Ho-nan director of education (Goodrich, *Ming Biography*, 1:823).

During the Ch'ing, this area was called the Yin Hamlet and belonged to a "Su family manor." The *Huai-ch'ing fu chih* of 1789 states (4/32a) that this site contained the tombs of all Han Yü's ancestors beginning with Han Mao of the Northern Wei. This seems extremely unlikely. The same work carries the fascinating story (27/19b) that the local peasants of the area destroyed the stele containing Huang-fu Shih's "Grave Inscription for Han Yü" (*Han Wen-kung shen-tao pei*) because they were too often disturbed by the endless stream of literati stopping to take rubbings. The same gazetteer also reprints (29/56-57b) the excellent essay "On Han Yü's Tomb at Meng-hsien" (*Meng-hsien Han Wen-kung mu k'ao*) by the early Ch'ing scholar Liu Ch'ing-li (1664-1709). This text relates that in the late Ming graverobbers unearthed from a tumulus south of the Yin Hamlet and then discarded in the bush a small stele that a woodcutter later found and took home for use as a chopping block. A local mandarin discovered and identified the stele as the funeral inscription of Han Yü's oldest son, Han Ch'ang, and it was placed in the Meng-hsien temple to Han Yü. People claiming to be Han Yü's descendants still lived in Meng-hsien in the mid-eighteenth century (19/33a).

Discussions on Han Yü's "native place" may be found in Ts'en Chung-mien, "T'ang chi chih i" [Notes on some texts of the T'ang dynasty], pp. 54-57, and in the excellent article by Chao Yü-ying, "Han Yü hsiang-li pien-lüeh" [On Han Yü's hometown], pp. 91-101. See also Lo Lien-t'ien, *Han Yü yen-chiu*, pp. 1-4.

9. William Hung, *Tu Fu*, pp. 90-91, 140-141.

10. Chao Yü-ying, "Han Yü," p. 100. Kubo Tenzui, *Kan Taishi*, p. 20, states flatly that Han Chung-ch'ing died in Lo-yang and that Han Yü was born there. Lo Lien-t'ien, *Han Yü yen-chiu*, p. 29, believes Han Yü was born in Ch'ang-an; Maeno Naoaki, *Kan Yu*, p. 16, suggests Han Chung-ch'ing may still have been in P'o-yang at the time.

11. "Ballad of the Three Constellations," *Poetry*, pp. 286-287, trans. in Edward H. Schafer, *Pacing the Void*, pp. 59-60. Su Shih (1036-1101) was born under the same moon sign and expressed sympathy with Han Yü's fate.

12. "Lament for Madam Cheng," *Prose*, pp. 194-195.

13. See especially Ch'ien Mu, "Tsa-lun T'ang-tai ku-wen yün-tung," pp. 126-132, and Lo Lien-t'ien, *Han Yü yen-chiu*, pp. 203-220.

14. "Postface on Some Tadpole Script Calligraphy," *Prose*, pp. 54-55. Li Ao, who married Han Yün-ch'ing's granddaughter, also praised his literary achievements in similar terms (*Li Wen-kung chi* [SPTK ed.] 15/69-70). For Han Yün-ch'ing's works see *Ch'üan T'ang wen* [Complete T'ang prose] 441/10b-17a. Cf. also Ts'en Chung-mien, "T'ang chi chih i," p. 47, and his *Yüan-ho hsing tsuan ssu-chiao chi*, 1:336.

15. Sometime between 761 and 768 Han Shen-ch'ing was on the staff of Ts'ui Yüan (703-768), the governor-general of Yang-chou. When he publicly reproached his superior for endangering his administration by conducting an open sexual relationship with a commoner, Ts'ui admitted his error and fined himself 500,000 cash. See *Prose*, p. 321.

16. *CTS* 130/3625. Han Yü's inscription for Lu Tung-mei commissioned by the latter's son in 807 (*Prose*, pp. 204-205) confirms this account of the "Four K'uei."

17. Bernard Karlgren, trans., "Book of Documents," p. 7.

18. See the *T'ang kuo-shih pu* completed by Li Chao in 825, p. 58. "Singing" (*ko*) is perhaps best understood in this context as "composing poetry with socially relevant content." Pulleyblank's "Neo-Confucianism," pp. 84-85, has an excellent discussion of these texts.

19. "Epitaph for Han P'ang" (Han Hui's grandson), *Prose*, pp. 322-323. Cf. the similar statement that Han Hui "was preeminent in his age for his moral and literary abilities" (*tao-te wen-hsüeh*), *Prose*, p. 204.

20. "Passing Hsi-lin Monastery, Written on the Old House of Hsiao Ts'un," *Poetry*, pp. 525-526. Cf. Chao Lin, *Yin hua lu*, pp. 23-24; *HTS* 202/5770; and Pulleyblank, "Neo-Confucianism," p. 86.

21. Lo Lien-t'ien, *Han Yü yen-chiu*, pp. 139-140. Cf. *HTS* 203/5779.

22. For instance *HTS* 203/5776, which says that Li Hua encouraged Han Hui and Han Yün-ch'ing. One T'ang reference often cited to demonstate a relationship between Han Hui and Liang Su is Liu Tsung-yüan's list of his father's friends, where both are mentioned (*Liu Tsung-yüan chi*, 1:301). Central to this question is a text known as the "Biography of Han Hui" (*Han Hui chuan*) by the late Northern Sung scholar Wang Chih, on which see the excellent note by Pulleyblank, "Neo-Confucianism," pp. 324-325.

The core of this text is the "Balance of Literature"(*Wen heng*), supposedly the only surviving work of Han Hui. Although I believe this text to be genuine, the surrounding "biography" consists of extracts from the *New T'ang History* and from Han Yü's own writings spliced together to emphasize Han Hui's, and thus Han Yü's, relationship to the Li-Hsiao group. Although the exact purpose of this overemphasis remains unclear, it is certainly related to the desire of the Sung Neo-Confucians to trace their intellectual heritage as far back as possible and to the resulting Sung interest, clearly reflected in the *New T'ang History*, in the Li-Hsiao group. On this latter point see David McMullen, "Historical and Literary Theory in the Mid-Eighth Century," pp. 320-321.

23. Li Hsi-chün was the father of Li Chi-fu; see *HTS* 146/4735-37. Li also employed Hsiao Ts'un (*HTS* 202/5770). On Ts'ui Tsao, see *CTS* 130/3625-27, *HTS* 150/4813-14, and *Cam. Hist.*, pp. 589-592. The diarists of activity and repose (sixth degree third class) recorded the emperor's words, proclamations, and edicts as source material for the state history (des Rotours, *Fonctionnaires*, 1:287).

24. *Cam. Hist.*, pp. 496-497, 576-579.

25. *CTS* 11/311; Szu-ma kuang, *Tzu-chih t'ung-chien* [hereafter cited as *TCTC*] 225/7241-43. The great Sung Han Yü scholar Fang Sung-ch'ing (1135-1194) observed that Han Hui's exile to distant Shao-chou in modern Kwangtung province was harsher than what the other members of the Yüan faction received. He speculates that Han Hui was actually exiled twice, and that the second exile was the work of the "slanderers" referred to both by Han Yü (*Prose*, p. 194) and by Liu Tsung-yüan (*Liu Tsung-yüan chi*, 1:301). This explanation would also explain why the Han family seems not to have arrived in Shao-chou until 779. See Lo Lien-t'ien, *Han Yü yen-chiu*, pp. 30-31.

26. Huang-fu Shih, "Epitaph for Han Yü," p. 117. For other texts confirming Han Yü's early literary ability see Ch'ien Mu, "Tsa-lun," pp. 128-131.

27. Ch'en Yin-k'o, "Lun Han Yü," p. 206; Yampolsky, *Platform Sutra*, pp. 27, 93, 125.

28. The exact date of Han Hui's death is conjecture. Maeno Naoaki (*Kan Yu*, p. 23) argues for 778; Ch'ien Mu ("Tsa-lun," p. 129) says 779. I follow Hanabusa Hideki, *Kan Yu kashi sakuin*, p. 377, and Shimizu Shigeru, *Kan Yu*, p. 190. For the 781-785 rebellions see *Cam. Hist.*, pp. 499-507; for the Hsüan-ch'eng estate see Pul-

leyblank, "Neo-Confucianism," p. 85 and p. 324 n.24, and *Poetry*, pp. 565-566.

29. *"Fu* Written in Response to Two Birds," *Prose*, p. 1. Cf. *Prose*, p. 177, for a similar statement. Han Yü also speaks about literature as a family "profession" in *Prose*, p. 205.

30. *Prose*, pp. 3-4. On this *fu* see Yamasaki Jun'ichi, "Kan Yu no kofu ni tsuite" [On Han Yü's old-style *fu*], pp. 28-32.

31. "Letter in Reply to Feng Su," written in 807; *Prose*, p. 112.

32. *Poetry*, p. 3; Mori Kainan, *Kanshi kōgi* [An exposition of Han Yü's poetry], 2:60-62; Yoshikawa Kōjirō, "Kan Yu," pp. 335-337.

33. The account is based mainly on Rgyal-bcan's biography in *Ts'e-fu yüan-kuei* 998/9a-11a, most of which is incorporated in the biographies of Li Sheng (*CTS* 133/3661ff., *HTS* 154/4863ff.), Ma Sui (*CTS* 134/3700-01, *HTS* 155/4889-90), and Hun Chen (*CTS* 134/3708-09, *HTS* 155/4894). See also *CTS* 12/357, *HTS* 7/195, and *CTS* 196B/5247-53, trans. in Paul Pelliot, *Histoire ancienne du Tibet*, pp. 43-54; also Paul Demiéville, *Le concile de Lhasa*, p. 182 n.3 and pp. 291-292 n.1. Most important is Li Kuan's "Elegy for Han Yen, Lost Among the Barbarians" composed in 791 (*T'ang wen ts'ui* 33B/615-6), which relates that five years after his disappearance there was still no definite word in Ch'ang-an as to the final fate of Han Yen. This information does not necessarily conflict with the statement of *CTS* 196B/5252 that Han Yen was killed by marauding soldiers, since this fact could have come to light after the composition of Li Kuan's "Elegy." This text is extremely important, however, because it confirms that at least before 791 it was not known whether Han Yen was dead or alive. This uncertainty may have contributed to the warm reception Han Yü received from Ma Sui. Many of those present at the debacle at P'ing-liang later influenced Han Yü's life: Lü Wen (772-811), later a prominent *ku-wen* writer, then aged fifteen, was wounded defending his superior and released by Rgyal-bcan; also released were the eunuch Chü Wen-chen, later instrumental in the ascension of Emperor Hsien-tsung to the throne, and Ma Yen, older brother of Ma Sui.

34. Han Yen's wife, née Wei (770-801), was later taken into Han Yü's household. Her daughter at age fourteen was married to Li Ao in 800. See note 14.

35. For Han Yen's *chin-shih* see Hung Hsing-tsu's *Han-tzu nien-p'u*

3/5b (p. 15). His name is not included in Hsü Sung, *Teng-k'o chi k'ao* 11/29b (p. 746).

36. "Epitaph for Ma Chi-tsu, Assistant Director of the Imperial Household Service," *Prose*, pp. 310-311. Ma Chi-tsu (785-821) was the grandson of Ma Sui and the son of Ma Ch'ang (767-812), the young friend whom Han Yü mentions. See Shimizu Shigeru, *Tō-Sō hakkabun*, 1:110-118, for a good explication of this text.

37. Following Ma Sui's death in 795, the eunuchs appropriated this mansion. The grounds were turned into the Feng-ch'eng gardens, and the buildings dismantled and their valuable woods confiscated into the inner palace (Li Chao, *T'ang kuo-shih pu*, p. 36). When Ma Ch'ang died in 812, the family property and fortune were exhausted (*CTS* 134/3701-02, *HTS* 155/4890-91). T'ang poets often used the sad fate of Ma Sui's mansion as an example of worldly impermanence. See Ch'en Yin-k'o's comments on Po Chü-i's "Apricot-wood are the Rafters" and "Grieving over a Mansion" in *Yüan Po shih chien cheng kao* [Draft notes on the poetry of Po Chü-i and Yüan Chen] in *Ch'en Yin-k'o hsien-sheng lun-wen chi*, 2:243-247. Cf. also Arthur Waley, *The Life and Times of Po Chü-i*, pp. 17-18 and 218.

38. I am inclined to believe Han Yü took his provincial examinations in Ch'ang-an. Graduates of the metropolitan district enjoyed greater literary renown than those who actually passed these examinations in the "provinces." They also had the extra advantage of direct access to the Ministry of Rites, which reviewed and approved results of the provincial examinations. For more information on the provincial examinations see Ku Li-san, "T'ang-tai chih kung-chü chih-tu" [The T'ang examination system], pp. 41-45; Hung, *Tu Fu*, p. 26; Waley, *Po Chü-i*, pp. 16-17; des Rotours, *Examens*, p. 37; and *HTS* 19/435ff.

39. For the examinations of 788 and 789 see Hsü Sung, *Teng-k'o chi k'ao* 11/21b-221 (pp. 790-791) and 12/26b (p. 800); for Liu T'ai-chen see *CTS* 137/3762-63, *HTS* 203/5781, and Yen Keng-wang, *T'ang p'u shang ch'eng lang piao*, 3:866-867.

40. "In Praise of the Trees with Interlocking Branches at Ho-chung," *Prose*, p. 46; "Letter to Governor Chia Tan of Hua-chou," *Prose*, pp. 383-384.

41. On Tu Huang-shang see *CTS* 147/3974-75, *HTS* 169/5145-47, and *Cam. Hist.*, pp. 622-624. For Han Yü's three *chih-shih* examination failures see Lo Lien-t'ien, *Han Yü yen-chiu*, pp. 33-40.

42. *T'ang hui-yao* 76/1384. On Ts'ui Yüan-han see *CTS* 137/3766-67, *HTS* 203/5783-84.
43. "Letter to Lu Ts'an, Auxiliary Secretary in the Bureau of Sacrifices," written in 802 when Han Yü recommended ten *chin-shih* candidates to Lu Ts'an, who was at that time assistant examiner to Ch'üan Te-yü (759-818), *Prose*, pp. 116-118. Han Yü says elsewhere (*The Veritable Record of the T'ang Emperor Shun-tsung*, trans. Bernard S. Solomon, p. 38) that Lu Chih's selection as prime minister was due to his successful supervision of the 792 examinations. The eight candidates recommended by Liang Su may be the same eight mentioned in the *HTS* biography (203/5787) of Ou-yang Chan as constituting the "Dragon-Tiger Board." These are, according to their ranking in the examination: Ou-yang Chan (d.801?, c.f. Lo Lien-t'ien, *Han Yü yen-chiu*, pp. 140-145), Li Kuan (766-794, cf. Lo Lien-t'ien, *Han Yü yen-chiu*, pp. 138-140), Feng Su (767-836), Wang Yai (c.760-835), Han Yü, Li Chiang (764-830), Yü Ch'eng-hsüan, and Ts'ui Ch'ün (772-832). A total of twenty-three candidates passed; Han Yü ranked fourteenth. See Hsü Sung, *Teng-k'o chi k'ao* 13/1a-5a. Ts'en Chung-mien, "Pa T'ang chih-yen," pp. 253-254, has shown that the anecdote recorded in the *T'ang chih-yen* (7/80-81) by Wang Ting-pao in which Li Kuan, Han Yü, Li Chiang, and Ts'ui Ch'ün waited three years to see Liang Su is problematic. He argues the story is an expanded version of the *CTS* 159/4190 account of an interview between Liang Su and Ts'ui Ch'ün. Even if true, the story hardly implies that Liang Su personally supported Han Yü.
44. On this examination see des Rotours, *Examens*, pp. 219-222; Waley, *Po Chü-i*, pp. 27-28; Solomon, *Veritable Record*, p. 38.
45. "Letter to Ts'ui Yüan-han of the Bureau of Scrutiny," *Prose*, pp. 384-386, and "Letter in Reply to Ts'ui Li-chih," *Prose*, pp. 96-98. The prime minister in question was probably Chao Ching (737-797) or Chia Tan. For the dispute between Lu Chih and P'ei Yen-ling see Solomon, *Veritable Record*, pp. 39-41, and *Cam. Hist.*, pp. 597-598. Cf. also Hsü Sung, *Teng-k'o chi k'ao* 13/16a, 13/25a, and 14/2a, and Lo Lien-t'ien, *Han Yü yen-chiu*, pp. 43-45.
46. "Letter to President Hsing at Feng-hsiang," *Prose*, pp. 118-119. Hsing Chün-ya assumed Li Sheng's position at Feng-hsiang after the debacle of 787 and remained at this post until his death in 798. See *CTS* 144/3925-26, *HTS* 156/4908-09.
47. For the three letters see *Prose*, pp. 89-95. The second letter, in which Han Yü compares himself to a man who is drowning or

on fire calling for help, is translated in Georges Margouliès, *Le kou-wen chinois*, pp. 203-205. There were three prime ministers during the spring of 795: Chao Ching, Chia Tan, and Lu Mao (739-798). See *HTS* 62/1706.

48. On May 29, 795 at the T'ung-kuan Pass about halfway to Lo-yang, Han Yü encountered a "tribute" mission from his native Ho-yang delivering two auspicious birds—an albino crow and an albino myna—to the court. The encounter resulted in the "*Fu* on Being Moved by Two Birds," a powerful allegory written in *sao* style that is probably Han Yü's best *fu* and traditionally the first piece in his collected works. See *Prose*, pp. 1-3; Margouliès, *Histoire*, p. 181; and Yamasaki Jun'ichi, "Kan Yu no kofu ni tsuite," pp. 23-28.

49. *Poetry*, pp. 17-19; Harada Kenyū, *Kan Yu*, pp. 49-52; Mori Kainan, *Kanshi kōgi*, 2:507-511. Ch'ien Chung-shu has a fine discussion of this poem in his review of *Poetry* in *Wen-hsüeh yen-chiu*, no.2 (1959): 181-182.

50. *Analects* XVII.17, "The Master said, 'I would prefer not speaking.' " *Chuang-tzu* 75/27/6; Watson trans., p. 304. For Ch'an references see Komazawa daigaku, *Zengaku daijiten*, 2:1204b.

51. A pun reinforces this interpretation. *Wan fen*, "a myriad grave mounds," could also mean "a myriad books" on the analogy of *san fen*, "the books of the three mythical emperors of Antiquity," as used in Han Yü's poem "Drunk: Sent to Secretary Chang," *Poetry*, p. 179.

52. See Han Yü's epitaph for his mother-in-law, née Miao (735-803), *Prose*, pp. 316-317, and for his brother-in-law Lu Yü-ling (772-807), *Prose*, pp. 318-319. For this branch of the Lu clan see *HTS* 73A/2923. Cf. also Lo Lien-t'ien, *Han Yü yen-chiu*, pp. 15-16.

53. *Prose*, pp. 252-253. Cf. also Han Yü's early poem "Green are the Rushes in the Water," which some critics understand as referring to his wife, *Poetry*, pp. 11-12. It is not possible to date Han Yü's marriage with certainty. The earliest reference to children is in 798.

54. This account is based on Han Yü's own life (*hsing-chuang*) of Tung Chin (*Prose*, pp. 331-336), which served as the base for his biographies in *CTS* 146/3934-37 and *HTS* 151/4819-21. Cf. also *TCTC* 235/7572, and *HTS* 214/6001-02. Chang Chi's "Poem on Lord Tung" (Ch'en Yen-chieh, ed., *Chang Chi shih chu*, pp. 138-140) confirms the account of Tung Chin's hurried entry into Pien-

chou. Several months later Teng Wei-kung was caught organizing a mutiny and exiled to the far South.

55. Li Ao had been trying to pass the *chin-shih* since 793 and did not succeed until 798. See Lo Lien-t'ien, "Li Ao yen-chiu," pp. 55–89.

56. Hua Ch'en-chih, *T'ang Meng Chiao nien-p'u* [A chronological biography of Meng Chiao of the T'ang], fol. 9a-28a. Cf. also Lo Lien-t'ien, *Han Yü yen-chiu*, pp. 155-162. Han Yü's early poems to Meng Chiao are translated by Stephen Owen: "Those Men Who Make Friends in Ch'ang-an: A Poem to Meng Chiao" (*Poetry*, pp. 5-6; Owen, *The Poetry of Meng Chiao and Han Yü*, pp. 40-42) and "Poem for Master Meng Chiao" (*Poetry*, pp. 6-10; Owen, "The Poetry of Meng Chiao [751-814] and Han Yü [768-824]," pp. 72-77).

57. Lo Lien-t'ien, "Chang Chi nien-p'u" [A chronological biography of Chang Chi]. Cf. also Arthur Waley, *Po Chü-i*, pp. 143-146. Han Yü's poem (*Poetry*, pp. 40-47) "How Sad This Day: A Poem Sent to Chang Chi" (Owen, *The Poetry*, pp. 74-80) describes Han Yü's first meeting with Chang Chi and his success at the examinations. Cf. also "While Sick: To Chang Chi" (*Poetry*, pp. 31-34; Owen, *The Poetry*, pp. 52-54).

58. *Prose*, p. 115.

59. *Poetry*, pp. 28-30, for poem and comment; Shimizu Shigeru, *Kan Yu*, pp. 22-26; Mori Kainan, *Kanshi kōgi*, 2:396-399.

60. See the biographies of Lu Ch'ang-yüan in *CTS* 145/3937-38, *HTS* 151/4822-23, also *TCTC* 235/7582. Anthropophagy as a means of revenge against obnoxious officers was common in the T'ang provincial armies of the period. Cf. Wang Tang, *T'ang yü-lin* 6/205 for an incident at Hsü-chou in the 790s.

61. The poem "How Sad This Day" (see note 57 above) has a moving account of these events.

62. *Prose*, p. 432. On Chang Chien-feng see *CTS* 140/3828-32, *HTS* 158/4939-41, and Li Chao, *T'ang kuo-shih pu*, p. 28.

63. *Poetry*, pp. 35-36; Mori Kainan, *Kanshi kōgi*, 2:74-77; Ch'en Yung-cheng, *Han Yü shih hsüan*, pp. 12-14; Owen, *The Poetry*, pp. 50-52.

64. *Poetry*, pp. 48-49; Mori Kainan, *Kanshi kōgi*, 2:79-83; Ch'en Yung-cheng, *Han Yü shih hsüan*, pp. 15-17. For the Ho River floods see *CTS* 13/391.

65. *Prose*, pp. 105-106.

66. See *Poetry*, pp. 49-51, "The Pien and the Ssu Flow Together:

To Chang Chien-feng" (Owen, *The Poetry*, pp. 87-89) and *Prose*,
p. 114, "A Second Letter to Chang Chien-feng."

67. *Poetry*, pp. 51-52; Mori Kainan, *Kanshi kōgi*, 2:106-108; Ch'en
Yung-cheng, *Han Yü shih hsüan*, pp. 18-19. Other poems of 799-
800 also utilize the avian escape motif, for instance, "The Crying
Wild Goose" (*Poetry*, pp. 52-53; Ch'en Yung-cheng, *Han Yü shih
hsüan*, pp. 20-21; trans. John Chalmers, "Han Wan-kung," p. 279)
in which the poet personifies himself as a solitary goose searching
for its flock; "The Pheasant Shot with an Arrow" (on which see
chapter four below); and "Ocean Waters" (*Poetry*, pp. 59-60; Ch'en
Yung-cheng, *Han Yü shih hsüan*, pp. 28-30).

68. See the "Lament for Ou-yang Chan" (*Prose*, pp. 177-178) and
the poem exchange between the two classmates written at this
time on the subject of "The Nag and the Thoroughbred" (*Poetry*,
pp. 55-57, both poems trans. in Chalmers, "Han Wan-kung," pp.
280-281). Ou-yang Chan died notoriously several years later lamenting the death of a T'ai-yüan courtesan. See Lo Lien-t'ien,
Han Yü yen-chiu, pp. 140ff.

69. *Poetry*, pp. 57-58; Owen, *The Poetry*, pp. 80-82. P'eng-ch'eng
was an older name for Hsü-chou.

70. Cf. notes 14 and 34 above.

71. See *Prose*, pp. 398-399. On Hou Hsi see Lo Lien-t'ien, *Han Yü
yen-chiu*, pp. 145-149.

72. For details see des Rotours, *Examens*, pp. 42-44. The *po-hsüeh
hung-tz'u* examination, which Han Yü failed three times, enabled
the office seeker to bypass the levy.

73. *Prose*, p. 428, preserves the text of the inscription (*t'i-ming*) re-
cording the date of this outing.

74. *Poetry*, pp. 68-69; Owen, *The Poetry*, pp. 83-85.

75. *Poetry*, pp. 69-71; Mori Kainan, *Kanshi kōgi*, 2:90-96; Yoshikawa
Kōjirō, "Kan Yu," pp. 345-348; Harada Kenyū, *Kan Yu*, pp. 60-
62; Ch'en Yung-cheng, *Han Yü shih hsüan*, pp. 34-37.

76. *Prose*, pp. 142-144; T'ung Ti-te, *Han Yü wen hsüan*, pp. 32-36;
trans. Yang Hsien-yi and Gladys Yang, "Prose Writings of Han
Yü," pp. 75-76; Georges Margouliès, *Anthologie raisonnée de la
littérature chinoise*, pp. 244-246.

77. The position carried rank of the seventh degree first class. See
des Rotours, *Fonctionnaires*, 1:452-453. For further details on the
college see des Rotours, *Examens*, pp. 132-133, 171-172, 179.

78. Li Chao, *T'ang kuo-shih pu*, p. 57. For the letter to Lu Ts'an see

Prose, pp. 116-118; on Lu Ts'an, cf. Lo Lien-t'ien, *Han Yü yen-chiu*, pp. 149-151, and "Li Ao yen-chiu," pp. 64-65.

79. *Prose*, pp. 98-100; T'ung Ti-te, *Han Yü wen hsüan*, pp. 27-32; trans. Zhang Xihou, "Prose Writings of Han Yü," pp. 93-94.

80. *Prose*, p. 84. The important "Preface Seeing Off Meng Chiao (*Prose*, pp. 136-137; T'ung Ti-te, *Han Yü wen hsüan*, pp. 44-52; trans. Margouliès, *Anthologie*, pp. 426, and Yang Hsien-yi and Gladys Yang, "Prose Writings of Han Yü," pp. 73-75), dating from 803, should also be included in this group.

81. *Prose*, pp. 24-25; T'ung Ti-te, *Han Yü wen hsüan*, p. 52-57; trans. Yang Hsien-yi and Gladys Yang, "Prose Writings of Han Yü," pp. 64-65, and Margouliès, *Anthologie*, pp. 130-131.

82. See *Cam. Hist.*, pp. 510-514 and 598-601, and Waley, *Po Chü-i*, pp. 50-63, for a summary of difficulties during these years.

83. Li Chao, *T'ang kuo-shih pu*, p. 38. Wang Tang, *T'ang yü lin* 4/148 (completed about 1100), which follows the same categories as *A New Account of Tales of the World (Shih-shuo hsin-yü)*, reprints this anecdote and places it in the category *ch'i-i*, "Living in Retirement" (trans. Richard B. Mather, pp. 331-339).

84. "Reply to Chang Ch'e" (*Poetry*, pp. 180-185, commentary to these lines on pp. 182-183; Owen, *The Poetry*, pp. 190-197, cf. lines 51-62 on pp. 192-193).

85. Shen Yen received the *chin-shih* during the *t'ien-fu* period (901-903). A collection of his writing in ten *chüan* titled *Ao shu* (Tortuous texts) existed in the Sung (*HTS* 60/1609). This tract was quoted in a variety of Sung compilations (cf. *Poetry*, pp. 183-184) and is now in *Ch'üan T'ang wen* 868/6b-7a.

86. The first incident clearly refers to the last entry in the *Spring and Autumn Annals* and the *Tso chuan* commentary where Confucius laments the untimely appearance of a unicorn and its implications for the political future of the state of Lu (James Legge, *The Chinese Classics*, vol. 5, pp. 833-835). The second incident relates to the following passage in *Huai-nan tzu* (*SPTK* ed. 17/14b): "The Sage's relation to objects is as though he looks at their forms in a mirror and so indirectly comes to understand their natures. Thus Yang-tzu saw a fork in the road and wept because it went either north or south. When Mo-tzu saw raw white silk, he wept because it could become either yellow or black." The third incident refers to the beginning of an account in the *Wei-shih ch'ün-ch'iu* concerning the famous encounter between the poet Juan Chi (210-263) and the recluse Sun Teng: "Juan Chi often went riding alone

wherever his fancy led him, not following the roads or byways, to the point where carriage tracks would go no farther, and always he would return weeping bitterly" (Mather, *New Account of Tales*, p. 331). The text goes on to relate that on one such outing Juan Chi encountered Sun Teng and attempted to engage him in philosophical discussion, but the latter "remained oblivious and never looked his way. Chi then with a shrill sound made a long whistling whose echoes reverberated through the empty stillness." This pleased the recluse who in turn treated Juan Chi to a display of virtuoso "whistling." The first text in the *Shih-shuo hsin-yü* chapter on "Living in Retirement" is a version of this encounter minus the preface about Juan Chi's following roads to their ends. Donald Holzman, *Poetry and Politics: The Life and Works of Juan Chi*, pp. 149-152, has a good discussion of this incident and the Taoist breath control technique known as "whistling." He observes that "like the Ch'an masters of the T'ang dynasty who, with their eructations and physical blows, resemble him [i.e. Sun Teng] so much, he knows that the Truth is beyond words. . . ."

87. *Poetry*, pp. 82-83; Mori Kainan, *Kanshi kōgi*, 2:145-148. "Seven lowlands" (*ch'i tse*) is an allusion to Szu-ma Hsiang-ju's "Tzu-hsü fu" (*Wen hsüan* [hereafter cited as *WH*] 7/18a; trans. Watson, *Records of the Grand Historian*, 2:302ff.) where it refers to the royal hunting domain of the kingdom of Ch'u. The term is best understood in Szu-ma Hsiang-ju's text, and here in Han Yü's poem, as a synecdoche for the country at large. Cf. David Hawkes, "The Quest of the Goddess," *Asia Major* 13 (1967): 91.

88. *CTS* 13/398.

89. "A Memorial Discussing This Year's Emergency Cancellation of the Examinations," *Prose*, pp. 337-338. The request was not granted; there were no examinations in 804. Cf. Hsü Sung, *Teng-k'o chi k'ao* 15/29b-30a (pp. 1002-1003). This memorial is studied and translated in Erich Haenisch, "Han Yü's Einspruch gegen die Prüfungssperre im Jahre 803, ein Kapital aus der Tang-Zeit," pp. 280-303.

90. See Hsü Sung, *Teng-k'o chi k'ao* 15/22a (p. 987). The day after Han Yü's memorial, Ch'i K'ang (740-804) resigned as prime minister, leaving Tu Yu the only functioning minister (*HTS* 62/1707, *TCTC* 236/7602). Both of Ch'i K'ang's biographies (*CTS* 136/3757, *HTS* 128/4471) describe him as a man of limited vision, interested only in the choicest positions, who became increasingly tyrannical in his later years.

91. Li Wen served as vice-president of the Censorate from 798 till his death in 804 and was doubtless a key figure in the early development of the Wang Shu-wen faction. Liu Tsung-yüan composed a funeral elegy for him on behalf of the Censorate staff (*Liu Tsung-yüan chi*, 3:1055–58). One can envision a scenario whereby Han Yü wrote the examination memorial as part of Tu Yu's efforts to oust Ch'i K'ang in return for Tu Yu's influence in obtaining a Censorate post for Han Yü. Tu Yu's relationship to the Wang faction at this time is well known. See Pulleyblank, "Neo-Confucianism," pp. 97–110, and Solomon, *Veritable Record*, p. xii.

92. For Han Yü's relations with these men see Lo Lien-t'ien, *Han Yü yen-chiu*, pp. 152–155, 162–174, and 180–184, respectively.

93. The basic reference on Wang Shu-wen and the history of 803–805 is Solomon, *Veritable Record*, which contains a complete translation of the *Shun-tsung shih-lu*. Cf. also Jack L. Dull, "Han Yü: A Problem in T'ang Dynasty Historiography," pp. 71–99; Pulleyblank, "Neo-Confucianism," pp. 107–113: William H. Nienhauser, Jr. et al., *Liu Tsung-yüan*, pp. 28–30; and Waley, *Po Chü-i*, pp. 36–37. An extended discussion of Wang Shu-wen and an attempt at a new interpretation of his political reforms in the light of Liu Tsung-yüan's allegories can be found in Charles Hartman, "*Alieniloquium*: Liu Tsung-yüan's Other Voice," pp. 23–73. A useful collection of traditional comment on Liu Tsung-yüan's association with Wang Shu-wen can be found in Lo Lien-t'ien, *Liu Tsung-yüan shih-chi hsi-nien chi tzu-liao lei-pien* [A chronological biography of Liu Tsung-yüan together with a classified compendium of reference materials], pp. 453–477. Also useful are Chiang Fan, "Han Yü yü Wang Shu-wen chi-t'uan te 'Yung-cheng kaike' " [Han Yü and the "805 Reforms" of the Wang Shu-wen faction], pp. 67–74, and Chang Hsiao-mei, "Liu Yü-hsi yü Wang-Wei chi-t'uan" [Liu Yü-hsi and the Wang-Wei faction], pp. 109–126.

94. *Poetry*, pp. 83–85; Mori Kainan, *Kanshi kōgi*, 2:460–468. For general information on such cults as background for this poem see Wolfram Eberhard, *The Local Cultures of South and East China*, pp. 229–248, and Edward H. Schafer, *The Divine Woman*, passim, but especially pp. 28–29. For more official dragon pools and rain deities see *T'ang hui-yao* 22/433–434 and Tu Yu, *T'ung tien*, chap. 120.

95. *Prose*, pp. 338–339; T'ung Ti-te, *Han Yü wen hsüan*, pp. 76–79.

96. Li Shih was related to the imperial family and was appointed mayor of Ch'ang-an on April 19, 803. Anecdotes about his cruelty

and extortion are legendary and derive mostly from his biography in the *Shun-tsung shih-lu* (Solomon, *Veritable Record*, pp. 7-8). His removal was a major goal of the Wang group.

97. See "On the Road to Chiang-ling, Sent to the Three Han-lin Scholars Wang Yai, Li Chien, and Li Ch'eng" (*Poetry*, pp. 132-141; trans. Chalmers, "Han Wan-kung," pp. 281-283). Relevant passages from this and the following poems are collected in Lo Lien-t'ien, *Han Yü yen-chiu*, pp. 61-69, and discussed briefly in Solomon, *Veritable Record*, pp. xiii-xiv.

98. "At Yüeh-yang Tower, Parting with Tou Hsiang" (*Poetry*, pp. 144-148; trans. Owen, *The Poetry*, pp. 103-106).

99. Wang Shu-wen was executed early in 806, and Liu Tsung-yüan feared the same fate for several years thereafter (see Hartman, "*Alieniloquium*," p. 41). There was considerable support in literati circles for the exiled "Eight Marshals." See for instance Ch'en Yin-k'o's reading of Po Chü-i's ballad "The Concubine by the Imperial Mausoleum" (*Ch'en Yin-k'o hsien-sheng lun-wen chi*, 2:236-239) as a poem written in sympathy for their fate.

100. *Poetry*, pp. 151-156; trans. Zach, *Han Yü's poetische Werke*, pp. 77-78. The Eight Marshals, of course, knew better; Liu Tsung-yüan's more private writings, for instance, reveal admiration and respect for Wang Shu-wen (see Hartman, "*Alieniloquium*," passim).

101. The present Yang-shan is about 150 miles northwest of Canton. Han Yü's journey there is described in his "Lament for Auxiliary Secretary Chang Shu of Honan" (*Prose*, pp. 182-184). Cf. also the "Epitaph for Chang Shu, Former Magistrate of Honan" (*Prose*, pp. 266-268).

102. Much of the poem is specifically inspired by the third in Tu Fu's series "Walking Alone and Visiting the Flowers on the Riverside" (Hung Yeh, *Tu Shih yin-te* 369/23/3C), which William Hung (*Tu Fu*, p. 175) translates: "A few houses stand where the river is deep and the bamboos are still; But too coquettish are these glowing flowers either red or white. I know my way of requiting the good spring: Some good wine to speed life on its course." Cf. also Erwin von Zach, *Tu Fu's Gedichte*, 1:254. For another Tu Fu imitation of this period see "T'ung-kuan Gorge" (*Poetry*, pp. 88-89; trans. Owen, *The Poetry*, pp. 108-109, and Chalmers, "Han Wan-Kung," pp. 339-340). Cf. also "Virgin Gorge" (*Poetry*, pp. 89-90; trans. Owen, *The Poetry*, p. 110, and Edward H. Schafer, *The Vermilion Bird*, p. 145) describing a fa-

mous defile on the Huang River northwest of Yang-shan, on which see *Shui ching chu* (*SPPY* ed.) 39/1a-2b.

103. *Poetry*, pp. 87-88; Ch'en Yung-cheng, *Han Yü shih hsüan*, pp. 48-49.

104. *Prose*, pp. 155-156; T'ung Ti-te, *Han Yü wen hsüan*, pp. 79-82.

105. *Poetry*, p. 90; Ch'en Yung-cheng, *Han Yü shih hsüan*, pp. 50-51; Mori Kainan, *Kanshi kōgi*, 2:312-315; Harada Kenyū, *Kan Yu*, pp. 72-75.

106. One such student, Ou Hung, perhaps identical or related to Ou Ts'e, actually followed Han Yü to Ch'ang-an but returned south after a short stay. See "Seeing Off Ou Hung on his Return South" (*Poetry*, pp. 252-255; Ch'en Yung-cheng, *Han Yü shih hsüan*, pp. 119-124; trans. Zach, *Han Yü's poetische Werke*, pp. 94-96).

107. See "An Account of the Pavilion of Feasting and Joy" (*Prose*, pp. 48-49), "Seeing Off Reverend Hui" (*Poetry*, pp. 91-94; trans. Owen, *The Poetry*, pp. 92-94), and "Seeing Off Reverend Ling" (*Poetry*, pp. 94-99; Harada Kenyū, *Kan Yu*, pp. 75-84; trans. Zach, *Han Yü's poetische Werke*, pp. 39-42). The poem "Spear Fishing" (*Poetry*, pp. 100-102; trans. Owen, *The Poetry*, pp. 112-113) was also composed in Yang-shan.

108. Solomon, *Veritable Record*, p. 15.

109. See the "Lament for Prefect Li of Ch'en-chou" (*Prose*, pp. 180-181). Cf. also Lo Lien-t'ien, *Han Yü yen-chiu*, p. 70.

110. Chü Wen-chen was an old acquaintance of the Han family. He was present on the Sino-Tibetan border when Han Yen was killed (or captured) in 787 (see Pelliot, *Histoire ancienne du Tibet*, pp. 52-53) and was later Han Yü's colleague at Pien-chou (cf. "Seeing Off Chü Wen-chen," *Poetry*, pp. 21-22, and Lo Lien-t'ien, *Han Yü yen-chiu*, pp. 52-53). On Chü Wen-chen's important role in the history of this period see Hartman, "*Alieniloquium*," pp. 34-37.

111. For these events see Solomon, *Veritable Record*, pp. 20-21 and 56-57.

112. *Poetry*, pp. 117-118; Mori Kainan, *Kanshi kōgi*, 2:131-134; Yoshikawa Kōjirō, "Kan Yu," pp. 341-342. Critics differ as to the identity of the "bright stars," some preferring to interpret them as lesser members of the Wang group whom the rising sun has already extinguished.

113. These are: "The Gentleman Models Himself on the Movements of Heaven," "The Daytime Moon," "After Drunkenness," "Mis-

cellaneous Poems, Four Selections," and "Shooting an Owl" (*Poetry*, pp. 110-111, 111, 112, 112-115, 116-117; Zach, *Han Yü's poetische Werke*, pp. 33-34, 296-297, 35, 186-187, 154-155).

114. *Poetry*, pp. 119-122; Ch'en Yung-cheng, *Han Yü shih hsüan*, pp. 61-65; Mori Kainan, *Kanshi kōgi*, 2:148-157. The opening quatrain describes the rise of the full moon and its reflection on calm river water. The Nine Doubts are mountains in southern Hunan (Schafer, *Vermilion Bird*, p. 140). Middle and higher grades of T'ang officials were exempt from corporal punishment. Chang Shu laments that their new positions will be too low to include them in this exemption. "The road to Heaven" is a metaphor for success in government service. This poem is included in the famous anthology *Three Hundred T'ang Poems* and has been translated by Witter Bynner, *Jade Mountain*, pp. 20-21.

115. For the post see des Rotours, *Fonctionnaires*, 2:698. On Yang P'ing see *CTS* 146/3967-68, *HTS* 160/4970-71; Nienhauser et al., *Liu Tsung-yüan*, p. 31; and Lo Lien-t'ien, *Han Yü yen-chiu*, pp. 175-177.

116. *Poetry*, p. 124; Ch'en Yung-cheng, *Han Yü shih hsüan*, p. 66.

117. *Poetry*, pp. 128-131; Ch'en Yung-cheng, *Han Yü shih hsüan*, pp. 67-71; Mori Kainan, *Kanshi kōgi*, 2:158-168; Harada Kenyū, *Kan Yu*, pp. 84-87. "To the Wooden Hermit, Two Poems" (*Poetry*, pp. 125-126) finely translated by Kenneth O. Hanson (Wuchi Liu and Irving Yucheng Lo, eds., *Sunflower Splendor* [New York: Doubleday, 1975], pp. 171-172) were also written at this time. Traditional critics read these poems as satires against Wang Shu-wen.

118. *Poetry*, pp. 131-132; Ch'en Yung-cheng, *Han Yü shih hsüan*, pp. 72-73; Mori Kainan, *Kanshi kōgi*, 2:168-171; Harada Kenyū, *Kan Yu*, pp. 88-89. Two English Victorian translators read this poem as a comedy; see Chalmers, "Han Wan-kung," p. 340, and James Legge, *The Chinese Classics*, vol. 3, prolegomena, pp. 68-69, which discusses the stele of Yü legend (pp. 67-73).

119. *Poetry*, p. 132; Harada Kenyū, *Kan Yu*, p. 89. The monk in question was Chieh Ying, who was also acquainted with Liu Tsung-yüan (see *Liu Tsung-yüan chi*, 1:173-174).

120. Cf. note 97 above.

121. See "Hindered by Winds at Lake Tung-t'ing: To Chang Shu" and "At Yüeh-lang Tower, Parting with Tou Hsiang" (*Poetry*, pp. 143-144, 144-150; Owen, *The Poetry*, pp. 102-103, 103-108).

122. *Poetry*, p. 156. A letter Liu Yü-hsi wrote the following year to

Tu Yu mentions his conversations with Han Yü in Chiang-ling and quotes Han Yü's advice to him at that time (see Liu Yü-hsi, *Liu Yü-hsi chi* 10/88-92).

123. *Poetry*, p. 151; Mori Kainan, *Kanshi kōgi*, 2:111-113; Yoshikawa Kōjirō, "Kan Yu," pp. 344-345. My interpretation of this poem follows that of Wang Yüan-ch'i (1714-1786).

124. "Letter to Li Sun, Vice-President of the Ministry of the Army" (*Prose*, pp. 83-84). On Li Sun see *CTS* 123/3521-23, *HTS* 149/4805-6, and Twitchett, *Financial Administration*, p. 56. Also important is the "Preface to Poems and Their Replies Between Ching and T'an," Han Yü's preface to a collection of poetic exchanges between P'ei Chün (750-811), Han Yü's superior at Chiang-ling (Ching), and Yang P'ing in Hunan (T'an) (cf. *HTS* 60/1624). For a translation and discussion of this preface see chapter four, pp. 233-234.

125. On the Act of Grace of 806 see *Cam. Hist.*, p. 621. Han Yü's biography in the *Old T'ang History* (160/4195) states that Cheng Yü-ch'ing praised his writings when he was a young man studying for the *chin-shih*. From 792 to 797 Cheng served in the Han-lin Academy and so was unable to promote Han Yü (cf. "Explanatory Words," *Prose*, p. 40). After a term as prime minister (798-800), Cheng spent five years in exile at Ch'en-chou where Han Yü certainly saw him. Although recalled by Wang Shu-wen, he was made prime minister by the new government on September 19, 805 (see *CTS* 158/4163-67, *HTS* 165/5059-61). Han Yü's position at the university carried the rank of fifth degree first class, a considerable promotion (des Rotours, *Fonctionnaires*, 1:447).

126. "Letter to Prime Minister Yü of Hsiang-yang," *Prose*, pp. 85-86. Yü Ti became prime minister in 808.

127. *Poetry*, pp. 177-180; Mori Kainan, *Kanshi kōgi*, 1:292-303. Secretary Chang is Chang Shu, who was also recalled to Ch'ang-an at this time. See Lo Lien-t'ien, *Han Yü yen-chiu*, pp. 153-154. For the linked verses see *Poetry*, pp. 186-193, 208-229, 259-269; trans. Owen, *The Poetry*, pp. 116-136, and his more detailed dissertation, "The Poetry," pp. 206-260.

128. Kao Pu-ying, *T'ang-Sung wen chü-yao*, 2:557. See also Charles Hartman, "Language and Allusion in the Poetry of Han Yü," p. 185.

129. Huang-fu Shih, "Spirit Inscription for Han Yü," *Huang-fu chih-cheng wen-chi* (*SPTK* ed.) 6/2a. Han Yü's "Explanatory Words" (*Prose*, pp. 40-41; trans. Hartman, "Language and Allusion," pp.

185-192) deals with these events in some detail, but Han Yü does not name his detractors. The beginning of this text mentions an interview Han Yü had immediately after his recall with "Prime Minister Cheng." It is uncertain whether this refers to Cheng Yü-ch'ing or to Cheng Yin (752-829). According to *CTS* 14/417, followed by *TCTC* 237/7633, Cheng Yü-ch'ing was dismissed from the prime ministership on June 7, 806 and thus did not hold this office when Han Yü returned to Ch'ang-an. Lo Lien-t'ien (*Han Yü yen-chiu*, p. 74) believes Cheng Yin wished to appoint Han Yü to the Han-lin Academy and that this appointment was slandered by "those who fought for this priority."

130. See Lo Lien-t'ien, *Han Yü yen-chiu*, pp. 14-15, 25. In 803 Han Yü had already taken in the family of his nephew Han Lao-ch'eng, son of Han Hui. The cousin who died in 807 was Han Yü (Mathews No. 7628), brother of Han Yen and son of Han Yün-ch'ing. The epitaph for his daughter (*Prose*, p. 321) implies Han Yü sought duty in Lo-yang to care for this family.

131. des Rotours, *Examens*, p. 179. See Waley, *Po Chü-i*, pp. 158-159, for a short vignette that describes ninth-century Lo-yang as "a sort of Leamington—the resort of aged generals and retired civil servants."

132. *Poetry*, pp. 297-304; trans. Owen, *The Poetry*, pp. 217-221; Zach, *Han Yü's poetische Werke*, pp. 100-102. On Huang-fu Shih see Lo Lien-t'ien, *Han Yü yen-chiu*, pp. 185-190, and the monograph by Chiang Kuo-chen, *Huang-fu chih-cheng hsüeh-shu yen-chiu* [Studies on Huang-fu Shih's scholarship]. On the examination controversy of 808 see *TCTC* 237/7649-50, *Cam. Hist.*, p. 649-651, and Eugene Feifel, *Po Chü-i as a Censor*, pp. 43-55, 189-194.

133. *Prose*, p. 429. On Fan Tsung-shih see Han Yü's "Epitaph for Fan Tsung-shih of Nan-yang" (*Prose*, pp. 311-312; Shimizu Shigeru, *Tō-Sō hakkabun*, 1:119-131) and *HTS* 159/4953, which is based on this text. Cf. also Ch'ien Chi-po, *Han Yü chih*, pp. 73-76. On Lu T'ung see *HTS* 176/5268 and *Han Yü chih*, pp. 107-108. For a partial translation of Lu T'ung's famous "Eclipse of the Moon" see A. C. Graham, *Poems of the Late T'ang*, pp. 81-88. Han Yü's reply, "The Eclipse of the Moon: An Imitation of a Work by Lu T'ung" (*Poetry*, pp. 324-333), is translated by Jerry D. Schmidt, "Han Yü and His *Ku-shih* Poetry," pp. 134-141. Both poems date from 810. Han Yü's "Sent to Lu T'ung" (*Poetry*, pp. 340-344; trans. Zach, *Han Yü's poetische Werke*, pp. 123-126) was written in the following year.

134. "Letter to Omissioner Li of Shao-shih" (*Prose*, pp. 386-387). On Li P'o see *CTS* 171/4437-42, *HTS* 118/4281-86 (which quotes Han Yü's letter).

135. des Rotours, *Fonctionnaires*, 1:87-91, 117-120. The appointment notice for this position was drafted by Han Yü's friend from his Yang-shan exile days, Wang Chung-shu (762-823), and is preserved in Hung Hsing-tsu's *Han-tzu nien-p'u* (cf. Lo Lien-t'ien, *Han Yü yen-chiu*, p. 75). The text acknowledges that the new appointment was given in recognition of Han Yü's literary achievements: "holding to the classics and devoted to their study, he has searched out their deepest meaning. Adhering to Antiquity when composing literature, he has attained its essence. . . . He has sought out his own Way and raised his voice from the darkness."

136. des Rotours, *Fonctionnaires*, 1:383, 388-389; *T'ang liu tien* 4/46b; *T'ang hui-yao* 49/860.

137. Huang-Fu Shih, "Spirit Inscription" (*SPTK* ed.) 6/2a (cf. Lo Lien-t'ien, *Han Yü yen-chiu*, p. 76).

138. "Report to the President, the Prime Minister Cheng" (*Prose*, pp. 86-87). For background on this incident see Kenneth Ch'en, "The Economic Background of the Hui-ch'ang Suppression of Buddhism," pp. 67-105.

139. Although this post carried rank of the fifth degree first class, Han Yü's transfer was probably considered a disciplinary action. A county magistracy, even in a capital district, was "provincial" and not a central government position. Like the western capital that comprised two counties—Wan-nien and Ch'ang-an—the eastern capital comprised Ho-nan and Lo-yang counties. See des Rotours, *Fonctionnaires*, 2:730.

140. Huang-fu Shih, "Spirit Inscription" (*SPTK* ed.) 6/2a. On the hostels see des Rotours's note (*Fonctionnaires*, 2:670-671). On Li Shih-tao see *CTS* 124/3538-39, *HTS* 213/5993-94, *TCTC* 239/7715-16, and Charles A. Peterson, "The Restoration Completed," pp. 166-167.

141. "Report to the Viceroy, the Prime Minister Cheng," *Prose*, pp. 87-88; T'ung Ti-te, *Han Yü wen hsüan*, pp. 104-107. For background on this incident see *Cam. Hist.*, pp. 598-599 and Waley, *Po Chü-i*, pp. 56-57.

142. *Prose*, pp. 34-35. Cf. J. D. Frodsham, *The Poems of Li Ho* (Oxford: Clarendon Press, 1970), pp. xvii-xxii.

143. See "Seeing Off Wu-pen on His Return to Fan-yang" (*Po-

etry, pp. 357-360; partial trans. Owen, *The Poetry*, pp. 224-225). Cf. Li Chia-yen, *Chia Tao nien-p'u* [Chronological biography of Chia Tao] (Shanghai: Shang-wu, 1947), pp. 4-7.

144. *Poetry*, pp. 315-316, 338-340; trans. Hans H. Frankel, *The Flowering Plum and the Palace Lady* (New Haven: Yale University Press, 1976), pp. 41-43, 47-49.

145. *Poetry*, pp. 346-352; trans. Owen, *The Poetry*, pp. 248-251; Witter Bynner, *Jade Mountain*, pp. 23-25. Jerry Schmidt has also studied two poems of 811: "The Son of Family X" and "Poem on the Two Birds" (*Poetry*, pp. 344-345 and 364-367; Schmidt, "Han Yü," pp. 142-143 and 144-148).

146. *CTS* 160/4196-97. Huang-fu Shih ("Spirit Inscription" [*SPTK* ed.] 6/2a) implies that the prime minister never actually granted Han Yü's request for an investigation and simply allowed the Censorate to approve the prefect's initial report. It is likely the first prefect cheated the populace in some way, and when Liu Chien detected him, conspired with the second prefect to have Liu charged with the embezzlement. On Liu Chien, cf. Hsü Sung, *Teng-k'o chi k'ao* 11/29b, and Hartman, "Language and Allusion," pp. 183-184.

147. In 813 Li Chi-fu was concurrently redactor-in-chief of the imperial history (*CTS* 148/3995), a post usually held by one of the prime ministers (des Rotours, *Fonctionnaires*, 1:15). He was almost certainly responsible for Han Yü's promotion (cf. Lo Lien-t'ien, *Han Yü yen-chiu*, p. 85). On the three ministers at this time see *Cam. Hist.*, pp. 624-629.

148. Solomon, *Veritable Record*, pp. xvi-xxiii; Dull, "Han Yü," pp. 98-99. Cf. also Erich Haenisch, "Das Ethos der chinesischen Geschichtschreibung," pp. 111-123.

149. "Epitaph for Master Chen-yao" (*Prose*, pp. 256-258; T'ung Ti-te, *Han Yü wen hsüan*, pp. 136-142) and "Letter to Prime Minister Cheng" (*Prose*, p. 129).

150. Detailed descriptions in des Rotours, *Examens*, pp. 50-55, and *Fonctionnaires*, 1:59-71.

151. des Rotours, *Examens*, p. 9, and *Fonctionnaires*, 1:18,182.

152. The following account is largely based on Charles A. Peterson, "Regional Defense Against the Central Power: The Huai-hsi Campaign, 815-817," pp. 123-150.

153. "Statement Discussing the Best Course of Action in the Huai-hsi Affair" (*Prose*, pp. 371-375), abridged in *TCTC* 239/7712. Han Yü noted the difficulty of coordinating the separate commands

and the high probability of defeat when one command acted alone. He encouraged use of local militia forces from the districts surrounding Huai-hsi and discouraged indiscriminate slaughter of the Huai-hsi population after the government victory. Cf. Peterson, "Regional Defense," pp. 139-140.

154. Waley, *Po Chü-i*, pp. 101ff.; Peterson, "The Restoration Completed," pp. 166-167.

155. des Rotours, *Fonctionnaires*, 1:180-187. The position carried rank of the fifth degree first class and conferred on Han Yü the "vermilion and the fish." Officials of the fourth and fifth degree wore vermilion robes; tallies shaped like fish, the official retaining the right half and the gatekeeper the left half, admitted the bearer to the imperial palace (*kung-ch'eng*) and the Ta-ming Palace. This was the first position Han Yü held that required access to these palaces, the actual residences of the T'ang emperors. Cf. *HTS* 24/526, 529; des Rotours, *Fonctionnaires*, 1:166-167.

156. des Rotours, *Fonctionnaires*, 2:594ff.; Waley, *Po Chü-i*, p. 90; Li Ao, "Life," in Kao Pu-ying, *T'ang-Sung wen chü-yao*, 2:559-560; Lo Lien-t'ien, *Han Yü yen-chiu*, pp. 90-91.

157. Han Yü was made administrative officer of the armies in the field (*hsing-chün szu-ma*) and conferred rank of the third degree (Li Ao, "Life," in Kao Pu-ying, *T'ang-Sung wen chü-yao*, 2:560). Others on P'ei Tu's staff included Ma Tsung (d.823), Li Cheng-feng, Feng Su, and Li Tsung-min (d.846). On September 22, 817, the top eight officials of the mission recorded their names and titles as they stopped their journey eastward to sacrifice at the imperial temple on Hua-shan (*Prose*, p. 430). On the same day as Han Yü's appointment, Ts'ui Ch'ün was made prime minister. Of the three ministers, two (Wang Yai and Ts'ui Ch'ün) were his classmates, and the third (P'ei Tu) was his patron. See *TCTC* 240/7737-38.

158. See *CTS* 156/4134-35; *TCTC* 239/7707; Peterson, "Regional Defense," p. 135. Han Hung went to great lengths to distract Li Kuang-yen. Searching out the most attractive girl in Pien-chou, he taught her singing, dancing, gambling, and other refinements appreciated by soldiers; clothing her in silks and pearls, he had a messenger present the girl, "her form and figure without parallel," to Li during a banquet for the general and his officers. Li instructed the messenger to thank Han Hung for his kind intentions but pointed out that since his troops had left their homes to fight for the government cause, it would hardly be proper for him alone

to enjoy himself in such a manner. Vowing "never to live under the sky with these bandits," he returned the girl—with tears in his eyes (*CTS* 161/4220, *HTS* 171/5185, *TCTC* 239/7717).

159. *Poetry*, p. 456.

160. *SC* 7/330ff.; trans. Chavannes, *Mémoires historiques*, 2:311ff.; Watson, *Records of the Grand Historian*, 1:68ff.

161. See Peterson, "Regional Defense," pp. 143-145, for details. Wu Yüan-chi's best troops were defending the borders, and the capital, Ts'ai-chou, was defended only by old men and boys. Li Su had this information from his defectors. Li Ao ("Life" in Kao Pu-ying, *T'ang-Sung wen chü-yao*, 1:560) and Huang-fu Shih ("Spirit Inscription" [*SPTK* ed.] 6/2b) both maintain that Han Yü was also aware of the same facts and urged P'ei Tu to launch the same kind of surprise attack against Ts'ai-chou. The reason for P'ei's hesitancy is not known. Lo Lien-t'ien (*Han Yü yen-chiu*, p. 95) speculates he did not wish to make his subordinates jealous by competing with them for military victories (?).

162. Cf. *Poetry*, pp. 469-475; trans. Owen, *The Poetry*, pp. 280-281, for poetry written on the return trip to Ch'ang-an.

163. *CTS* 160/4198. The biography of Wu Yüan-chi in the *New T'ang History* (214/6008-12) records the complete text of Han Yü's inscription and implies that Han's version conformed to the emperor's opinion that P'ei Tu's tenacity and skill in executing the emperor's unpopular policies made him the long-range architect of victory. Although Li Su's daring raid ended the war, that action would not have been possible without the constant political and military pressure marshaled against Huai-hsi for over three years. Peterson, "Regional Defense," p. 145, comes to much the same conclusion, quoting the Huai-hsi general Tung Chung-chih's admission that even without the Li Su raid government pressure would have collapsed the Huai-hsi defenses within another year.

164. The *HTS* (214/6011) adds that the emperor ordered Han Yü's text effaced because he was unwilling to oppose the sentiments of the military. There is a short story by the late T'ang author Lo Yin (833-909) that narrates how a soldier who had served with Li Su became so incensed reading Han's account of the Huai-hsi campaign that he pushed over the stone. In jail he killed a guard and was ultimately brought before the emperor, to whom he related the injustice done to Li Su. The emperor pardoned the soldier and ordered a new account written. See *T'ang wen-ts'ui* 100/9a-10a and a shorter version in Wang Tang, *T'ang yü lin* 6/

21b. Cf. also Lo Lien-t'ien, *Han Yü yen-chiu*, pp. 97-98, and Li Shang-yin's famous poem, "The Memorial Inscription by Han Yü," James Liu, *The Poetry of Li Shang-yin*, pp. 191-195. Neither Li Ao nor Huang-fu Shih mentions the Huai-hsi inscription incident.

165. *CTS* 160/4198. *CTS* 15/466 is less graphic. Li Ao ("Life," in Kao Pu-ying, *T'ang-Sung wen chü-yao*, 1:561) says that "people burned their fingers and the tops of their heads to pray for blessings."

166. This account follows *CTS* 160/4200, which is accepted by Szu-ma Kuang (*TCTC* 240/7758-59). For the text of the "Memorial on the Buddha Relic," see *Prose*, pp. 354-356; T'ung Ti-te, *Han Yü wen hsüan*, pp. 172-179; Shimizu Shigeru, *Tō-Sō hakkabun*, 1:234-255. There are many translations: readily available is that by J. K. Rideout in Cyril Birch, ed., *Anthology of Chinese Literature*, pp. 250-253. Closer to the original is that by Homer H. Dubs in "Han Yü and the Buddha's Relic," pp. 5-17.

167. See *Cam. Hist.*, pp. 632-633. In this connection there is a fascinating statement in *CTS* 168/4389 that Huang-fu Po suspected the memorial's real author was Feng Su and so exiled him at the same time as prefect of Hsi-chou. Han Yü may also have misjudged the level of hysteria the relic would cause in Ch'ang-an. Its last appearance had been in 790 (*CTS* 13/369) when Han Yü was absent from the capital.

168. *Poetry*, pp. 484-487; Ch'en Yung-cheng, *Han Yü shih hsüan*, pp. 194-196; Shimizu Shigeru, *Kan Yu*, pp. 114-117; Harada Kenyū, *Kan Yu*, pp. 327-328; Yoshikawa Kōjirō, "Kan Yu," pp. 365-368. When the Taoists later immortalized Han Hsiang as one of the "Eight Transcendents," this poem became an integral part of his biography. There is a sizable literature on the subject, some of which has been collected by Ch'ien Chung-lien in his headnote to this poem. See also Ch'ien Chi-po, *Han Yü chih*, pp. 51-54; W. Perceval Yetts, "The Eight Immortals," *JRAS* (1916): 799-802, explains the essentials of the legend. Cf. also Sawado Mizuho, "Kan Shōshi densetsu to zoku bungaku" [The Han Hsiang-tzu legend and popular literature], *Chung-kuo hsüeh-chih* 5 (1969): 145-180. There are a number of articles on Han Yü's Ch'ao-chou exile; most useful is Lin Yü-ling, "Han T'ui-chih che Ch'ao-chou k'ao" [A study of Han Yü's exile to Ch'ao-chou], pp. 132-144.

169. *Poetry*, pp. 487; Shimizu Shigeru, *Kan Yu*, pp. 117-118.

170. *Prose*, p. 323; Shimizu Shigeru, *Tō-Sō hakkabun*, 1:104-10. Cf.

also the "Lament for My Daughter Na" (*Prose*, pp. 199-200) composed for her reburial at Ho-yang in 823.

171. *Poetry*, pp. 489-490; Ch'en Yung-cheng, *Han Yü shih hsüan*, pp. 199-200; Shimizu Shigeru, *Kan Yu*, pp. 118-119. Cf. Also Han Yü's "Account of the I-ch'eng Post Station" (*Prose*, pp. 397-398), composed March 1, 819, which describes the setting of the poem.

172. This king is best known for having once offered a position to Confucius. Although his advisors opposed the plan, which was abandoned, King Chao had saved his state from extinction, and his virtue drew from Confucius the remark that "King Chao of Ch'u understands the great Way; it is right he should not lose his state" (*SC* 40/1717; Chavannes, *Mémoires historiques*, 4:379-380; cf. also *SC* 47/1932; Chavannes, *Mémoires historiques*, 5:371-373; *Tso chuan*, trans. Legge, *Chinese Classics*, 5:810; Maspero, *China in Antiquity*, pp. 218-219).

173. *Poetry*, pp. 494-495; Ch'en Yung-cheng, *Han Yü shih hsüan*, p. 201; Shimizu Shigeru, *Kan Yu*, p. 132. Ch'ao-yang was a seaside county in Ch'ao-chou.

174. *Poetry*, p. 496; Harada Kenyū, *Kan Yu*, pp. 339-340.

175. *Prose*, pp. 356-358. Han Yü's biographies in both the *CTS* (160/4201-02) and *HTS* (176/5261-62) reproduce this text and relate that when the emperor read it he realized Han Yü had written his earlier memorial "out of love for me . . . but it was still not proper for him to say that the ruler of men by serving the Buddha would shorten his life." He wished to recall Han Yü, but Huang-fu Po, "loathing his honesty and directness," suggested instead that his sentence be reduced by moving his place of exile one province closer to the capital.

176. *Prose*, pp. 329-331. Complete translation by J. K. Rideout in Birch, *Anthology*, pp. 253-255.

177. Chalmers, "Han Wan-kung," p. 347.

178. *Prose*, pp. 185-187, has five such texts composed at Ch'ao-chou; *Prose*, p. 187, has three more composed the following year at Yüan-chou. Cf. also Schafer, *Vermilion Bird*, pp. 94-95.

179. See the "Epitaph for Liu Tsung-yüan" (*Prose*, pp. 294-297; T'ung Ti-te, *Han Yü wen hsüan*, pp. 180-188): trans. Yang Hsien-yi and Gladys Yang, "Prose Writings of Han Yü," p. 82. Cf. also Nienhauser et al., *Liu Tsung-yüan*, p. 41, and Schafer, *Vermilion Bird*, pp. 56-57.

180. See his "Inscription for the Temple to Han Yü at Ch'ao-chou"

(in *Prose*, pp. 446-448). Cf. also Han Yü's official letter requesting the establishment of the school, *Prose*, pp. 401-402. Chao Te later gathered seventy-five of Han Yü's writings into an anthology called the *Literary Record (Wen-lu)*. The work disappeared in the Sung, but the preface survives (in *Prose*, p. 445). See Hartman, "Preliminary Bibliographical Notes," p. 95 n.17.

181. *Prose*, pp. 389-391. Han Yü scholars have long contested the authenticity of these letters. Ou-yang Hsiu believed they were genuine; Su Shih thought the style "so crude, even a servant in Han Yü's household would not have spoken thus"; Chu Hsi thought them genuine but acknowledged serious questions concerning their transmission: Lu Yu considered them simple fakes. Lo Lien-t'ien (*Han Yü yen-chiu*, pp. 108-109) concludes the letters are genuine but the texts have been altered. The present text of the letters is certainly in bad condition; several passages are barely intelligible. The originals were certainly intended as short informal notes and were not included in Han Yü's collected works. The present texts supposedly derive from rubbings obtained by Ou-yang Hsiu from stone engravings made by Ta-tien's disciples and preserved on Ling Mountain. See Hartman, "Preliminary Bibliographical Notes," p. 96 n.23. The crudeness of style and textual corruption may have resulted from a number of sources: (1) as Su Shih implied, a subordinate may have dictated or written the letters; (2) the monks who carved the texts on stone may have "embellished" the originals; (3) routine textual corruption may have followed Ou-yang Hsiu's printing of the letters in his edition of 1062; and (4) enthusiastic Neo-Confucians solicitous of Han Yü's reputation as an anti-Buddhist may have willfully altered the texts. For evidence of this latter process in the "Letter to Meng Chien," see Ch'ien Mu, ed., *Chu-tzu hsin hsüeh-an*, 5:262 (*Prose*, pp. 124-125).

There is a sizable secondary literature on these letters and the larger question of Han Yü and Ta-tien. See Tung Fan, "Han Yü yü Ta-tien" [Han Yü and Ta-tien], pp. 79-87; Lo Hsiang-lin, "Ta-tien Wei-yen yü Han Yü Li Ao kuan-hsi k'ao" [A Study of the relationships between Ta-tien and Han Yü, and Wei-yen and Li Ao], pp. 177-193; and Ch'ien Chung-shu, *T'an i lu*, pp. 77-82. See also Komazawa daigaku, *Zengaku daijiten*, 2:808, 1138.

182. Meng Chien, an avid Buddhist, took part in the translation of Sanskrit texts (*CTS* 4257-58, *HTS* 160/4968-69). A "name inscription" (*t'i-ming*) on the T'ang Buddhist reading house at Kuei-

lin records his presence there in 806 (see Lo Hsiang-lin, *Buddhist Rock Sculptures of the T'ang Dynasty at Kweilin* [Hong Kong: Institute of Chinese Culture, 1958], p. 128).

183. "Letter to Meng Chien," *Prose*, pp. 124-126.

184. This work disappeared in China in the eleventh century. The wood blocks of a unique Korean edition of 1245 were discovered by Japanese scholars in 1933, and the work eventually became known to the scholarly world in the 1960s. For a full discussion and bibliography see Paul Demiéville, "Le recueil de la salle des patriarches," pp. 262-286. To my knowledge, no Han Yü scholar has noticed this relevant material in the *Tsu-t'ang chi* despite the Japanese translation and study by Yanagida Seizan, "Bukkotsu no hyō (Kan Yu to Daiten). *Sodō shū* monogatari" [The memorial on the Buddha relic (Han Yü and Ta-tien). A story from the *Tsu-t'ang chi*], pp. 24-32. Arthur Waley, "A Sung Colloquial Story from the *Tsu-t'ang chi*," pp. 245-246, makes brief mention of this passage. I have also called attention to the importance of this passage for the biography of Han Yü in Ts'ai Han-mo [Charles Hartman], "Ch'an-tsung *Tsu-t'ang chi* chung yu kuan Han Yü te hsin tzu-liao" [New source material concerning Han Yü in the *Tsu-t'ang chi* of the Ch'an school], pp. 19-21.

185. "Buddha-light" is radiance emanating from the body and mind of a Buddha. It is a conventional symbol for wisdom (*prajñā*), and Ta-tien later uses it as a euphemism for enlightenment.

186. That is, they congratulated the emperor, attributing the appearance of the light to the influence of his sagacious virtue. Yanagida Seizan understands "they greeted the miraculous manifestation of His Majesty's belief." The idea seems to be that the combination of the relic of the Buddha's true body and the sagacious virtue of His Majesty resulted in the appearance of the Buddha-light.

187. "The five sorts of vision" (*pañca-cakṣu*) are (1) human vision; (2) divine vision, which sees all material objects in lightness or darkness; (3) wisdom vision, which sees with eyes of the *hīnayāna* enlightened; (4) dharma vision, which sees with the eyes of a bodhisattva; and (5) Buddha vision or omniscience. "The two sorts of hearing" are human and divine. Cf. Komazawa daigaku, *Zengaku daijiten*, 1:338, and William Edward Soothill and Lewis Hodous, *A Dictionary of Chinese Buddhist Terms*, p. 123.

188. The poem would seem to be a polite way of saying that Ta-tien wished to return home. The palace of pine creepers under the

moon refers both to the monk's retreat and to his mind. This he has not "locked with golden chains," a metaphor for binding the mind with the desire for *bodhi* or nirvana (Komazawa daigaku, *Zengaku daijiten*, 1:235–236). The "white clouds" represent something free, unimpeded, and unattached and are often a metaphor for the recluse (*Zengaku daijiten*, 2:1013–14). The *P'ei-wen yün-fu* (58/2 under *pai-yün feng*) attributes this last couplet to an unidentified poem of Ch'en Po (c.906–989), on whom see Ch'ang Pi-te et al., eds., *Sung-jen chuan-chi tzu-liao so-yin*, pp. 2504–05. I have been unable to locate the full text of Ch'en Po's poem.

189. The advice is a direct quotation from the *Nirvāṇa sutra*. Speaking of suffering and delusion, the Buddha preaches that "as when rooting up a strong tree, first one loosens it with the hands, then it comes up easily, so is the meditation (*samādhi*) and wisdom (*prajñā*) of the bodhisattva. First one loosens [suffering] through meditation, then one roots up [delusion] through wisdom" (*Taishō*, No. 374, vol. 12, p. 548b). The two are of course to be conceived as one process. The identity of meditation and wisdom is fundamental to Ch'an. See Yampolsky, *Platform Sutra*, p. 135ff.

190. The ritual of "paying homage" (*li-pai*) consisted of the disciple prostrating or bowing before the master.

191. *Tsu-t'ang chi* (Kyoto 1960 ed.), 2:1–3; (Taipei 1972 ed.), pp. 93–94.

192. *Poetry*, pp. 521–522; Harada Kenyū, *Kan Yu*, p. 356.

193. Tu Sung-po, *Ch'an-hsüeh yü T'ang-Sung shih-hsüeh*, pp. 228–229, and the same author's "P'o Ku te yü-Ch'an tz'u" [*Tz'u* poems concerning Ch'an by Su Tung-p'o and Huang T'ing-chien].

194. See *CTS* 16/481, which shows that Han Yü's recall was part of a series of appointments and emoluments for the political faction he associated with in the later years of Hsien-tsung's reign. Others affected were P'ei Tu, Ts'ui Ch'ün, Li Chiang, Li Kuang-yen, Li Su, and Li Tsung-min.

195. "Chi-tzu of Yen-ling had gone to Ch'i, and his eldest son having died, on the way back (to Wu), he buried him between Ying and Po. Confucius (afterwards) said, 'Chi-tzu was the one man in Wu most versed in the rules of propriety, so I went and saw his manner of interment. The grave was not so deep. . . . When the mound was completed, he bared his left arm; and, moving to the right, he went round it thrice, crying out, "That the bones and flesh should return again to the earth is what is appointed. But the soul in its energy can go anywhere; it can go

anywhere" (*Li chi chu-shu* [*SPPY* ed.] 10/10b-11a; trans. Legge, *Rites*, 1:192-193). Confucius comments on the appropriateness of Chi-tzu's makeshift burial for his son. Han Yü's allusion is "reversed" (*fan-yung*): there was *not* even time to call out three times. This irony heightens the pathetic inappropriateness of the burial for his daughter and thus intensifies his own feelings of guilt and failed responsibility. Han Yü often uses allusion in this way, called by one critic "the live use of a dead classic" (*szu tien huo yung*).

196. *Poetry*, pp. 529-531; Harada Kenyū, *Kan Yu*, pp. 358-360.

197. The College for the Sons of the State was to have 300 students whose fathers held third degree rank or above; the College of Superior Studies was to have 500 students whose fathers held at least eighth degree rank; and the College of the Four Gates was to have 500 students from the general population. See "Memorial Requesting the Return of Students to the Imperial University" (*Prose*, pp. 339-340). For background on this text see des Rotours, *Examens*, pp. 131ff., 179ff. This memorial is traditionally dated 803, which Hanabusa Hideki follows. The text, however, has a clear reference to the ascension of a new emperor (Mu-tsung), and, moreover, Han Yü could not have had the authority to request such sweeping changes in 803. Cf. Lo Lien-t'ien, *Han Yü yen-chiu*, p. 117.

198. *Prose*, p. 369. He also requested that his old protégé and friend Chang Chi be appointed professor in the College of the Sons of the State (*Prose*, p. 364).

199. *Prose*, p. 371. There is no evidence Mu-tsung acted on this advice, although Huang-fu Shih ("Spirit Inscription" [*SPTK* ed.] 6/3a) writes that after Han Yü's return from Yüan-chou a release order was issued and transmitted to the prefects.

200. "Memorial on the Proper Disposition of the Huang Family Rebels," *Prose*, pp. 369-371. For background see Schafer, *Vermilion Bird*, pp. 50ff. and 64ff., and Eberhard, *The Local Cultures of South and East China*, pp. 438-455.

201. *HTS* 222/6329-32.

202. On T'ien Hung-cheng see *CTS* 141/3848-52, *HTS* 148/4781-84. T'ien was born into the ruling family of Wei-po, and his defection to the government cause in 812 was a major policy success for Hsien-tsung (see Peterson, "The Restoration Completed," pp. 164ff.); his cooperation helped to subdue the remaining Ho-pei separatists during 818-819. T'ien was reputed to be highly educated and to have possessed a library of 10,000 *chüan*.

203. On Wang T'ing-ts'ou see *CTS* 142/3884-88, *HTS* 211/5959-61. Wang was an Uighur descended from the mid-eighth-century person or tribe known as A-pu-ssu (Edwin G. Pulleyblank, *The Background of the Rebellion of An Lu-shan*, pp. 101, 167-168). Six of Wang's descendants ruled Ch'eng-te until the collapse of the T'ang in 907 (see Jonathan Mirsky, "Structure of Rebellion," p. 82); one was probably the patron of the great Ch'an teacher Lin-chi at Chen-chou (see Paul Demiéville, trans., *Entretiens de Lin-tsi*, pp. 22-24).

204. On Niu Yüan-i see *HTS* 148/4788-89; on T'ien Pu see *CTS* 141/3852-53, *HTS* 148/4785-86, and Waley, *Po Chü-i*, pp. 137ff. The general progress of these events can be followed in *TCTC* 242/7796-7813.

205. *Poetry*, p. 546; Harada Kenyü, *Kan Yu*, p. 360.

206. The soldiers are referring to Wang Wu-chün (735-801), governor of Ch'eng-te from 782-801. Wang joined the 782 revolt against the crown but later defected to the government and killed Chu T'ao, a major leader of the separatists, in 784. His descendants ruled Ch'eng-te until T'ien Hung-cheng was appointed in 820. See *CTS* 142/3871-76, *HTS* 211/5951-55, *TCTC* 231/7436, and *Cam. Hist.*, pp. 503-507.

207. T'ien was created honorary president of the secretariat in 820 (*CTS* 141/3851). For his wealth see *TCTC* 242/7812.

208. Li Ao, "Life," in Kao Pu-ying, *T'ang-Sung wen chü-yao*, 2:562-566. Huang-fu Shih ("Spirit Inscription" [*SPTK* ed.] 6/3a) relates these events in less detail but specifically indicates that Mu-tsung wished to appoint Han Yü prime minister. Other accounts of the mission to Chen-chou based on Li Ao's "Life" are *HTS* 176/5264 and *TCTC* 242/7812-13. Wang T'ing-ts'ou's *CTS* biography (142/3887) relates that Niu Yüan-i and ten horsemen broke out of the Shen-chou siege in the third lunar month (3/27-4/24) of 822. When a eunuch envoy came in the fifth month (5/22-6/22) to escort Niu's family and the body of T'ien Hung-cheng back to the capital, Wang replied he would send the Niu family along in the autumn, but he did not know where T'ien's body was. When Niu suddenly died, Wang slaughtered his family. Lo Lien-t'ien (*Han Yü yen-chiu*, pp. 121-122) believes this passage contradicts Li Ao's statement that Wang released Niu after the negotiations with Han Yü. But the two accounts are not totally irreconcilable. I suspect that Niu's dramatic escape was simply arranged as a face-saving gesture

for Wang. This is implied in *TCTC* 242/7813 where Niu's escape follows the narrative of the Wang-Han Yü interview.

209. Waley, *Po Chü-i*, pp. 139-140.

210. The only other prime minister with literary pretensions during Mu-tsung's reign was Niu Seng-ju (779-847). He held the office for five days.

211. *Poetry*, pp. 547-548.

212. Wang Tang, *T'ang yü lin* 2/220. The tradition supposedly derived from an anonymous T'ang comment on a stone engraving of the two poems unearthed at Shou-yang station in the eleventh century (*Poetry*, p. 548). According to this source, Han Yü's concubines were named Graceful Peach and Wind Willow.

213. "Statement Concerning the Proper Course of Action Regarding Reform of the Salt System," *Prose*, pp. 375-380; trans. Twitchett, *Financial Administration*, pp. 165-172.

214. Li Ao, "Life," in Kao Pu-ying, *T'ang-Sung wen chü-yao*, 2:566.

215. He was conjointly president of the Censorate, which carried rank of the third degree first class. This was the highest rank Han Yü attained in government service. See des Rotours, *Fonctionnaires*, 1:281, 2:680-684.

216. On this custom see *T'ang hui-yao* 60/1046. Maeno Naoaki (*Kan Yu no shōgai*, p. 182) argues that Han Yü requested this dispensation because his joint appointment as president of the Censorate made the ritual superfluous. Much more probable is the suggestion of the Sung scholar Fang Sung-ch'ing (cf. Lo Lien-t'ien, *Han Yü yen-chiu*, pp. 126-127) that Han Yü did not wish to pay a courtesy call on a former student. The presidency of the Censorate during this period was a sinecure; the vice-president was in actual control.

217. Li Ao, "Life," in Kao Pu-ying, *T'ang-Sung wen chü-yao*, 2:567; Huang-fu Shih ("Spirit Inscription" [*SPTK* ed.] 6/3a-b). For background on the former incident see des Rotours, *Fonctionnaires*, 2:861-863.

218. The above account in the main follows Huang-fu Shih ("Spirit Inscription" [*SPTK* ed.] 6/3a-b) and Li Ao, "Life," in Kao Pu-ying, *T'ang-Sung wen chü-yao*, 2:567. The biographies of Li Shen (*CTS* 173/4497-4500, *HTS* 181/5347-50, cf. also *CTS* 16/503) imply that Li Feng-chi specifically arranged for Han Yü's appointment as metropolitan prefect with the courtesy call dispensation in order to precipitate a quarrel between Li and Han and then used this as a pretext to engineer Li Shen's removal from Ch'ang-an. Li Feng-chi's biographies (*CTS* 167/4365, *HTS* 174/5221-23),

which are strongly biased against him, have a similar story. Fang Sung-ch'ing (cf. Lo Lien-t'ien, *Han Yü yen-chiu*, pp. 126-127), however, hesitated to attribute such long-range maliciousness to Li Feng-chi, pointing out that Han Yü himself requested the dispensation and that although Li Feng-chi certainly took advantage of the affair and misrepresented it to the emperor, he probably did not plot it himself. Although Li was an enemy of his patron P'ei Tu, Han Yü seems to have maintained a polite social relationship with him; he addressed four poems to Li between 820 and 823 (*Poetry*, pp. 528, 553, 559, and 561). Finally, it seems highly unlikely that Han Yü, who at this point in his career had certainly seen his share of bureaucratic intrigue, would have allowed himself to be duped by such an obvious ploy of Li Feng-chi.

219. *Poetry*, pp. 566-569; Ch'en Yung-cheng, *Han Yü shih hsüan*, pp. 217-221; Shimizu Shigeru, *Kan Yu*, pp. 147-154; Harada Kenyū, *Kan Yu*, pp. 360-366.

220. Statues in force during this period allowed officials a hundred days of sick leave before mandatory resignation due to illness. See *T'ang hui-yao* 82/1519-20.

221. "Elegy for T'ui-chih," Ch'en Yen-chieh (ed.), *Chang Chi shih chu* 7/152. The poem (7/149-153) chronicles the lifelong relationship between the two poets, but over half the text concerns the last months of Han Yü's life.

222. *Poetry*, pp. 569-570; Harada Kenyū, *Kan Yu*, pp. 366-368. Librarian Wang is Wang Chien (768?-830?).

223. The dates are from Huang-fu Shih ("Spirit Inscription" [*SPTK* ed.] 6/3b). Cheng Ch'ien, "Ku chin fei Han k'ao-pien" [An investigation of defamations of Han Yü ancient and modern], pp. 3-22, contains a detailed study of Han Yü's illness. Cheng believes the "weakened legs" of the third "South Stream" poem (*Poetry*, p. 568) is a T'ang medical term for the modern *chiao-ch'i* or beriberi. He notes that Han Yü's nephew, the famous *shih-erh-lang* (*Prose*, pp. 196-197) as well as Liu Tsung-yüan (*Liu Tsung-yüan chi*, 3:872) also suffered from this disease, which is caused by a deficiency of vitamin B1. Cheng points out that the Han family had a history of premature death and suggests that Han Yü's childhood years spent in southern exile and the early adult years in military camps may have permanently damaged his health. In addition, his bad teeth—they began to fall out at age thirty and by age forty two-thirds were gone, a condition often mentioned

in his writings and not usual in the T'ang—certainly influenced his diet. Beri-beri has always been more prevalent in south than in north China because the vitamin B1 content of the rice husks is destroyed if the rice is first milled then stored in its polished form (see Lu Gwei-djen and Joseph Needham, "A Contribution to the History of Chinese Dietetics," pp. 13-20). There is evidence that Han Yü took sulphur for his illness (Cheng Ch'ien, "Ku chin fei Han k'ao-pien," pp. 14-16). Sulphur dissolved in boiled milk was a common prescription for *chiao-ch'i* since the fourth century. Ingestion of herbs accompanied by dietary changes was another. Yet neither Lu and Needham nor Schafer (*Vermilion Bird*, p. 133) mention sulphur as a cure for the disease, and this suggests that this pseudo-cure was more common in the T'ang than these scholars have realized and that Han Yü may perhaps have received bad medical advice. To summarize, it is possible to surmise that Han Yü's dental problems forced him to curtail his normal diet to the point where he developed beri-beri, perhaps during his 819-820 exile. Prescription of sulphur did not improve and perhaps worsened his condition. Finally, Cheng insists that Han Yü's ingestion of sulphur was not connected with alchemy nor was it intended as a remedy for syphilis, which, being native to the New World, did not appear in China until the sixteenth century.

224. Lo Lien-t'ien, *Han Yü yen-chiu*, pp. 23-27, collects the major texts relating to Han Yü's economic situation.

225. Even members of the wealthy and aristocractic Po-ling Ts'ui clan faced death and starvation when the An Lu-shan rebellion forced them from their home base in Lo-yang. See Patricia Buckley Ebrey, *The Aristocratic Families of Early Imperial China: A Case Study of the Po-ling Ts'ui Family* (Cambridge: Cambridge University Press, 1978), pp. 96-99.

226. This table does not include the value of the considerable number of servants that also came with official position. Also, it should be remembered that these figures represent only Han Yü's official income. The family certainly received income of some kind from its private landholdings. Finally, Han Yü, especially during his later years, earned sizable sums from literary commissions. Liu Yü-hsi mentions, rhetorically, that one character of a funeral inscription by Han Yü was worth "a mountain of gold" (*Liu Yü-hsi chi* 40/404). For instance, Han Yü himself states that he received 500 bolts of silk, worth about 400,000 cash, from Han Hung as a token of the latter's appreciation for Han Yü's favorable mention

of him in the "Inscription on the Pacification of Huai-hsi." The sum was almost a third of Han Yü's yearly salary at the time.

227. *CTS* 160/4203.
228. On Han Yü's Ch'ang-an mansion and his pride in it, see "Shown to My Sons" (*Poetry*, pp. 418-421). On the villa see the commentary to "First Trip to South Stream" (*Poetry*, pp. 566-569).
229. Twitchett, *Financial Administration*, pp. 80-81; Waley, *Po Chü-i*, pp. 60-61. For the 817 edict against cash hoarding and its effect on Ch'ang-an real estate see Denis Twitchett, "Merchant, Trade, and Government in Late T'ang," p. 94 n.123.
230. "Eulogy for Vice-President Han," *T'ang wen-ts'ui* 33B/618.

Chapter Two

1. *TCTC* 198/6247.
2. *TCTC* 193/6074-78; *Cam. Hist.*, pp. 222-223. Cf. Fu Lo-ch'eng, "T'ang-tai i-hsia kuan-nien chih yen-pien" [The development of racial attitudes in the T'ang], p. 6, and F. A. Bischoff, *Interpreting the Fu*, pp. 115-187. In 644, T'ai-tsung settled another contingent of submitted Turks south of the Yellow River, proclaiming, "The I and the Ti are men also and their natures are no different from the Chinese" (*TCTC* 197/6215-16), which passage Bischoff (p. 119) cites as an example of the "cultural broadmindedness of T'ang T'ai-tsung." Cf. also Liu Mau-ts'ai, *Die chinesischen Nachrichten zur Geschichte der Ost-Türken (T'u-küe)*, 1:197 (translating *HTS* 215A/6038) for yet another example of T'ai-tsung's belief that the natures of Hua and I were identical. Edwin G. Pulleyblank, "The An Lu-shan Rebellion and the Origins of Chronic Militarism in Late T'ang China," pp. 37-40, has some excellent observations on T'ai-tsung's conception of the T'ang as a "joint Sino-barbarian polity":

> We may, in fact, think of the T'ang ruler not as seeking to impose Chinese sovereignty outward from the Middle Kingdom, as the Han emperors had sought to do, but rather as seeking to substitute himself for the Turkish *qaghan* as lord of the steppe. Where the Hsiung-nu ruler Mao-tun and Han Kao-tsu had agreed to divide the world into two halves, leaving the southern agricultural world for the Han emperor and reserving the lordship over those who draw

the bow for the Hsiung-nu, T'ai-tsung wanted to look both ways and combine the two dignities in his own person.

This aspiration of T'ai-tsung was symbolized in the title T'ien k'o-han "Heavenly Qaghan" which was proffered to him in 630 by the chieftains of the various nomadic tribes. Though we may hold legitimate doubts as to whether the offering of this title was wholly spontaneous, the fact that it was adopted by the Chinese emperor was symbolically very important. It established a separate basis of legitimacy for his rule beyond the Great Wall, with its roots in nomad traditions, and was not simply an extension of universalist claims by the Chinese Son of Heaven. Moreover, it had as its corollary the assumption, quite contrary to Chinese traditional attitudes, of the equality of barbarian and Chinese as subjects. This was a point consciously maintained and expressed by T'ai-tsung. (p. 38)

3. "Wall Inscription for the Governor of Shou-chou," *Wen-yüan ying-hua* 801/1b.

4. Wang Shou-nan, *T'ang-tai fan-chen yü chung-yang kuan-hsi chih yen-chiu* [A study of the relations between the regional commanders and the central government during the T'ang], p. 312. Considerable evidence also supports the contention that T'ang terms such as *hu, fan, lu, jung,* and *chieh,* all routinely rendered into English as "barbarian," do not necessarily designate physical racial features as much as they do cultural characteristics. In other words, behavior not birthplace or physical appearance determined which of these epithets might be applied to a given individual. Wang Shou-nan (p. 314) cites several interesting examples. When Ko-shu Han (d.756), a Turkish general in the service of the T'ang, defeated the Tibetans in 753, the poet Kao Shih (706?-765) lauded his achievement with the couplet, "The streams surge forth with the blood of the many *jung*; the wind drives along the ghosts of the dead *lu*." These terms would hardly have been possible in a poem praising a Turkish general had they been simply racial epithets for non-Chinese. For a full translation of this poem see Marie Chan, *Kao Shih,* p. 37. On the contrary, in 642, one Ho-li, a Turk of the Ch'i-pi tribe that had submitted to the T'ang, was abducted by a faction within his tribe hostile to the T'ang and ordered to forswear this allegiance. He replied in a loud voice, "This T'ang warrior will never accept such indignity at the hands of a *lu* court,"

referring to himself as a "T'ang warrior" and his own tribesmen as *lu* (see *TCTC* 196/6180).

5. Denis Twitchett has a good paragraph describing this pre-T'ang northern society:

These centuries of political and social dominance by non-Chinese peoples left deep marks on the society and institutions of northern China. The nobility of the various foreign ruling houses constantly intermarried with the Chinese elite. This was particularly the case in the north-west, where two aristocratic groups emerged to form an elite very different from the traditional Chinese ruling class. These groups, the Tai-pei aristocracy of central and northern Shansi, and the far more powerful Kuan-lung aristocracy with its power bases in southwest Shansi, Shensi and Kansu, were not only of mixed blood. They had a life style strongly influenced by nomadic customs; even well into the T'ang period many of them still spoke Turkish as well as Chinese; they were essentially a military group rather than a civilian elite, living a hard, active outdoor life; and, as among the nomads, their womenfolk were far more independent and powerful than in traditional Chinese society. (*Cam. Hist.*, pp. 3-4)

6. On the *fu-ping* see Pulleyblank, *Background*, pp. 61-74, for a description of the system, its relation to the Kuan-lung aristocracy, and its breakdown in the later seventh and early eighth centuries. Arthur F. Wright in *Cam. Hist.*, pp. 96-103, has some good pages on the origins of the *fu-ping*. Cf. ibid., pp. 207-208, for details of its organization under T'ai-tsung. The "aristocracy" of course provided only the officers of the *fu-ping*; its troops were peasants, probably from the same localities as their officers.

7. Howard Wechsler concludes his discussion of T'ai-tsung's ministers with this paragraph:

Li Ching and Li Shih-chi were examples of a type of official which remained common throughout the seventh century, the man who was equally at home as a court official or as a commander-in-the-field. These officials are a reminder that the new T'ang ruling group still came from a society in which a leader needed not only to be adept as an administrator and a scholar, but also to be trained in the martial arts, as was the emperor himself. (*Cam. Hist.*, p. 200)

8. Kao Pu-ying, *T'ang-Sung wen chü-yao*, 1:16.
9. From an untitled text attributed to Shen Chi-chi in the commentary to Tu Yu, *T'ung tien* 15/84a. Shen's longer memorial of 779 proposing reform of the examination system is included in *T'ung tien* 18/101a-102a and in *HTS* 45/1178-79, trans. in des Rotours, *Examens*, pp. 269-274.
10. Larry W. Moses, "T'ang Tribute Relations with the Inner Asian Barbarians," p. 72, makes a direct connection between Empress Wu's moves against the old northwest aristocracy and the resurgence of the Turkish empire under Qutluq Elterish in 683: "Her support came from those who opposed the ranks and positions of Türks in the T'ang administration. Those opposed to the Empress were western Chinese gentry, who were not adverse to seeing Türks at the upper levels of government and the army. The ensuing struggle at court spun off a Türk revolt that led to the re-creation of the great Türk Empire of 552." It seems highly suggestive that this Turkish disaffection with the T'ang followed hard on the heels of Empress Wu's espousal of basically Hua and *wen* values through the examination system.
11. *Hua* means racially Chinese. Technically, *Hu* referred to the Indo-European-speaking peoples of Central Asia, especially the Sogdians. Yet since these were the purveyors of written culture and civilization throughout Central Asia, the term *Hu* evolved into a general designation for the distinctly non-Chinese cultures of the north and west. Cf. Pulleyblank, *Background*, pp. 10-11; Hsieh Hai-p'ing, *T'ang-tai fan-hu sheng-huo chi ch'i tui wen-hua chih ying-hsiang* [Foreigners in the T'ang dynasty and their cultural influence], pp. 1-4; Moses, "T'ang Tribute Relations," p. 76.
12. Cf. Pulleyblank, "The An Lu-shan Rebellion," p. 40:

By 750, what remained of T'ai-tsung's combined nomad and Chinese empire? No longer equal partnership (if this had ever really existed) presided over by an emperor with one foot in each camp and an impartial regard for the interests of both. There was still a kind of partnership, but it was based upon a division of roles in which the barbarians acted, to use a common Chinese metaphor, as the "claws and teeth," while the Chinese were the "heart and belly," i.e., the directing mind and the main economic beneficiaries of protection. Unfortunately, the "claws and teeth" showed that they had minds of their own and, instead of protecting the Chinese, decided to move in and try to appropriate or at least share in the spoils. Hence the cancerous growth of militarism within the country which, as the *Hsin T'ang-shu* says, ended by destroying the dynasty, through the institutions which it had itself set up.

13. Denis Twitchett, "Varied Patterns of Provincial Autonomy in the T'ang Dynasty," pp. 98-105, describes the varied relations between the T'ang court and the military powers in each provincial area. The spectrum ranged from a total confrontation between imperialism and separatism in the northeast to almost complete court control in the south. A key factor was the ability of the court to prevent the practice of hereditary succession to military position within a particular provincial army. In the northeast, the Turkish military and nomad ethic encouraged the transmission of position from father to son; this was not a factor among the sedentary agricultural tribes of the south.

14. On T'u-t'u Ch'eng-ts'ui see Hartman, "*Alieniloquium*," pp. 65-67. Hsieh Hai-p'ing, *T'ang-tai fan-hu sheng-huo chi ch'i tui wen-hua chih ying-hsiang*, pp. 87-88, notes that although T'u-t'u's ethnic origin is omitted from his biographies in the T'ang histories, the *Yüan-ho hsing tsuan* (ed. Ts'en Chung-mien), a contemporary genealogy, identifies him as a *tai-jen* (2:633), perhaps a designation for some tribal division of Thai stock.

15. See Ch'en Yin-k'o, *Ch'en Yin-k'o hsien-sheng lun-wen chi*, 1:178, 195ff., and Pulleyblank, *Background*, pp. 75-81, for discussions of the ethnic migrations of non-Chinese into Hopei. Most significant seems to have been the revival of the Eastern Turkish confederation under Qapaghan Qaghan (d.716) in the early eighth century, which momentarily united the nomadic tribes north of China and thus provided a conduit for the migrations of Central Asian Hu into Hopei.

16. *TCTC* 224/7222 records the proposed erection of a shrine to the "Four Sages" (*szu sheng*)—An Lu-shan, Shih Szu-ming (d.761) his successor, and their two sons—at Wei-po in 773. There seem to have been other such "shrines" throughout the northeast. Cf. Pulleyblank, *Background*, p. 17.

17. "Words to Find Fault With" (*Tsui-yen*), *Ch'üan T'ang wen* 754/12a.

18. *Ch'üan T'ang wen* 755/1a-2b. The text continues to relate that Lu P'ei (809-839) made a secret plan with his mother and brother to escape Chen-chou. He stole a horse, rode 300 *li* to the border, then walked to the Wang-wu Mountains in the Huai-chou area of

Honan where he took refuge in a Taoist monastery. After ten years of study, at age twenty-nine, he traveled to Ch'ang-an in 838 to sit for the *chin-shih* examination, which he passed and thereby won immediate renown. Ironically, on his return from a trip north the next year, he was killed by bandits around Chin-chou.

19. *CTS* 129/3611. Cf. Pulleyblank, "The An Lu-shan Rebellion," pp. 50-51.

20. "Epitaph for Chang Ch'e of Ch'ing-ho, Posthumous Grand Secretary in the Department of the Chancellery and Former Administrative Officer for the Military Region of Yu-chou," *Prose*, pp. 314-316; T'ung Ti-te, *Han Yü wen hsüan*, pp. 204-210. Cf. the commentary in *TCTC* 242/7795 for other texts relating to these events. Han Yü's account indirectly condemns Chang Hung-ching's conduct in Yu-chou as responsible for Chang Ch'e's death. On the other hand, Han Yü enhances the image of Chang Ch'e as a defender of the T'ang by creating a verbal parallel between Chang's cursing of the Yu-chou soldiers and that passage in the *Han shu* [hereafter cited as *HS*] (Peking: Chung-hua, 1962; 54/2462) biography of the Han patriot Su Wu, where Su, during his imprisonment among the Hsiung-nu, cursed Wei Lü, a Turk originally in Han service who had defected to the Hsiung-nu.

21. Quoted from Liu Yü-hsi's "Spirit Inscription" (*shen tao pei*) for Shih Hsiao-chang, *Liu Yü-hsi chi* 3/36. Cf. also *CTS* 181/4686-87; *HTS* 148/4790-91 adds that Shih's father was a "crude military" (*ts'u-wu*) and did not heed his son's advice.

22. "Letter Congratulating Administrator of the Army Lu Ch'ang-yüan," *Li Wen-kung chi* (*SPTK* ed.) 8/60a. On this incident see *TCTC* 235/7573-76 and Barrett, "Buddhism," pp. 182-183.

23. See Arthur F. Wright, "T'ang T'ai-tsung and Buddhism," pp. 239-263. Although there seems to be no direct evidence that T'ai-tsung adopted the T'o-pa Wei policy of equating emperor and Buddha under the title "Son of Heaven Bodhisattva" (*p'u-sa t'ien-tzu*) as did Sui Wen-ti, the later Lamaist tradition often includes him among its reincarnation lineages of bodhisattva-emperors. See David M. Farquhar, "Emperor as Bodhisattva in the Governance of the Ch'ing Empire," p. 17, and Herbert Franke, *From Tribal Chieftain to Universal Emperor and God*, pp. 52-53.

24. T'ang Chen-ch'ang, "Han Yü p'ai Fo-Lao i" [Han Yü's anti-Buddhist and anti-Taoist opinions], pp. 178-179, notes the frivolous nature of these "debates," calling attention to an account

from the *hsien-t'ung* period (860-873), in which a court jester named Li K'o-chi staged a mock "debate" among adherents of the "three religions" at which he and his cohorts proved by recourse to deft and salacious citation that the Buddha, Lao-tzu, and Confucius were all women! Cf. Lo Hsiang-lin, "T'ang-tai san-chiao chiang-lun k'ao" [A study of the debates between the three religions during the T'ang], pp. 172-173.

25. In this connection, it is interesting to note that Ch'an, the only Buddhist school to flourish and survive the ninth century, diminished and even denied the personal role of the Buddha in individual salvation.

26. See Li Ao's "Letter Recommending Some Acquaintances to Vice-President Chang Chien-feng" (*Li Wen-kung chi* 8/54a-b) written in 798; the letter recommends Li Kuan, Han Yü, Meng Chiao, Chang Chi, and Li Ching-chien, and is also included in *T'ang chih-yen* 6/70-72. Li Ao's "Miscellaneous Persuasions" (*Tsa-shuo*) also attribute such achievements to Kuan Chung and lament that even Tseng Hsi and Mencius (cf. *Mencius*, Lau trans., p. 74) did not realize their significance (*Li Wen-kung chi* 5/34a). Cf. also Barrett, "Buddhism," p. 285. For background on Kuan Chung see Maspero, *China in Antiquity*, pp. 180-191, especially p. 184, for the wars against the Jung and the Ti. The *Kuan-tzu* also mentions these wars; see W. Allyn Rickett, *Kuan-tzu: A Repository of Early Chinese Thought*, pp. 61-65.

27. *Prose*, p. 60.

28. Pulleyblank, "Neo-Confucianism," p. 101. The quotation is from Tu Yu's *T'ung tien* 12/68a. Han Yü and Li Ao's approbation of Kuan Chung, evidence of Neo-Legalist influence on their political thought, was a departure from the earlier Confucian castigation of Kuan. For example, Yüan Chieh, in his 757 essay titled "On Kuan Chung" (*Kuan Chung lun* in *T'ang wen-ts'ui* 35/645-46), counters the contemporary argument that the T'ang needs a minister like Kuan Chung to combat the rise of militarism (i.e. the An Lu-shan rebellion). Yüan maintained that Kuan Chung was not suitable as an exemplum for the T'ang because he had devoted all his energies to the aggrandizement of his own state of Ch'i rather than to the strengthening of the Chou royal house (cf. David McMullen, "Historical and Literary Theory," pp. 328-329, for a synopsis of this essay). Yüan's argument follows the opinion of Szu-ma Ch'ien in his comment to Kuan Chung's biography in the *Shih chi* (62/2136).

29. Lest the reader be tempted to dismiss the "Poem on the Sagacious Virtue of Primal Harmony" as specious flattery, it should be pointed out that there is among Han Yü's contemporaries no surviving poem even remotely like it in scope or style.

30. On Hsien-tsung's avarice see Tuan Hsing-min, *Liu Tzu-hou yü-yen wen-hsüeh t'an-wei*, pp. 226-228, and Feifel, *Po Chü-i as a Censor*, pp. 105-107.

31. It is significant that Han Yü's first, and perhaps only, criticism of Hsien-tsung seems to be "On the Temple of King Chao of Ch'u" written on the way to exile in 819. I do not mean to imply by the above paragraph that Hsien-tsung was personally aware of Han Yü's larger political concerns, only that Han Yü perhaps attached his own motives to Hsien-tsung's anti-separatism.

32. On this system see Donald Holzman, "Les débuts du système médiéval de choix et de classement des functionnaires," pp. 387-414.

33. See Hartman, "*Alieniloquium*," pp. 37-38; *Cam. Hist.*, pp. 586-611; and F. A. Bischoff, *La Forêt des pinceaux*, p. 10.

34. *CTS* 160/4203.

35. *Poetry*, pp. 384-385.

36. *Cam. Hist.*, p. 345.

37. See Ch'en Erh-tung, "Han Yü 'Yu T'ai-p'ing kung-chu shan-chuang' so yin" [An exposé of Han Yü's poem "An Excursion to the Mountain Villa of the Princess of Great Tranquillity"], pp. 272-274. The Ch'ing commentators Chu I-tsun and Ho Ch'o had previously noted the "satirical" intent of this poem.

38. *Prose*, p. 273.

39. *Prose*, p. 232. For more quotations in this vein see Chiang Fan, "Han Yü yü Wang Shu-wen chi-t'uan te 'Yung-chen kai-ke' " [Han Yü and the "805 Reforms" of the Wang Shu-wen faction], p. 70. Cf. also Teng T'an-chou, "Lun Han Yü chi yu-kuan te chi-ke wen-t'i" [On Han Yü and several related questions], p. 27, for a list of poems that Teng reads as attacks on the aristocracy. These include "Bitter Cold" (*Poetry*, pp. 74-77; trans. Owen, *The Poetry*, pp. 213-215; Schmidt, "Han Yu," pp. 100-104), "In the Southern Mountains There Is a Tall Tree: A Ballad Presented to Li Tsung-min" (*Poetry*, pp. 535-538), "On Reading the Miscellaneous Affairs of Tung-fang Shuo" (*Poetry*, pp. 394-397; trans. Schmidt, "Han Yu," pp. 149-152), "I Reprimand the Malaria Demon" (*Poetry*, pp. 122-124; trans. Schmidt, "Han Yu," pp. 109-112), and

"Describing the Snow, Presented to Chang Chi" (*Poetry*, pp. 77-82).

40. Many scholars have rightly cautioned against too simplistic an interpretation of the conflict between aristocrats and career bureaucrats in the T'ang. See for instance Denis Twitchett, "The Government of T'ang in the Early Eighth Century," pp. 322-323.

41. Hartman, "*Alieniloquium*," pp. 37-40.

42. For policies common to Han Yü and the Wang Shu-wen group see Chiang Fan, "Han Yü yü Wang Shu-wen," pp. 69-71.

43. See *TCTC* 240/7752-53; Huang-fu Po's biographies in *CTS* 135/3738-43 and *HTS* 167/5113-15; Ch'eng I's biograhies in *CTS* 135/3737-38 and *HTS* 168/5142-43. Cf. also *Cam. Hist.*, pp. 632-633.

44. It is interesting to note that the *CTS* (135/3713-44) groups Huang-fu Po and Ch'eng I with Wang Shu-wen and Wang Pei. Others included in this chapter are Lu Ch'i, the nefarious prime minister during the early 780s (*Cam. Hist*, p. 586), the infamous P'ei Yen-ling (728-796, cf. *Cam. Hist.*, pp. 597-598), and Li Shih, the imperial relative and metropolitan governor of Ch'ang-an with whom Han Yü clashed in 803. All three entered government service through the *yin* privilege, and their actions undermined the regular bureaucratic structure.

45. Ch'en Yin-k'o, *Ch'en Yin-k'o hsien-sheng lun-wen chi*, 2:173-174; Bischoff, *Forêt des pinceaux*, pp. 10-17; Sun Kuo-t'ung, *T'ang-tai chung-yang chung-yao wen-kuan ch'ien-chuan t'u-ching yen-chiu* [Researches on career paths of important civil officials in the central government of the T'ang dynasty], pp. 198-212; and *Cam. Hist.*, pp. 595-596.

46. Wu Yüan-heng (*CTS* 158/1159-60) was a major opponent of the Wang Shu-wen party; P'ei Tu's prowar policies were consistently opposed by the Han-lin scholars (*CTS* 170/4415). This antagonism between Han Yü's party and the Han-lin probably accounts for the lack of meaningful literary interchange between Han Yü and Po Chü-i or Yüan Chen, both of whom were Han-lin scholars and intimately associated with its policies.

47. For a collection of antieunuch passages from Han Yü's writings see Chiang Fan, "Han Yü yü Wang Shu-wen," pp. 70-71. Much ink has been spilled contending that Han Yü's poem "Seeing Off the Pien-chou Military Superintendent Chü Wen-chen" (*Poetry*, pp. 21-22; preface in *Prose*, p. 391) proves his adherence to this eunuch and his faction. It is true that Chü Wen-chen was central

to Emperor Hsien-tsung's victory over the Wang Shu-wen coalition (see Hartman, "*Alieniloquium,*" pp. 34-37) and that Han Yü would have been sympathetic to this eunuch's pro-Hsien-tsung policy. But this poem, a perfunctory social piece written in 797, hardly proves Han Yü's support for Chü himself or the eunuchs in general. Besides being his colleague on the staff of Tung Chin at Pien-chou, Chü had been present on the Tibetan border in 787 and had been captured together with Han Yen. What is remarkable about the relationship is that Han Yü seems *not* to have profited during the early years of the *yüan-ho* period when Chü Wen-chen's influence was at its peak. On Chü's later career see Feifel, *Po Chü-i as a Censor,* pp. 75-79 and 205-206. For the traditional defense of Han Yü against charges of complicity with Chü Wen-chen see Wang Ming-sheng's comments quoted in the note under the title at *Poetry,* p. 21, and Lo Lien-t'ien, *Han Yü yen-chiu,* pp. 52-53. A particularly flagrant example of the lengths to which this eight-line poem has been stretched to demonstrate Han Yü's supposed proeunuch sentiments is Yang Jung-kuo, "Han Yü ssu-hsiang p'i-p'an," pp. 10ff., in which the author contends that "Essentials of the Moral Way" was written to support the power of the eunuch establishment!

48. *Prose,* pp. 42-45; T'ung Ti-te, *Han Yü wen hsüan,* pp. 82-97; Kao Pu-ying, *T'ang-Sung wen chü-yao,* 1:164-173; trans. in Liu Shih Shun, *Chinese Classical Prose,* pp. 60-67. On the siege of Sung-chou during the An Lu-shan rebellion see the biographies of Chang Hsün and Hsü Yüan in *CTS* 187B/4899-4903 and *HTS* 192/5534-42, which quotes from Han Yü's "Postface." Cf. also *Cam. Hist.,* p. 478. Li Han's memorial on Chang Hsün is excerpted in *HTS* 203/5777-78; cf. the full text in *T'ang wen-ts'ui* 25/455-457.

49. It is not entirely fortuitous that Han Yü took interest in the heroes of the siege of Sung-chou. *HTS* 192/5541 includes a list of officials who, along with Li Han, had promoted the posthumous merits of Chang Hsün after the rebellion. These included Chang Chien-feng and others who are elsewhere (*HTS* 203/5776) linked with Han Yün-ch'ing and Han Hui. In short, the Han family in the generation before Han Yü was already involved in the effort to secure a proper historical assessment for the defenders of Sung-chou, and some political benefits, certainly Han Yü's relationship with Chang Chien-feng, resulted from these contacts.

50. *Prose,* pp. 244-249; Kao Pu-ying, *T'ang-Sung wen chü-yao,* 1:313-333. On Li Kao, cf. *CTS* 131/3637-41.

51. *Prose*, pp. 154-55; T'ung Ti-te, *Han Yü wen hsüan*, pp. 108-111; Kao Pu-ying, *T'ang-Sung wen chü-yao*, 1:215-220. On Liu Chi see *CTS* 143/3900-01, *HTS* 212/5974-75. Li Fan (754-811) was prime minister from 809 to 811; see *CTS* 148/3997-4001, *HTS* 169/5150-52. On Li I see *CTS* 137/3771-72, *HTS* 203/5784-85, and the fine monograph by Wang Meng-ou, *T'ang shih-jen Li I sheng-p'ing chi ch'i tso-p'in* [The life and works of the T'ang poet Li I].

52. See, for instance, *HTS* 212/5975 where one T'an Chung uses the same argument to rationalize the capitulation of Liu Chi's son Liu Tsung to the T'ang. It is possible Liu Chi was actually considering such a move in 810, for he was murdered by his son shortly after Li I's return to Yu-chou. This son, in turn, became a Buddhist monk over remorse at the murder of his father and died in 821. See *TCTC* 241/7788-90, and *Cam. Hist.*, p. 538.

53. See Han Yü's poem "Alas for Master Tung: A Ballad" composed in 799 (*Poetry*, pp. 38-40) trans. in the text, pp. 264-265.

54. The phrase refers to the distressed song of men driven to desperate political circumstances. The reference is probably to the song sung by Ching K'o as he crossed the Yi River on his journey to assassinate Ch'in Shih Huang-ti. See *SC* 86/2534, translated by Burton Watson in Birch, *Anthology*, pp. 106-118. Cf. also *WH* 28/28b, trans. in Erwin von Zach, *Die chinesische Anthologie*, 1:510. Songs of Yen and Chao were often characterized as "songs of sorrow and indignation" (*pei-ko k'ang-k'ai*) and later formed a distinct subgenre of *yüeh-fu* poetry. Cf. the *Shih chi* biography of Hsiang Yü (*SC* 7/333; Watson, *Records of the Grand Historian*, 1:70), *WH* 27/19a (Zach, *Anthologie*, 1:480), and Jao Tsung-i, "Chan-kuo wen hsüeh," *BIHP* 48 (1976): 154.

55. Yüeh I was named commander-in-chief of the forces of Yen in 284 B.C. and led a successful campaign against Ch'i the next year. When King Chao of Yen died and was succeeded by his son King Hui in 279 B.C., however, the latter replaced Yüeh I, who then fled to Chao. When Ch'i forces counterattacked, Yüeh I was summoned back to Yen. See *SC* 34/1558 (trans. Chavannes, *Mémoires historiques*, 4:145), Yüeh I's biography in *SC* 80/2427-36, and Maspero, *China in Antiquity*, pp. 262-263. Cf. also Liu Tsung-yüan's "Lament for Yüeh I" (*Liu Tsung-yüan chi*, 2:519-521), which seems to indicate that during this period Yüeh I was a prototype of the meritorious servitor whose deeds go unknown and who is harmed by slander.

56. The "dog butcher" was an anonymous resident of the Yen mar-

ketplace and an early confidant of Ching K'o. The allusion returns to the theme of "songs of sorrow and indignation." Thus *SC* 86/2528, as translated by Burton Watson (in Birch, *Anthology*, p. 106):

> In the course of his travels, Ching K'o reached the state of Yen, where he became close friends with a dog butcher and a man named Kao Chien-li, who was good at playing the lute. Ching K'o was fond of wine, and every day he would join the dog butcher and Kao Chien-li to drink in the marketplace of the Yen capital. After the wine had begun to take effect, Kao Chien-li would strike up the lute and Ching K'o would join in with a song. In the middle of the crowded marketplace they would happily amuse themselves, or if their mood changed they would break into tears, exactly as though there were no one else about.

57. *Prose*, pp. 144-145; Shimizu Shigeru, *Tō-Sō hakkabun*, 1:51-57; T'ung Ti-te, *Han Yü wen hsüan*, pp. 68-70; Kao Pu-ying, *T'ang-Sung wen chü-yao*, 1:210-212.

58. See especially the comment of Szu-ma Kuang in *TCTC* 240/7759, where the historian remarks that Han Yü's expression of his anti-Buddhist sentiment in the "Memorial on the Buddha Relic" is "inflammatory and excessive" and that the concluding passage of this preface, which Szu-ma Kuang quotes, constitutes a more measured opinion. Cf. also the collected critical comment on this text in Lo Lien-t'ien, *Han Yü yen-chiu*, pp. 335-336, and Shih Shu-nü, "Han Yü shih wen hui-p'ing" [A collection of critical comments on Han Yü's prose and poetry], p. 217. The text is in *Prose*, pp. 147-148.

59. Han Yü refers to *Fa yen* (*SPPY* ed.) 3/4a: "Someone asked, 'If there were a man leaning against the wall of Confucius's house playing the music of Cheng and Wei and reciting the books of Han fei-tzu and Chuang-tzu would you invite him to enter the gate?' Yang Hsiung replied, 'Among the barbarians, I would invite him to enter; but if he were leaning on the wall by the gate, I would bar his entry.' "

60. The translation here follows the K'ung Ying-ta commentary, which interprets this passage as follows: to make their thoughts true, the ancients first drew upon their knowledge of what was closest to them, using this as a base from which to proceed to a knowledge of the more distant, thus tying together the various links in the catenation. But knowledge can be either of good or of evil. Knowledge of good stimulates good "objects" to be at-

tracted to its possessor. Likewise, a knowledge of evil attracts evil happenings and events to its possessor. Thus by observing the moral quality of the "objects" that he attracts, the Sage determines the quality of his knowledge and adjusts his actions accordingly. Perfection is attained when the Sage encounters and practices only good. Cf. *Li chi chu-shu* (*SPPY* ed.) 60/2b, and Barrett, "Buddhism," pp. 255-257.

61. This theme is ubiquitous among Han Yü's detractors. An early example is Wang An-shih; see Ch'ien Chung-shu, *T'an i lu*, p. 75. Some Sung Neo-Confucians still equated the political extension of *jen* with "universal love"; see the remarks of Yang Shih (1053-1135) quoted in Chan, trans., *Reflections on Things at Hand*, pp. 80-81. Most modern Chinese articles on Han Yü's "thought" contain a selection of quotations arranged to demonstrate the "contradictions" of his attitude toward Mo-tzu. Homer H. Dubs, "The Development of Altruism in Confucianism," pp. 52-53, notes the influence of both Buddhism and Mohism on Han Yü's idea of *jen*, arguing that *po-ai* is identical to the Mohist "universal love." Wing-tsit Chan, "The Evolution of the Confucian Concept *Jen*," pp. 303-304, argues that Han Yü's real interest was not to define the nature of *jen* but to emphasize its superior utility in a Confucian rather than a Buddhist system: "the Confucian Way . . . consists of 'giving life to and supporting one another' and 'ordering the state and regulating the family.' It was the way of 'having activity.' In short, the Buddhist and Taoist Way was nothing but an empty state of mind and inactivity." Chan is certainly correct in his observation that Han Yü's extension of *jen* is not a redefinition of the essential concept of "love with distinction" but rather an enlarging of its functional sphere. He continues, however, to translate *po-ai* as "universal love," somewhat confusing the issue.

62. *Prose*, pp. 22-23; T'ung Ti-te, *Han Yü wen hsüan*, pp. 242-245. The four divisions of Han Yü's text—"unity with the superior" (*shang t'ung*), "universal love" (*chien ai*), "elevation of the worthy" (*shang hsien*), and "explanation of ghosts" (*ming kuei*)—are all chapter headings from the *Mo-tzu*. They are also major Mohist teachings; see Burton Watson, *Basic Writings of Mo tzu, Hsün tzu, and Han fei tzu* (New York: Columbia University Press, 1967), pp. 6-10, 18-49, 94-109. The first and third constitute the major Mohist teachings on political order. "Therefore the sage kings of ancient times took great pains to elevate the worthy and employ the capable, showing no special consideration for their

own kin, no partiality for the eminent and rich, no favoritism for the good-looking and attractive. They promoted the worthy to high places, enriched and honored them, and made them heads of government; the unworthy they demoted and rejected, reduced to poverty and humble station, and condemned to penal servitude. Thus the people encouraged by the hope of reward and awed by the fear of punishment, led each other on to become worthy, so that worthy men increased in number and unworthy men became few. This is what is called elevation of the worthy" (pp. 22-23). "When all these officials had been installed, the Son of Heaven proclaimed the principle of his rule to the people of the world, saying, 'Upon hearing of good or evil, one shall report it to his superior. What the superior considers right all shall consider right; what the superior considers wrong all shall consider wrong. If the superior commits any fault, his subordinates shall remonstrate with him; if his subordinates do good, the superior shall reward them. To form unity with one's superior and not to form cliques on the lower levels—such conduct as this shall be rewarded by those above and praised by those below.' " Such subordination began with the village heads and proceeded through the county heads and lords of each region to the Son of Heaven. "If we examine the reason why the world was well ordered, we find that it was simply that the Son of Heaven was able to unify the standards of judgment throughout the world, and this resulted in order" (pp. 35-37). One can easily see from these passages that the impartial application of moral standards to the selection of officials and the strict hierarchical ordering of these officials under the Son of Heaven probably attracted Han Yü to Mo-tzu more than did the latter's doctrine of "universal love." Indeed, this Mohist structure of ascending levels of authority recalls the *Great Learning* catenation.

63. See Ch'eng Shu-te, *Lun yü chi-shih*, 1:372-374, for collected commentaries on this passage. Arthur Waley's translation (*The Analects of Confucius*, p. 122) emphasizes the text's political tone:

Tzu-kung said, If a ruler not only conferred wide benefits upon the common people, but also compassed the salvation of the whole State, what would you say of him? Surely, you would call him Good? The Master said, It would no longer be a matter of 'Good.' He would without doubt be a Divine Sage. Even Yao and Shun could hardly criticize him. As for Goodness—you yourself desire rank and standing; then help others to get rank and standing. You want to turn your own merits to account; then help others to turn theirs to account—in fact, the ability to take one's own feelings as a guide—that is the sort of thing that lies in the direction of Goodness.

Richard Wilhelm, on the other hand (*Kung-futse Gespräche*, p. 60), translates in spiritual, almost religious, terms:

Dsï Gung sprach: "Wenn einer dem Volke reiche Gnade spendete und es vermöchte, die gesamte Menschheit zu erlösen, was wäre ein solcher?" Der Meister sprach: "Nicht nur sittlich, sondern göttlich wäre der zu nennen. Selbst Yao und Shun waren in diesem Stück sich mit Schmerzen (ihrer Unvollkommenheit) bewusst. Was den Sittlichen anlangt, so festigt er andere, da er selbst wünscht gefestigt zu sein, und klärt andre auf, da er selbst wünscht aufgeklärt zu sein. Das Nahe als Beispiel nehmen können (nach sich selbst die anderen zu beurteilen verstehn), das kann als Mittle zur Sittlichkeit bezeichnet werden."

It is possible of course to construe the passage both ways, and Han Yü took advantage of this ambiguity to stress the identity of moral and political action. This certainly explains the later Neo-Confucian emphasis on this passage, which they used to unite the extension of *jen* to "disinterestedness" (*kung*), itself leading to the view that "by *jen* heaven and earth and the innumerable things are regarded as one substance, so that nothing is not oneself" (Ch'eng Hao commentary to *Analects* VI.30, trans. in A. C. Graham, *Two Chinese Philosophers*, p. 98. Cf. also Chan, *Reflections on Things at Hand*, p. 19, and "The Evolution of the Confucian Concept of Jen," pp. 308-309).

64. *Kuang Hung-ming chi* (*SPPY* ed.) 16/2a. See E. Zürcher, *The Buddhist Conquest of China*, p. 177.

65. See Ch'eng Shu-te, *Lun yü chi-shih*, 1:374, and Chan, "The Evolution of the Confucian Concept *Jen*," p. 295.

66. Ch'en Yin-k'o, "Lun Han Yü," p. 107. On *ko-i* see T'ang Yung-t'ung, "On 'ko-yi,' the Earliest Method by Which Indian Buddhism and Chinese Thought Were Synthesized," in W. R. Inge et al., eds., *Radhakrishnan* (London: Allen and Unwin, 1951). pp. 276-286. Cf. also Zürcher, *Buddhist Conquest*, p. 184.

67. *Kuang Hung-ming chi* 36/11b. This passage is partially translated in Jacques Gernet, *Les aspects économiques du bouddhisme*, p. 289,

where the text is wrongly attributed to Emperor Wu of Ch'en (r. 557-559).

68. *Hsün-tzu*, ch. 22 "Rectifying Names"; see Watson, *Basic Writings*, p. 144. Cf. also J.J.L. Duyvendak, "Hsün-tzu on the Rectification of Names," *TP* 23 (1924): 221-254.

69. See Joseph R. Levenson and Franz Schurmann, *China: An Interpretive History*, pp. 47-48: "One cannot say that a son has murdered his father, because it is essential that a son respect his father: *essential*, not in the sense that filial piety is binding on a son, but in the sense that he *is* not (he does not have the essence of) a son without it. A king does not starve or slaughter his people, because it is of the essence of kingship that a king brings harmony to the realm. If one fails in this and yet is called a king, that name must be 'rectified.' As the great Confucianist, Mencius, said, speaking of Shou Hsin, or Chou (the last ruler of Shang, that legendary monster of evil), he knew no monarch, Chou—only a villain, Chou."

70. Han Yü often uses "rectification of names" as a dialectical and rhetorical technique. See, for instance, his 795 letters to the prime ministers in chapter one above, also his "Discourse on Teachers." Cf. also Barrett, "Buddhism," pp. 282-283.

71. See the note in Kao Pu-ying, *T'ang Sung wen chü-yao*, 1:154. The rhymes belong to the *yang, tung,* and *keng* categories of the traditional *Ch'ieh yün* classification. Similar cross-rhyming occurs in Han Yü's poem "How Sad This Day," written in 799 (*Poetry*, pp. 40-47, with an ample selection of commentary on the rhyme scheme).

72. See Bernhard Karlgren, *The Poetical Parts in Lao-tsï*, and Lung Yü-ch'ün, "Hsien-Ch'in san-wen chung te yün-wen" [Rhyme in pre-Ch'in prose texts].

73. Unfortunately, it is impossible to translate this famous concluding passage without destroying these features. Literally, the text says "[If there is] no blocking [of that], [there will be] no flowing [of this]; [if there is] no stopping [of that], [there will be] no moving [of this]. Humanize these humans, fire their books, make homes of their dwellings, enlighten the words of former kings to moralize them. . . ." For further rhetorical notes on the "Essentials of the Moral Way" see Lo Lien-t'ien, *Han Yü yen-chiu*, pp. 221-223, 225-226, 230-231.

74. This was Lu Chün (774-860), who served from 846 to 850 as governor of the Hsüan-wu military region headquartered at Pien-

chou, the ancient Ta-liang. Lu Chün received the *chin-shih* in 809 and was enfeoffed as Duke of Fan-yang in 850. Cf. *CTS* 177/ 4591-93; *HTS* 182/5367-69.

75. Lu Wan (247-194 B.C.) was born on the same day in the same village as Liu Pang, first emperor of the Han Dynasty, whom he faithfully served for many years. Yet he finally defected to the Hsiung-nu, where he died. See *SC* 93/2637-39; Watson, *Records of the Grand Historian*, 1:238-241.

76. Chin Jih-ti (d. 86 B.C.) was a Hsiung-nu nobleman taken prisoner by the Han. He served Han Wu-ti with distinction and together with Ho Kuang (d. 68 B.C.) acted as guardian for the young Emperor Chao. See *HS* 68/2959-67.

77. *Ch'üan T'ang wen* 767/27a-b. Hsieh Hai-p'ing, *T'ang-tai fan-hu sheng-huo chi ch'i tui wen-hua chih ying-hsiang*, pp. 90-91, states that Li Yen-sheng received the *chin-shih* in 848. One finds the same argument, this time worked in the opposite direction, in Huang-fu Shih's dissertation "On the Legitimacy of the Eastern Chin and the T'o-pa Wei Dynasties":

> Historians of today all take the Eastern Chin as illegitimate, which is a great error. To those who maintain that the T'o-pa held the central states, I reply that rites and propriety are what constitute the central states and that the lack of these is what constitutes the barbarians. How could it depend solely on geography? If the state of Chi (in Honan) uses barbarian rites, then it is barbarian. And if a Sage dwells among the Nine Barbarian tribes, then the barbarians are not rude. (*Huang-fu chih-cheng wen-chi*, SPTK ed. 2/4a)

Cf. also Chiang Kuo-chen, *Huang-fu chih-cheng hsüeh-shu yen-chiu*, pp. 83-84.

78. Ch'en Yin-k'o, "Lun Han Yü," pp. 105-106. No point in this article has generated more controversy. See, for instance, Huang Yün-mei, "Tu Ch'en Yin-k'o hsien-sheng 'Lun Han Yü,'" pp. 68-71, and Chi Chen-huai, "Han Yü te chi-pen ssu-hsiang chi ch'i mao-tun," p. 71. Neither author's objections merit rebuttal. There are many valuable observations, however, in Barrett's discussion of the question: "Buddhism," pp. 76-77, 287-293, 297. For the history of the Ch'an "transmission of the dharma" see Yampolsky, *Platform Sutra*, pp. 1-57.

79. Barrett, "Buddhism," pp. 291-292.

80. "Letter in Reply to Chang Chi," *Prose*, p. 77.

81. *Prose*, pp. 76-79, which prints Chang Chi's two letters in the

headnotes. Han Yü's two letters have been translated in Bruno Hermann Luebeck, "Han Yü, the Champion of Confucianism," pp. 67-74. Chang Chi's letters are translated in Chuen-tang Chow, "Chang Chi the Poet," pp. 67-84, with some discussion. A recent article fixing the composititon of the letters in the winter of 798 and containing much useful analysis is Lo Lien-t'ien, "Chang Chi shang Han Ch'ang-li shu te chi-ke wen-t'i" [Several problems concerning Chang Chi's letters to Han Yü], pp. 353-385. Cf. also Charles Hartman, "Han Yü and T. S. Eliot—a Sinological Essay in Comparative Literature," pp. 74-75.

82. *Analects* VII.20: "The Master said, 'I was not born with knowledge but, being fond of Antiquity, I am quick to seek it' " (Lau trans., p. 88).

83. *Analects* XIX.22: "Kung-sun Ch'ao of Wei asked Tzu-kung: 'From whom did Confucius learn?' Tzu-kung said, 'The way of King Wen and King Wu has not yet fallen to the ground but is still to be found in men. The worthy realize what is of major significance; the unworthy realize what is of minor significance. Yet all have something of the way of King Wen and King Wu in them. So the Master learned everywhere; and therefore he had no constant teacher.' " The susceptibility of this passage to Ch'an interpretation is obvious. For instance, the Sung dynasty *Record of Returning to the Self* (*Fan-shen lu*) comments: "When Confucius studied, he had no constant teacher; and this is why he was a Sage. If everyone could perfect this teaching, then one could draw something of benefit everywhere, and everyone would become Confucius" (quoted in Ch'eng Shu-te, *Lun yü chi-shih*, 2:1158).

84. For what Confucius learned from T'an-tzu see *Commentary of Tso* (trans. Legge, *Chinese Classics*, vol. 5, text p. 666/5, trans. p. 668a). Confucius studied music under Ch'ang Hung (d.492 B.C.): see *Li chi chu-shu* 39/4b (trans. Legge, *Rites*, 2:122, equals Chavannes, *Mémoires historiques*, 3:279; cf. also 3:402, 428). He studied the lute under Master Hsiang: see *SC* 47/1935-36 (Chavannes, 5:349-351), and James R. Hightower, trans., *Han shih wai chuan*, pp. 167-168. For the Master's discipleship to Lao-tzu, see *SC* 47/1919 (Chavannes, 5:299-301, with an extensive note reviewing the literature on the Lao-tzu/Confucius relationship).

85. *Analects* VII.22: "Even when walking in the company of two other men, I am bound to be able to learn from them. The good points of the one I copy; the bad points of the other, I correct in myself" (Lau trans., p. 88).

86. *Prose*, pp. 24-25; T'ung Ti-te, *Han Yü wen hsüan*, pp. 52-57; Shimizu Shigeru, *Tō-Sō hakkabun*, 1:256-267; trans. Margouliès, *Anthologie*, pp. 130-131; Yang Hsien-yi and Gladys Yang, "Prose Writings of Han Yü," pp. 64-65; Liu Shih Shun, *Chinese Classical Prose*, pp. 34-37.

87. There are some indications that prior to Han Yü's innovation, "lectures" at the Imperial University were delivered only on occasions of high ritual such as a visit of the emperor or the heir apparent to the school. See des Rotours, *Fonctionnaires*, 1:445 n. 1.

88. "Letter to Professor I of the Imperial University," Hsiao Ti-fei, ed., *P'i-tzu wen-sou* [Literary marsh of Master P'i] (Peking: Chunghua, 1959), pp. 96-97. I am indebted to Professor David McMullen for this and the following reference.

89. *Ch'üan T'ang wen* 735/15b-16a. This preface can be dated to 816. "Deficient conduct" (*tuan hsing*) presumably refers to the Ch'an practice of outlandish gesture and action as a technique to awaken the mind.

90. *Erh-Ch'eng i-shu* (*SPPY* ed.) 2A/9b; reference from Barrett, "Buddhism," p. 428 n. 40. Ch'en Yin-k'o was of course not the first to suspect Ch'an influence on the *tao-t'ung* concept. Buddhist authors as early as the Sung protested the Confucian appropriation of their concept. The similarity also troubled later Confucians. Itō Jinsai (1627-1703) "rejected it [the *tao-t'ung*] as a shallow attempt on the part of Confucians to emulate the Zen Buddhist doctrine of the transmission of the dharma directly from patriarch to patriarch" (Barrett, p. 76).

91. "Letter in Reply to Wei Chung-li Concerning the Tradition of Teachers," *Liu Tsung-yüan chi*, 3:871-872.

92. Komazawa daigaku, *Zengaku daijiten*, 1:12, cites the Sung compendium *Tsu-t'ing shih yüan* [The Garden of Events from the Courtyard of the Patriarchs]. For a contemporary reference see Tsung-mi's preface to his *Yüan-jen lun* [Discussion on the Origins of Human Beings], *Taishō*, No. 1886, vol. 45, p. 708a; trans. Paul Masson-Oursel, "Le Yuan Jen Louen," pp. 299-354.

93. For this formulation, the ultimate epistemological expression of the *Great Learning* catenation, see Chan, *Reflections on Things at Hand*, pp. 88-122; Graham, *Two Chinese Philosophers*, pp. 74-82; and Graf, *Tao und Jen*, pp. 116-125.

There is some evidence that Confucian scholars had begun to appropriate the Ch'an master-disciple relationship in the genera-

tion before Han Yü. See McMullen, "Historical and Literary Theory," pp. 310-311. The term used to express this relationship in
a Confucian context was *shih-yu* ("teacher and friends," or more
accurately "those united [through the same] teacher"). Chang Chi
uses the term in his second letter to Han Yü, "Now the tradition
of 'teacher and friends' (*shih-yu*) is gone" (*Prose*, p. 78). Wang
Ting-pao, *T'ang chih yen* chapter four (pp. 47-52), has an entire
section titled *shih-yu* composed almost entirely of anecdotes involving Hsiao Ying-shih, Li Hua, Ch'i Yang, Tu Fu, Ts'ui Ch'ün,
Lu Chih, and Han Yü. The section also contains a version of the
account of the "Four K'uei" (p. 48). The term also occurs in Ch'an
contexts; see the quotation from the *Tsu-t'ing shih yüan* cited in
the previous note.

94. See *CTS* 136/3750-51, *HTS* 150/4814-15.

95. See *Commentary of Tso*; trans. Legge, *Chinese Classics*, vol. 5,
text p. 418, trans. p. 420.

96. *Analects* XII.6: "Tzu-chang asked about clarity. The Master said,
'To be unmoved by slanders that slowly seep in and by denunciations that build up like dirt on the skin can be called clarity. It
can also be called far-sightedness.' " As Waley correctly notes
(*Analects of Confucius*, p. 164), a passage in the *I Chou shu* provides
the context: "He whom neither slander nor denunciation can influence is called clearsighted, i.e. in his choice of subordinates."
This interpretation concurs with Han Yü's meaning: when the
ruler is not influenced by wrongful denunciations in his choice of
subordinates, there will be no cause for false accusations against
these subordinates from among the people.

97. *Analects* XII.4: "At forty I was free from doubts, at fifty I knew
the will of Heaven."

98. *Prose*, pp. 140-142.

99. Levenson, *China: An Interpretive History*, pp. 92-93.

100. Pairing of these two terms is very old. The earliest reference
is to common versus private land, so *Book of Poetry* 52/212/3, "it
rains on our public fields, and then comes to our private fields"
(trans. Bernhard Karlgren, *The Book of Odes*, p. 166). The *Book
of Documents* (trans. Legge, *Chinese Classics*, 3:531) contains an
address to the officers of early Chou: "By your public feeling
extinguish all selfish aims, and the people will have confidence in
you, and be gladly obedient."

101. See Graham, *Two Chinese Philosophers*, pp. 96ff. For example,
Ch'eng Hao wrote, "To sum up the way of benevolence (*jen*), it

333

is enough to say the one word 'disinterested.' " "Where there is disinterestedness there is unity, where there is selfishness there are innumerable divisions."

102. This passage constitutes to my knowledge the only occurrence in Han Yü's writings of the much overused term *fu-ku*. As can be clearly seen, its implications are primarily political, not literary.

103. *Prose*, pp. 13-14; T'ung Ti-te, *Han Yü wen hsüan*, pp. 229-233; translated by J. K. Rideout in Birch, *Anthology*, pp. 255-257, and Margouliès, *Anthologie*, pp. 159-161. *Hui* fundamentally means "to break, destroy; diminish, enfeeble," an overtone Han Yü certainly intended. Thus Margouliès translates *Yüan hui* as "Origine de la corruption."

104. See his "Explanatory Words" (*Shih yen*) in *Prose*, pp. 40-41, trans. Hartman, "Language and Allusion," pp. 185-192.

105. See above, chapter one, note 11.

106. *HTS* 46/1182; des Rotours, *Fonctionnaires*, 1:4. During the period of Han Yü's lifetime it was customary for the emperor to appoint three prime ministers, each selected for his affiliation to major coalitions and interest groups within the bureaucracy. Their effectiveness depended on the power of the group they represented, on individual ability and energy, and on their personal relationship with the sovereign. The stature of the office lost ground toward the end of Te-tsung's reign when the "inner court" appropriated many of its duties. The Wang Shu-wen faction, for instance, regarded the office and its occupants lightly. Hsien-tsung, in accordance with his reassertion of central power, renewed the authority of the prime ministership and appointed highly capable officers to staff it.

107. See Ho Peng Yoke, *The Astronomical Chapters of the Chin shu* (Paris: Mouton, 1966), pp. 69-71. This text states that "when these stars fail to appear horses are in short supply."

108. See *Chuang-tzu*, chapter nine (Watson trans., pp. 104-106); *Ch'u tz'u* (*SPPY* ed.) 4/22a (trans. David Hawkes, *Ch'u Tz'u: Songs of the South*, p. 71); *Han shih wai chuan* (Hightower trans., pp. 227-230); *Chan-kuo ts'e* (Shanghai: Ku-chi, 1978), pp. 572-573 (J. I. Crump, trans., *Chan-Kuo Ts'e*, pp. 273-274) and pp. 1092-1093 (Crump, p. 514). Han Yü also used the figure in his "Preface Seeing Off the Scholar Wen Upon His Departure for the Ho-yang Army" (*Prose*, pp. 164-165; trans. Liu Shih Shun, *Chinese Classical Prose*, pp. 77-79) and in the "Letter Seeking a Recommendation on Another's Behalf" (*Prose*, pp. 119-120).

109. *Prose*, p. 20; T'ung Ti-te, *Han Yü wen hsüan*, pp. 236-238; Kao Pu-ying, *T'ang-Sung wen chü-yao*, 1:157-159; Shimizu Shigeru, *Tō-Sō hakkabun*, 1:198-202; trans. Liu Shih Shun, *Chinese Classical Prose*, pp. 28-29, and Zhang Xihou, "Prose Writings of Han Yü," p. 92

Chapter Three

1. Wing-tsit Chan, ed., *Source Book in Chinese Philosophy*, p. 450. Chan continues, "As philosophers they [Han Yü and Li Ao] are quite negligible. There is nothing new in their theories of human nature, and their dualism of good nature and evil feelings is but a continuation of a worn-out theory some eight hundred years old. Han Yü's discussion of the Way is superficial and, unlike that of the Taoists and Buddhists, does not touch on its deeper aspects." Fung Yu-lan, *A History of Chinese Philosophy*, 2:410, writes that "Han Yü is more famous as a stylist than as a speculative thinker, and in the above quotation [from the *Yüan tao*] there is little of purely philosophical interest." Han Yü fares much better in Hou Wai-lu et al.'s *Chung-kuo ssu-hsiang t'ung-shih* [Comprehensive history of Chinese thought], 4:319-351, presumably because the scope of this work is considerably wider than that of those whose interests are "purely philosophical." On the other hand, the heavy-handed Marxist readings of Hou Wai-lu and his collaborators contort much of the material in the section on Han Yü and Li Ao into almost comical caricatures of the original texts.
2. Li Ao's "Life of Han Yü" (Kao Pu-ying, *Tang-Sung wen chü-yao*, 2:556) records that "when he grew up, he could recite all he had ever learned since birth." The *New T'ang History* (*HTS* 176/5255) writes that "ever since he learned to read, he committed several thousand words per day to memory, and when he grew up, he understood perfectly the *Six Classics* and the hundred philosophers."
3. Ch'en Yen-chieh, *Chang Chi shih chu* 7/150.
4. See the "Song of the Stone Drums" (*Poetry*, pp. 346-352; trans. Owen, *The Poetry*, pp. 248-251). The *Hsüan-shih chih* by the late T'ang author Chang Tu records that an earthquake in the mountains south of Ch'üan-chou brought to light a rock inscription written in old "tadpole" characters that only Han Yü could decipher (quoted in Ch'ien Chi-po, *Han Yü chih*, p. 49).

5. Pulleyblank, "Neo-Confucianism," p. 112, argues along more conventional lines that "Han Yü seems to have concerned himself very little" with the new classical scholarship and goes on to speak of Han Yü's "mediocre attainment in scholarship."

6. Barrett, "Buddhism," p. 286.

7. Han Yü's writings in this genre also include discourses on *Hsün-tzu, Ho-kuan-tzu*, and the *I-li* (*Prose*, pp. 20-23). Liu Tsung-yüan's surviving efforts in a similar genre, the "judgement" (*pien*), can be found in his *Liu Tsung-yüan chi*, 1:105-116, and include comments on the *Lieh-tzu, Wen-tzu, Kuei-ku-tzu, Lun yü, Yen-tzu ch'un-ch'iu*, and the *Ho-kuan-tzu*.

8. The *tao-t'ung* concept is first mentioned in the correspondence of 798, between Chang Chi and Han Yü, where Chang Chi introduces Yang Hsiung as the model of one who succeeded in such a reexamination of Antiquity in his own day. See Barrett, "Buddhism," p. 288. The actual phrase, *tao-t'ung*, was a Sung coinage and not used by Han Yü.

9. Han Yü's clearest exposition of this distinction is contained in his famous "Letter to Li I," discussed in detail in the following chapter, pp. 242-244.

10. Liu Tsung-yüan, *Liu Tsung-yüan chi*, 1:105-106; Kao Pu-ying, *T'ang-Sung wen chü-yao*, 1:460-462; Shimizu Shigeru, *Tō-Sō hakkabun*, 1:348-354; Liu Shih Shun, *Chinese Classical Prose*, pp. 102-105. Liu Tsung-yüan's arguments run as follows: If the baby brother had actually been entitled to a fief, the Duke of Chou would have mentioned it earlier and not waited until a mistake had been made to effect the enfeoffment. If the brother were not so entitled, the Duke would never have insisted that the jest be carried through. Furthermore, the Duke would not have so acted simply to impress the king with the seriousness of his position. What if the king had "enfeoffed" a woman or a eunuch instead? Surely the Duke would never have insisted that such an act be carried out. The king had the right, and the Duke the duty, to correct the mistake that had been made. To insist thus on carrying through with the mistake rather than correcting it must have been the action of a small-minded, minor functionary. Liu then refers to the account in *SC* 39/1635 (trans. Chavannes *Mémoires histo-riques*, 4:249-251), according to which a petty annalist called Yin-i, not the sainted Duke of Chou, insisted on the king actually enfeoffing his baby brother.

11. Sakata Shin, " 'Shih chih hsü i' kō" [A study of the "Disquisition on the Preface to the *Book of Poetry*"], pp. 58-59.

12. Barrett, "Buddhism," p. 261.

13. Ibid., pp. 235, 239-240, 407 n. 139, and 408 n. 141. Emperor Wu of the Liang Dynasty (r. 502-549) wrote a commentary on the *Chung yung* (see Legge, *The Chinese Classics*, vol. 1, p. 35; *CTS* 46/1974; *HTS* 57/1432). He also summarized his view of the text at the end of the preface to his "*Fu* on Pure Karma": "The *Rites* maintain that at birth men possess the tranquil nature of Heaven, but as the world influences them their natures are moved by desire. When there is movement, the mind is stirred; but where there is tranquillity, the mind is pure. When movement from outside has ceased, the mind inside becomes bright (*ming*). This is the beginning of enlightenment, and there is no way for suffering to arise. Thus I have made the '*Fu* on Pure Karma' " (*Kuang Hung-ming chi, Taishō* ed., vol. 52, p. 336b). Liu Yü-hsi wrote in the preface to his "Poem Seeing Off the Monk Ch'ün-su" that "when I was young, I studied the *Doctrine of the Mean* and when I came to the passage 'the man of integrity (*ch'eng*) hits what is right without effort and knows what is right without thought,' then awe-struck did I realize that the moral strength of the Sage was through learning that had attained to the state of no learning." Liu then equates this state with "enlightenment that depends on no man, only on the mind alone" (*Liu Yü-hsi chi* 29/268).

14. *Ou-yang hsing-chou chi* (*SPTK* ed.) 6/63a-64b, and *T'ang wen-ts'ui* 35/650-1. Cf. also Barrett, "Buddhism," pp. 273-274.

15. Li Ao, of course, quotes both texts in his *Fu-hsing shu* (Barrett, "Buddhism," pp. 255-257), although the emphasis is more "cosmic" than "social," according to Barrett.

16. des Rotours, *Examens*, pp. 30, 32, 136-137.

17. Fung Yu-lan, "The Rise of Neo-Confucianism and Its Borrowings from Buddhism and Taoism," p. 96. Cf. also Tu Sung-po, "Sung-tai li-hsüeh yü Ch'an-tsung chih kuan-hsi" [Relations between the Sung school of principle and Ch'an], pp. 118-119.

18. Cf. *Chuang-tzu*, chap. 21, "T'ien Tzu-fang"; Watson trans., pp. 221-233.

19. Cf. *SC* 67/2211.

20. Cf. *Mencius* IV.B.31: " 'The way followed by Tseng-tzu and Tzu-ssu,' commented Mencius, 'was the same' " (Lau trans., p. 136).

21. *Prose*, pp. 152-153; T'ung Ti-te, *Han Yü wen hsüan*, pp. 257-260.

22. See *Fu-hsing shu* section 5.3; Barrett, "Buddhism," pp. 244-246 and 292.

23. *Prose*, pp. 20-21; Kao Pu-ying, *T'ang-Sung wen chü-yao*, 1:159-164; T'ung Ti-te, *Han Yü wen hsüan*, pp. 238-241; trans. Liu Shih Shun, *Chinese Classical Prose*, pp. 42-43.

24. See Kao Pu-ying, *T'ang-Sung wen chü-yao*, 1:159. The *SPPY* edition of *Hsün-tzu* contains citations of Han Yü at 1/5a, 1/12a, 3/6a, 15/1b, 17/7a-b (which quotes the entire *Yüan hsing*), 18/2b, and 18/3b-4a. Most of these citations are technical notes on textual matters.

25. The first chapter of the *Lun yü pi-chieh*, for example, comments on *Analects* I.13,14; II.2,4,11,12,13,23.

26. For example, Han Yü joins *Analects* II.12 and 13 (*Lun yü pi-chieh* 1/4a-b).

27. Han Yü and Li Ao, *Lun yü pi-chieh* 1/3a-4b; Ch'eng Shu-te, *Lun yü chi-shih*, 1:84.

28. *Doctrine of the Mean* XXVII.6 reads: "The superior man (*chün-tzu*) treasures his virtuous nature and pursues it through inquiry and study. By attaining its breadth and greatness, he perfects it in every detail. By bringing it to its highest brilliance, he sets it on the Way of equilibrium and harmony. *By recalling the old, he knows the new.* And by honesty and diligence [in his studies] he honors the rites" (*Li chi chu-shu* 53/5a; trans. Legge, *Rites*, 2:323). According to K'ung Ying-ta, the entire passage concerns "the man of perfect integrity" (*chih ch'eng*).

29. Chu Hsi comments: "It means that if in study one can review what he has already learned each time he acquires something new, then what he has studied will be within himself and the responses (*ying*) will be endless. One can then be a teacher. If the text means only 'study by rote memory,' then nothing will be attained in the mind and one's understanding will be limited. For this reason the 'Record of Studies' [chapter of the *Rites*] castigates this as 'not qualifying one to be a teacher' " (quoted in Ch'eng Shu-te, *Lun yü chi-shih*, 1:84).

30. Han Yü and Li Ao, *Lun yü pi-chieh* 7/3a-4b; Ch'eng Shu-te, *Lun yü chi-shih*, 2:831.

31. See above, chapter two, note 89.

32. Han Yü and Li Ao, *Lun yü pi-chieh* 4/1b-2a; Ch'eng Shu-te, *Lun yü chi-shih*, 1:402.

33. Before proceeding further, it will perhaps be useful to address two questions that are crucial to a proper understanding of the *Lun yü pi-chieh*. The first concerns the nature of Han Yü's relationship to Li Ao; the second concerns the authenticity of the text itself. Since the Northern Sung, there have been suggestions that Han Yü and Li Ao were not on the best of terms (cf. references in Barrett, "Buddhism," pp. 318-319 nn. 8 and 9). In modern times, J. K. Rideout, "The Context of the Yüan Tao and Yüan Hsing," pp. 403-408, has suggested that Han Yü was angered "to see the essentially Buddhist doctrine of self-annihilation coming under the guise of Confucianism" in Li Ao's *Fu-hsing shu* and so composed the *Yüan tao* and *Yüan hsing* to refute Li's opinion. These assertions are totally without foundation, and Barrett (pp. 193-196) has effectively disposed of them. Futhermore, by demonstrating the basically Confucian stance of the *Fu-hsing shu*, Barrett has, on the contrary, shown that this work is more subtly and correctly read as a response from Li Ao to Chang Chi's call for an anti-Buddhist tract from Han Yü (pp. 292 and 428 n. 44). To these observations one might add that Li Ao married into Han Yü's family in 800, that Han Yü composed the epitaph for Li Ao's grandfather in 801 (*Prose*, pp. 317-318), that except for their early years together in Pien-chou and brief periods in Lo-yang in 807-809 and Ch'ang-an in 818-819 and 823-824 Li Ao's and Han Yü's bureaucratic careers kept them separated, and that in spite of this separation Li Ao composed Han Yü's official "biographical sketch" and a eulogy, both of which show great affection for Han Yü and a real understanding of his life and achievements. I believe the rumors of discord between them that arose in the Northern Sung are best interpreted as attempts to enchance Han Yü's stature as an anti-Buddhist polemicist by distancing him from the supposedly Buddhist-influenced Li Ao and his *Fu-hsing shu*.

This brings us to the *Lun yü pi-chieh*. It is obvious that this text, purporting as it does to be a joint Han Yü–Li Ao commentary on the *Analects*, would not have been welcomed by Sung or later Neo-Confucian scholars anxious to preserve Han Yü's reputation from contamination with Li Ao. Despite many unresolved questions about the provenance of the present text, it cannot be dismissed as a late Northern Sung forgery (cf. Ch'eng Shu-te, *Lun yü chi-shih*, 1:45, 65). First, Han Yü himself in an early letter to Hou Hsi implies he has been working on a commentary to the *Analects* (*Prose*, p. 425). Chang Chi in his "Elegy for T'ui-chih" wrote that "his *Analects* commentary was unfinished, / the hand-writing already fading away" (Ch'en Yen-chieh, *Chang Chi shih chu*, p. 152). Li Han's preface to Han Yü's collected works states that there was "also a commentary to the *Lun yü* in ten *chüan* for instructing students" (see Hartman, "Preliminary Bibliographical Notes," p. 90). The *New T'ang History* (*HTS* 57/1444) lists a *Lun yü* commentary by Han Yü in ten *chüan*. A work by Li K'uang-i of the *t'ai-chung* period (847-859) quotes two passages from the work, one of which is in the present text, one of which is not (see Chi Yün et al., eds., *Ssu-k'u ch'üan-shu tsung-mu t'i-yao* [Rpt. Shanghai: Shang-wu, 1933], p. 715, for citations). The earliest printed edition, now in the Palace Museum Library in Taipei, dates from the reign of Emperor Hsiao-tsung (r.1163-1189) of the Southern Sung but reprints an earlier text by one Hsü Po (978-1047), whose preface it contains (see Wu Che-fu, "Ku-kung shan-pen-shu chih: *Lun yü pi-chieh*" [Notes on rare books in the Palace Museum. The *Lun yü pi-chieh*], pp. 49-50). This association of the *Lun yü pi-chieh* with Hsü Po affords an important clue to the book's early history and influence, for Hsü Po was among the intellectual predecessors and early confidants of the Ch'eng brothers (see Huang Tsung-hsi, *Sung-Yüan hsüeh-an* [*SPPY* ed.] 12/22a; the *Erh-Ch'eng i-shu* [*SPPY* ed.] 3/5a, 6a, contains anecdotes concerning Hsü Po). The epitaph for Hsü Po composed by Fan Ch'un-jen (1027-1101) mentions that Hsü, just before his death, left two letters for his offspring. Their "major import was all in the phrase 'to develop one's nature to perfection through the investigation of Principle' " (*ch'iung-li chin-hsing*) (*Fan Chung-hsüan chi, Ssu-k'u ch'üan-shu chen-pen, pa-chi* ed., 12/11b). This phrase, as will be seen shortly, is central to the *Lun yü pi-chieh*, a fact that suggests that Hsü Po may have been the vehicle through which Han Yü's philosophical positions, as manifested in the *Lun yü pi-chieh*, influenced early Neo-Confucian thinkers, especially the Ch'eng brothers.

All later editions seem to derive from this early edition of Hsü Po. Most, however, are divided into two *chüan*. The *Sung History* bibliography (*Sung shih* [*SPPY* ed.] 202/13a) mentions the *Lun yü pi-chieh* by Han Yü in two *chüan*, and the editors of the Harvard-Yenching Institute Sinological Index Series (*Combined Indices to Twenty Historical Bibliograhies* [Peking: Harvard-Yenching Institute, 1933], 4:200) equate this entry with the prior entry of a ten-*chüan Analects* commentary by Han Yü in the *New T'ang History*.

Neither the *Ssu-k'u* editors nor later bibliographers, however, knew of the Sung ten-*chüan* edition, and its existence weakens many of their arguments against the authenticity of the present *Lun yü pi-chieh*. The *Ssu-k'u* editors maintained, for example, that since both Li Han and the *New T'ang History* bibliograpy mentioned a Han Yü *Analects* commentary in ten *chüan* and the *Lun yü pi-chieh* was only two *chüan*, these early references could not be to the *Lun yü pi-chieh*. Yet since this title was certainly added later to describe the random nature of the work, there is no valid argument against the validity of these early references, especially when one remembers Chang Chi's testimony that Han Yü's *Analects* commentary was unfinished. Ch'eng Shu-te (*Lun yü chi-shih*, 1:65) objects to the pronounced Neo-Confucian flavor of the text, arguing that such sentiments cannot predate the eleventh century. In one case (2:680), he refuses to print the *Lun yü pi-chieh* commentary on *Analects* XI.20 because its overt use of Buddhist vocabulary contradicts "what Han Yü could have said." On the contrary, the greatest argument in favor of the ultimate authenticity of the *Lun yü pi-chieh* is the close correlation between its exegesis, in technique, vocabulary, and style, and Han Yü's and Li Ao's existing works. It fits the iconoclastic and irreverent yet searchingly spiritual tenor of their age. Both the history of the book and its text obviously merit a detailed study. Finally, it is interesting to note that Hou Wai-lu et al., *Chung-kuo ssu-hsiang t'ung-shih*, 4:344, insists on the unity of opinion between Han Yü and Li Ao and accepts (pp. 347-350) the *Lun yü pi-chieh* as a valid source for the ideas of both thinkers.

34. Other surviving examples of Han Yü's exegetical labors are the "Letter in Reply to Master Hou's Inquiry Concerning the *Analects*" (*Prose*, p. 425) and the "Essay in Response to the Departmental Examination on the Topic 'Yen-tzu Did Not Repeat Errors' " (*Prose*, pp. 72-73). Both of these works will be discussed in detail below. Hints survive of much more extensive projects. The conclusion to the "Letter to Master Hou" can be read as implying that Han Yü was at work on a commentary on *Mencius*, and a manuscript purporting to be a joint Han Yü–Li Ao commentary on *Mencius* seems to have existed in the Sung (see Barrett, "Buddhism," pp. 215 and 393 n.3). There are also the existing fragments of Han Yü's comments on *Hsün-tzu* in the standard Yang Liang commentary, mentioned above in note 24.

35. Inaba Ichirō, "Chūtō ni okeru shinjugaku undō no ichi kōsatsu:

Ryū Chiki no keisho hihan to Tan-Chō-Riki shi no *Shunjūgaku*" [A study of the Neo-Confucian movement of the mid-T'ang: The classical criticism of Liu Chih-chi and the *Spring and Autumn* studies of Masters Tan, Chao, and Lu], pp. 377-403.

36. Ma Ch'i-ch'ang points out four instances in his note under the title in *Prose*, p. 425. These are *Analects* V.10, VII.14, XI.21, and XI.24. None of these proposed emendations was accepted by Chu Hsi.

37. Han Yü and Li Ao, *Lun yü pi-chieh* 6/4a-b; Ch'eng Shu-te, *Lun yü chi-shih*, 2:685, notes Ch'eng I's acceptance of this emendation and its rejection by Chu Hsi.

38. See chapter two, note 103.

39. Soothill and Hodous, *Dictionary of Chinese Buddhist Terms*, pp. 76-77, explains the varying interpretations of the Three Truths. All involve a pseudo-dichotomy between *k'ung* and *chia* that is ultimately resolved in the unity of the "mean" (*chung*).

40. *T'ang wen-ts'ui* 61/1018-19; cf. also Fung Yu-lan, "The Rise of Neo-Confucianism," pp. 111-112. For the history of the *Chih-kuan t'ung-li* and its influence on Li Ao see Barrett, "Buddhism," pp. 176-180.

41. *Li chi chu-shu* 53/2a; trans. Legge, *Rites*, 2:319. This passage is one of the few extensive, and thus important, quotations in Li Ao's *Fu-hsing shu*; see Barrett, "Buddhism," pp. 238-240, with excellent commentary on the T'ang understanding of this passage.

42. *Chou-i chu-shu* 7/19b. The quotation is abridged and slightly changed. The whole text reads: "In silence to fulfill them, confidence without words, these depend on the practice of moral strength." The subject is the Sage's understanding of the *Changes*.

43. *Chou-i chu-shu* 7/10a-b. Once again, the subject is the Sage using the *Changes* to understand the world.

44. *Chou-i chu-shu* 8/11a. The context is again the *Changes*. Wilhelm (p. 348) translates as follows:

> The Changes is a book
> From which one may not hold aloof.
> Its tao is forever changing—
> Alteration, movement without rest,
> Flowing through the six empty places;
> Rising and sinking without fixed law,
> Firm and yielding transform each other.
> They cannot be confined within a rule;
> It is only change that is at work here.

45. *Shih ching* 67/255/7; trans. Karlgren, *The Book of Odes*, p. 217.
46. *Li chi chu-shu* 36/2a; trans. Legge, *Rites*, 2:83-84. The context concerns the progress made by students at the colleges of Antiquity. "In the first year it was seen whether they could read the classics and determine the meaning; in the third year, whether they were reverently attentive to their work, and what companionship was most pleasant to them; in the fifth year, how they extended their studies and sought the company of their teachers; in the seventh year, how they could discuss the subjects of their studies and select their friends. They were now said to have made some small attainments. In the ninth year, when they knew the different classes of subjects and had gained a general intelligence, were firmly established and would not fall back, they were said to have made great attainments."
47. Han Yü and Li Ao, *Lun yü pi-chieh* 6/1b-2a; Ch'eng Shu-te, *Lun yü chi-shih*, 2:644-645.
48. This is still the usual interpretation. Cf. *Han shih wai chuan* 2/16 (Hightower trans., pp. 54-55); Lau, *Analects*, p. 154; and Waley, *Analects of Confucius*, p. 226.
49. Han Yü and Li Ao, *Lun yü pi-chieh* 10/1a-b; Ch'eng Shu-te, *Lun yü chi-shih*, 2:1140-1141. The distinction between the Sage and the Worthy Man is detailed in the K'ung Ying-ta subcommentary to *Doctrine of the Mean* sections 22 and 23 (*Li chi chu-shu* 53/2a-b; cf. also Barrett, "Buddhism," p. 238-240). Han Yü's interpretation of this *Analects* passage is based on this distinction.
50. *T'ang wen-ts'ui* 61/1020. Cf. also Barrett, "Buddhism," p. 242. Li Ao is no less clear on this point in his *Fu-hsing shu*. Speaking of the nature of the Sage, he writes: "So, then do common folk not have this nature? The nature of the common folk is no different from that of the sage . . ." (Barrett, p. 229).
51. Yampolsky, *Platform Sutra*, p. 151. Cf. p. 151 n.136 for references to other Ch'an literature. The same idea also occurs on p. 158. For the quotations, the last from the *Vimalakīrti Sutra*, see p. 141.
52. *Chou-i chu-shu* 9/2a; Wilhelm, *Changes*, p. 262.
53. Wilhelm's translation strongly emphasizes this dichotomy: "By thinking through the order of the outer world to the end, and by exploring the law of their nature to the deepest core, they arrived at an understanding of fate" (*Changes*, p. 262).
54. *Taishō*, No.2145, vol. 55, p. 54c. This preface is dated 408. On

Seng-Jui see A. F. Wright, "Seng-jui alias Hui-jui," *Sino-Indian Studies* 5 (1957): 272-292.

55. *Taishō*, No. 1775, vol. 38, p. 410a. This commentary, although attributed to Seng-chao, is a composite of remarks by many of Kumārajīva's disciples. See Étienne Lamotte, trans., *L'Enseignement de Vimalakīrti*, p. 445 n.25. In Seng-chao's *Nirvāṇa Is Unnameable* (*Nieh-p'an wu-ming lun*), *ch'iung-li chin-hsing* is quoted as a description of *nirvāṇa*. See Walter Liebenthal, *Chao lun* (Hong Kong: University of Hong Kong Press, 1968), p. 118. There is an earlier, non-Buddhist usage of the phrase in the opening lines of the *Discussions of the Different Types of Literature* (*Wen-chang liu-pieh lun*) by Chih Yü (d. 311), where *ch'iung-li chin-hsing* is said to be a function of literature. But Joseph Roe Allen's translation of *chin-hsing* as "express one's emotions" considerably muddles the intent of the passage. See his "Chih Yü's *Discussions of Different Types of Literature*," p. 16.

56. Cf. Yanagida Seizan, *Rinzai roku*, p. 290.

57. *Taishō*, no. 1886, vol. 45, p. 708a; Paul Masson-Oursel, "Le *Yuan Jen Louen*," p. 321.

58. On Tsung'mi's Confucian-Buddhist syncretism see Kenneth Ch'en, *The Chinese Transformation of Buddhism*, pp. 29ff. Cf. also Peter Nielsen Gregory, "Tsung-mi's *Inquiry into the Origins of Man*: A Study of Chinese Buddhist Hermeneutics."

59. Li Chao, *T'ang kuo-shih pu*, p. 24. Ching-shan Fa-ch'in, a master of the Ox-head school of Ch'an, gained fame by preaching to Emperor Tai-tsung in 768. He counted among his disciples the Prime Minister Ts'ui Huan (730-791), an acquaintance of Han Yü's father, Ts'ui Yüan-han, Han Yü's examination patron, and P'ei Tu. Li Chi-fu composed his epitaph. See Komazawa daigaku, *Zengaku daijiten*, 2:1126a, for full references.

60. *Chou-i chu-shu* 8/11b; trans. Wilhelm, *Changes*, p. 349. Han Yü's use here of the phrase *yüan-shih yao-chung* seems to confine its meaning to a technical understanding of the line configurations in the hexagrams. On this phrase as a T'ang cliché see William Hung, "A T'ang Historiographer's Letter of Resignation," p. 20 n.29.

61. The opening sentence of the *Doctrine of the Mean*, *Li chi chu-shu* 52/1a; trans. Legge, *Rites*, 2:300.

62. A paraphrase of the opening of the last book of *Mencius*: "He who develops his mind to perfection knows his own nature; and to know one's own nature is to know Heaven." See Legge, *The Chinese Classics*, vol. 2, pp. 448-449; Lau trans., p. 182. Ch'eng I

adopted this equation of *ch'iung-li chin-hsing* and *Mencius* VII.A.1.
In response to a question on *Mencius* VII.A.1, he replied, "Developing the mind to perfection means that if one can perfect his own mind, then he will as a matter of course know his own nature and know Heaven. It is like 'developing one's nature to perfection through the understanding of Principle and thereby attaining to the will of Heaven.' One must accomplish this according to the stated sequence; for, in fact, only one who has Principle can then perfect his nature and attain to the will of Heaven" (*Erh-Ch'eng i-shu* [*SPPY* ed.] 22A/11b).

63. Han Yü and Li Ao, *Lun yü pi-chieh* 1/3a; Ch'eng Shu-te, *Lun yü chi-shih*, 1:65.

64. This gloss of "understanding the will of Heaven" with *ch'iung-li chin-hsing* was also adopted by Ch'eng I in his comments on the *Analects*; see *Ho-nan Ch'eng-shih ching-shuo* (*Erh-Ch'eng ch'üan-shu* [*SPPY* ed.]) 6/2a.

65. Han Yü and Li Ao, *Lun yü pi-chieh* 10/3a-b; Ch'eng Shu-te, *Lun yü chi-shih*, 2:1192.

66. See *Ho-nan Ch'eng-shih ching-shuo* 5/1a-5b. Ch'eng Hao's reconstruction is closer to the traditional *Li chi* text; Ch'eng I's is closer to Chu Hsi's final version. Legge's tanslation of the *Li chi* follows the old version; his translation of the *Four Books* follows Chu Hsi's new version. For a general discussion of these issues see Chan, *Source Book*, pp. 84-89.

67. *Erh-Ch'eng i-shu, wai-shu* 4/1a. Restatements and elaborations of this basic equation can be found on folios 15/11a (trans. Graham, *Two Chinese Philosophers*, p. 77, and Chan, *Source Book*, p. 556), 18/5b (Graham, p. 76; Fung Yu-lan, *History of Chinese Philosophy*, 2:529-530), 19/1a (Graham, p. 75), 22A/1a, 25/1a and *wai-shu* 2/4a (Graham, p. 74). For Chu Hsi on this equation see Ch'ien Mu, *Chu-tzu hsin hsüeh-an*, 1:246ff.

68. *Huang-chi ching-shih shu* [Supreme Principles Governing the World] (*SPPY* ed.) 5/7a and 6/26a (trans. Chan, *Source Book*, pp. 485, 487-488; Fung Yu-lan, *History of Chinese Philosophy*, 2:466). *Chen-chih* is a Taoist term: "There must first be a True Man before there can be true knowledge" (*Chuang-tzu* 15/6/4; Watson trans., p. 77). Cf. also Graham, *The Book of Lieh-tzu* (London: John Murray, 1960), p. 76.

69. *Heng-chü I-shuo* [Heng-chü's Explanations of the *Changes*], *Chang Tsai chi* (Peking: Chung-hua, 1978 ed.), pp. 234-235 (equals *SPPY* ed. 11/29a-b): "The paths toward knowledge and toward

attainment are far apart. One first comprehends human nature (*chin-hsing*) and only then attains to the will of Heaven (*chih yü ming*). The two cannot be said to be one." Likewise, "the understanding of Principle must be gradual. The more things (*wu*) one sees, the more one understands their Principles. One then proceeds to link these together and so comprehends the nature of men and of things. The Principles in the world (*t'ien-hsia chih li*) are thus inexhaustible, yet if one bases himself on the Principle of Heaven (*t'ien li*), then each can be handled in the proper way. Nature (*hsing*) in the phrase *ch'iung-li chin-hsing* means one has already approached the nature of others; *ming* in *chih yü ming* refers to oneself." Cf. also *Cheng-meng* [Correcting Youthful Ignorance], ibid., p. 21 (trans. Chan, *Source Book*, pp. 508–509).

70. *Erh-Ch'eng i-shu* 2A/2b: "These three activities are simultaneous; there is no basic sequence among them. The understanding of Principle cannot be taken simply as a matter of obtaining knowledge; for, if Principle is really understood, then nature and decree (*ming*) will also be had" (trans. Graham, *Two Chinese Philosophers*, pp. 74–75; Chan, *Source Book*, p. 531; Fung Yü-lan, *History of Chinese Philosophy*, 2:527). Cf. also 11/3b (trans. Chan, p. 539) for a more concise statement; also 12/1b, which insists on the effortlessness of this process: "When one attains to the will of Heaven, this is accomplished totally without effort. The idea is the same as that 'for one who has perfected himself in music joy is born of itself'" (cf. *Analects* VIII.8 and *Mencius* IV.A.27).

71. *Erh-Ch'eng i-shu* 18/9a (trans. Chan, *Source Book*, p. 563, and Fung Yü-lan, *History of Chinese Philosophy*, 2:531). Cf. also 22A/11b translated above in note 62.

72. *Erh-Ch'eng i-shu* 10/5a. Cf. the note by Chan, *Source Book*, pp. 539–540.

73. There are many enumerations and descriptions of the *daśabhūmi* in mahāyāna literature. See Zürcher, *Buddhist Conquest of China*, pp. 382–383 n.157; Luis O. Gomez, "The Bodhisattva as Wonderworker," in Lewis Lancaster, ed., *Prajñāpāramitā and Related Systems*, pp. 248–257, contains a translation of the "ten birth-stages" from the *Gaṇḍavyūha-sūtra*. Cf. also Paul Demiéville, "Le chapitre de la Bodhisattvabhūmi sur la perfection du Dhyāna," pp. 109–128.

74. *Li chi chu-shu* 53/2a. Cf. also Soothill and Hodous, *Dictionary of Chinese Buddhist Terms*, p. 444.

75. Kao Pu-ying, *T'ang-Sung wen chü-yao*, 1:151–152, quotes a pas-

sage from Huang Chen (1213-1280) that castigates Ch'eng I for criticizing Han Yü for not including *chih-chih ko-wu* in "Essentials of the Moral Way." I can find no such criticism in the *SPPY* edition of the *Erh-Ch'eng i-shu*.

76. *Mencius* II.A.2.20: "I have heard that Tzu-hsia, Tzu-yu, and Tzu-chang each had one part of the Sage. Jan Niu, Min Tzu, and Yen Yüan had all the parts, though in lesser degree." Mencius is here playing on the multiple meanings of *t'i* "the body, a member or part of the body; the essence of a thing; a part of a whole." Han Yü's exegesis transfers this metaphor over to the text "the Sage fulfills his body" by introducing the gloss "body" expresses "completeness," meaning that the Sage is complete in his wisdom as the body is complete with all its parts.

77. *Prose*, p. 425.

78. This passage was of course central to the eleventh-century Neo-Confucians. See Graf, *Tao und Jen*, p. 102, and *Erh-Ch'eng i-shu* 2B/6b.

79. Han Yü's explications of this *Mencius* passage was accepted by the Ch'eng brothers and Chu Hsi. Ch'eng I writes: " 'Only the Sage can fulfill his body' means the Sage completely obtains the way of men (*jen tao*). Men are born with the true ether (*cheng ch'i*) of Heaven and Earth and are different from the myriad things. Since they are men, they must completely obtain the Principle of men (*jen li*). All men have this but do not realize it. The worthy man (*hsien jen*) fulfills it but not completely. Only the Sage can fulfill his body" (*Erh-Ch'eng i-shu* 18/22b). Cf. also *Erh-Ch'eng i-shu, wai-shu* 2/3a, 4/1a.

80. *Li chi chu-shu* 53/2a; trans. Legge, *Rites*, 2:318-319. This is one of the most important passages in the *Doctrine of the Mean*. Han Yü follows K'ung Ying-ta's explication that the former—"Enlightenment that proceeds from integrity is ascribed to nature"—refers to the Sage, whereas the latter refers to the worthy man (*hsien jen*). Ou-yang Chan begins his "Essay on Integrity from Enlightenment" with the following definitions: "To arrive at an understanding of things through one's nature (*hsing*) is called integrity (*ch'eng*). To arrive at an understanding of integrity through study is called enlightenment (*ming*). The highest Sage follows integrity to stimulate enlightenment. Below him, is one who investigates enlightenment to obtain integrity" (*T'ang wen-ts'ui* 35/650). Chang Tsai fused this distinction between (1) an inner wisdom (*ch'eng*) that one applied to "enlighten" (*ming*) outside events,

and (2) "enlightenment" about the outside world that one then used to cultivate inner integrity (*ch'eng*) with the phrase *ch'iung-li chin-hsing*. In chapter six, "Integrity and Enlightenment," of the *Cheng-meng* he wrote, " 'Integrity that proceeds from enlightenment' is to develop one's [inner] nature to perfection through the understanding of Principle; 'enlightenment that proceeds from integrity' is to understand the Principle [of outer things] through the development of one's own nature" (*Chang Tsai chi*, Peking 1978 ed., p. 21; cf. also Chan, *Source Book*, p. 508). Cf. also Graham, *Two Chinese Philosophers*, p. 75, for Ch'eng I's view that "integrity" and "enlightenment" are identical.

81. Also *Doctrine of the Mean, Li chi chu-shu* 53/1a. Cf. also Li Ao's *Fu-hsing shu* (Barrett, "Buddhism," pp. 258-259), which maintains a similar distinction and characterizes Yen Hui as an exemplar of the secondary or "worthy man" status.

82. *Chou-i chu-shu* 8/8a; trans. Wilhelm, *Changes*, p. 342. Li Ao quotes the same passage; cf. Barrett, "Buddhism," p. 253.

83. *Prose*, pp. 72-73.

84. Barrett, "Buddhism," p. 243.

85. It is interesting to note that Ch'eng I's position on Yen Hui, as recorded in Chan, *Reflections on Things at Hand*, pp. 35-39, 96, is taken from Han Yü.

86. *Fu-hsing shu* (*T'ang wen-ts'ui* ed.) 44A/767-68; Barrett "Buddhism," p. 252. Barrett notes that "Han Yü was already using such language before Li Ao" (p. 251) and refers to the essay on Yen Hui. Barrett also notes the obvious Ch'an parallels.

87. This is the interpretation of K'ung An-kuo, who comments: "Although the good man does not simply follow in old tracks, his accomplishments are few, and so he cannot enter the profound inner room of the Sages." See Ch'eng Shu-te, *Lun yü chi-shih*, 2:680.

88. The "mind-ground" (*hsin-ti*) is an important Ch'an concept that occurs often in T'ang Ch'an texts. The *Tsu-t'ang chi* biography of Nan-yüeh Huai-jang defines the term: "You should understand the doctrine of the mind-ground, which teaches that this mind-ground is as if planted with seeds. When I expound the essentials of the Dharma to you, it will be like rain falling upon that ground. Because the circumstances of your makeup join with the rain, therefore you are able to see the Way" (trans. Yampolsky, *Platform Sutra*, p. 164 n.210). The term also occurs in the *Platform Sutra* (Yampolsky trans., pp. 158, 164, 178) where it is equated with

the self-nature" (*tzu-hsing*). Lin-chi preaches to his followers: "What Dharma do I teach? I teach the Dharma of the mind-ground, through which one can enter the profane and the Sage, the pure and the impure, the true and the vile . . . (*Lin-chi lu*: Yanagida Seizan ed., *Rinzai roku*, p. 93; trans. Demiéville, *Entretiens de Lin-tsi*, p. 69). Demiéville comments on the expression, "l'esprit comparé à la terre nourricière, productrice de toutes choses." Cf. also Yanagida, p. 142; Demiéville, p. 121, and Komazawa daigaku, *Zengaku daijiten*, 1:619. Hou Wai-lu and company, who quote this passage from the *Lun yü pi-chieh* (*Chung-kuo ssu-hsiang t'ung shih*, 4:347-348), err seriously in connecting *hsin-ti* with the "mind-fasting" of Chuang-tzu (*Chuang-tzu* 9/4/25ff.; Watson trans., pp. 57-58).

89. Han Yü and Li Ao, *Lun yü pi-chieh* 6/3a-b. Ch'eng Shu-te (*Lun yü chi-shih*, 2:680-682) omits this entry from the *Lun yü pi-chieh*, claiming that "these opinions cannot be accepted." Li Ao's concluding phrase plays on the phrase *t'ang-t'ang-hu* "majestic, grand," which describes Tzu-chang in *Analects* XIX.16. *T'ang* "outer hall" can be contrasted with *shih* "the inner room," which increases the ironic overtones of Li Ao's concluding sentence: "A man of the outer hall was Tzu-chang! He could in truth never attain to this."

90. No major commentator or translator of the *Analects* follows such an interpretation, which is, incidentally, a good example of Han Yü's "layering" of the text.

91. *Prose*, pp. 11-13; Margouliès, *Anthologie*, pp. 400-401; Chan, *Source Book*, pp. 451-454.

92. Cf. note under title, *Prose*, p. 11.

93. Cf. the *Vijñaptimātratāsiddhi* (*Taishō*, no. 1585, vol. 31, p. 23), trans. Louis de La Vallée Poussin, *Le siddhi de Hiuan tsang* (Paris: Geuthner, 1928), p. 265.

94. *Scripture of the Lotus Blossom of the Fine Dharma*, trans. Leon Hurvitz, p. 103: "The living beings dwell on a variety of grounds. Only the Thus Come One sees them for what they are and understands them clearly and without obstruction. Those grasses and trees, shrubs, and forests, and medicinal herbs do not know themselves whether their nature is superior, intermediate, or inferior; but the Thus Come One knows this Dharma of a single mark and a single flavor . . . finally reducing itself to Emptiness. The Buddha, knowing this, observes the heart's desire of each of the beings, and guides them protectively. For this reason he does not im-

mediately preach to them the knowledge of all modes. . . ." Cf. Barrett, "Buddhism," pp. 243-244, for a translation and discussion of a *Fu-hsing shu* passage influenced by this metaphor. Barrett makes a rare error when he attributes the last line of this passage— "These are explanations of 'correct nature and decree' "—to the Buddhist concept of "right life." The reference is to *Chou-i chu-shu* 1/4a. Cf. note 98 below.

95. *Huang-fu chih-cheng wen-chi* (*SPTK* ed.) 2/4b-5b and Chiang Kuo-chen, *Huang-fu chih-cheng hsüeh-shu yen-chiu,* p. 84. Barrett, "Buddhism," pp. 221ff., points out the relation between Han Yü's text and the *Fu-hsing shu*, suggesting that Han Yü may have written the *Yüan hsing* to supplement Li Ao's discussion of *hsing* and *ch'ing* (cf. p. 397 n.43).

96. Han Yü and Li Ao *Lun yü pi-chieh* 3/2b-3a; Ch'eng Shu-te, *Lun yü chi-shih,* 1:279. Li Ao's comment begins with the opening of the *Doctrine of the Mean*: " 'What Heaven decrees is called human nature' means that Heaven and man are together as if one. For Heaven also has its nature. In the spring it is humane (*jen*), in the summer decorous (*li*), in the autumn just (*i*), and in the winter wise (*chih*). Men follow this nature, and this is the way of the Five Norms."

97. This passage was a common topic of discussion during the period. The *fu* for the *chin-shih* examination of 800 was upon this passage. Cf. des Rotours, *Examens,* pp. 335-342, and Bischoff, *Interpreting the Fu,* pp. 57-111.

98. *Chou-i chu-shu* 1/4a; trans. Wilhelm, *Changes,* p. 371. The text continues, "Thus everything comes into accord with the Great Harmony, and this is what furthers and what perseveres." The *Fu-hsing shu* quotes this *Changes* passage as the proof-text that "the emotions are false and perverse (*hsieh*). . . . When these false emotions are destroyed and cease, the basic nature (*pen hsing*) will be clear and bright . . . which is the reason why this is termed being able to return to the true nature" (*fu ch'i hsing*). See Barrett, "Buddhism," p. 266, and discussion following. For the phrase in a Neo-Confucian context see Graham, *Two Chinese Philosophers,* pp. 60, 134.

99. *Chou-i chu-shu* 1/11a; trans. Wilhelm, *Changes,* p. 377, which is part of the *wen-yen* commentary to the passage quoted above.

100. *Chou-i chu-shu* 7/7a-b; trans. Wilhelm, *Changes,* pp. 297-298. The *Fu-hsing shu* also quotes this passage as a gloss on the *Great Learning* catenation: see Barrett, "Buddhism," pp. 256ff. For a

Neo-Confucian citation see Graham, *Two Chinese Philosphers*, p. 132 translating *Erh-Ch'eng i-shu* 1/7b, which equates this line with the Mencian concept of good human nature.

101. *Chou-i chu-shu* 7/14b; trans. Wilhelm, *Changes*, p. 315. For Li Ao, and for later Neo-Confucians, this was among the most important phrases in the *Changes*. It occurs often in the *Fu-hsing shu* (see Barrett, "Buddhism," pp. 227ff., 234ff., 244, 254) as an attribute of the Sage.

102. The first state (*tso-wang*) refers to the well-known passage in *Chuang-tzu* 16/9/92; Watson trans., p. 90. I have been unable to identify the phrase *i-chao* "to pass on the image."

103. The "Commentary on the Decision" to hexagram 24 "Return (The Turning Point)" reads, "In the hexagram of RETURN one sees the mind of Heaven and Earth" (*Chou-i chu-shu* 3/11b; trans. Wilhelm, *Changes*, p. 505).

104. Han Yü, probably to balance the repeated quotation from the hexagram "Creative" (*Ch'ien*), associated with Heaven, introduces two quotations from the following hexagram "Receptive" (*K'un*), associated with Earth. *Chou-i chu-shu* 1/15b and 1/14b (trans. Wilhelm, *Changes*, p. 392 and p. 389). These quotations reinforce the symmetry of the argument.

105. Han Yü and Li Ao, *Lun yü pi-chieh* 9/1a-2b; Ch'eng Shu-te, *Lun yü chi-shih*, 2:1026.

106. Barrett, "Buddhism," p. 16. Cf. also Li Ao's own words in *Fu-hsing shu* 2.1, "The nature is the decree of Heaven: the Sage is he who obtains it and is not deluded," which echoes the opening of the *Doctrine of the Mean* (Barrett, p. 226). After describing the Sage as "absolutely still and unmoving," the text continues, "so, then do the common folk not have this nature? The nature of the common folk is no different from that of the Sage. However, they are darkened by the emotions and under successive attack from them, and this goes on for ever, so that even to the end of their lives they do not themselves view their true natures" (Barrett, p. 229; cf. also pp. 263ff.).

This *Random Notes* commentary on *Analects* XVII.2 constitutes further evidence for the authenticity of the text. The Sung scholars apparently felt Li Ao's solution to the contradictions inherent in this *Analects* text was too "Buddhist" and preferred to develop the line first suggested by Han Yü that there are two different natures. The "endowed nature" that each individual receives at birth, the Neo-Confucians called his "capacity," or "talent" (*ts'ai*) to distinguish it from the nature that was identical to the decree of Heaven (see Graham, *Two Chinese Philosophers*, pp. 48-49). The Ch'eng brothers repeatedly state that when Yang Hsiung and Han Yü talk about nature they mean talent (see *Erh-Ch'eng i-shu* 19/4b, 22A/10b). If *Random Notes* was indeed a product of the Sung Neo-Confucian school, it is unlikely they would have forged a text in which Han Yü contradicted a basic, orthodox tenet of their school.

107. For a brief survey of the history of *li* as a Chinese philosophical term see Paul Demiéville, "Études sur la formation du vocabulaire philosophique chinois," pp. 151-157. On the two periods in question Demiéville observes "in the fourth century A.D. with the advent of Buddhism into the Chinese literary world and its integration into the highest currents of the philosophical tradition, the word *li* detached itself firmly from all naturalism and became a technical designation for a pure, transcended absolute in the manner of the Buddhist *tathatā* or of the Neo-Platonic One or Being or of the divine essence such as it was conceived at about the same time by certain Greek fathers of the Christian church" (p. 154). Speaking of Chu Hsi's understanding of the term, Demiéville writes "he made it then a principle of the natural order, at once cosmic, social, and moral; but he conserved at the same time its Buddhist sense as a metaphysical absolute immanent in each of us" (p. 156). Similarly, Graham writes that "the great innovation of the Ch'eng brothers is to claim that 'the innumerable principles amount to one principle,' for which 'heaven,' the 'decree,' and the 'Way' are merely different names, thus transforming a natural order conceived after the analogy of human society into a rational order. Such an achievement can only have been the result of long development, and a study of the gradual emergence of the idea of *li* during the preceding fifteen hundred years would no doubt reveal that the way had been prepared for them by earlier thinkers" (*Two Chinese Philosophers*, p. 11). Also, "the great innovation of the Ch'engs . . . is the elevation of principle to the place formerly occupied by heaven; and this involves treating 'heaven' and its 'decree,' as well as the 'Way,' as merely names for different aspects of principle" (p. 23).

108. Chan, *Source Book*, p. 493 n.26.

109. Graf, *Tao und Jen*, p. 100.

110. Adumbrations of a similar position abound in Li Ao's *Fu-hsing shu*, which early introduces the notion of *ch'eng* as "the nature of the Sage, 'absolutely still and unmoving' " (Barrett, "Buddhism,"

pp. 234ff.). Cf. Barrett, pp. 257-258, for the identification of *ch'eng* with the unity of the *tao*; p. 262, for its relation to *ming* "brightness"; and p. 264, for its equation with Sagehood. Barrett also writes (p. 283) of Li Ao's "substitution of sincerity as a basic metaphysical principle in the place of non-being." For Li Ao's bold equation of sincerity and unity see pp. 252-253 and 416 n. 248. Similarly, Graham (*Two Chinese Philosophers*, p. 67), describing Ch'eng I's idea of *ch'eng*, writes that "to be *ch'eng* is to be an integral whole, all of one piece." And "integrity is not conceived as a substance like the mind and nature, and the principles of which they consist; it is the state of man when all these are as they should be."

Chapter Four

1. *Liu pin-k'o chia hua lu* [Record of Counselor Liu's best stories] (*TSCC* ed.), p. 11. Cf. also Ch'ien Chi-po, *Han Yü chih*, p. 48. The *Liu pin-k'o chia hua lu* purports to be a record, composed in 856 by one Wei Hsüan, of stories told to him by his then teacher Liu Yü-hsi in K'uei-chou in 821. On this text see des Rotours, *Examens*, pp. 107-108, and Lo Lien-t'ien, "T'ang Sung san-shih-ssu chung tsa-shih pi-chi chieh-t'i" [Notes on thirty-four T'ang and Sung semi-historical and anecdotal works], p. 59. Des Rotours has misconstrued the title as *Recueil des belles paroles dites par monsieur Lieou à ses hôtes*. *Pin-k'o* is not *à ses hôtes* but the title of Liu Yü-hsi's last post, counselor to the heir apparent. See des Rotours, *Fonctionnaires*, 2:572, and Lo Lien-t'ien, "Liu Meng-te nien-p'u" [A chronological biography of Liu Yü-hsi], pp. 290-293. Wei Hsüan was the son of Wei Chih-i, chief minister during the Wang Shu-wen government (*HTS* 598/1542).

2. This famous quotation is from Su Shih's "Inscription for the Temple to Han Yü at Ch'ao-chou," reprinted in *Prose*, p. 447.

3. The expression "literature is a vehicle for the Way" (*wen i tsai tao*) was formulated by Chou Tun-i. See James J. Y. Liu, *Chinese Theories of Literature*, p. 114. The original text and considerable commentary are reprinted in Kuo Shao-yü, ed., *Chung-kuo li-tai wen-lun hsüan*, 2:60-64.

4. See Han Yü's "Letter to Feng Su Discussing Literature," *Prose*, p. 115, quoted in chapter one above, pp. 37-38. This struggle for public acceptance of *ku-wen* is a key motif in Li Han's preface

to Han Yü's collected works. See Hartman, "Preliminary Biblio-graphical Notes," pp. 89-91. Related to Han Yü's concept of lit-erary unity and certainly significant is the fact that his generation was the first in Chinese history whose writers' surviving works comprise relatively equal portions of prose and verse: Po Chü-i, Yüan Chen, Liu Tsung-yüan, and Liu Yü-hsi are all represented by copious collections of prose and verse, unlike Li Po, Tu Fu, or even Ch'en Tzu-ang. This probably represents a change in the social conception of the literary value of various genres: as the Six Dynasties, "dilletantish," view of literature and the genres declined and the concept of the Neo-Confucian civil servant began to emerge, it became increasingly acceptable to regard official doc-uments and chancery pieces as works with literary value. Thus, the concept of a man's "collected works" as a total representation of his private and public life would seem to date from this period.

5. *Prose*, p. 178. T'ung Ti-te, *Han Yü wen hsüan*, p. 64, dates this work shortly after Ou-yang Chan's death about 801 (see Lo Lien-t'ien, *Han Yü yen-chiu*, pp. 140-145); Hanabusa Hideki, *Kan Yu kashi sakuin*, p. 46, on the other hand dates the work about 823.

6. *Analects* XIX.12 (Lau trans., p. 154): "It is futile to try to give such a false picture of the way of the gentleman."

7. "Letter to My Younger Cousin, Correcting His Writings," quoted in Kuo Shao-yü, *Chung-kuo li-tai wen-lun hsüan*, 1:477-478.

8. *Prose*, pp. 72-73. Cf. chapter three above, note 80. Li Ao's use in this passage of the contrast between "nature" (*hsing*) and "prac-tice" (*hsi*) also recalls the commentary on *Analects* XVII.2 in *Lun-yü pi-chieh* 9/1a-2b, discussed above pp. 207-208.

9. For these see James R. Hightower, "The *Wen hsüan* and Genre Theory," pp. 512-533.

10. Wei Ch'ing-chih, comp., *Shih-jen yü hsieh* [Jade chips of the poet], 2:323-324. Cf. Volker Klöpsch, *Die Jadesplitter der Dichter*, pp. 37-38. The earliest record of this conversation seems to be in the *Leng-chai yeh hua* [Evening conversations in the cold studio] by the Buddhist monk Hui Hung (1071-?). See Kuo Shao-yü, *Sung shih-hua k'ao*, pp. 14-15.

11. See Ch'eng Ch'ien-fan, "Han Yü i-wen-wei-shih shuo" [Han Yü's theory of "making poetry out of prose"], p. 193.

12. *Ch'üan T'ang wen chi-shih*, chap. 69, quoted in Wang Yün-hsi, "Han Yü san-wen te feng-ke t'e-cheng ho t'a te wen-hsüeh hao-hsiang" [The stylistic distinctiveness of Han Yü's prose and his

literary preferences], p. 93. This attitude toward Han Yü's literary corpus continues to surface among contemporary scholars anxious to expose his "contadictions." Cf. Huang Yün-mei's "Tu Ch'en Yin-k'o hsien-sheng 'Lun Han Yü,' " rpt. in his *Han Yü Liu Tsung-yüan wen-hsüeh p'ing-chia*, p. 98. Wang's article is an eloquent attack on this attitude. Wang also points out (p. 104) that the Sung *ku-wen* authors accepted only partial elements of Han Yü's prose style.

13. Quoted in Kuo Shao-yü, *Chung-kuo li-tai wen-lun hsüan*, 1:441.

14. See Ch'ien Mu, "Tsa-lun T'ang-tai ku-wen yün-tung," pp. 123-125. Tu Fu, Li Hua, Liu Tsung-yüan, and Po Chü-i also traced the beginnings of their own concerns with a distinctly T'ang moral force in literature to Ch'en Tzu-ang, whose series marked the first meaningful shift in content toward a literature of "allegorical lodging" since the beginning of the dynasty. On these poems see Richard M. W. Ho, *Ch'en Tzu-ang kan-yü shih-chien* (Hong Kong: Hsüeh-chin, 1978) and William H. Nienhauser's careful exegesis of the opening poem of the series in "Diction, Dictionaries, and the Translation of Classical Chinese Poetry," pp. 53-66, which demonstrates what T'ang readers saw as "allegorical lodging."

15. Ch'ien Mu's full argument is as follows. Prior to the age of Han Yü and Liu Tsung-yüan, literature was divided into two large segments: (1) prose, consisting of (a) larger, book-length works (the classics, histories, and philosophies) and (b) shorter practical works such as government memorials, scholarly prefaces, and socially necessary pieces like stele inscriptions and letters; and (2) verse, consisting of (a) the *Book of Songs*, the *Ch'u tz'u*, and the *fu*, and (b) the five-word verse of the Han and its descendants. These versified genres constituted the "pure literature" of the Six Dynasties as the popularity of the *Wen hsüan* bears witness, and shorter prose pieces were written in the *p'ien-t'i* form popular at that time. Ch'en Tzu-ang began to reform the content of poetry; Han Yü and Liu Tsung-yüan reformed both the content and style of the shorter prose genres by infusing these genres with the ideals of "pure literature" that had hitherto existed only in the verse genres. The result was to expand the scope of the shorter prose genres by allowing them a much greater range of emotional expression than had been customary when these were tied to more narrow social and practical uses. See Ch'ien Mu, "Tsa-lun," pp. 145-156.

16. Chiang Ch'iu-hua, " 'I-wen-wei-shih' yü 'i-shih-wei-wen' " ["Making poetry from prose" and "making prose from poetry"],

p. 19-32, is a useful summary of these two critical approaches to Han Yü.

17. Owen, "The Poetry," p. 565. This passage is omitted from the published version of Owen's study.

18. Wilhelm, *Changes*, pp. 97-100, 504-509.

19. See Han Yü's "Preface Seeing Off the Master-in-Charge Li I of Yu-chou," *Prose*, pp. 154-155, trans. in the text, pp. 143-144.

20. Barrett, "Buddhism," p. 245. Cf. also Barrett, p. 430 n. 57 for further contemporary references to the idea of cyclical return. Both Li Ao and Han Yü comment on the spiritual significance of "return" in their *Analects* commentary. See *Lun-yü pi-chieh* 9/1a-2b discussed in chapter three above, pp. 207-208.

21. See *Prose*, pp. 140-142, and chapter two above, pp. 166-68.

22. On the importance of *ch'eng* in Han Yü's literary theory see the excellent note by Hu Shih-hsien, "Ch'ang-li 'ku-wen' chih chen-i" [The true meaning of Han Yü's *ku-wen*], pp. 111-112. This article also makes the important point that Han Yü's theory of the unity of *tao* and *wen* mandated a change in the content as well as the style of Six Dynasties literature and thus differed from earlier reformist theories.

23. *Prose*, p. 84. The first paragraph of this letter echoes the diction and sentiment of *Great Learning* chapter six, which contains the explication of "making true one's thoughts" (*ch'eng ch'i i*): " 'Making true one's thoughts' means no self-deception: when we detest a vile stench or admire a lovely view, we are then at peace with ourselves; and so the superior man is attentive to his private life.

"The petty man commits all manner of evils when he lives apart, but when he sees the superior man he covers himself, concealing his evil and displaying what is good. Yet when others look at him, it is as if they see into his very soul, and his dissembling profits him nothing. This means that when there is integrity at the core, it will manifest itself to the outside, so the gentleman is attentive to his private life" (*Li chi chu-shu* 60/1b-3a). *Shih* "actuality, reality" was a common gloss for *ch'eng* "integrity" in the K'ung Ying-ta subcommentaries. Cf. the above passage and also *Chou-i chu-shu* 1/8a and Barrett's note ("Buddhism"), p. 408 n.152. This gloss was accepted by Chu Hsi who interpreted *ch'eng* as *chen shih* "truth and reality." See Legge, *Chinese Classics*, 1:415.

24. Barrett's remark ("Buddhism," pp. 236-237) that Li Ao's conjunction of returning (*fu*) and sincerity (*ch'eng*) was probably new with this generation seems significant in this context.

25. Text quoted in Kuo Shao-yü, *Chung-kuo li-tai wen-lun hsüan* (Peking: Chung-hua, 1962), 1:382-383. For a monograph on Chiao-jan see Thomas P. Nielson, *The T'ang Poet-Monk Chiao-jan*. Cf. also Iriya Yoshitaka's "T'ang Hu-chou Chu-shan Chiao-jan chuan" (an annotated translation of the biography of Chiao-jan from Tsan-ning's *Sung kao-seng chuan* completed in 988), pp. 625-635.

26. Chiao-jan is elsewhere on record as condemning contemporary attempts to write "ancient poetry." See Richard Bodman, "Poetics and Prosody in Early Medieval China," p. 406. For an excellent paragraph on *pien* as a concept in Han Yü's prose see Wu Hsiao-lin, "Shih-lun Han Yü san-wen te ch'uang-hsin t'e-se" [On the innovative features of Han Yü's prose], p. 156.

27. See K. L. Thern, *Postface of the Shuo-wen chieh-tzu, the First Comprehensive Chinese Dictionary*, pp. 11, 13-16. The term also referred specifically to the "archaic script" classics supposedly found in the walls of Confucius's house in the second century B.C. See Wang Kuo-wei, "*Shuo-wen* so-wei ku-wen shuo" [Discussion of the term *ku-wen* in the *Shuo-wen*], in *Kuan-t'ang chi-lin* (rpt. Taipei: Wen-hua, 1968), 1:296-299. Prominent among these texts was the *Ku-wen shang-shu* or *Book of Documents in Archaic Script*, on which see Paul Pelliot, "Le *Chou king en caractèrs ancien* et le *Chang chou che wen*," *Mémoires concernant l'Asie Orientale* (Paris: L'Académie des inscriptions et belles lettres, 1916), 2:123-177, and William Hung, "A Bibliographical Controversy at the T'ang Court A.D. 719," pp. 99-104. It has been suggested that the redaction of the *Shang-shu shih-wen* in 744 and the subsequent disappearance of the *ku-wen* text of the *Book of Documents* may have freed the term *ku-wen* for adoption of a wider meaning. See Georges Margouliès, "L'origine de l'acception actuelle de l'expression *kou-wen*," in *Le kou-wen chinoise*, pp. xvii-cx. Around mid-century, Wang Ch'ang-ling (698-756) used the term to refer in a general way to "ancient literature"; see Bodman, "Poetics and Prosody," p. 368. A similar usage occurs in a Chiao-jan poem from about 773; see Ichihara Kōkichi, "Chūtō shoki ni okeru kōsa no shisō ni tsuite" [On the poet-monks south of the Yangtze in the early mid-T'ang period], p. 230.

28. For a good example of this usage see the "Letter to Feng Su Discussing Literature," *Prose*, p. 115, and chapter one above, p. 38.

29. "Letter to Lu Ts'an," *Li Wen-kung chi* (*SPTK* ed.) 7/50a. This

passage continues, "his diction is in accord with his thought; and since the death of Mencius none have surpassed this achievement." The letter can be dated about 800-801; see Lo Lien-t'ien, "Li Ao yen-chiu," p. 78.

30. "Letter in Reply to Master Li," *Prose*, p. 102. Cf. also the 802 "Letter to Master Ch'en Shang," *Prose*, p. 103: "What I aim at is the Way of the ancients; and I also enjoy their language."

31. *Prose*, p. 152. My discussion of this passage is based on the excellent remarks in Chien T'ien-hsing, "Han Yü chih ssu-hsiang chi ch'i wen-lun" [Han Yü's thought and his literary theory], pp. 79-80.

32. See Graham, *Two Chinese Philosophers*, p. 12, for the relation between *tao* and *li*.

33. Cf. the remark of Liu Hsi-tsai quoted in Kuo Shao-yü, *Chung-kuo li-tai wen-lun hsüan*, 1:442, for further argument that this passage presumes the unity of *tao* and *wen*.

34. For Yang Shu see *Commentary of Tso*: trans. Legge, *Chinese Classics*, vol. 5, text p. 456, trans. p. 458; Cook Ting: *Chuang-tzu* 7/3/2 (Watson trans., pp. 50ff.); Master K'uang: *Mencius* IV.A.1 (Lau trans., p. 117); Pien Ch'üeh: *SC* 105/2785-94; Hsiung I-liao: *Chuang-tzu* 67/24/67 (Watson trans., p. 272); I-ch'iu: *Mencius* VI.A.9 (Lau trans., p. 165); Liu Ling: Mather, *Shih-shuo hsin-yü*, p. 551.

35. Chang Hsü, noted for his cursive calligraphy, was active during the mid-eighth century and was an acquaintance of Tu Fu. See *CTS* 190B/5034, *HTS* 202/5764; Hung, *Tu Fu*, p. 251.

36. *Prose*, pp. 157-159; Kao Pu-ying, *T'ang Sung wen chü-yao*, 1:220-225; T'ung Ti-te, *Han Yü wen hsüan*, pp. 260-265; trans. Yang Hsien-yi and Gladys Yang, "Prose Writings of Han Yü," pp. 77-78.

37. My reading of this text is based on the observations of Ch'ien Mu, "Tsa-lun," pp. 144-145, who was in turn enlarging on a comment of Tseng Kuo-fan. Cf. also Chien T'ien-hsing, "Han Yü chih ssu-hsiang chi ch'i wen-lun," pp. 91-95.

38. Liu Tsung-yüan, *Liu Tsung-yüan chi*, 3:873. On this difference between Han Yü and Liu Tsung-yüan see Ch'ien Mu, "Tsa-lun," p. 143.

39 See Obi Kōichi, "Ryū Ben no bunron" [The stylistics of Liu Mien], pp. 30-31.

40. See for instance Kuo Shao-yü, *Chung-kuo wen-hsüeh p'i-p'ing shih* [History of Chinese literary criticism], 1:238.

41. *Prose*, pp. 85-86. This letter comments on four texts that Yü Ti had sent to Han Yü for review. These were (1) the text of a dance presentation or masque, (2) a poem on the Yang Kuei-fei theme, (3) a "Poem on Reading Ts'ai Yen's Songs for the Tartar Flute," and (4) a letter to the metropolitan governor of Ch'ang-an concerning the transplantation of refugees. Han Yü's reply reveals that he considered each item of this miscellaneous collection *ku-wen*. Cf. also Hartman, "Han Yü and T.S. Eliot," p. 66. On this masque see Feifel, *Po Chü-i as a Censor*, pp. 65-66, 199-200.

42. A proof-text is the following passage from the *Chung-shan shih-hua* of Liu Pin (1022-1088): "Mei Yao-ch'en said of Yin Shu (1001-1088) that although he was famous for his *ku-wen*, he had no talent for poetry." See Helmut Martin, comp., *Index to the Ho Collection of Twenty-Eight Shih-hua*, 1:175.

43. See for instance Sun Ch'ang-wu, "T'ang-tai 'ku-wen yün-tung' ch'ien-i" [My views on the T'ang "*ku-wen* movement"], pp. 42-45.

44. See Ichihara Kōkichi, "Chūtō shoki ni okeru kōsa no shisō ni tsuite," pp. 222-223, and Arthur Waley, *Po Chü-i*, pp. 171-172. *Upāyajñāna* is the wisdom or knowledge of using expedient means as a way to lead others to salvation. This text has marked similarities to Po Chü-i's concept expressed in his "Preface to the New Yüeh-fu" (cf. Kuo Shao-yü, *Chung-kuo li-tai wen-lun hsüan*, 1:421) that these poems "were written for the sovereign, for his ministers, for the people, for the world, and for specific events—not for the sake of literature." For the expression *wen i tsai tao* in a Ch'an context see *Pi yen lu* case 12, Wang Chin-jui, *Pi yen lu chiang-i* [Lectures on the *Blue Cliff Records*] (Tainan: Ta-hsin, 1972), p. 323, and Wilhelm Gundert, trans., *Bi-yän-lu: Meister Yüan-wu's Niederschrift von der Smaragdenen Felswand*, p. 240.

45. See Liu Tsung-yüan, *Liu Tsung-yüan chi*, 2:578-581, and Ch'ien Mu, "Tsa-lun," pp. 136-138.

46. For the primacy of the Way in the *tao/wen* dialectic see Li Chia-yen, "Han Yü fu-ku yün-tung te hsin t'an-so" [A new inquiry into Han Yü's *fu-ku* movement], pp. 104-106. This primacy among ultimate equals seems similar to the relation common at this time between "integrity" (*ch'eng*) as a hallmark of the Sage and "enlightenment" (*ming*) as a hallmark of the Worthy Man. See chapter three notes 80-81 above.

47. See Han Yü and Li Ao, *Lun yü pi-chieh* 6/1b-2a and chapter three above, pp. 188-190.

48. This text is contained in the *Han Hui chuan*, on which see chapter one note 22. The *Han Hui chuan* was printed as *chüan* eight of the *Han Wen lei-p'u* edited by Wei Chung-chü and appended to his *Hsin-k'an wu-pai-chia chu yin-pien Ch'ang-li hsien-sheng wen-chi* printed in 1200. The Commercial Press reprinted this work in 1912. A much more accessible text of the *Han Hui chuan* is the *Ch'üan T'ang wen chi-shih* 39/503-505.

49. Text in Konishi Jin'ichi, *Bunkyō hifuron kō* [Studies in the *Bunkyō hifuron*], 3:162. Cf. also the translation and comment in Bodman, "Poetics and Prosody," pp. 363-368, and the synopsis in Joseph J. Lee, *Wang Ch'ang-ling*, pp. 51-53.

50. These are the traditional "eight voices" (*pa-yin*) of classical Chinese music. See Kenneth J. DeWoskin, *A Song for One or Two*, pp. 52-53.

51. The idea seems to be that these natural sounds here associated with the four seasons signal imbalances between *yin* and *yang* that result in seasonal change.

52. Kao Yao and Yü were both legendary ministers to whom various sections of the *Book of Documents* were attributed.

53. A reference to *Book of Documents* (S. Couvreur, *Les Annales de la Chine*, pp. 29-30). *Shao* was the court music of Emperor Shun. See *Analects* VII.14 (Lau trans., p. 87).

54. "Songs of the Five Sons" is a section of the *Book of Documents* (Couvreur, *Les Annales*, pp. 91-95). Yi Yin, minister to Emperor T'ang of the Shang, and the Duke of Chou are both reputed authors of several pieces in the *Book of Documents*.

55. *Analects* III.24 (Lau trans., p. 71): "The border official of Yi requested an audience, saying, 'I have never been denied an audience by any gentleman who has come to this place." The followers presented him. When he came out, he said, 'What worry have you, gentlemen, about the loss of office? The Empire has long been without the Way. Heaven is about to use your Master as the wooden tongue for a bell [to rouse the Empire].' "

56. On Tsang-sun Ch'en (d.617 B.C.), a counselor of the state of Lu see *Commentary of Tso* (trans. Legge, *Chinese Classics*, 5:507) and *Analects* V.18 (Lau trans., p. 78).

57. On Shen Tao and T'ien P'ien see Fung Yu-lan, *History of Chinese Philosophy*, 1:132-133.

58. Su Yüan-ming (d.762) was a literatus active during the *t'ien-pao* period (742-755) and a good friend of Tu Fu. See Hung, *Tu Fu*,

p. 296, and *A Supplementary Volume*, p. 27. Su was also an advocate of Yüan Chieh and Liang Su. See *HTS* 202/5771-73.

59. Shimizu Shigeru (*Tō-Sō hakkabun*, 1:38) suggests it is also possible to interpret this passage as follows: "The best of his work surpasses the Wei and Chin, and when he exerts himself to the utmost he can attain the Ancients. In his other works he has immersed himself in the Han."

60. *Prose*, pp. 136-137; T'ung Ti-te, *Han Yü wen hsüan*, pp. 44-52; Shimizu Shigeru, *Tō-Sō hakkabun*, 1:23-42. For dating see Hua Ch'en-chih, *T'ang Meng Chiao nien-p'u*, 30b-31a.

61. Wu Wen-chih, "Lüeh-lun Han Yü te ku-wen li-lun" [A brief discussion of Han Yü's *ku-wen* theory], pp. 18-19.

62. Ch'ien Chung-shu, "Shih k'o-i yüan" [Our sweetest songs], pp. 18-19. Ch'ien traces this reading of the text to Huang T'ing-chien. Narrower interpretations are traced to Hung Mai, Ch'ien Ta-hsin, and others (see Ch'ien's note 9, p. 21). Ch'ien demonstrates that water roiled into waves as a metaphor for human nature (*hsing*) excited into emotion (*ch'ing*) was common at this time: "The relation between human nature and emotion is like that between waves and water. At rest, there is water; but moving, it becomes waves. At rest, there is human nature; but moving, it becomes emotion" (K'ung Ying-ta subcommentary to *Doctrine of the Mean*, *Li-chi chu-shu* 52/1b). See also Ch'ien Chung-shu, *Kuan-chui pien*, 3:1211-1213, for an extended discussion of this metaphor and its Buddhist and Taoist parallels.

63. The "Preface Seeing Off the Monk Kao-hsien" insists on the ability of the artist to make use of the range of his emotions and has other points in common with this text. See the excellent commentary of the Ch'ing critic Lin Yün-ming quoted in Lo Lien-t'ien, *Han Yü yen-chiu*, pp. 325-326.

64. *Prose*, pp. 153-154. On P'ei Chün see *HTS* 108/4091; on Yang P'ing see *CTS* 146/3967, *HTS* 160/4970. This latter was a political adversary of Han Yü. See chapter one above and Lo Lien-t'ien, *Han Yü yen-chiu*, pp. 175-177.

65. From Percy Shelley's "To a Skylark"; see Ch'ien Chung-shu, "Shih k'o-i yüan," p. 19.

66. This is not of course to imply that no change occurred. There is obviously an enormous difference in form and meaning between the oracle-bone script and modern "simplified characters." I simply wish to emphasize the continuity and stability of the Chinese written character in the period between the Ch'in language reform

and the introduction and spread of written vernacular Chinese in the twentieth century.

67. Han Yü's own epitaph for his son-in-law's father Li P'ing records that when Li "was fourteen or fifteen he could recite from memory the *Lun yü, Shu ching, Shih ching, Tso chuan*, and the *Wen hsüan*—in all, several million words" (*Prose*, p. 313). The autobiographical funeral inscription of Han Yü's own son, Han Ch'ang, touches on several interesting aspects of his early education and reveals the difficulties of those who could not master the required memorization:

> When he began his studies as a young boy he spoke and laughed little and did not play with other boys. He could not memorize, so when he grew older he could not recite even a passage of several hundred characters and his classmates laughed at him. At the age of six or seven he had not yet learned to hold a brush and write characters. And yet by nature he was fond of literature and could compose orally. This was different from what others did. Chang Chi marveled at him and taught him poetry. When he was a little over ten, they studied one *chüan* per day, which surprised Chang greatly. And when Chang tried this with his other students, none could match it. He was also able, based on what he heard, to ask detailed questions about the meaning, which often Chang could not answer. When he had mastered three or four *chüan* of poetry, then he could compose on his own.
>
> At age eleven or twelve, Fan Tsung-shih marveled at him. Fan was a teacher of composition, and his style was different from that of normal men. Ch'ang read and admired it. One morning he was composing, and Fan was surprised because among his characters were some that did not come from the classics and histories. And when Fan read, he could not understand.

Noteworthy in this self-revelation are the points in which Han Ch'ang's education differed from the norm: (1) he could not memorize, (2) he asked detailed questions about the meanings of texts studied, and (3) his compositions used expressions not from the "classics and histories."

68. See Huang T'ing-chien's "Letter to Hung Chü-fu" in Kuo Shao-yü, *Chung-kuo li-tai wen-lun hsüan*, 2:87-88. Cf. also Yoshikawa Kōjirō, "Tu Fu's Poetics and Poetry," *Acta Asiatica* (Tokyo) 16

(1969): 9, where the phrase in question is rendered more freely "There is not a single word without a history in Tu Fu or Han Yü." Cf. also Adele Austin Rickett, "Method and Intuition: The Poetic Theories of Huang T'ing-chien," in her edited volume, *Chinese Approaches to Literature*, pp. 109-110.

69. Hung Yeh, *Tu Shih yin-te*, 2:369.

70. For a good description of parallel prose see James R. Hightower, *Topics in Chinese Literature*, pp. 38-42, and "Some Characteristics of Parallel Prose," pp. 108-139. For the relation between the *Wen hsüan* and parallel prose see David R. Knechtges, trans., *Wen Xuan*, pp. 45-52.

71. *CTS* 119/3430. See also *Ts'e-fu yüan-kuei* 640/5a-b. Abbreviated versions of this memorial in *HTS* 44/1166 (trans. des Rotours, *Examens*, pp. 187-188) and *TCTC* 222/7143 substitute the idea of *t'ieh-kuo* "citation collections" in place of the last passage of this text. "Citations" were short passages, usually three characters long, that the candidate was required to recognize and place in their original contexts in the classic texts. But instead of memorizing the classic texts, candidates selected and arranged the most difficult and most frequently asked citations into versified and easily memorized jingles. These were the "citation collections." See des Rotours, *Examens*, p. 188 n.1.

72. *Poetry*, p. 246; Hartman, "Language and Allusion," pp. 135-136. For Tu Fu's memorization of the *Wen hsüan* and Li Shan commentary see Yoshikawa Kōjirō, "Tu Fu's Poetics and Poetry," pp. 8-9. On the importance of the *Wen hsüan* for T'ang examination studies see Liu Su, *Ta T'ang hsin-yü* (completed 807; *TSCC* ed.), pp. 95-96, and Knechtges, *Wen Xuan*, pp. 1, 54.

73. Wang Yün-hsi, "Han Yü san-wen te feng-ke t'e-cheng ho t'a te wen-hsüeh hao-hsiang," pp. 95ff.

74. *CTS* 139/3792. See also Denis Twitchett, "Lu Chih (754-805)," p. 96, and Solomon, *The Veritable Record*, pp. 37-38, for further testimony on Lu Chih's literary prowess. It should be stressed that Wang Yün-hsi's inclusion of Lu Chih's memorials as examples of parallel prose is not meant to question their rhetorical power; Wang intends only to demonstrate the ubiquity of parallel prose at all social levels from the court chancery to popular literature.

75. On this work see the translation and study by Howard S. Levy, *The Dwelling of Playful Goddesses* (Tokyo: Dai Nippon Insatsu, 1965). Levy discusses the work's parallel prose style on pp. 1-3.

76. Much of this literature exhibits parallel prose features. See es-

pecially the *pien-wen* on Wang Chao-chün and the "*Fu* on the Swallow and the Sparrow," Wang Chung-min, ed., *Tun-huang pien-wen chi* (rpt. Taipei: Shih-chieh, 1969), 1:98-108, 249-266; Arthur Waley, *Ballads and Stories from Tun-huang*, pp. 11-24.

77. *Ch'üan T'ang wen chi-shih*, chap. 76, quoted in Wang Yün-hsi, "Han Yü san-wen," p. 98. Arthur Waley, "China's Greatest Writer," pp. 163-168, also points out that in contrast to *ku-wen*, the rigid parallelism, semantic reduplication, and rhyme of *p'ien-wen* made the latter much easier to memorize.

78. See "Letter to Auxiliary Secretary Lu in the Bureau of Sacrifices," *Prose*, pp. 116-117. Li I was the last of ten students recommended.

79. *Prose*, pp. 98-100; Kao Pu-ying, *T'ang-Sung wen chü-yao*, 1:199-203; T'ung Ti-te, *Han Yü wen hsüan*, pp. 27-32. For other translations see Zhang Xihou, "Prose Writings of Han Yü," pp. 93-94, and Diana Yu-shih Mei, "Han Yü as a *Ku-wen* Stylist," pp. 184-186. "To establish one's words" (*li yen*) means to achieve an enduring reputation through excellence in literature. It is the third in a triad of methods to achieve historical immortality. The first is to "establish one's virtue" (*li te*), and the second is to "establish one's public service" (*li kung*). See *Commentary of Tso*; trans. Legge, *Chinese Classics*, vol. 5, text p. 505/3, trans. p. 507a.

80. The sentence in which the phrase "to remove old clichés" (*ch'en-yen chih wu ch'ü*) occurs is often understood "I wanted to rid myself of all stereotyped phrases, but I found this an arduous task" (Zhang Xihou, "Prose Writings of Han Yü," p. 93; so also Mei, "Han Yü as a *Ku-wen* Stylist," p. 185: "It came so hard, as it were, with much creaking and sq[u]ealing"). Both understand the "difficulty" to be that of the author during the act of composition. I believe, however, that the full context of the passage makes it more probable that Han Yü's compositions resulting from the elimination of the "old cliches" were difficult for the contemporary audience. *Chia-chia-hu*, the descriptive phrase that modifies "difficult" (*nan*), refers primarily to sound: "the sound of objects being struck together" (*Chung-wen ta tzu-tien* 4/11870/2), thus Mei's "creaking and squealing" and my "cacophonous." Furthermore, *chia-chia* also occurs in the phrase *chia-chia tu-tsao* "difficult and uniquely created," which refers to writing that departs from established stylistic standards. Finally, Han Yü is describing here his earliest attempts at composition; "cacophonous and difficult" tallies quite well with

modern appreciations of these earliest surviving works. See Owen, *The Poetry*, pp. 36-48.

81. Cf. the "Orientations" section, note 11 above.

82. *Mencius* II.A.2 (Lau trans., pp. 76-80): "*Ch'i* unites rightness (*i*) and the Way. Deprive it of these and it will collapse. It is born of accumulated rightness (*i*). . . ." For *ch'i* as "style" see James Liu, *Chinese Theories of Literature*, pp. 12-13. For a survey of the various meanings of *ch'i* in relation to literature see Ch'ien Chung-lien, "Shih 'ch'i' " [On *ch'i*], pp. 129-150.

83. Hu Shih-hsien, "Ch'ang-li 'ku-wen' chih chen-i," p. 111, defined these rather broadly as "expressions that do not possess the *tao*." Wu-Wen-chih, "Lüeh-lun Han Yü te ku-wen li-lun," pp. 15-16, and Wu-Hsiao-lin, "Shih-lun Han Yü san-wen te ch'uang-hsin t'e-se," p. 155, on the basis of the remark of the Ch'ing critic Hsüeh Hsüeh (1681-1763?) that "if you do not remove old clichés there will never be new ideas," argue that "old clichés" embrace stereotyped ideas as well as diction.

84. *Analects* XVII.3 (Lau trans., p. 143): "The Master with a grin laughed and said. . . ."

85. *Chou-i chu-shu* 5/13b (trans., Wilhelm, *Changes*, p. 197): "Laughing words—ha, ha!"

86. *Ku-liang Commentary* (*SPPY* ed.) 17/2b: "The soldiers all guffawed and laughed."

87. Pan Ku, "Response to a Guest's Jest," *WH* 45/13b: "The host chortled and laughed."

88. Tso Szu, "*Fu* on the Wu Capital," *WH* 5/1a (trans. Knechtges, *Wen Xuan*, p. 373): "The Prince of Wu on the east laughed heartily."

89. Kuo Shao-yü, *Chung-kuo li-tai wen-lun hsüan*, 1:472-473.

90. For a good account of "remove old clichés" as an effort to abandon the *Wen hsüan* as a source of "poetic diction" see Iguchi Takashi, "Gyoku-sen-shi no shi" [the poetry of Lu T'ung], pp. 55-60.

91. Li Chao, *T'ang kuo-shih pu* 3/57.

92. For bibliographical notes on Fan Tsung-shih's two surviving works see Ch'ien Chi-po, *Han Yü chih*, pp. 73-76.

93. *Prose*, pp. 311-312; Kao Pu-ying, *T'ang-Sung wen chü-yao*, 1:379-384; Shimizu Shigeru, *Tō-Sō hakkabun*, 1:119-131; T'ung Ti-te, *Han Yü wen hsüan*, pp. 210-215.

94. Kao Pu-ying, *T'ang-Sung wen chü-yao*, 2:568.

95. For a further discussion of *tsao-yü* in Han Yü see Hartman, "Language and Allusion," pp. 68-71.

96. Quoted in *Poetry*, p. 37. See also Chiang Hsin-mei, "Lun Han Yü shih te chi-ke wen-t'i" [A discussion of several questions relating to Han Yü's poetry], p. 243.

97. See his preface to the *Han-wen k'ao-i* in *Hui-an hsien-sheng Wen-kung wen-chi* (*SPTK* ed.) 76/29a-30a, trans. Hartman, "Preliminary Bibliographical Notes," pp. 97-98.

98. Quoted in Chien T'ien-hsing, "Han Yü chih ssu-hsiang chi ch'i wen-lun," pp. 83-84.

99. *Prose*, p. 55.

100. Tu Chung-ling, "Lüeh-lun Han Yü te shu-mien yü-yen yü tang-shih k'ou-yü te kuan-hsi" [A brief study of the relation between Han Yü's literary language and contemporary colloquial language], pp. 55-63; Kuo Hsi-liang, "Han Yü tsai wen-hsüeh yü-yen fang-mien te li-lun ho shih-chien" [The theory and practice of Han Yü's literary language], pp. 51-73, esp. 67-71.

101. See Shinohara Hisao, "Tōdai bunjin no Bukkyō rikai ni tsuite" [The comprehension of Buddhism among T'ang literati], pp. 229-230.

102. Cf. Hartman, "Han Yü and T.S. Eliot," pp. 73-75, and above pp. 106-108.

103. T. S. Eliot, *Selected Essays* (New York: Harcourt, Brace, and World, 1932), p. 444.

104. *Prose*, pp. 121-122; T'ung Ti-te, *Han Yü wen hsüan*, pp. 120-123. The letter was probably written between 811 and 813. Liu Cheng-fu was the son of Liu P'o-chiu, a Lo-yang acquaintance of Han Yü.

105. "Letter to Prime Minister Yü of Hsiang-yang," *Prose*, p. 86. Cf. also "Letter in Reply to Master Hu," *Prose*, p. 107: "To adhere to reality in forming expressions was precisely what the ancient authors did"; also the "Memorial Presenting the 'Inscription on the Pacification of Huai-hsi'" (*Prose*, p. 350), in which Han Yü writes that the *Shih ching* is a classic because in it "language and reality suit each other."

106. Hu Shih-hsien, "Ch'ang-li 'ku-wen' chih chen-i," p. 111, notes that the images of free-flowing productivity that follow literary "enlightenment" in the "Letter to Li I" are related to the *Doctrine of the Mean*'s definition of the "man of integrity" as one who "hits what is right without any effort, and apprehends without any exercise of thought" (*Li chi chu-shu* 53/1a; trans. Legge, *Rites*,

2:317). The Ch'an parallel is obvious, and similar ideas on literary style can be traced back to the earliest attempts to apply the ideology of Ch'an spirituality to literature. Wang Ch'ang-ling notes, for instance, that "writing is neither difficult nor toilsome" (Bodman, "Poetics and Prosody," p. 423); Chiao-jan refuses to enjoin the use of parallel prose: "the ancients put language last and meaning first. They created language from their meaning, and did not permit language to influence meaning. Sometimes they would use parallel couplets, sometimes free periods . . ." (Bodman, pp. 415-416).

107. Kuo Shao-yü, *Chung-kuo li-tai wen-lun hsüan*, 1:479, 482; cf. also Wang Ting-pao, *T'ang chih-yen* 5/57-58 and Chiang Kuo-chen, *Huang-fu chih-cheng hsüeh-shu yen-chiu*, pp. 58-61, 86-87.

108. See Wang Yün-hsi, "Han Yü san-wen," pp. 95ff., and the excellent article by Ku I-sheng, "Shih-t'an Han Yü te shang ch'i chi Han wen yü tz'u-fu p'ien-wen te kuan-hsi" [On Han Yü's adulation of *ch'i* and the relation between his prose and earlier *fu* and *p'ien-wen*], pp. 66-72.

109. See for instance P'ei Tu's famous "Letter to Li Ao," in Kuo Shao-yü, *Chung-kuo li-tai wen-lun hsüan*, 1:464-469, which protests against Han Yü and Li Ao's insistence that parallelism "is the greatest evil of literature and therefore you would remedy it with violent diction and far-off meanings. . . ." On this letter see Wang Yün-hsi, "Han Yü san-wen," pp. 94-95; Ch'eng Ch'ien-fan, "Han Yü i-wen-wei-shih shuo," p. 213 n.7; and Su Wen-cho, *Han wen ssu lun* [Four essays on Han Yü's works], pp. 146ff. As early as the Sung Dynasty, Hung Mai pointed out that this letter should be dated fairly early, before P'ei Tu's rise to political power. See Ch'ien Chi-po, *Han Yü chih*, pp. 50-51. Lo Lien-t'ien, "Li Ao yen-chiu," p. 66, places the letter in 802-803.

110. See Chien T'ien-hsing, "Han Yü chih ssu-hsiang chi ch'i wen-lun," pp. 102ff.

111. Liu Tsung-yüan, *Liu Tsung-yüan chi*, 3:882. Cf. also ibid., 1:301.

112. Han Yü's "Explication of 'Progress in Learning,' " for instance, is directly modeled on Yang Hsiung's "Explication of Ridicule," included in the latter's biography in *Han shu* 87B. For translations see Franklin Melvin Doeringer, "Yang Hsiung and His Formulation of a Classicism," pp. 281-291, and David Knechtges, *The Han Rhapsody*, pp. 97-103.

113. Knechtges, *Han Rhapsody*, p. 108. A reading of Doeringer's

dissertation, especialy pp. 142-179, reveals a multitude of similarities between Yang Hsiung and Han Yü. Thus Yang "viewed his work as an attempt to rescue ancient values from the verbal chaos into which they had been cast by generations of later writers" (p. 142). He revered and identified with Mencius (pp. 144-145). His eclectic approach to Taoism compares with Han Yü's eclectic approach to Ch'an (p. 147). He emphasized the role of the Sage as one whose "main task was to evaluate and assimilate ideas in the long tradition to which he was heir" (pp. 148ff.) and discoursed on human nature (pp. 151-152), mind (p. 153), enlightenment (pp. 155ff.), and teachers (p. 160). Literature was "a means to convey moral value" (p. 164), and there were no distinctions between "artistic and informative writing" (p. 165). Literary style was to be "terse and unembellished" (p. 168), and "good writing had to incorporate a precise balance of form and content." " 'When facts and rhetoric are in balance,' he proclaimed, 'then it will be a classic' " (p. 169)! Finally, the study of Yang Hsiung was also popular among Han Yü's acquaintances: Wang Yai wrote a surviving commentary on the *Classic of Great Mysterey (T'ai hsüan ching)* and Liu Tsung-yüan wrote an unfortunately lost commentary on the *Exemplary Words (Fa yen)*. See *HTS* 59/1512. Liu Tsung-yüan (*Liu Tsung-yüan chi*, 2:673-674) argued that Han Yü's admiration for the Buddhist-related ideas in the *Changes* and *Analects* was parallel to Yang Hsiung's adoption of ideas from Chuang-tzu, Mo-tzu, Shen Pu-hai, and Han Fei. Cf. also Barrett, "Buddhism," p. 314 n.33.

114. This scheme is adapted from Ting Chi-han, *Han Yü wen-t'i fen-lei yen-chiu* [Studies in the classification of Han Yü's literary genres], pp. 15-108. I have retained the author's nine major divisions but condensed his many subdivisions.

115. See Liu Hsieh, *Wen-hsin tiao-lung*, ed. Wang Li-ch'i (Peking: Centre franco-chinois d'études sinologiques, 1950), pp. 37-38; Knechtges, *Wen Xuan*, p. 47.

116. Ch'en Yin-k'o juxtaposed two popular epitaphs excavated from the Lo-yang area to demonstrate these features. See "Ch'ang-hen ko chien-cheng" [Notes on the "Song of Everlasting Remorse"], *Ch'en Yin-k'o hsien-sheng lun-wen chi*, 2:2-3.

117. See chapter one note 36 above.

118. See *Prose*, pp. 294-297; Kao Pu-ying, *T'ang Sung wen chü-yao*, 1:350-361; T'ung Ti-te, *Han Yü wen hsüan*, pp. 180-188; trans.

Yang Hsien-yi and Gladys Yang, "Prose Writings of Han Yü," pp. 81-84; Liu Shih Shun, *Chinese Classical Prose*, pp. 90-97.

119. See *Prose*, pp. 284-286; Kao Pu-ying, *T'ang-Sung wen chü-yao*, 1:307-313; T'ung Ti-te, *Han Yü wen hsüan*, pp. 197-203. For an analysis and translation see Mei, "Han Yü as a *Ku-wen* Stylist," pp. 164-173, 182-184. Cf. also James R. Hightower, "Han Yü as Humorist," pp. 24-26. On the *chih-kuai* fiction see Kenneth J. DeWoskin, "The Six Dynasties *Chih-kuai* and the Birth of Fiction," in Andrew H. Plaks, ed., *Chinese Narrative* (Princeton: Princeton University Press, 1977), pp. 21-52.

120. See *Prose*, pp. 280-283; Kao Pu-ying, *T'ang-Sung wen chü-yao*, 1:296-307; trans. Edward H. Schafer, "Notes on T'ang Culture," pp. 203-221.

121. See the "Memorial Presenting the 'Inscription on the Pacification of Huai-hsi,' " *Prose*, pp. 350-351, and the partial translation in Mei, "Han Yü," pp. 159-160. Cf. also the excellent analysis in Yeh Ch'ing-ping, "Ts'ung 'P'ing Huai-hsi pei' k'an Han Yü ku-wen" [On Han Yü's *ku-wen* as seen in the "Inscription on the Pacification of Huai-hsi"], pp. 168-172.

122. See Victor H. Mair, *Tun-huang Popular Narratives*, pp. 14ff.

123. See James Liu, *The Poetry of Li Shang-yin*, pp. 191-195, and Zach, *Han Yü's poetische Werke*, pp. 363-365. Cf. also Mei, "Han Yü," pp. 158-163.

124. For the letters in the *Wen hsüan* see Knechtges, *Wen Xuan*, pp. 43-44, and Ch'ien Mu, "Tsa-lun," pp. 147-148.

125. *Prose*, pp. 79-80, 108-110; trans. Margouliès, *Kou-wen chinois*, pp. 205-206, and Yang Hsien-yi and Gladys Yang, "Prose Writings of Han Yü," pp. 70-73.

126. See Knechtges, *Wen Xuan*, pp. 49-50; Ch'ien Mu, "Tsa-lun," pp. 148-151; Ting Chi-han, *Han Yü wen-t'i fen-lei yen-chiu*, pp. 59-67; Mei, "Han Yü," pp. 150-151.

127. Shih Shu-nü, "Han Yü shih wen hui-p'ing," p. 216.

128. Ch'ien Mu, "Tsa-lun," p. 151.

129. *Poetry*, pp. 38-40; Harada Kenyū, *Kan Yu*, pp. 53-57; Mori Kainan, *Kanshi kōgi*, 2:62-70. Notes to the poem are as follows: 1.7—the *chen-yüan* period was 785-805. 1.9—*Analects* XVI.11: "Confucius said, 'I live in retirement in order to attain my purpose and practice what is right in order to realize my way.' " 1.27—The Old Man of Heaven (T'ien-weng) was a T'ang popular deity. See Tuan Ch'eng-shih, *Yu-yang tsa tsu* (Peking: Chung-hua, 1981), p. 128.

130. Ch'en Yin-k'o, "Han Yü and the T'ang Novel," *HJAS* 1 (1936): 37-43. The best comprehensive study of the issues involved is Y. W. Ma, "Prose Writings of Han Yü and *Ch'uan-ch'i* Literature," pp. 195-223, which includes a full bibliography. Ch'en's 1936 article was only a brief series of observations, and although he returned to aspects of the problem in later works (cf. *Ch'en Yin-k'o hsien-sheng lun-wen chi*, 2:2-4, 102-103, 534-535, 598), he seems never to have finalized his thinking on the issue. A useful summary of Ch'en's ideas along with a thoughtful critique is Wang Yün-hsi, "Shih-lun T'ang ch'uan-ch'i yü ku-wen yün-tung te kuan-hsi" [On the T'ang *ch'uan-ch'i* and their relation to the *ku-wen* movement], pp. 321-332.

131. See for example Kung Shu-ch'ih, *Han Yü chi ch'i ku-wen yün-tung* [Han Yü and his *ku-wen* movement], pp. 119-124.

132. William H. Nienhauser, Jr., "A Structural Reading of the *Chuan* in the *Wen-yüan ying-hua*," pp. 443-456.

133. See T'ai Ching-nung, "Lun pei-chuan wen chi ch'uan-ch'i wen" [On biographical stone inscriptions and *ch'uan-ch'i* literature], pp. 219-227. On "Ying-ying chuan" see James R. Hightower, "Yüan Chen and 'The Story of Ying-ying,' " pp. 90-123, and Angela Palandri, *Yüan Chen*, pp. 145-155.

134. For the "Biography of Fur Point," see *Prose*, pp. 325-327; Kao Pu-ying, *T'ang-Sung wen chü-yao*, 1:260-269; T'ung Ti-te, *Han Yü wen hsüan*, pp. 97-104; Shimizu Shigeru, *Tō-Sō hakkabun*, 1:170-189; trans. with excellent analysis in William H. Nienhauser, Jr., "An Allegorical Reading of Han Yü's 'Mao-Ying Chuan' (Biography of Fur Point)," pp. 153-174; cf. also Hightower, "Han Yü as Humorist," pp. 10-14. On the "Biography of Wang Ch'eng-fu, the Mason," see *Prose*, pp. 30-31; T'ung Ti-te, *Han Yü wen hsüan*, pp. 21-27; trans. Yang Hsien-yi and Gladys Yang, "Prose Writings of Han Yü," pp. 65-67; Margouliès, *Anthologie*, pp. 178-180; and Hightower, "Han Yü as Humorist," pp. 17-19. For the prose and verse portions of the "Preface to the Linked Verses on the Stone Tripod," see *Prose*, pp. 171-174; *Poetry*, pp. 371-375; T'ung Ti-te, *Han Yü wen hsüan*, pp. 123-128; Shimizu Shigeru, *Tō-Sō hakkabun*, 1:150-169; Harada Kenyū, *Kan Yu*, pp. 253-268; trans. Yang Hsien-yi and Gladys Yang, "Prose Writings of Han Yü," pp. 79-81; Zach, *Han Yü's poetische Werke*, pp. 305-307.

135. The texts on the stone tripod are probably Han Yü's most daring attempt to combine prose and verse into a single unified composition. The original version seems to have been a prose

narrative account of the composition of some linked verses on a stone tripod, into which the verses themselves were inserted at proper junctures in the story. Since the traditional *Collected Works* lacked an appropriate niche for such a work, Han Yü's editors separated the prose and verse sections and included the former among the prefaces.

136. The phrase occurs in the *Yün-lu man-ch'ao* [Rambling notes from the clouded foothills] by Chao Yen-wei (fl. 1195) (Shanghai: Ku-tien, 1957), 8/111. This often cited passage links *ch'uan-ch'i* and *wen-chüan* "keeping the scrolls warm," a practice of scroll presentation to their examiners by T'ang examination candidates. Two recent studies, however, have proved conclusively that *ch'uan-ch'i* were not used for this purpose. See Victor H. Mair, "Scroll Presentation in the T'ang Dynasty," pp. 35–60, and Lo Lien-t'ien, "T'ang-tai wen-hsüeh shih liang-ke wen-t'i t'an-t'ao" [An investigation of two questions in T'ang literary history], pp. 11–21. Chao Yen-wei's use of the term *neng pei chung t'i*, however, does represent a genuine desire for stylistic catholicity among mid-T'ang authors. Liu Yü-hsi, for instance, applied the phrase to describe the works of Chiao-jan. See *Liu Yü-hsi chi* 19/174; trans. Stephen Owen, *The Great Age of Chinese Poetry*, p. 282. Cf. also Ch'en Yin-k'o, *Ch'en Yin-k'o hsien-sheng lun-wen chi*, 2:4.

137. For a useful survey of fictional elements in Han Yü's prose see Ma, "Prose Writings," pp. 213–219.

138. Quoted in *Poetry*, p. 38, from the *Ou-pei shih-hua* of Chao I.

139. Chao I's thesis is the starting point for many discussions of Han Yü's poetry. See for instance Graham, *Poems of the Late T'ang*, pp. 71–72; Ch'eng Ch'ien-fan, "Han Yü i-wen-wei-shih shuo," pp. 200ff.; and Chiang Ch'iu-hua, " 'I-wen-wei-shih' yü 'i-shih-wei-wen,' " p. 20. Han Yü often mentions Li Po and Tu Fu in his works, but his fullest tribute to their influence on him is the poem "Taunting Chang Chi," *Poetry*, pp. 434–436; Shimizu Shigeru, *Kan Yu*, pp. 26–33; Ch'en Yung-cheng, *Han Yü shih hsüan*, pp. 171–175; Mori Kainan, *Kanshi Kōgi*, 2:485–490. There is a sizable bibliography on Han Yü's poetry. In addition to articles already mentioned, three general surveys are Ch'ien Tung-fu, "Kuan-yü Han Yü te shih" [On the poetry of Han Yü], pp. 140–164; Teng T'an-chou, "T'an Han Yü te shih" [The poetry of Han Yü], pp. 81–100; and Shu Wu, "Lun Han Yü shih" [On Han Yü's poetry], pp. 199–210.

140. See *Liu-i shih-hua*, ed. Martin, *Index*, p. 162; Ch'eng Ch'ien-

fan, "Han Yü i-wen-wei-shih shuo," pp. 196-197; Klöpsch, *Die Jadesplitter*, p. 105.

141. See *Hou-shan shih-hua*, ed. Martin, *Index*, p. 182; Klöpsch, *Die Jadesplitter*, pp. 104-105. Cf. also a passage in the same work (Martin, p. 185): "When Han Yü makes poetry from prose and Su Shih makes *tz'u* from poetry, these are like the music academy dance of Lei Ta-shih: although it may be very skilled, it lacks its own distinctive flavor." I have been unable to identify "the dance of Lei Ta-shih," and so the point of the simile is not totally clear to me.

142. See Ch'eng Ch'ien-fan, "Han Yü i-wen-wei-shih shuo," pp. 199-200.

143. See Ch'ien Chung-shu, *T'an i lu*, pp. 74ff.; Yoshikawa Kōjirō, *An Introduction to Sung Poetry*, p. 92; Ch'eng Ch'ien-fan, "Han Yü i-wen-wei-shih shuo," p. 198.

144. Yeh Hsieh, *Yüan shih*, p. 8.

145. Hu Shih, *Pai-hua wen-hsüeh shih* [A history of literature in the colloquial language], pp. 133-180, esp. pp. 169-171; for Hu Shih's remarks on Han Yü see pp. 351-360.

146. See Ch'en Yin-k'o, "Lun Han Yü," pp. 112-113; Iguchi Takashi, "Gyoku-sen-shi no shi," pp. 49-50; and the excellent summary in Chiang Ch'iu-hua, " 'I-wen-wei-shih' yü 'i-shih-wei-wen,' " pp. 23-27. See also Jao Tsung-i, "Han Yü 'Nan-shan shih' yü T'an-wu-ch'an i Ma-ming *Fo-so hsing-tsan*" [Han Yü's "Poem on the Southern Mountains" and T'an-wu-ch'an's translation of Aśvaghoṣa's *Buddhacarita*], pp. 98-101, for specific evidence of textual affiliation between the *Buddhacarita* and Han Yü's poetry.

147. See Schmidt, "Han Yü and His *Ku-shih* Poetry," pp. 60-63.

148. *Poetry*, p. 179; for a full translation see chapter one above, pp. 69-70.

149. *Poetry*, p. 179. Cf. also Owen, *The Poetry*, p. 189, and Hartman, "Han Yü and T.S. Eliot," pp. 68-69.

150. *Poetry*, p. 359; Mori Kainan, *Kanshi kōgi*, 2:436-437; cf. also Owen, *The Poetry*, pp. 224-225, where the translation differs considerably. I have followed Mori Kainan and Zach, *Han Yü's poetische werke*, p. 129.

151. For the concept of *p'ing tan* as an important force in Sung poetry see Jonathan Chaves, *Mei Yao-ch'en and the Development of Early Sung Poetry*, pp. 114-125.

152. *Poetry*, p. 568; cf. chapter one above, pp. 111-113.

153. *Poetry*, pp. 51-52; cf. chapter one above, p. 43.

154. For Han Yü's use of *fu* techniques in poetry see Schmidt, "Han Yü and His *Ku-shih* Poetry," pp. 38-39; Ku I-sheng, "Shih-t'an Han Yü te shang ch'i chi Han wen yü tz'u-fu p'ien-wen te kuan-hsi," pp. 66-72; and Wang Ch'i-hsing, "Han Yü shih-ko i-shu ch'u-t'an" [An initial inquiry into Han Yü's poetic art], pp. 165-169.

155. Cf. note 150. Ch'ien Chung-shu, *Sung shih hsüan chu* [Sung poems selected and annotated], p. 72, mentions these lines as an example of Han Yü's repeated metaphors, a stylistic feature that greatly influenced the poetry of Su Shih.

156. *Poetry*, p. 204.

157. *Poetry*, pp. 53-54; Ch'en Yung-cheng, *Han Yü shih hsüan*, pp. 22-23; Mori Kainan, *Kanshi kōgi*, 2:114-116; Yoshikawa Kōjirō, "Kan Yu," pp. 342-344; trans. Owen, *The Poetry*, p. 21; Chalmers, "Han Wan-kung," p. 280.

158. See J. D. Frodsham, *New Perspectives in Chinese Literature* (Canberra: Australian National University Press, 1970), pp. 11-13.

159. See Hartman, "Han Yü and T.S. Eliot," pp. 59-60. Cf. also Russell McLeod, "The Baroque as a Period Concept in Chinese Literature," pp. 185-211. By far the most thoughtful review of the question is Wong Tak-wai, "Toward Defining Chinese Baroque Poetry," pp. 25-72.

160. See Morris W. Croll, "The Baroque Style in Prose," rpt. in Stanley E. Fish, ed., *Seventeenth-Century Prose* (New York: Oxford University Press, 1971), pp. 26-52, whose analysis of the Senecan, anti-Ciceronian prose of the century 1575-1675 into a "curt style" (*stile coupé*) that valued "novelty and unexpectedness" and a "loose style" that reflected "the movements of a mind discovering truth as it goes, thinking while it writes" brings to mind analogies with Han Yü's prose style.

161. Owen, *The Poetry*, p. 278; Yanagida Seizan, "The 'Recorded Sayings' Texts of Chinese Ch'an Buddhism," p. 190.

162. Similar concerns can be traced to Tu Fu. See Yoshikawa Kōjirō, "Tu Fu's Poetics and Poetry," pp. 1-26, which pinpoints "minuteness" and "transcendence" as basic qualities of Tu Fu's poetics. For the relation between Ch'an and poetry see Paul Demiéville, "Le Tch'an et la poésie chinoise," pp. 123-136, and Iriya Yoshitaka, "Chinese Poetry and Zen," pp. 54-67.

A Note on Han Yü Bibliography

There are numerous studies on the history of Han Yü's *Collected Works* and on the relation of the various traditional editions. Hartman, "Preliminary Bibliographical Notes," attempts to establish the early history of the collection. Ch'ien Mu, *Chu-tzu hsin hsüeh-an*, 5:228–265, discusses Chu Hsi's important work on Han Yü's text. Useful surveys of the field are Wan Man, *T'ang chi hsü-lu*, pp. 167–183, and *Poetry*, pp. 64–65. Cf. also Wu Wen-chih, "Han chi ch'u-i erh t'i" [My opinion on two questions concerning *Han Yü's Collected Works*], pp. 48–49.

There is no fully adequate biography of Han Yü. The Sung dynasty chronological biographies (*nien-p'u*) are collected in the *Han Liu nien-p'u* edited by Ch'en Ching-yün (1670–1747). This collection is reprinted in the *Yüeh-ya t'ang ts'ung-shu*, and is readily available in Chou K'ang-hsieh, ed., *Han Liu wen-hsüeh yen-chiu ts'ung-k'an* and *Han Yü yen-chiu lun-ts'ung*. Most of this traditional material, along with later revisions and corrections, is incorporated into the biographical studies by Lo Lien-t'ien, *Han Yü yen-chiu*, pp. 1–136, which is to date the most detailed and careful study of Han Yü's life. A general work in Japanese is Maeno Naoaki, *Kan Yu no shōgai*, now also available in Chinese translation. Ōta Tsugio, "Kan Yu ni tsuite no ichi kōsatsu," is a more specialized study of Han Yü's career as a T'ang civil servant.

The standard texts of Han Yü's writings now in use are Ch'ien Chung-lien, *Poetry* (1957 ed.) and Ma Ch'i-ch'ang, *Prose* (1957 ed.). Of these, the former is much the superior work. Ch'ien meticulously lists textual variants and supporting evidence for preferred readings. The poems are arranged chronologically, and each is preceded by a headnote in which Ch'ien gives the reasons for his placement and carefully quotes other arguments. A selection of general critical comment follows each poem. The interlinear commentary is particularly strong on identifying allusions and has even been criticized as somewhat excessive in this regard (cf. Ch'ien Chung-shu's review in *Wen-hsüeh yen-chiu*). *Prose*, on the other hand, is the first-time printing of a manuscript by the late Ch'ing scholar

Ma Ch'i-ch'ang (1855–1930) and appears to have been left unfinished. Collation notes and selection of previous commentary are sketchy and uneven. For collections of general critical comment on specific prose texts, readers may refer to Lo Lien-t'ien, *Han Yü yen-chiu*, pp. 263–283, and to Shih Shu-nü, "Han Yü shih wen hui-p'ing." A new edition of Han Yü's complete works, conforming to modern standards of textual scholarship and with a generous collection of earlier commentary, is urgently needed. Wu Wen-chih is reportedly working on a Han Yü edition to parallel his four-volume 1979 edition of Liu Tsung-yüan. The same author's monumental *Han Yü tzu-liao hui-pien* unfortunately appeared too late for me to make use of in this book. It is certain, however, that this compendium will have a major impact on future Han Yü studies. A useful digest of these volumes' riches is Wu Wen-chih, "Han Yü yen-chiu shu-p'ing" [An account of studies on Han Yü], pp. 23–29.

An excellent modern anthology of Han Yü's poetry is Ch'en Yung-cheng, *Han Yü shih hsüan*, which has a fine selection of poems and copious annotation, mostly selected from *Poetry*. Ch'en, however, steers clear of Han Yü's longer poems; for these, readers may consult Mori Kainan, *Kanshi Kōgi*, which contains a brilliant commentary on longer poems, mostly from the first two *chüan* of Han Yü's *Collected Works*. A more recent, though less insightful, Japanese anthology is Harada Kenyū, *Kan Yu*. Shimizu Shigeru, *Kan Yu*, is the best small anthology of Han Yü's poetry, yet one that well represents his scope as a poet. The volume contains a good introduction and a postscript by Yoshikawa Kōjirō. Invaluable is the full concordance to Han Yü's poetry by Hanabusa Hideki, *Kan Yu kashi sakuin*, which also includes a useful table of Han Yü's writings, listing their locations in a variety of traditional editions and anthologies as well as their suspected date and place of composition. Han Yü's poetry has been completely translated into German by Erwin von Zach, *Han Yü's poetische Werke*, a monumental achievement by one of the great sinologists of the twentieth century. Translations of selected Han Yü poems into English are Stephen Owen's unpublished dissertation and published book, *The Poetry of Meng Chiao and Han Yü*; Jerry Schmidt, "Han Yü and His Ku-shih Poetry"; and Kenneth O. Hanson, trans., *Growing Old Alive*.

A good recent anthology of Han Yü's prose is T'ung Ti-te, *Han Yü wen hsüan*, a chronological selection of fifty-four texts, probably intended for use as a textbook. Although the political comment is sometimes obtrusive, the philology is basic and sound. More traditional is the generous selection from Han Yü in Kao Pu-ying, *T'ang-Sung wen chü-yao*. The commentary is especially strong on historical background. There are many anthologies of Han Yü's prose in Japanese series and collectaneas of Chinese literature; I have used with profit Hoshikawa Kiyotaka, *Tō-Sō hachidaikabun tokuhon*. Especially good is Shimizu Shigeru, *Tō-Sō hakkabun*, which shares all the virtues of the same author's anthology of Han Yü's poetry. Despite his importance, there is no really adequate selection of Han Yü prose translations into a European language. The largest selection is Bruno Hermann Luebeck, "Han Yü, the Champion of Confucianism," but the translations are not reliable and the work is inaccessible. More accurate is Liu Shih Shun, *Chinese Classical Prose*, which, however, suffers from the lack of commentary. Selections of varying length and quality may be found in almost all anthologies of Chinese literature in translation, such as Cyril Birch, ed., *Anthology of Chinese Literature*. Cf. also G. Margouliès, *Le kou-wen chinois* and *Anthologie raisonnée de la littérature chinoise*.

Chou K'ang-hsieh, *Han Liu wen-hsüeh yen-chiu ts'ung-k'an*, is a multi-volume collectanea of works relating to Han Yü and Liu Tsung-yüan. The same author's *Han Yü yen-chiu lun-ts'ung* is a one-volume reprinting of the *Han Liu nien-p'u* along with twenty modern articles on various aspects of Han Yü. There is no comprehensive bibliography of Han Yü studies. Lo Lien-t'ien, *T'ang-tai wen-hsüeh lun-chu chi-mu* [A bibliography of articles on T'ang literature] (Taipei: Hsüeh-sheng shu-chü, 1979), pp. 69–76, constitutes a good beginning.

Chinese and Japanese Works

Chang Hsiao-mei 張肖梅. "Liu Yü-hsi yü Wang-Wei chi-t'uan" 劉禹錫與王韋集團 [Liu Yü-hsi and the Wang-Wei faction]. *Kuo-li pien-i-kuan kuan-k'an* 11, no. 2 (December 1982): 109–126.

Chang Meng-chi 張夢機. "T'an Han Yü wu-ku te chang-fa" 談韓愈五古的章法 [A discussion of structure in Han Yü's five-character old style poetry]. *Chung-hua wen-hua fu-hsing yüeh-k'an* 8, no. 6 (January 1975): 56–60.

———. "Tu Fu 'Pei cheng' yü Han Yü 'Nan-shan shih' te pi-chiao" 杜甫北征與韓愈南山詩的比較 [A comparison of Tu Fu's "Northern Journey" and Han Yü's "Poem on the Southern Mountain"]. *Hsüeh-ts'ui* 學粹 (Taiwan) 17, no. 2 (June 1975): 8–15.

Chang San-hsi 張三夕. "Lüeh-t'an Han Yü te yü-yen i-shu" 略談韓愈的語言藝術 [On Han Yü's verbal art]. *Nan-ching ta-hsüeh hsüeh-pao*, no. 2 (1981): pp. 15–19.

Chang Shih-chao 章士釗. *Liu wen chih-yao* 柳文指要 [Essentials of Liu Tsung-yüan's writings]. Peking: Chung-hua shu-chü, 1974.

Ch'ang Pi-te 昌彼德 et al., eds. *Sung-jen chuan-chi tzu-liao so-yin* 宋人傳記資料索引 [Index to biographical materials of Sung figures]. 6 vols. Taipei: Ting-wen shu-chü, 1974–1976.

Chao Lin 趙璘 (mid-ninth century). *Yin hua lu* 因話錄 [A record of stories]. Rpt. Shanghai: Ku-tien wen-hsüeh ch'u-pan-she, 1957.

Chao Yü-ying 趙毓英. "Han Yü hsiang-li pien-lüeh" 韓愈鄉里辯略 [On Han Yü's hometown]. *Kuo-wen yüeh-k'an* 39–40 (December 1945–January 1946). Rpt. Chou K'ang-hsieh, *Han Yü yen-chiu lun-ts'ung*, pp. 91-101.

Ch'en Ching-yün 陳景雲 (1670–1747), ed. *Han Liu nien-p'u* 韓柳年譜 [Chronological biographies of Han Yü and Liu Tsung-yüan]. *Yüeh-ya t'ang ts'ung-shu* ed. Rpt. in Chou K'ang-hsieh, ed., *Han Liu wen-hsüeh yen-chiu ts'ung-k'an* and *Han Yü yen-chiu lun-ts'ung*.

Ch'en Erh-tung 陳邇冬. *Han Yü shih hsüan* 韓愈詩選 [Selections from Han Yü's poetry]. Peking: Jen-min wen-hsüeh ch'u-pan-she, 1984.

————. "Han Yü 'Yu T'ai-p'ing kung-chu shan-chuang' so-yin" 韓愈游太平公主山莊索隱 [An exposé of Han Yü's poem "An Excursion to the Mountain Villa of the Princess of Great Tranquillity"]. *T'ang-tai wen-hsüeh* 1 (1981): 272–274.

Ch'en Hsiao-ch'iang 陳曉薔. "Han Yü chi ch'i shih" 韓愈及其詩 [Han Yü and his poetry]. *Hsien-tai hsüeh-yüan* 5, no. 11 (December 1968): 11-16.

Ch'en Kuang-ch'ung 陳光崇. "Kuan-yü p'ing-chia Han Yü te chi-ke wen-t'i" 關于評價韓愈的幾個問題 [On several questions concerning criticism of Han Yü]. *Kuang-ming jih-pao*, January 19, 1978. Rpt. Chou K'ang-hsieh, *Han Yü yen-chiu lun-ts'ung*, pp. 1-3.

Ch'en Tso-lung 陳祚龍. "Liu Yü-hsi yü Fo-chiao" 劉禹錫與佛教 [Liu Yü-hsi and Buddhism]. *Fo-kuang hsüeh-pao* 2 (1977): 83-110.

Ch'en Yen-chieh 陳延傑, ed. *Chang Chi shih chu* 張籍詩注 [Chang Chi's poems annotated]. Rpt. Taipei: Shang-wu, 1967.

Ch'en Yin-k'o 陳寅恪. *Ch'en Yin-k'o hsien-sheng lun-wen chi* 陳寅恪先生論文集 [Collected works of Ch'en Yin-k'o]. 2 vols. Taipei: San-jen hsing ch'u-pan-she, 1974.

————. "Lun Han Yü" 論韓愈 [On Han Yü]. *Li-shih yen-chiu*, no. 2 (1954): 105-114. Rpt. Chou K'ang-hsieh, *Han Yü yen-chiu lun-ts'ung*, pp. 1-10.

Ch'en Yun-chi 陳允吉. "Lun T'ang-tai ssu-miao pi-hua tui Han Yü shih-ko te ying-hsiang" 論唐代寺廟壁畫對韓愈詩歌的影響 [The influence of T'ang dynasty monastic frescoes on Han Yü's poetry]. *Fu-tan hsüeh-pao*, no. 1 (1983): 72-80.

Ch'en Yung-cheng 陳永正 [Chih Shui 止水]. *Han Yü shih hsüan* 韓愈 詩選 [Selections from Han Yü's poetry]. Hong Kong: San-lien shu-chü, 1980.

Cheng Chih-chou 鄭芝周. *Huai-ch'ing fu chih* 懷慶府志 [Gazetteer of Huai-ch'ing prefecture]. Ming edition of 1518 preserved in National Central Library, Taipei.

Cheng Ch'ien 鄭騫. "Ku chin fei Han k'ao-pien" 古今誹韓考辨 [An investigation of defamations of Han Yü ancient and modern]. *Shu-mu chi-k'an* 11, no. 4 (March 1978): 3–22.

Ch'eng Ch'ien-fan 程千帆. "Han Yü i-wen-wei-shih shuo" 韓愈 以文爲詩說 [Han Yü's theory of "making poetry out of prose"]. *Ku-tai wen-hsüeh li-lun yen-chiu ts'ung-k'an* 1 (1979): 193–215.

Ch'eng Shu-te 程樹德. *Lun yü chi-shih* 論語集釋 [Collected commentary on the *Analects*]. 2 vols. Rpt. Taipei: Ting-wen shu-chü, 1973.

Chi Chen-huai 季鎮淮. "Han Yü te chi-pen ssu-hsiang chi ch'i mao-tun" 韓愈的基本思想及其矛盾 [Han Yü's basic thought and its contra-dictions]. *Wen-hsüeh yen-chiu*, no. 1 (1959): 69–78.

————. "Pi-chiao Han Yü ho Liu Tsung-yüan te liang shou shih" 比較韓 愈和柳宗元的兩首詩 [Comparing two poems of Han Yü and Liu Tsung-yüan]. *Kuang-ming jih-pao*, April 22, 1978. Rpt. Chou K'ang-hsieh, *Han Yü yen-chiu lun-ts'ung*, pp. 75–76.

Chiang Ch'iu-hua 蔣秋華. "'I-wen-wei-shih' yü 'i-shih-wei-wen'" 以文 爲詩與以詩爲文 ["Making poetry from prose" and "making prose from poetry"]. *Hsin ch'ao* 新潮 (Dept. of Chinese, National Taiwan University) 39 (1979): 19–32.

Chiang Fan 蔣凡. "Han Yü yü Wang Shu-wen chi-t'uan te 'Yung-cheng kai-ke'" 韓愈與王叔文集團的永貞改革 [Han Yü and the "805 Reforms" of the Wang Shu-wen faction]. *Fu-tan hsüeh-pao* 4 (July 1980): 67–74.

Chiang Hsin-mei 江辛眉. "Lun Han Yü shih te chi-ke wen-t'i" 論韓愈 詩的幾個問題 [A discussion of several questions relating to Han Yü's poetry]. In *Wen-hsüeh yen-chiu ts'ung-pien*, vol. 2., pp. 237–263. Taipei: Mu-to ch'u-pan-she, 1983.

Chiang Kuo-chen 江國貞. *Huang-fu chih-cheng hsüeh-shu yen-chiu* 皇甫 持正學術研究 [Studies on Huang-fu Shih's scholarship]. Taipei: Yu-shih wen-hua shih-yeh kung-szu, 1975.

Chiang Li-ts'ai 蔣勵材. "Han Yü 'Nan-shan shih' yen-shih" 韓愈南 山詩研釋 [An explication of Han Yü's "Poem on the Southern Mountains"]. *Chien-she tsa-chih* 8, no. 1 (June 1959): 32–37; no. 2 (July 1959): 27–31; no. 3 (August 1959): 31–32; no. 4 (September

378

1959): 31–32; nos. 5, 6 (October–November 1959): 37–39; no. 7 (December 1959): 30–31; no. 9 (February 1960): 27–30.

Chien T'ien-hsing 簡添興. "Han Yü chih ssu-hsiang chi ch'i wen-lun" 韓愈之思想及其文論 [Han Yü's thought and his literary theory]. Master's thesis, National Taiwan Normal University, 1978.

Ch'ien Chi-po 錢基博. Han Yü chih 韓愈志 [Monograph on Han Yü]. 1930. Rev. ed. 1957. Rpt. Taipei: Ho-lo t'u-shu ch'u-pan-she, 1975.

Ch'ien Chung-lien 錢仲聯, ed. Han Ch'ang-li shih hsi-nien chi-shih 韓昌黎詩繫年集釋 [The poetry of Han Yü arranged chronologically with collected annotations]. Shanghai: Ku-tien wen-hsüeh ch'u-pan-she, 1957. Rpt. Taipei: Shih-chieh shu-chü, 1966. (Poetry)

———. "Han Yü" 韓愈 [Han Yü]. Tz'u shu yen-chiu, no. 4 (1980): 66–73.

———. "Shih 'ch'i'" 釋氣 [On ch'i]. Ku-tai wen-hsüeh li-lun yen-chiu 5 (1981): 129–150.

Ch'ien Chung-shu 錢鍾書. Kuan-chui pien 管錐編 [Pipe-awl chapters]. 4 vols. Peking: Chung-hua, 1979.

———. Review of Ch'ien Chung-lien, Han Ch'ang-li shih hsi-nien chi-shih. Wen-hsüeh yen-chiu 2 (1958): 179–183.

———. "Shih k'o-i yüan" 詩可以怨 [Our sweetest songs]. Wen-hsüeh p'ing-lun, no. 1 (1981): 16–21.

———. Sung shih hsüan chu 宋詩選註 [Sung poems selected and annotated]. Rpt. Peking: Jen-min wen-hsüeh ch'u-pan-she, 1979.

———. T'an i lu 談藝錄 [Discourses on art]. Shanghai: K'ai-ming shu-chü, 1948. Rpt. Taipei: K'ai-ming, n.d.

Ch'ien Mu 錢穆, ed. Chu-tzu hsin hsüeh-an 朱子新學案 [A new casebook for Chu Hsi]. 5 vols. Taipei: San-min shu-chü, 1971.

———. "Han Liu chiao i" 韓柳交誼 [The friendship between Han Yü and Liu Tsung-yüan]. Chung-kuo wen-hsüeh chiang-yen chi, pp. 102–104. Kowloon: Jen-sheng ch'u-pan-she, 1963.

———. "Tsa-lun T'ang-tai ku-wen yün-tung" 雜論唐代古文運動 [Notes on the ku-wen movement of the T'ang]. Hsin-ya hsüeh-pao 3 (1957): 123–168.

Ch'ien Tung-fu 錢冬父. Han Yü 韓愈 [Han Yü]. Peking: Chung-hua shu-chü, 1980.

———. "Kuan-yü Han Yü te shih" 關于韓愈的詩 [On the poetry of Han Yü]. Wen-hsüeh i-ch'an tseng-k'an 4 (1957): 140–164. Rpt. Chou K'ang-hsieh, Han Yü yen-chiu lun-ts'ung, pp. 50–74.

———. T'ang-tai ku-wen yün-tung 唐代古文運動 [The T'ang dynasty ku-wen movement]. Shanghai: Ku-chi ch'u-pan-she, 1962.

Chou K'ang-hsieh 周康燮, ed. Han Liu wen-hsüeh yen-chiu ts'ung-k'an

韓柳文學研究叢刊 [A collectanea of studies on the writings of Han Yü and Liu Tsung-yüan]. Chung-kuo wen-hsüeh yen-chiu ts'ung-pien. Series 2. Hong Kong: Lung-men shu-tien, 1969.

————, ed. *Han Yü yen-chiu lun-ts'ung* 韓愈研究論叢 [Collected studies on Han Yü]. Hong Kong: Ta-tung t'u-shu kung-szu yin-hang, 1978.

Chou Yin-t'ang 周蔭棠. "Han Po Lun" 韓白論 [On Han Yü and Po Chü-i]. *Chin-ling hsüeh-pao* 1, no. 1 (May 1931): 189–203.

Chou-i chu-shu 周易注疏 [The *Changes of Chou* with commentary and subcommentary]. Completed by K'ung Ying-ta in 659. *SPPY* ed.

Ch'u tz'u pu chu 楚辭補注 [The *Ch'u tz'u* with supplementary commentary]. By Hung Hsing-tsu 洪興祖 (1070–1135). *SPPY* ed.

Chuang-tzu yin-te 莊子引得 [A concordance to *Chuang-tzu*]. Harvard-Yenching Institute Sinological Index Series Supplement No. 20. Rpt. Cambridge, MA: Harvard University Press, 1956.

Ch'üan T'ang wen 全唐文 [Complete T'ang prose]. Completed 1814. Rpt. Taipei: Ta-t'ung shu-chü, 1979.

Fu Lo-ch'eng 傅樂成. "T'ang-tai i-hsia kuan-nien chih yen-pien" 唐代夷夏觀念之演變 [The development of racial attitudes in the T'ang]. *Ta-lu tsa-chih* 25, no. 8 (October 1962): 6–12.

Fukushima Shunnō 福島俊翁. "Ri Kō no gakuzen to *Fukuseisho*" 李翱の学禅と復性書 [Li Ao's study of Ch'an and the *Fu-hsing shu*]. *Zengaku kenkyū* 51 (1961): 32–44.

Han T'ing-i 韓廷一. *Han Ch'ang-li ssu-hsiang yen-chiu* 韓昌黎思想研究 [Studies in Han Yü's thought]. Taipei: Shang-wu, 1982.

Han Yü 韓愈, and Li Ao 李翱. *Lun yü pi-chieh* 論語筆解 [Random notes on the *Analects*]. Edited by Hsü Po (978–1047). Late twelfth-century Southern Sung edition preserved in Palace Museum Library, Taipei.

Hanabusa Hideki 花房英樹. *Kan Yu kashi sakuin* 韓愈詩歌素引 [A concordance to the poems of Han Yü]. Kyoto: Kyotō furitsu daigaku jimbun gakkai, 1964.

Harada Kenyū 原田憲雄. *Kan Yu* 韓愈 [Han Yü]. Kanshi taikei, vol. 11. Tokyo: Shūeisha, 1965.

Ho T'ang 何瑭 (1474–1543). *Ho Wen-ting kung wen-chi* 何文定公文集 [Collected works of Ho T'ang]. 1576 edition preserved in National Central Library, Taipei.

Hoshikawa Kiyotaka 星川清孝. *Tō-Sō hachidaikabun tokuhon* 唐宋八大家文讀本 [A reader in the eight great prose masters of T'ang and Sung]. Tokyo: Meiji shoten, 1976.

Hou Wai-lu 侯外廬 et al. *Chung-kuo ssu-hsiang t'ung-shih* 中國思想通史 [A comprehensive history of Chinese thought]. 5 vols. Peking: Jen-min, 1959.

Hsieh Hai-p'ing 謝海平. *T'ang-tai fan-hu sheng-huo chi ch'i tui wen-hua chih ying-hsiang* 唐代蕃胡生活及其對文化之影響 [Foreigners in the T'ang dynasty and their cultural influence]. Taiwan: privately printed, n.d.

————. *T'ang-tai shih-jen yü tsai Hua wai-kuo jen chih wen-tzu chiao* 唐代詩人與在華外國人之文字交 [Literary relations between T'ang dynasty poets and foreigners in China]. Taipei: Wen shih che ch'u-pan-she, 1981.

Hsü Sung 徐松 (1781–1848). *Teng-k'o chi k'ao* 登科記考 [A study of the registers of those received at the examinations]. Nan-ch'ing shu-yüan ts'ung-shu edition of 1888. Rpt. 3 vols. with index. Taipei: Ching-sheng wen-wu kung-ying kung-szu, 1972.

Hsün-tzu 荀子. *SPPY* ed.

Hu Ch'u-sheng 胡楚生, ed. *Han-wen hsüan hsi* 韓文選析 [Prose of Han Yü, selected and explained]. Taipei: Hua-cheng shu-chü, 1983.

Hu Shih 胡適. *Pai-hua wen-hsüeh shih* 白話文學史 [A history of literature in the colloquial language]. Rpt. Taipei: Hu Shih chi-nien-kuan, 1969.

Hu Shih-hsien 胡時先. "Ch'ang-li 'ku-wen' chih chen-i" 昌黎古文之眞義 [The true meaning of Han Yü's *ku-wen*]. *Kuo-wen yüeh-k'an* 76 (February 1949). Rpt. Chou k'ang-hsieh, *Han Yü yen-chiu lun-ts'ung*, pp. 111–112.

Hua Ch'en-chih 華忱之. *T'ang Meng Chiao nien-p'u* 唐孟郊年譜 [A chronological biography of Meng Chiao of the T'ang]. Peking: Kuo-li Pei-ching ta-hsüeh t'u-shu-kuan, 1940.

Huai-ch'ing fu chih 懷慶府志 [Gazetteer of Huai-ch'ing prefecture]. Ch'ing edition of 1789. Rpt. Taipei: Hsüeh-sheng shu-chü, 1968.

Huang Yün-mei 黃雲眉. *Han Yü Liu Tsung-yüan wen-hsüeh p'ing-chia* 韓愈柳宗元文學評價 [A critical evaluation of the literature of Han Yü and Liu Tsung-yüen]. Shan-tung, 1957. Rpt. Chi-nan: Chi-Lu shu-chü, 1979.

————. "Han Yü wen-hsüeh te p'ing-chia" 韓愈文學的評價 [A critical evaluation of Han Yü's literature]. *Wen shih che. Shan-tung ta-hsüeh hsüeh-pao* (November 1956), pp. 1–10; (December 1956), pp. 43–57.

————. "Tu Ch'en Yin-k'o hsien-sheng 'Lun Han Yü'" 讀陳寅恪先生 '論韓愈' [Reading Ch'en Yin-k'o's "On Han Yü"]. *Wen shih che. Shan-tung ta-hsüeh hsüeh-pao* (August 1955), pp. 23–35.

Huang-fu Shih 皇甫湜. *Huang-fu chih-cheng chi* 皇甫持正集 [Collected works of Huang-fu Shih]. *SPTK* ed.

Hung Hsing-tsu 洪興祖 (1090–1155). *Han-tzu nien-p'u* 韓子年譜 [A

chronological biography of Master Han]. Rpt. in Ch'en Ching-yün, ed., *Han Liu nien-p'u*.

Hung Yeh 洪業 [William Hung]. *Tu shih yin-te* 杜詩引得 [A concordance to the poems of Tu Fu]. Harvard-Yenching Institute Sinological Index Series Supplement No. 14. 3 vols. Rpt. Taipei: Chinese Materials and Research Aids Service Center, 1966.

Ichihara Kōkichi 市原亨吉. "Chūtō shoki ni okeru kōsa no shisō ni tsuite" 中唐初期における江左の詩僧について [On the poet-monks south of the Yangtze in the early mid-T'ang period]. *Tohō gakuhō* 28 (1958): 219–248.

Iguchi Takashi 井口孝. "Gyoku-sen-shi no shi" 玉川子の詩 [The poetry of Yü-ch'uan-tzu (Lu T'ung)]. *Chūgoku bungaku hō* 28 (October 1977): 32–70.

Inaba Ichirō 稲葉一郎. "Chūtō ni okeru shinjugaku undō no ichi kōsatsu: Ryū Chiki no keisho hihan to Tan-Chō-Riki shi no *Shunjūgaku*" 中唐における新儒学運動の一考察—劉知幾の経書批判と啖・趙・陸氏の春秋学 [A study of the Neo-Confucian movement of the mid-T'ang: The classical criticism of Liu Chih-chi and the *Spring and Autumn* studies of Masters Tan, Chao, and Lu]. In Chūgoku chūseishi kenkyūkai, ed., *Chūgoku chūseishi kenkyū: Rikuchō Sui Tō no shakai to bunka*, pp. 377–403. Tokyo: Tōkai daigaku shuppankai, 1970.

Iriya Yoshitaka 入矢義高. "T'ang Hu-chou Chu-shan Chiao-jan chuan" 唐湖州杼山皎然傳 [Biography of Chiao-jan of Chu-shan in Hu-chou]. In Ogawa Tamaki, ed., *Tōdai no shijin: Sono denki* [Biographies of T'ang poets], pp. 625–635. Tokyo: Taishokan shoten, 1975.

Jao Tsung-i 饒宗頤. "Han Yü 'Nan-shan shih' yü T'an-wu-ch'an i Ma-ming *Fo-so hsing-tsan*" 韓愈南山詩與曇無讖譯馬鳴佛所行讚 [Han Yü's "Poem on the Southern Mountains" and T'an-wu-ch'an's translation of Aśvaghoṣa's *Buddhacarita*]. *Chūgoku bungaku hō* 19 (1963): 98–101.

Jen Fang-ch'iu 任訪秋. "Lun Han Yü ho Liu Tsung-yüan te san-wen" 論韓愈和柳宗元的散文 [On the prose writings of Han Yü and Liu Tsung-yüan]. *Hsin chien-she* (September 1957), pp. 47–50. Rpt. Chou K'ang-hsieh, *Han Yü yen-chiu lun-ts'ung*, pp. 37–42.

Kanda Kiichirō 神田喜一郎. "Ryō Shuku nempu" 梁肅年譜 [A chronological biography of Liang Su]. In *Tōhōgaku ronshū*. Twenty-fifth Anniversary Volume, pp. 259–274. Tokyo: Tōhō gakkai, 1972.

Kao Pu-ying 高步瀛, ed. *T'ang-Sung wen chü-yao* 唐宋文舉要 [Essential T'ang and Sung prose]. Shanghai: Chung-hua, 1962. Rpt. 3 vols. Hong Kong: Chung-hua, 1976.

Katō Minoru 加藤實. "Kan Yu 'Shih chih hsü i' yakuchu" 韓愈詩之序議譯注 [Han Yü's "Disquisition on the Preface to the *Book of Poetry*" translated and annotated]. *Shikyō kenkyū* 1 (1974): 23–26.

Komazawa daigaku 駒沢大学. *Zengaku daijiten* 禅学大辞典 [The great dictionary of Ch'an]. 3 vols. Tokyo: Taishokan shoten, 1971.

Konishi Jin'ichi 小西甚一. *Bunkyō hifuron kō* 文鏡秘府論考 [Studies on the *Bunkyō hifuron*]. 3 vols. Kyoto: Dai Nihon yūbenkai kōdansha, 1948–1953.

Ku I-sheng 顧易生. "Shih-t'an Han Yü te shang ch'i chi Han wen yü tz'u-fu p'ien-wen te kuan-hsi" 試談韓愈的尚奇及韓文與辭賦駢文的關係 [Han Yü's adulation of *ch'i* and the relation between his prose and (earlier) *fu* and *p'ien-wen*]. *Wen-hsüeh i-ch'an tseng-k'an* 10 (1962): 66–72. Rpt. Chou K'ang-hsieh, *Han Yü yen-chiu lun-ts'ung*, pp. 43–49.

Ku Li-san 顧立三. "T'ang-tai chih kung-chü chih-tu" 唐代之貢舉制度 [The T'ang examination system]. *Kuo-li pien-i-kuan kuan-k'an* 5, no. 1 (June 1976): 41–67.

Kubo Tenzui 久保天隨. *Kan Taishi* 韓退之 [Han Yü]. Osaka: Shōbidō, 1901.

———. *Kan Taishi shishū* 韓退之詩集 [The collected poetry of Han Yü]. Zoku kokuyaku kanbun taisei vols. 7 and 8. Tokyo: Kokumin bunko kankōkai, 1929.

Kung P'eng-ch'eng 龔鵬程. "K'ung Ying-ta Chou-i cheng-i yü Fo-chiao chih kuan-hsi" 孔穎達周易正義與佛教之關係 [The relation between Buddhism and the *Chou-i cheng-i* of K'ung Ying-ta]. *K'ung Meng hsüeh-pao* 39 (1980): 137–154.

Kung Shu-chih 龔書熾. *Han Yü chi ch'i ku-wen yün-tung* 韓愈及其古文運動 [Han Yü and his *ku-wen* movement]. Ch'ung-ch'ing: Shang-wu, 1945.

Kuo Hsi-liang 郭錫良. "Han Yü tsai wen-hsüeh yü-yen fang-mien te li-lun ho shih-chien" 韓愈在文學語言方面的理論和實踐 [The theory and practice of Han Yü's literary language]. *Yü-yen hsüeh lun-ts'ung* (Shanghai) 1 (1957): 51–73.

Kuo Shao-yü 郭紹虞, ed. *Chung-kuo li-tai wen-lun hsüan* 中國歷代文論選 [An anthology of Chinese literary criticism]. 3 vols. Rpt. Hong Kong: Chung-hua, 1979.

———. *Chung-kuo wen-hsüeh p'i-p'ing shih* 中國文學批評史 [History of Chinese literary criticism]. 2 vols. Shanghai: Shang-wu, 1934–1947.

———. *Sung shih-hua k'ao* 宋詩話考 [Researches on the Sung *shih-hua*]. Peking: Chung-hua, 1979.

Kuo Yü-heng 郭預衡. "Chieh-ch'u te san-wen-chia Han Yü" 杰出的

散文家韓愈 [The outstanding prose writer Han Yü]. In Kuo Yü-heng, *Ku-tai wen-hsüeh t'an-t'ao chi*, pp. 160–176. Peking: Pei-ching shih-fan ta-hsüeh ch'u-pan-she, 1981.

———. "Han Yü p'ing-chia te chi-ke wen-t'i" 韓愈評價的幾個問題 [Several questions concerning the evaluation of Han Yü]. In *Ku-tai wen-hsüeh t'an-t'ao chi*, pp. 143–159.

Li Ao 李翱. *Li Wen-kung chi* 李文公集 [Collected works of Li Ao]. *SPTK* ed.

Li Chao 李肇 (d. 836?). *T'ang kuo-shih pu* 唐國史補 [Supplement to the state history of the T'ang]. Rpt. Shanghai: Ku-tien wen-hsüeh ch'u-pan-she, 1957.

Li Ch'ang-chih 李長之. *Han Yü* 韓愈 [Han Yü]. Ch'ung-ch'ing, 1945. Rpt. Chou K'ang-hsieh, *Han Liu wen-hsüeh yen-chiu ts'ung-k'an.*

Li chi chu-shu 禮記注疏 [*Record of Rites* with commentary and subcommentary]. Completed by K'ung Ying-ta in 659. *SPPY* ed.

Li Chia-yen 李嘉言. "Han Yü fu-ku yün-tung te hsin t'an-so" 韓愈復古運動的新探索 [A new inquiry into Han Yü's *fu-ku* movement]. *Wen-hsüeh* 6 (1934). Rpt. Chou K'ang-hsieh, *Han Yü yen-chiu lun-ts'ung,* pp. 102–110.

Li Chuang-chia 李莊甲. "Yang Hsiung wen-hsüeh ssu-hsiang shu-p'ing" 揚雄文學思想述評 [A critique of Yang Hsiung's literary thought]. In *Ku-tien wen-hsüeh lun-ts'ung. Fu-tan hsüeh-pao (she-hui k'e-hsüeh pan) tseng-k'an*, pp. 69–81. Shanghai: Jen-min, 1980.

Liang Jung-jo 梁容若. *Wen-hsüeh shih-chia chuan* 文學十家傳 [Biographies of ten Chinese authors]. T'ai-chung: Tung-hai University, 1966.

Liang P'ing-chü 梁平居. "Lun Han T'ui-chih tui T'ang Sung i-hou wen-chang chih ying-hsiang" 論韓退之對唐宋以後文章之影響 [Han Yü's influence on T'ang and post-T'ang literature]. *Wen-shih hsüeh-pao* (Hong Kong) 2 (1965): 112–125.

Lien-ho pao 聯合報 [United Daily News]. *Fei Han an lun-ts'ung* 誹韓案論叢 [A collection of articles on the defamation of Han Yü case]. Taipei: Lien-ho pao she, 1977.

Lin Tzu-sen 林自森. "Han Yü te ssu-hsiang" 韓愈的思想 [Han Yü's thought]. *Hsin ch'ao* (Dept. of Chinese, National Taiwan University) 36 (June 1978): 32–53.

Lin Yü-ling 林玉玲. "Han T'ui-chih che Ch'ao-chou k'ao" 韓退之謫潮州考 [A study of Han Yü's exile to Ch'ao-chou]. *Wen-shih hsüeh-pao* (Hong Kong) 2 (1965): 132–144.

Liu Hsü 劉昫. *Chiu T'ang shu* 舊唐書 [Old T'ang history]. Completed 945. Rpt. Peking: Chung-hua shu-chü, 1975.

Liu Kuo-ying 劉國盈. "Li Ao ho ku-wen yün-tung" 李翱和古文運動 [Li Ao and the *ku-wen* movement]. *T'ang-tai wen-hsüeh* 3 (1983): 170–184.

Liu Tsung-yüan 柳宗元 (773–819). *Liu Tsung-yüan chi* 柳宗元集 [Collected works of Liu Tsung-yüan]. Wu Wen-chih et al., eds. 4 vols. Peking: Chung-hua, 1979.

Liu Yü-hsi 劉禹錫 (772–842). *Liu Yü-hsi chi* 劉禹錫集 [Collected works of Liu Yü-hsi]. Shanghai: Jen-min, 1975.

Lo Hsiang-lin 羅香林. "Ta-tien Wei-yen yü Han Yü Li Ao kuan-hsi k'ao" 大顛惟儼與韓愈李翱關係考 [A study of the relationships between Ta-tien and Han Yü, and Wei-yen and Li Ao]. *T'ang-tai wen-hua shih* [A history of T'ang culture], pp. 177–193. Rpt. Taipei: Shang-wu, 1974 [article first published 1937].

———. "T'ang-tai san-chiao chiang-lun k'ao" 唐代三教講論考 [A study of the debates between the three religions during the T'ang]. *T'ang-tai wen-hua shih*, pp. 159–176. Rpt. Taipei: Shang-wu, 1974 [article first published 1953].

Lo K'e-tien 羅克典. *Lun Han Yü* 論韓愈 [On Han Yü]. Taipei: Kuo-chia ch'u-pan-she, 1982.

Lo Lien-t'ien 羅聯添. "Chang Chi nien-p'u" 張籍年譜 [A chronological biography of Chang Chi]. *Ta-lu tsa-chih* 25, no. 4 (August 31, 1962): 14–19; no. 5 (September 15, 1962): 15–22; no. 6 (September 30, 1962): 20–29.

———. "Chang Chi shang Han Ch'ang-li shu te chi-ke wen-t'i" 張籍上韓昌黎書的幾個問題 [Several problems concerning Chang Chi's letters to Han Yü]. In *T'ai Ching-nung hsien-sheng pa-shih shou-ch'ing lun-wen chi* [A collection of essays in honor of the eightieth birthday of Professor T'ai Ching-nung], pp. 353–385. Taipei, 1981.

———. *Han Yü* 韓愈 [Han Yü]. Taipei: Ho-lo t'u-shu ch'u-pan-she, 1977.

———. *Han Yü yen-chiu* 韓愈研究 [Han Yü studies]. Taipei: Hsüeh-sheng shu-chü, 1977. 2d rev. ed. 1981. This latter edition incorporates some material from the author's 1977 *Han Yü*. I quote the 1977 edition.

———. "Li Ao yen-chiu" 李翱研究 [Li Ao studies]. *Kuo-li pien-i-kuan kuan-k'an* 2, no. 3 (December 1973): 55–89.

———. "Liu Meng-te nien-p'u" 劉夢得年譜 [A chronological biography of Liu Yü-hsi]. *Wen shih che hsüeh-pao* 8 (1958): 181–295.

———. "Liu Tsung-yüan erh p'ien i-lun wen fen-hsi" 柳宗元二篇議論文分析 [An analysis of two argumentative texts by Liu Tsung-yüan]. *Chung-wai wen-hsüeh* 97 (December 1980): 34–61.

———. *Liu Tsung-yüan shih-chi hsi-nien chi tzu-liao lei-pien* 柳宗元事蹟繫年暨資料類編 [A chronological biography of Liu Tsung-yüan together with a classified compendium of reference materials]. Tai-pei: Kuo-li Pien-i-kuan chung-hua ts'ung-shu pien-shen wei-yüan hui, 1981.

———. "T'ang Sung san-shih-ssu chung tsa-shih pi-chi chieh-t'i" 唐宋三十四種雜史筆記解題 [Notes on thirty-four T'ang and Sung semihistorical and anecdotal works]. *Shu-mu chi-k'an* 12, nos. 1 and 2 (September 1978): 57–66.

———. "T'ang-tai shih wen chi te chiao-k'an wen-t'i" 唐代詩文集的校勘問題 (Collation problems in collections of T'ang verse and prose]. *Kuo-li pien-i-kuan kuan-k'an* 12, no. 2 (1983): 1–16.

———. "T'ang-tai wen-hsüeh shih liang-ke wen-t'i t'an-t'ao" 唐代文學史兩個問題探討 [An investigation of two questions in T'ang literary history]. *Shu-mu chi-k'an* 11, no. 3 December 1977): 11–21.

———. "Tu-ku Chi k'ao-cheng" 獨孤及考證 [Notes on Tu-ku Chi]. *Ta-lu tsa-chih* 48, no. 3 (March 1974): 21–42.

Lun yü yin-te 論語引得 [A concordance to the *Analects* of Confucius]. Harvard-Yenching Institute Sinological Index Series Supplement No. 16. Peking: Harvard-Yenching Institute, 1940.

Lung Yü-ch'ün 龍宇純. "Hsien-Ch'in san-wen chung te yün-wen" 先秦散文中的韻文 [Rhyme in pre-Ch'in prose texts]. *The Chung Chi Journal* 2, no. 2 (May 1963): 137–168; 3, no. 1 (November 1963): 55–87.

Ma Ch'i-ch'ang 馬其昶, ed. *Han Ch'ang-li wen chi chiao-chu* 韓昌黎文集校注 [Han Yü's prose, collated and annotated]. Shanghai: Ku-tien wen-hsüeh ch'u-pan-she, 1957. Rpt. Taipei: Shih-chieh shu-chü, 1967. (*Prose*)

Ma Ch'i-hua 馬起華. *Han Wen-kung nien-p'u* 韓文公年譜 [A chronological biography of Han Yü]. Taipei: Shang-wu, 1978.

Maeno Naoaki 前野直彬. *Kan Yu no shōgai* 韓愈の生涯 [The life of Han Yü]. Tokyo: Akiyama shoten, 1976. Chinese trans. by T'an Chi-shan 譚繼山. *Han Yü* 韓愈 [Han Yü]. Taipei: Wan-sheng ch'u-pan kung-szu, 1984.

———. *Tōdai no shijintachi* 唐代の詩人達 [T'ang poets]. Tokyo: Tōkyōdō shuppan, 1971.

Meng-tzu yin-te 孟子引得 [A concordance to *Meng-tzu*]. Harvard-Yenching Institute Sinological Index Series Supplement No. 17. Peking: Harvard-Yenching Institute, 1941.

Mori Kainan 森槐南. *Kanshi kōgi* 韓詩講義 [An exposition of Han Yü's poetry]. 2 vols. Tokyo: Bunkaidō shoten, 1915.

Mou Jun-sun 牟潤孫. "Lun Ju-Shih liang chia chih chiang-ching yü i-shu"

論儒釋兩家之講經與義疏 [On Confucian and Buddhist exegesis and commentary]. *Hsin-ya hsüeh-pao* 4, no. 2 (February 1960): 353–415.

———. "T'ang-ch'u nan-pei hsüeh-jen lun hsüeh chih i-ch'u chi ch'i ying-hsiang" 唐初南北學人論學之異趣及其影響 [The differences of academic approach between the northern and southern scholars in the early T'ang, and their influence]. *Bulletin of the Institute of Chinese Studies of the Chinese University of Hong Kong* 1 (1968): 50–88.

Murayama Yoshihiro 村山吉廣. "Kaidai Kan Yu 'Shih chih hsü i'" 解題韓愈詩之序議 [A synopsis of Han Yü's "Disquisition on the Preface to the *Book of Poetry*"]. *Shikyō kenkyū* 1 (1974): 21–22.

Obi Kōichi 小尾郊一. "Ryū Ben no bunron" 柳冕の文論 [The stylistics of Liu Mien]. *Shinagaku kenkyū* 27 (March 1962): 27–37.

Ogawa Tamaki 小川環樹, ed. *Tōdai no shijin: Sono denki* 唐代の詩人 ─ その伝記 [Biographies of T'ang poets]. Tokyo: Taishokan shoten, 1975.

Ono Shihei 小野四平. "Kan Yu no sekibaku" 韓愈の寂寞 [Han Yü's loneliness]. *Tōyōgaku* 29 (1972): 29–42.

———. "Yōsan ni okeru Kan Yu" 陽山における韓愈 [Han Yü in Yang-shan]. *Tōyōgaku* 30 (1973): 59–78.

Ōta Teizō 太田悌蔵. "Kan Yu no haibutsu no Sōgaku e no eikyo" 韓愈の排仏の宋学への影響 [The influence of Han Yü's anti-Buddhism on Sung thought]. *Indogaku Bukkyōgaku kenkyū* 15, no. 1 (1966): 50–55.

Ōta Tsugiō 太田次男. "Kan Yu ni tsuite no ichi kōsatsu—toku-ni sono kanjin seikatsu o chūshin toshite" 韓愈についての一考察─特にその官人生活を中心として [A study of Han Yü with special reference to his official life]. *Shidō bunko ronshū* 1 (1962): 85–192.

Ou-yang Hsiu 歐陽修, and Sung Ch'i 宋祁. *Hsin T'ang-shu* 新唐書 [New T'ang history]. Completed 1060. Rpt. Peking: Chung-hua shu-chü, 1975.

P'an Lü Ch'i-ch'ang 潘呂棋昌. *Hsiao Ying-shih yen-chiu* 蕭穎士研究 [Hsiao Ying-shih studies]. Taipei: Wen shih che ch'u-pan-she, 1983.

P'ei-wen yün-fu 佩文韻府 [Rhymed treasury from the P'ei-wen studio]. Rpt. 7 vols. Taipei: Shang-wu, 1974.

P'i Jih-hsiu 皮日修 (c. 834–c. 883). *P'i-tzu wen-sou* 皮子文藪 [Literary marsh of Master P'i]. Edited by Hsiao Ti-fei. Peking: Chung-hua shu-chü, 1959.

Sakata Shin 坂田新. "'Shih chih hsü i' kō. Kobun fukkō undō no ichimen ni furete" 「詩之序議」考. 古文復興運動の一面にふれて [A study of the "Disquisition on the Preface to the *Book of Poetry*." Commentary on an aspect of the *ku-wen* renaissance movement]. *Chūgokukoten kenkyū* 20 (1975): 50–61.

Shih Shu-nü 施淑女, ed. "Han Yü shih wen hui-p'ing" 韓愈詩文彙評 [A collection of critical comments on Han Yü's prose and poetry]. Originally published in six parts, *Wen-shih chi-k'an* 1, no. 1–2, no. 2 (October 1970–January 1972). Rpt. Chou K'ang-hsieh, *Han Yü yen-chiu lun-ts'ung*, pp. 184–244.

Shimizu Kiyoshi 清水潔. "Kan Yu no bungaku ni okeru odoke to yūmoa" 韓愈の文学における諧謔とユーモア [Wit and humor in the writings of Han Yü]. *Kaitoku* 32 (1961): 1–30.

———. "Kan Yu no haibutsuron o meguru ichi kōsatsu" 韓愈の排仏論をめくる一考察 [A study of Han Yü's anti-Buddhist discourses]. *Ōsaka daigaku namboku bunkō kenkyū shūroku (Jimbun shakai kagaku)* 2 (March 1954): 47–57.

Shimizu Shigeru 清水茂. *Kan Yu* 韓愈 [Han Yü]. Chūgoku shijin zenshū vol. 11. Tokyo: Iwanami shoten, 1958.

———. *Tō-Sō hakkabun* 唐宋八家文 [Eight prose masters of the T'ang and Sung dynasties]. 2 vols. Tokyo: Asahi shimbunsha, 1966.

Shinohara Hisao 篠原壽雄. "Tōdai bunjin no Bukkyō rikai ni tsuite" 唐代文人の仏教理解について [The comprehension of Buddhism among T'ang literati]. *Indogaku Bukkyōgaku kenkyū* 10, no. 2 (March 1962): 227–232.

———. "Tōdai zen to Ryū Sōgan" 唐代禅と柳宗元 [T'ang Zen and Liu Tsung-yüan]. *Indogaku Bukkyōgaku kenkyū* 11, no. 2 (March 1963): 126–130.

Shu Wu 舒蕪. "Lun Han Yü shih" 論韓愈詩 [On Han Yü's poetry]. *Chung-kuo she-hui k'o-hsüeh*, no. 5 (1982): 199–210.

Shui Yüan 蜕園. "Han Yü yü Yüan Po te kuan-hsi" 韓愈與元白的關係 [The relationship between Han Yü and Yüan Chen and Po Chü-i]. *I-lin ts'ung-lu* 7 (January 1973): 146–148. Rpt. Chou K'ang-hsieh, *Han Yü yen-chiu lun-ts'ung*, pp. 245–247.

Su Wen-cho 蘇文擢. *Han wen ssu lun* 韓文四論 [Four essays on Han Yü's works]. Hong Kong: Hua-nan yin-shua chih-pan kung-szu, 1978.

———. "Han Yü tui Fo-t'u chih chieh-ch'u yü t'ai-tu" 韓愈對佛徒之接觸與態度 [Han Yü's contacts with and attitude toward Buddhists]. *Lien-ho shu-yüan hsüeh-pao* 11 (1973): 33–42.

Sun Ch'ang-wu 孫昌武. "T'ang-tai 'ku-wen yün-tung' ch'ien-i" 唐代古文運動淺議 [My views on the T'ang "ku-wen movement"]. *T'ang-tai wen-hsüeh* 3 (1983): 28–45.

Sun Kuo-t'ung 孫國棟. *T'ang-tai chung-yang chung-yao wen-kuan ch'ien-*

chuan t'u-ching yen-chiu 唐代中央重要文官遷轉途徑研究 [Researches on the career paths of important civil officials in the central government of the T'ang dynasty]. Hong Kong: Hsin-ya yen-chiu-so, 1978.

————. "Ts'ung *Meng-yu lu* k'an T'ang-tai wen-jen ch'ien-kuan te tsui-yu t'u-ching" 從夢遊錄看唐代文人遷官的最優途徑 [Channels of promotion in the T'ang dynasty as seen in the *Meng-yu lu* (Record of Rambling Dreams), a T'ang period novel]. *Journal of Oriental Studies* 10, no. 2 (July 1972): 188–196.

Szu-ma Ch'ien 司馬遷 (145–c.86 B.C.). *Shih chi* 史記 [Records of the historian]. Rpt. Peking: Chung-hua shu-chü, 1959.

Szu-ma Kuang 司馬光. *Tzu-chih t'ung-chien* 資治通鑑 [The complete mirror: An aid to government]. Completed 1085. Rpt. Peking: Ku-chi ch'u-pan-she, 1956.

T'ai Ching-nung 臺靜農. "Lun pei-chuan wen chi ch'uan-ch'i wen" 論碑傳文及傳奇文 [On biographical stone inscriptions and *ch'uan-ch'i* literature]. In Liu Shao-t'ang et al., *Shen-me shih chuan-chi wen-hsüeh*, pp. 219–227. Taipei: Chuan-chi wen-hsüeh ch'u-pan-she, 1967.

Taishō shinshu daizōkyo 大正新修大藏經 [The Buddhist canon of the *taishō* period]. Edited by Takakusa Junjirō and Watanabe Kaikyoku. 85 vols. Tokyo: Taishō Issaikyō kankōkai, 1924–1934.

T'ang Chen-ch'ang 唐振常. "Han Yü p'ai Fo-Lao i" 韓愈排佛老議 [Han Yü's anti-Buddhist and anti-Taoist opinions]. In *Ku-tien wen-hsüeh lun-ts'ung*, vol. 1, pp. 177–208. Chi-nan: Chi-Lu shu-she, 1980.

T'ang hui-yao 唐會要 [Collected essentials of the T'ang]. Completed 961. Rpt. Taipei: Shih-chieh shu-chü, 1968.

T'ang liu tien 唐六典 [T'ang administrative institutions]. Completed 739. Rpt. Taipei: Wen-hai ch'u-pan-she, 1974.

T'ang wen-ts'ui 唐文粹 [Best of T'ang literature]. Completed by Yao Hsüan (968–1020). Basic Sinological Series ed. Rpt. Taipei: Shang-wu, 1968.

Teng T'an-chou 鄧潭洲. "Lun Han Yü chi yu-kuan te chi-ke wen-t'i" 論韓愈及有關的幾個問題 [On Han Yü and several related questions]. *Jen-wen tsa-chih* 1, no. 3 (June 1958): 36–49.

————. "T'an Han Yü te shih" 談韓愈的詩 [The poetry of Han Yü]. *Wen-hsüeh i-ch'an tseng-k'an* 6 (1958): 81–100.

Ting Chen-chia 丁振家. "Tui Han Yü chi ch'i wen-hsüeh te p'ing-chia" 對韓愈及其文學的評價 [On Han Yü and an assessment of his writings]. *Wen-hsüeh i-ch'an tseng-k'an* 5 (1957): 176–190. Rpt. Chou K'ang-hsieh, *Han Yü yen-chiu lun-ts'ung*, pp. 77–92.

Ting Chi-han 丁記涵. *Han Yü wen-t'i fen-lei yen-chiu* 韓愈文體分類研究 [Studies on the classification of Han Yü's literary genres]. Taipei: Chi-wen shu-chü, 1976.

Tokiwa Daijō 常盤大定. *Shina ni okeru Bukkyō to Jukyō Dōkyō* 支那における仏教と儒教道教 [Buddhism and Confucianism and Taoism in China]. Tokyo: Tōyō bunko, 1930.

Ts'ai Han-mo 蔡涵墨 [Charles Hartman]. "Ch'an-tsung *Tsu-t'ang chi* chung yu kuan Han Yü te hsin tzu-liao" 禪宗祖堂集中有關韓愈的新資料 [New source material concerning Han Yü in the *Tsu-t'ang chi* of the Ch'an school]. *Shu-mu chi-k'an* 17, no. 1 (June 1983): 19–21.

Ts'e-fu yüan-kuei 册府元龜 [The grand tortoise: A repository of documents]. Completed 1013. Ming 1642 edition. Rpt. Taipei: Chung-hua shu-chü, 1965.

Ts'en Chung-mien 岑仲勉. "Pa *T'ang chih-yen*" 跋唐摭言 [Notes on the *T'ang chih-yen*]. *BIHP* 9 (1947): 243–264.

———. "T'ang chi chih i" 唐集質疑 [Notes on some texts of the T'ang dynasty]. *BIHP* 9 (1947): 1–82.

———, ed. *Yüan-ho hsing tsuan ssu-chiao chi* 元和姓纂四校記 [A compendium of surnames from the Yüan-ho period]. Academia Sinica, Institute of History and Philology, Monograph 29. 2 vols. Shanghai, 1948. Rpt. Taipei: T'ai-lien kuo-feng ch'u-pan-she, 1975.

Tsu-t'ang chi 祖堂集 [Collection from the hall of the patriarchs]. Completed 952. Edited by Yanagida Seizan from a Korean edition of 1245. Kyoto: Hanazono daigaku, 1960. Rpt. Taipei: Kuang-wen shu-chü, 1972.

Tu Chung-ling 杜仲陵. "Lüeh-lun Han Yü te shu-mien yü-yen yü tang-shih k'ou-yü te kuan-hsi" 略論韓愈的書面語言與當時口語的關係 [A brief study of the relation between Han Yü's literary language and contemporary colloquial language]. *Yü-yen yen-chiu* 4 (September 1959): 55–63.

Tu Sung-po 杜松柏. *Ch'an-hsüeh yü T'ang-Sung shih-hsüeh* 禪學與唐宋詩學 [Ch'an and T'ang-Sung poetics]. Taipei: Li-ming wen-hua ch'u-pan-she. 1976.

———. "P'o Ku te yü–Ch'an tz'u" 坡谷的寓禪詞 [*Tz'u* poems concerning Ch'an by Su Tung-p'o and Huang T'ing-chien]. *Chung-hua jih-pao*, literary page, June 21, 1983.

———. "Sung-tai li-hsüeh yü Ch'an-tsung chih kuan-hsi" 宋代理學與禪宗之關係 [Relations between the Sung school of principle and Ch'an]. *K'ung Meng hsüeh-pao* 30 (1975): 111–136.

Tu Yu 杜佑 (735–812). *T'ung tien* 通典 [Complete institutions]. Completed 801. Rpt. Taipei: Hsin-hsing shu-chü, 1963.

Tuan Hsing-min 段醒民. *Liu Tzu-hou yü-yen wen-hsüeh t'an-wei* 柳子厚寓言文學探微 [Studies in Liu Tsung-yüan's allegorical writings]. Taipei: Wen-chin ch'u-pan-she, 1978.

———. "Yu Han Yü 'Kan ch'ün shih' p'ing-chih Han Yü jen-ke hsing-t'ai te fa-chan li-ch'eng" 由韓愈感春詩評隲韓愈人格型態的發展歷程 [An investigation of the development of Han Yü's personality based on his "Poems in Response to Spring"]. *T'ai-pei shang-chuan hsüeh-pao* 14 (June 1980): 97–141.

Tung Chin-yü 董金裕. "Li-hsüeh te hsien-tao: Han Yü yü Li Ao" 理學的先導—韓愈與李翱 [The forerunners of the school of principle: Han Yü and Li Ao]. *Shu-mu chi-k'an* 16, no. 2 (September 1982): 33–40.

Tung Fan 董璠. "Han Yü yü Ta-tien" 韓愈與大顛 [Han Yü and Ta-tien]. *Wen-hsüeh nien-pao* 3 (1937): 79–87. Rpt. Chou K'ang-hsieh, *Han Yü yen-chiu lun-ts'ung*, pp. 248–256.

T'ung Ti-te 童第德. *Han Yü wen hsüan* 韓愈文選 [A selection of Han Yü's prose]. Peking: Jen-min, 1980.

Wan Man 萬曼. *T'ang chi hsü-lu* 唐集叙錄 [Notes on collected works of the T'ang dynasty]. Peking: Chung-hua, 1980. See pp. 167–183 for a discussion of Han Yü's *Collected Works*.

Wang Ch'i-hsing 王啓興. "Han Yü shih-ko i-shu ch'u-t'an" 韓愈詩歌藝術初探 [An initial inquiry into Han Yü's poetic art]. *Ku-tien wen-hsüeh lun-ts'ung*, vol. 1, pp. 164–176. Chi-nan: Chi-Lu shu-she, 1980.

———. "Ju-ho p'ing-chia Han Yü shih-ko te ssu-hsiang i-i" 如何評價韓愈詩歌的思想意義 [How to assess Han Yü's poetic thought]. *T'ang-tai wen-hsüeh* 1 (1981): 207–220.

Wang Meng-ou 王夢鷗. *T'ang shih-jen Li I sheng-p'ing chi ch'i tso-p'in* 唐詩人李益生平及其作品 [The life and works of the T'ang poet Li I]. Taipei: I-wen, 1973.

Wang Shou-nan 王壽南. *T'ang-tai fan-chen yü chung-yang kuan-hsi chih yen-chiu* 唐代藩鎮與中央關係之研究 [A study of the relations between the regional commanders and the central government during the T'ang]. Taipei: Chia-hsin shui-ni kung-szu, 1969.

Wang Tang 王讜 (early twelfth century). *T'ang yü lin* 唐語林 [Forest of anecdotes from the T'ang]. Rpt. Shanghai: Ku-tien wen-hsüeh ch'u-pan-she, 1957.

Wang Ting-pao 王定保 (870–?). *T'ang chih-yen* 唐摭言 [Collected anecdotes from the T'ang]. Rpt. Shanghai: Ku-tien wen-hsüeh ch'u-pan-she, 1954.

Wang Yün-hsi 王運熙. "Han Yü san-wen te feng-ke t'e-cheng ho t'a te wen-hsüeh hao-hsiang" 韓愈散文的風格特徵和他的文學好尚

[The stylistic distinctiveness of Han Yü's prose and his literary preferences]. In *Ku-tien wen-hsüeh lun-ts'ung. Fu-tan hsüeh-pao (she-hui k'o-hsüeh pan) tseng-k'an*, pp. 93–104. Shanghai: Jen-min ch'u-pan-she, 1980.

———. "Shih-lun T'ang ch'uan-ch'i yü ku-wen yün-tung te kuan-hsi" 試論唐傳奇與古文運動的關係 [On the T'ang *ch'uan-ch'i* and their relation to the *ku-wen* movement]. Rpt. *Wen-hsüeh i-ch'an hsüan-chi*, vol. 3, pp. 321–332. Peking: Chung-hua, 1960.

Wei Ch'ing-chih 魏慶之, comp. *Shih-jen yü-hsieh* 詩人玉屑 [Jade chips of the poet]. Preface dated 1244. 2 vols. Shanghai: Ku-tien wen-hsüeh ch'u-pan-she, 1958.

Wen hsüan 文選 [Anthology of literature]. Compiled by Hsiao Tung (501–531); commentary by Li Shan (?–689): edited by Yu Mao (1127–1194) and Hu K'e-chia (1757–1816). 1869 edition. Rpt. Taipei: Cheng-chung shu-chü, 1971.

Wen-yüan ying-hua 文苑英華. Completed 987. Ming 1567 ed. Rpt. Taipei: Hua-wen shu-chü, 1965.

Wu Che-fu 吳哲夫. "Ku-kung shan-pen-shu chih: *Lun yü pi-chieh*" 故宮善本書志：論語筆解 [Notes on rare books in the Palace Museum: The *Lun Yü pi-chieh*]. *Ku-kung t'u-shu chi-k'an* 1, no. 1 (July 1970): 49–50.

Wu Hsiao-ju 吳小如. "Han-wen so-cha" 韓文瑣札 [Notes on Han Yü's prose]. *Wen-hsien* 11 (March 1982): 38–42.

Wu Hsiao-lin 吳小林. "Shih-lun Han Yü san-wen te ch'uang-hsin t'e-se" 試論韓愈散文的創新特色 [On the innovative features of Han Yü's prose]. *T'ang-tai wen-hsüeh* 3 (1983): 153–169.

Wu Ta-yün 吳達芸. "Han Yü sheng-p'ing chi ch'i shih chih yen-chiu" 韓愈生平及其詩之研究 [A study of Han Yü's life and his poetry]. Master's thesis, National Taiwan University, 1972.

Wu Wen-chih 吳文治. "Han chi ch'u-i erh t'i" 韓集芻議二題 [My opinion on two questions concerning *Han Yü's Collected Works*]. *Chiang Han lun-t'an*, no. 1 (1983): 48–49.

———. *Han Yü tzu-liao hui-pien* 韓愈資料彙編 [A compendium of materials on Han Yü]. 4 vols. Peking: Chung-hua, 1984.

———. "Han Yü yen-chiu shu-p'ing" 韓愈研究述評 [An account of studies on Han Yü]. *Su-chou ta-hsüeh hsüeh-pao (che-hsüeh she-hui k'o-hsüeh pan)*, no. 2 (1982): 23–29.

———. "Lüeh-lun Han Yü te ku-wen li-lun" 略論韓愈的古文理論 [A brief discussion of Han Yü's *ku-wen* theory]. *T'ang-tai wen-hsüeh* 1 (1981): 10–23.

———. "Lüeh-lun T'ang-tai ch'ien-ch'i te ku-wen li-lun" 略論唐代

前期的古文理論 [Brief remarks on *ku-wen* theory in the early T'ang]. *Wen-i lun-kao*, vol. 2, pp. 134–153. Chi-lin: Chi-lin sheng wen-lien wen-i li-lun yen-chiu-shih, 1980.

Yamasaki Jun'ichi 山崎純一. "Kan Yu no kofu ni tsuite" 韓愈の古賦について [On Han yü's old-style *fu*]. *Tōyō bungaku kenkyū* 19 (1971): 22–34; 20 (1972): 1–13.

———. "Kan Yu no setsuron nihen. Toku-ni sono kokkeikan ni tsuite" 韓愈の設論二篇. とくにその滑稽感について [Two essays of Han Yü; his sense of humor]. *Chūgokukoten kenkyū* 18 (1971): 20–42.

———. " 'Mei-ei den' shoko" 毛穎傳小考 [A study of the "Biography of Fur Point"]. *Chūgokukoten kenkyū* 20 (1975): 33–49.

Yanagida Seizan 柳田聖山. "Bukkotsu no hyō (Kan Yu to Daiten). *Sodō shū* monogatari" 仏骨の表 (韓愈と大顛)―祖堂集ものがたり [The memorial on the Buddha relic (Han Yü and Ta-tien). A story from the *Tsu-t'ang chi*]. *Zen bunka* 51 (January 1969): 24–32.

———. *Rinzai roku* 臨濟錄 [Dialogues of Lin-chi]. Tokyo: Daizō shuppan, 1972.

———. *Shoki zenshū shisho no kenkyū* 初期禅宗史書の研究 [Studies in early Ch'an historical texts]. Kyoto: Hōzōkan, 1967.

Yang Jung-kuo 楊榮國. "Han Yü ssu-hsiang p'i-p'an" 韓愈思想批判 [An appraisal of Han Yü's thought]. *Li-lun yü shih-chien*, nos. 11, 12 (1958). Rpt. Chou K'ang-hsieh, *Han Yü yen-chiu lun-ts'ung*, pp. 4–36.

Yeh Ch'ing-ping 葉慶炳. "Ts'ung 'P'ing Huai-hsi pei' k'an Han Yü ku-wen" 從平淮西碑看韓愈古文 [On Han Yü's *ku-wen* as seen in the "Inscription on the Pacification of Huai-hsi"]. *Hsien-tai wen-hsüeh* 35 (November 1968): 168–172.

Yeh Hsieh 葉燮 (1627–1703). *Yüan shih* 原詩 [The essentials of poetry]. Edited by Huo Sung-lin. Peking: Jen-min, 1979.

Yen Ch'i 閻琦. "P'ing-chia Han Yü han Yung-cheng ke-hsin kuan-hsi te chi-tien ch'ien-chien" 評價韓愈和永貞革新關係的幾點淺見 [Several opinions assessing Han Yü's relationship to the 805 reforms]. *T'ang-tai wen-hsüeh* 1 (1981): 254–267.

Yen Keng-wang 嚴耕望. *T'ang p'u-shang-ch'eng-lang piao* 唐僕尙丞郞表 [Tables of high officials in the Department of Affairs of State during the T'ang]. Academia Sinica, Institute of History and Philology, Monograph 36. 4 vols. Taipei: Academia Sinica, 1956.

Yen K'un-yang 顔崑陽. "Ts'ung 'Nan-shan shih' t'an Han Yü shan-shui shih te feng-ke" 從南山詩談韓愈山水詩的風格 [A discussion of style in Han Yü's landscape poetry based on the "Poem on the Southern Mountains"]. *Hsüeh ts'ui* (Taiwan) 17, no. 1 (April 1975): 18–22.

Young Yung 楊勇 [Yang Yung]. "Lun Han Yü chih yung tzu yung yün yü yung su-yü" 論韓愈之用字用韻與用俗語 [Diction, rhyme, and colloquialisms in Han Yü's writings]. In *Ch'ien Mu hsien-sheng pa-shih sui chi-nien lun-wen chi*, pp. 275–286. Kowloon: Hsin-ya yen-chiu-so, 1974.

Yoshikawa Kōjirō 吉川幸次郎. "Kan Yu" [section on Han Yü]. In his *Shin Tō-shi sen* 新唐詩選 [New anthology of T'ang verse]. Rpt. *Yoshikawa Kōjirō zenshū* 11: 328–369. Tokyo: Chikuma, 1974.

Yü Mei-yün 餘美雲. "Lun T'ang T'ai-tsung shih" 論唐太宗詩 [On the poetry of T'ang T'ai-tsung]. *T'ang-tai wen-hsüeh* 3 (1983): 56–67.

Yüan Fei-han 袁飛翰. "Han Yü san chih Kuang-tung chi ch'i ying-hsiang" 韓愈三至廣東及其影響 [Han Yü: Three times to Kuang-tung and his influence there]. *Chu-hai hsüeh-pao* 8 (1975): 125–137.

Western-language Works

Allen, Joseph Roe. "Chih Yü's *Discussions of Different Types of Literature:* A Translation and Brief Comment." In *Two Studies in Chinese Literary Criticism*, Parerga no. 3, pp. 3–36. Seattle: Institute for Foreign Area Studies, 1976.

Barrett, Timothy Hugh. "Buddhism, Taoism and Confucianism in the Thought of Li Ao." Ph.D. dissertation, Yale University, 1978.

Birch, Cyril, ed. *Anthology of Chinese Literature from Early Times to the Fourteenth Century*. New York: Grove Press, 1965.

Bischoff, F. A. *Interpreting the Fu: A Study in Chinese Literary Rhetoric*. Münchener ostasiatische Studien vol. 13. Wiesbaden: Franz Steiner, 1976.

―――. *La Forêt des pinceaux: Étude sur l'Académie du Han-lin sous la Dynastie des T'ang et traduction du Han lin tche*. Paris: Presses Universitaires des France, 1963.

Bodman, Richard. "Poetics and Prosody in Early Medieval China: A Study and Translation of Kūkai's *Bunkyō hifuron*. Ph.D. dissertation, Cornell University, 1978.

Bynner, Witter, trans. *Jade Mountain*. Rpt. New York: Doubleday, 1964.

Chalmers, John. "Han Wan-kung: A Study in Chinese Biography." *The China Review* 1 (1872–1873): 275–283, 339–347.

Chan, Marie. *Kao Shih*. Boston: Twayne, 1978.

Chan, Wing-tsit. "The Evolution of the Confucian Concept *Jen*." *PEW* 4 (1954): 295–319.

―――, trans. *Reflections on Things at Hand: The Neo-Confucian Anthology*

Compiled by Chu Hsi and Lü Tsu-ch'ien. New York: Columbia University Press, 1967.

———, ed. *Source Book in Chinese Philosophy.* Princeton: Princeton University Press, 1963.

Chang, Carsun. "Buddhism as Stimulus to Neo-Confucianism." *Oriens Extremus* 2 (1955): 157–166.

———. *The Development of Neo-Confucian Thought.* New York: Bookman Associates, 1957.

Chang Chung-yuan, trans. *Original Teachings of Ch'an Buddhism.* New York: Random House, Vintage Books, 1971.

Chavannes, Édouard, trans. *Les mémoires historiques de Se-ma Ts'ien.* 5 vols. 1895–1905. Rpt. Paris: Maisonneuve, 1967.

Chaves, Jonathan. *Mei Yao-ch'en and the Development of Early Sung Poetry.* New York: Columbia University Press, 1976.

Ch'en, Kenneth. *The Chinese Transformation of Buddhism.* Princeton: Princeton University Press, 1973.

———. "The Economic Background of the Hui-ch'ang Suppression of Buddhism." *HJAS* 19 (1956): 67–105.

Ch'en Yin-k'o. "Han Yü and the T'ang Novel." *HJAS* 1 (1936): 39–43.

Chi Chen-huai. "Han Yü's Life and His Prose." *Chinese Literature*, no. 2 (1959): 55–87.

Chow, Chuen-tang. "Chang Chi the Poet." Ph.D. dissertation, University of Washington, 1968.

Convreur, S. *Les Annales de la Chine.* Rpt. Paris: Cathasia, 1950. Originally published 1897.

Creel, H. G. *Shen Pu-hai: A Chinese Political Philosopher of the Fourth Century B.C.* Chicago: University of Chicago Press, 1974.

Crump, J. I., Jr., trans. *Chan-Kuo Ts'e.* Oxford: Clarendon Press, 1970.

Demiéville, Paul. "Études sur la formation du vocabulaire philosophique chinois" [Course resumé]. *Annuaire du Collége de France* 47 (1947): 151–157.

———. "La pénétration du bouddhisme dans la tradition philosophique chinoise." *Cahiers d'Histoire mondiale* 3.1 (1956): 19–38.

———. "Le chapitre de la *Bodhisattvabhūmi* sur la perfection du Dhyāna." *Rocznik Orientalistyczny* 21 (1957): 109–128.

———. *Le concile de Lhasa.* Paris: Presses Universitaires de France, 1952.

———. "Le recueil de la salle des patriarches." *TP* 56 (1970): 262–286.

———. "Le Tch'an et la poésie chinoise." *Hermès* 7 (1970): 123–136.

———. "Les entretiens de Lin-tsi." *Hermès* 7 (1970): 1–20.

———, trans. *Entretiens de Lin-tsi.* Paris: Fayard, 1972.

———. "Nécrologie: Tch'en Yin-k'o." *TP* 57 (1971): 136–143.

des Rotours, Robert, trans. *Histoire de Ngan Lou-chan*. Paris: Presses Universitaires de France, 1962.

————, trans. *Le Traité des examens*. Paris: Ernest Leroux, 1932.

————, trans. *Traité des fonctionnaires et traité de l'arméé*. 2 vols. Leiden: Brill, 1948.

DeWoskin, Kenneth J. *A Song for One or Two: Music and the Concept of Art in Early China*. Ann Arbor: Center for Chinese Studies, 1982.

Doeringer, Franklin Melvin. "Yang Hsiung and His Formulation of a Classicism." Ph.D. dissertation, Columbia University, 1971.

Dubs, Homer H. "The Development of Altruism in Confucianism." *PEW* 1, no. 1 (1951): 48–55.

————. "Han Yü and the Buddha's Relic: An Episode in Medieval Chinese Religion." *The Review of Religion* 11 (November 1946): 5–17.

Dull, Jack L. "Han Yü: A Problem in T'ang Dynasty Historiography." In International Association of Historians of Asia, *Second Biennial Conference. Proceedings*, pp. 71–99. Taipei: Taiwan Provincial Museum, 1962.

Eberhard, Wolfram. *Das Toba-Reich Nordchinas*. Leiden: Brill, 1949.

————. *The Local Cultures of South and East China*. Leiden: Brill, 1968.

Erkes, Eduard. "Das Mädchen vom Hua-shan." *AM* 9 (1933): 591–596.

Farquhar, David M. "Emperor as Bodhisattva in the Governance of the Ch'ing Empire." *HJAS* 38, no. 1 (June 1978): 5–34.

Feifel, Eugene. *Po Chü-i as a Censor*. 's-Gravenhage: Mouton, 1961.

Franke, Herbert. *From Tribal Chieftain to Universal Emperor and God: The Legitimation of the Yüan Dynasty*. Munich: Bayerische Akademie der Wissenschaften, 1978.

Frankel, Hans H. "The Date and Authorship of the *Lung-ch'eng lu*." In *Silver Jubilee Volume of the Zinbun-kagaku-kenkyūsho*, pp. 129–149. Kyoto: Zinbun-kagaku kenkyūsho, 1954.

Fung Yu-lan. *A History of Chinese Philosophy*. Translated by Derk Bodde. 2 vols. Princeton: Princeton University Press, 1952–1953.

————. "The Rise of Neo-Confucianism and Its Borrowings from Buddhism and Taoism." *HJAS* 7 (1942): 89–125.

Gernet, Jacques, trans. *Entretiens du Maître de Dhyāna Chen-houei de Ho-tsö*. Hanoi: École française d'Extrême-Orient, 1949.

————. *Les aspects économiques du bouddhisme dans la société chinoise de V^e au Xe siècle*. Saigon: École française d'Extrême-Orient, 1956.

Graf, Olaf. *Tao und Jen: Sein und Sollen im sungchinesischen Monismus*. Wiesbaden: Harrassowitz, 1970.

Graham, A. C. *Poems of the Late T'ang*. Harmondsworth: Penguin, 1965.

————. *Two Chinese Philosophers: Ch'eng Ming-tao and Ch'eng Yi-ch'uan*. London: Lund Humphries, 1958.

Gregory, Peter Nielsen. "Tsung-mi's *Inquiry into the Origins of Man:* A Study of Chinese Buddhist Hermeneutics." Ph.D. dissertation, Harvard University, 1981.

Gundert, Wilhelm, trans. *Bi-yän-lu: Meister Yüan-wu's Niederschrift von der Smaragdenen Felswand*. Rpt. 3 vols. Munich: Hanser, 1977.

Haenisch, Erich. "Das Ethos der chinesischen Geschichtschreibung." *Saeculum* 1 (1950): 111–123.

————. "Der Zensor: Tao und Amtsauftrag." *ZDMG* 104 (1954): 412–431.

————. "Han Yü's Einspruch gegen die Prüfungssperre im Jahre 803, ein Kapital aus der Tang-Zeit." *ZDMG* 102 (1952): 280–303.

Hanson, Kenneth O., trans. *Growing Old Alive: Poems by Han Yü*. Port Townsend: Copper Canyon Press, 1978.

Hartman, Charles. "*Alieniloquium*: Liu Tsung-yüan's Other Voice." *CLEAR* 4 (January 1982): 23–73.

————. "Han Yü and T. S. Eliot—a Sinological Essay in Comparative Literature." *Renditions* 8 (1977): 59–76.

————. "Language and Allusion in the Poetry of Han Yü: The 'Autumn Sentiments.'" Ph.D. dissertation, Indiana University, 1975.

————. "Preliminary Bibliographical Notes on the Sung Editions of Han Yü's *Collected Works*." In William H. Nienhauser, Jr., ed., *Critical Essays on Chinese Literature*, pp. 86–100. Hong Kong: The Chinese University of Hong Kong, 1976.

Hawkes, David, trans. *Ch'u Tz'u: Songs of the South*. London: Oxford University Press, 1959.

Hightower, James R., trans. *Han shih wai chuan: Han Ying's Illustrations of the Didactic Application of the Classic of Songs*. Cambridge, MA: Harvard University Press, 1952.

————. "Han Yü as Humorist." *HJAS* 44, no. 1 (June 1984): 5–27.

————. "Some Characteristics of Parallel Prose." Rpt. in John L. Bishop, ed. *Studies in Chinese Literature*, pp. 108–139. Cambridge, MA: Harvard University Press, 1965.

————. *Topics in Chinese Literature*. Rev. ed. Cambridge, MA: Harvard Unversity Press, 1953.

————. "The *Wen hsüan* and Genre Theory." *HJAS* 20 (1957): 512–533.

————. "Yüan Chen and 'The Story of Ying-ying.'" *HJAS* 33 (1973): 90–123.

Holzman, Donald. "Les débuts du système médiéval de choix et de classement des fonctionnaires: Les Neuf Catégories et l'Impartial et

Juste." In *Mélanges publiés par l'Institut des Hautes Études Chinoises*, pp. 387–414. Paris: Institut des Hautes Étudies Chinoises, 1957.

————. *Poetry and Politics: The Life and Works of Juan Chi*. Cambridge: Cambridge University Press, 1976.

Hung, William. "A Bibliographical Controversy at the T'ang Court A.D. 719." *HJAS* 20 (1957): 74–134.

————. *A Supplementary Volume of Notes for Tu Fu: China's Greatest Poet*. Cambridge, MA: Harvard University Press, 1952.

————. "A T'ang Historiographer's Letter of Resignation." *HJAS* 29 (1969): 5–52.

————. *Tu Fu: China's Greatest Poet*. Cambridge, MA: Harvard University Press, 1952.

Hurvitz, Leon, trans. *Scripture of the Lotus Blossom of the Fine Dharma. Translated from the Chinese of Kumārajīva*. New York: Columbia University Press, 1976.

Huters, Theodore. *Qian Zhongshu*. Boston: Twayne, 1982.

Iriya Yoshitaka. "Chinese Poetry and Zen." *Eastern Buddhist* 6, no. 1 (May 1973): 54–67.

Karlgren, Bernhard. "The *Book of Documents*." *BMFEA* 22 (1950): 1–81.

————. *The Book of Odes*. Stockholm: Museum of Far Eastern Antiquities, 1950.

————. *The Poetical Parts in Lao-tsï*. Göteborgs högskolas årsskrift, vol. 38. Göteborg: Elanders boktryckeri aktiebolag, 1932.

Klöpsch, Volker. *Die Jadesplitter der Dichter: Die Welt der Dichtung in der Sicht eines Klassikers der chinesischen Literaturkritik*. Bochum: Brockmeyer, 1983.

Knechtges, David R. *The Han Rhapsody*. Cambridge: Cambridge University Press, 1976.

————, trans. *Wen Xuan, or Selections of Refined Literature*. Vol. One: *Rhapsodies on Metropolises and Capitals*. Princeton: Princeton University Press, 1982.

Lai, Whalen, and Lewis Lancaster, eds. *Early Ch'an in China and Tibet*. Berkeley: Asian Humanities Press, 1983.

Lamont, H. G. "An Early Ninth-Century Debate on Heaven: Liu Tsung-yüan's *T'ien Shuo* and Liu Yü-hsi's *T'ien lun*." *AM* 18 (1973): 181–208; 19 (1974): 37–85.

Lamotte, Étienne, trans. *L'Enseignement de Vimalakīrti*. Bibliothèque du Muséon. Vol. 51. Louvain: Publications Universitaires, 1962.

Lancaster, Lewis, ed. *Prajñāpāramitā and Related Systems: Studies in Honor of Edward Conze*. Berkeley: Berkeley Buddhist Studies Series, 1977.

Lau, D. C., trans. *The Analects*. Harmondsworth: Penguin, 1979.

————, trans. *Mencius*. Harmondsworth: Penguin, 1970.

Lee, Joseph J. *Wang Ch'ang-ling*. Boston: Twayne, 1982.

Legge, James, trans. *The Chinese Classics*. Vol. 1: *Confucian Analects, The Great Learning, and the Doctrine of the Mean*. Rpt. Hong Kong: Hong Kong University Press, 1960. Originally published 1861.

————. *The Chinese Classics*. Vol. 2: *The Works of Mencius*. Rpt. Hong Kong: Hong Kong University Press, 1960. Originally published 1861.

————. *The Chinese Classics*. Vol. 3: *The Shoo King*. Rpt. Hong Kong: Hong Kong University Press, 1960. Originally published 1865.

————. *The Chinese Classics*. Vol. 4: *The She King*. Rpt. Hong Kong: Hong Kong University Press, 1960. Originally published 1871.

————. *The Chinese Classics*. Vol. 5: *The Ch'un Ts'ew with the Tso Chuen*. Rpt. Hong Kong: Hong Kong University Press, 1960. Originally published 1872.

————. *Li Chi: Book of Rites*. Rpt. 2 vols. New Hyde Park, NY: University Books, 1967. Originally published 1885.

Levenson, Joseph R., and Franz Schurmann. *China: An Interpretive History. From the Beginnings to the Fall of Han*. Berkeley: University of California Press, 1969.

Liu, James J. Y. *Chinese Theories of Literature*. Chicago: University of Chicago Press, 1975.

————. *The Poetry of Li Shang-yin*. Chicago: University of Chicago Press, 1969.

Liu Mau-ts'ai. *Die chinesischen Nachrichten zur Geschichte der Ost-Türken (T'u-küe)*. 2 vols. Wiesbaden: Harrassowitz, 1958.

Liu Shih Shun [劉師舜 Liu Shih-shun]. *Chinese Classical Prose: The Eight Masters of the T'ang-Sung Period*. Hong Kong: The Chinese University Press, 1979.

Lu Gwei-djen, and Joseph Needham. "A Contribution to the History of Chinese Dietetics." *Isis* 42 (April 1951): 13–20.

Luebeck, Bruno Hermann. "Han Yü, the Champion of Confucianism." Ph.D. dissertation, Hartford Seminary Foundation, 1938.

Ma, Y. W. "Prose Writings of Han Yü and *Ch'uan-ch'i* Literature." *Journal of Oriental Studies* 7, no. 2 (1969): 195–223.

McLeod, Russell. "The Baroque as a Period Concept in Chinese Literature." *Tamkang Review* 7, no. 2 (October 1976): 185–211.

McMullen, David. "Historical and Literary Theory in the Mid-Eighth Century." In Arthur F. Wright and Denis Twitchett, eds., *Perspectives on the T'ang*, pp. 307–342. New Haven: Yale University Press, 1973.

Mair, Victor H. "Scroll Presentation in the T'ang Dynasty." *HJAS* 38, no. 1 (June 1978): 35–60.

———. *Tun-huang Popular Narratives*. Cambridge: Cambridge University Press, 1983.

Margouliès, Georges. *Anthologie raisonnée de la littérature chinoise*. Paris: Payot, 1948.

———. *Histoire de la littérature chinoise. Prose*. Paris: Payot, 1949.

———. *Le kou-wen chinois*. Paris: Geuthner, 1926.

Martin, Helmut, comp. *Index to the Ho Collection of Twenty-Eight Shih-hua*. 2 vols. Taipei: Chinese Materials and Research Aids Service Center, 1973.

Maspero, Henri. *La Chine antique*. Paris: Boccard, 1927; rev. ed. 1965. English trans. by Frank A. Kierman, *China in Antiquity*. Boston: University of Massachusetts Press, 1978.

Masson-Oursel, Paul. "Le *Yuan Jen Louen*." *Journal asiatique* Ser. 11, vol. 5 (March–April 1915): 299–354.

Mather, Richard B., trans. *Shih-shuo hsin-yü: A New Account of Tales of the World*. Minneapolis: University of Minnesota Press, 1976.

———. "Wang Chin's 'Dhūta Temple Stele Inscription' as an Example of Buddhist Parallel Prose." *JAOS* 83 (1963): 338–359.

Mei, Diana Yu-shih. "Han Yü as a *Ku-Wen* Stylist." *Tsing Hua Journal of Chinese Studies* NS 7, no. 1 (August 1968): 143–207.

Mirsky, Jonathan. "Structure of Rebellion: A Successful Insurrection during the T'ang." *JAOS* 89 (1969): 67–87.

Moses, Larry W. "T'ang Tribute Relations with the Inner Asian Barbarians." In John Curtis Perry and Bardwell L. Smith, eds., *Essays on T'ang Society: The Interplay of Social, Political, and Economic Forces*, pp. 61–89. Leiden: Brill, 1976.

Needham, Joseph. *Science and Civilization in China*. Vol. 2: *History of Scientific Thought*. London: Cambridge University Press, 1956.

Nielson, Thomas P. *The T'ang Poet-Monk Chiao-jan*. Occasional Paper No. 3. Center for Asian Studies. Tempe, Arizona: Arizona State University, 1972.

Nienhauser, William H., Jr. "An Allegorical Reading of Han Yü's 'Mao-Ying Chuan' (Biography of Fur Point)." *Oriens Extremus* 23, no. 2 (December 1976): 153–174.

———. "Diction, Dictionaries, and the Translation of Classical Chinese Poetry." *TP* 64 (1978): 47–109.

——— et al. *Liu Tsung-yüan*. New York: Twayne, 1973.

———. *P'i Jih-hsiu*. Boston: Twayne: 1979.

————. "A Structural Reading of the *Chuan* in the *Wen-yüan ying-hua*," *JAS* 36, no. 3 (May 1977): 443–456.

Owen, Stephen. *The Great Age of Chinese Poetry: The High T'ang*. New Haven: Yale University Press, 1981.

————. "The Poetry of Meng Chiao (751–814) and Han Yü (768–824): A Study of a Chinese Poetic Reform." Ph.D. dissertation, Yale University, 1972.

————. *The Poetry of Meng Chiao and Han Yü*. New Haven: Yale University Press, 1975.

Palandri, Angela C. Y. Jung. *Yüan Chen*. Boston: Twayne, 1977.

Pelliot, Paul. *Histoire ancienne du Tibet*. Paris: Maisonneuve, 1961.

Peterson, Charles A. "Regional Defense Against the Central Power: The Huai-hsi Campaign, 815–817." In Frank A. Kierman, Jr., ed. *Chinese Ways in Warfare*, pp. 123–150. Cambridge, MA: Harvard University Press, 1974.

————. "The Restoration Completed: Emperor Hsien-tsung and the Provinces." In Arthur F. Wright and Denis Twitchett, eds. *Perspectives on the T'ang*, pp. 151–191. New Haven: Yale University Press, 1973.

Pulleyblank, Edwin G. "The An Lu-shan Rebellion and the Origins of Chronic Militarism in Late T'ang China." In John Curtis Perry and Bardwell L. Smith, eds., *Essays on T'ang Society: The Interplay of Social, Political, and Economic Forces*, pp. 33–60. Leiden: Brill, 1976.

————. *The Background of the Rebellion of An Lu-shan*. London: Oxford University Press, 1955.

————. "Liu K'o, a Forgotten Rival of Han Yü." *AM* NS 7 (1959): 145–160.

————. "Neo-Confucianism and Neo-Legalism in T'ang Intellectual Life, 755–805." In Arthur F. Wright, ed., *The Confucian Persuasion*, pp. 77–144. Stanford: Stanford University Press, 1960.

Rickett, Adele Austin, ed. *Chinese Approaches to Literature*. Princeton: Princeton University Press, 1978.

Rickett, W. Allyn, trans. *Kuan-tzu. A Repository of Early Chinese Thought*. Hong Kong: Hong Kong University Press, 1965.

Rideout, J. K. "The Context of the Yüan Tao and the Yüan Hsing." *BSOAS* 12, no. 2 (1947): 403–408.

Schafer, Edward H. *The Divine Woman: Dragon Ladies and Rain Maidens in T'ang Literature*. Berkeley: University of California Press, 1973.

————. "Notes on T'ang Culture." *Monumenta Serica* 21 (1962): 194–221; 24 (1965): 130–154.

Schafer, Edward H. *Pacing the Void: T'ang Approaches to the Stars.* Berkeley: University of California Press, 1977.

———. *The Vermilion Bird: T'ang Images of the South.* Berkeley: University of California Press, 1967.

Schloegl, Irmgard, trans. *The Record of Rinzai.* London: The Buddhist Society, 1975.

Schmidt, Jerry D. "Han Yü and His *Ku-shih* Poetry." Master's thesis, University of British Columbia, 1969.

Solomon, Bernhard S. *The Veritable Record of the T'ang Emperor Shun-tsung.* Cambridge, MA: Harvard University Press, 1955.

Soothill, William Edward, and Lewis Hodous. *A Dictionary of Chinese Buddhist Terms.* London: Kegan Paul, 1934. Rpt. Taipei: Ch'eng-wen, 1976.

South, Margaret T. "Han Yü—'Guide, Philosopher and Friend.'" *Journal of the Oriental Society of Australia* 5, nos. 1 and 2 (December 1967): 158–175.

Stein, Rolf. "Illumination subite ou saisie simultanée: Note sur la terminologie chinoise et tibétaine." *Revue de l'histoire des religions* 179, no. 1 (1971): 3–30.

Tang Yung-tung. "On 'Ko-yi,' the Earliest Method by which Indian Buddhism and Chinese Thought Were Synthesized." In W. R. Inge et al., eds., *Radhakrishnan: Comparative Studies in Philosophy Presented in Honour of his Sixtieth Birthday,* pp. 276–286. London: Allen and Unwin, 1951.

Thern, K. L. *Postface of the* Shuo-wen chieh-tzu, *the First Comprehensive Chinese Dictionary.* Madison, WI: Dept. of East Asian Languages and Literatures, University of Wisconsin, 1966.

Twitchett, Denis, ed. *The Cambridge History of China.* Vol. 3: *Sui and T'ang China, 589–906, Part 1.* Cambridge: Cambridge University Press, 1979.

———. "Chinese Social History from the Seventh to the Tenth Centuries: The Tunhuang Documents and their Implications." *Past and Present* 35 (December 1966): 28–53.

———. "The Composition of the T'ang Ruling Class: New Evidence from Tunhuang." In Arthur F. Wright and Denis Twitchett, eds., *Perspectives on the T'ang,* pp. 47–85. New Haven: Yale University Press, 1973.

———. *Financial Administration under the T'ang Dynasty.* 2d ed. Cambridge: Cambridge University Press, 1970.

———. "The Government of T'ang in the Early Eighth Century." *BSOAS* 18, no. 2 (1956): 322–330.

———. "Lu Chih (754–805): Imperial Adviser and Court Official." In

Arthur F. Wright and Denis Twitchett, eds. *Confucian Personalities*, pp. 24–64. Stanford: Stanford University Press, 1962.

———. "Merchant, Trade, and Government in Late T'ang." *AM* 14 (1968): 63–95.

———. "The Monasteries and China's Economy in Medieval Times." *BSOAS* 19, no. 1 (1957): 526–549.

———. "Varied Patterns of Provincial Autonomy in the T'ang Dynasty." In John Curtis Perry and Bardwell L. Smith, eds., *Essays on T'ang Society: The Interplay of Social, Political, and Economic Forces*, pp. 90–109. Leiden: Brill, 1976.

Waley, Arthur, trans. *The Analects of Confucius*. London: Allen and Unwin, 1938.

———. *Ballads and Stories from Tun-huang*. London: Allen and Unwin, 1960.

———. "China's Greatest Writer." In Arthur Waley, *Secret History of the Mongols*, pp. 163–168. London: Allen and Unwin, 1963.

———. *The Life and Times of Po Chü-i*. London: Allen and Unwin, 1949.

———. "A Sung Colloquial Story from the *Tsu-t'ang chi*." *AM* 14 (1968): 242–246.

Watson, Burton, trans. *The Complete Works of Chuang-tzu*. New York: Columbia University Press, 1968.

———. *Records of the Grand Historian of China*. 2 vols. New York: Columbia University Press, 1961.

Watters, Thomas. "The Life and Works of Han Yü or Han Wen-kung." *Journal of the North China Branch of the Royal Asiatic Society* 7 (1871–72): 165–181.

Wilhelm, Richard, trans. *The I Ching, or Book of Changes*. 3d ed. Princeton: Princeton University Press, 1967.

Wong Tak-wai [黄德偉 Huang Te-wei]. "Toward Defining Chinese Baroque Poetry." *Tamkang Review* 8, no. 1 (April 1977): 25–72.

Wright, Arthur F. "Buddhism and Chinese Culture: Phases of Interaction." *JAS* 17 (November 1957): 17–42.

———. "Fu I and the Rejection of Buddhism." *Journal of the History of Ideas* 12 (1951): 33–47.

———. Review of Jacques Gernet, *Les aspects économique du Bouddhisme*. *JAS* 16 (1957): 408–414.

———. "T'ang T'ai-tsung and Buddhism." In Arthur F. Wright and Denis Twitchett, eds., *Perspectives on the T'ang*, pp. 239–263. New Haven: Yale University Press, 1973.

Yampolsky, Philip B., trans. *The Platform Sutra of the Sixth Patriarch*. New York: Columbia University Press, 1967.

Yanagida Seizan. "The 'Recorded Sayings' Texts of Chinese Ch'an

Buddhism." In Whalen Lai and Lewis R. Lancaster, eds., *Early Ch'an in China and Tibet*, pp. 185–205. Berkeley: Berkeley Buddhist Studies Series, 1983.

Yang Hsien-yi and Gladys Yang, trans. "Prose Writings of Han Yü." *Chinese Literature*, no. 2 (1959): 64–87.

Yoshikawa Kōjirō. *An Introduction to Sung Poetry*. Translated by Burton Watson. Cambridge, MA: Harvard University Press, 1967.

———. "Tu Fu's Poetics and Poetry." *Acta Asiatica* (Tokyo) 16 (1969): 1–26.

Zach, Erwin von. *Die chinesische Anthologie: Ubersetzungen aus dem Wen hsüan*. 2 vols. Cambridge, MA: Harvard University Press, 1958.

———, trans. *Han Yü's poetische Werke*. Harvard-Yenching Institute Studies 7. Cambridge, MA: Harvard University Press, 1952.

———. *Tu Fu's Gedichte*. 2 vols. Cambridge, MA: Harvard University Press, 1952.

Zhang Xihou, trans. (?). "Prose Writings of Han Yü." *Chinese Literature*, no. 9 (1979): 92–94.

Zürcher, E. *The Buddhist Conquest of China*. Leiden: Brill, 1959.

This list contains all works of Han Yü referred to in this book. The list follows the numerical order assigned to Han Yü's writings in Hanabusa Hideki, *Kan Yu kashi sakuin* (cf. above p. 375). This order in turn is based on the sequence in traditional editions of Han Yü's *Collected Works*: 001–004, *fu*; 005–216, old-style poetry; 217–227, linked verses; 228–391, regulated poetry; 392–455, miscellaneous prose tracts; 456–507, letters; 508–543, prefaces; 544–580, laments; 581–655, epitaphs; 656–707, memorials and official documents; 708–775, addenda.

Page numbers in bold type indicate works translated in full in this book. Roman type in parentheses indicates a translated excerpt. Plain roman type indicates a summary or paraphrase of the whole text. Italics indicate a simple mention or reference to the text in question. In some instances, it has been difficult to maintain these distinctions, but I hope readers will find useful this attempt to indicate how extensively a particular text of Han Yü is discussed at any one place in this book.

Finally, an asterisk indicates a work scheduled for inclusion in my *Major Works of Han Yü*, a forthcoming volume of annotated translations of Han Yü's more important longer works.

inl

GENERAL INDEX
AND GLOSSARY

General Index and Glossary

n.86, 348–349 n.88, 359 n.44; and
Confucian humanism, 6–8, 277 n.5,
278 n.14; and *"ku-wen* movement,"
5–8; and literary style, 366–367
n.106; and poetry, 373 n.162; Han
Yü's interest in, 93–100, 198; influence on Han Yü's concept of
mind, 204; literature of, 269, 274–
275, 343 n.51; *logia*, 178–179, 184,
193, 195; master-disciple relationship, 332–333 n.93; Northern and
Southern schools, 161, 198, 203; oral
transmission of a teaching method,
160–162, 251; use of paradox, 158;
vision of the Sage, 186

Chan, Marie, 315 n.4
Chan, Wing-tsit, 280 n.24, 326 n.61,
328 n.63, n.65, 332 n.93, 335 n.1,
345 n.66, n.67, n.68, 346 n.69, n.70,
n.71, n.72, 348 n.80, n.85, 349 n.91,
352 n.108
ch'an-jan 囅然 "heartily," 246
Chan-kuo ts'e 戰國策 *Intrigues of the
Warring States*, 334 n.108
Ch'ang-an 長安, 9, 17, 18, 22, 24, 26,
27, 28, 30, 41, 43–44, 47, 49, 53, 56–
57, 64–65, 68–70, 72, 74–79, 81,
83–84, 86–87, 91–92, 99–100,
105–106, 108, 110, 115–116, 120,
123–126, 142, 147, 166, 230, 234,
283 n.10, 286 n.33, 287 n.38, 294
n.96, 296 n.106, 298 n.127, 299
n.129, 300 n.139, 303 n.162, 304
n.167, 311 n.218, 319 n.18, 322 n.44,
339 n.33; real estate in, 314 n.229
Chang Ch'e 張徹 (d. 821), 127–128,
259, 319 n.20
Chang Cheng-ts'e 張正則, friend of
Han Hui, 21
Chang Chi 張籍 (766–829?), 37–40,
43, 69–70, 78, 111, 113–115, 161,
164, 174, 232, 290 n.57, 309 n.198,
320 n.26, 322 n.39, 330–331 n.81,
333 n.93, 336 n.8, 339–340 n.339;
anti-Buddhism and anti-Taoism of,

161–162; "Elegy for T'ui-chih,"
113–115, 174, 312 n.221, 339–340
n.33; "Poem on Lord Tung," 289
n.54; tutor to Han Ch'ang, 362 n.67
Chang Chien-feng 張建封 (735–800),
40–44, 273–274, 290 n.62, 291 n.66,
320 n.26, 323 n.49
Chang Chung-yuan, 278 n.10
Chang Heng 張衡 (78–139), "*Fu* on
the Western Capital," 249
Chang Hsiao-mei, 294 n.93
Chang Hsü 張旭 (eighth-century
calligrapher), 222–224, 358 n.35
Chang Hsün 張巡 (709–757),
141–142, 323 n.48, n.49
Chang Hung 張鴻 (nineteenth-
century critic), 39
Ch'ang Hung 萇弘 (d. 492 B.C.), 164,
331 n.84
Chang Hung-ching 張弘靖 (760–
824), 80, 126–127, 141, 319 n.20
Chang I 張儀 (d. 310 B.C.), 231
Chang Liang 張良 (d. 187 B.C.), 82
Chang Shu 張署 (758–817), 52,
56–58, 61–62, 64–65, 297 n.114,
n.121, 298 n.127
Chang Tsai 張載 (1020–1076),
196–197, 347–348 n.80
Chang Tsu 張鷟 (657?–730), 239
Chang Ts'ung-hou 張宗厚, 126
Chang Tu 張讀 (late ninth century),
335 n.4
Changes. See I-ching
Chao 趙, ancient state, 124–125, 144
Chao, Emperor of Han 漢昭帝 (95–74
B.C.), 330 n.76
Chao, King of Ch'u 楚昭王 (r. 515–
489 B.C.), 88–89, 305 n.172
Chao, King of Yen 燕昭王 (d. 279
B.C.), 324 n.55
Chao Ching 趙憬 (737–797), 288
n.45, 289 n.47
Ch'ao-chou 潮州, T'ang prefecture in
modern Kuangtung, 85–99, 104,
304 n.168, 305 n.178, n.180

424

Ch'in Shih Huang-ti 秦始皇帝 (259–210 B.C.), First Emperor of Ch'in, 11, 111, 324 n.54

"Chinese." See *Hua*

Chinese characters, 235; Han Yü's use of, 252. *See also* written word

ching 靜 "quiescence," 187

ching 景 "scene," 46–47

ch'ing 情 "emotions," 204–209, 350 n.95, 361 n.62; as source of literature, 323–335, 259

Ching-an 靖安, ward in Ch'ang-an, 113, 116

Ching-chou 涇州, T'ang prefecture in modern Kansu, 26

Ching K'o 荊軻 (d. 227 B.C.), 145, 324 n.54, 325 n.56

Ching-shan Fa-ch'in 徑山法欽 (714–792), 194, 344 n.59

Ching-tsung 敬宗 (r. 824–827), thirteenth T'ang emperor, 111

chiu-p'in chung-cheng 九品中正 "the nine categories and the impartial and just," 136

Chiu T'ang shu 舊唐書 *Old T'ang History*, 29, 77, 83, 116, 118, 126, 137

ch'iung chih wu li 窮格物理, 196

ch'iung-li 窮理, as public endeavor of the Sage, 192; equated with *ko-wu*, 196

ch'iung-li chin-hsing 窮理盡性 "to develop one's nature to perfection through the understanding of Principle," 187, 191–199, 207–208, 340 n.33, 344 n.55, 346 n.69, 348 n.80; and *Mencius*, 345 n.62; as description of *nirvāṇa*, 344 n.55; as function of literature, 344 n.55; as metaphysical Absolute, 193–199; equivalent to *prajñāpāramitā* and Buddhahood, 193–194; in *Random Notes on the Analects*, 194–199; Neo-Confucian interpretation of, 195–199; Wilhelm translation of, 343 n.53

ch'iung-li chin-hsing i chih yü ming 窮理盡性以至於命, 198, 209

Chou, Duke of, 周公, 125, 147, 149, 169, 176, 231, 336 n.10, 360 n.54

Chou dynasty, 130, 181, 186–187

Chou i 周易 *Changes of Chou.* See *I-ching*

Chou K'ang-hsieh, 277 n.2

Chou li 周禮 *Rituals of Chou*, 136

Chou Tun-i 周敦頤 (1017–1073), 15, 353 n.3

Chow, Chuen-tang, 331 n.81

chü 懼 "fear," 205

Ch'u 楚, Warring States kingdom, 88–89, 231, 293 n.87

Chu Hsi 朱熹 (1130–1200), 195–196, 205, 250, 281 n.24, 306 n.181, 338 n.29, 342 n.36, n.37, 345 n.66, n.67, 347 n.79; interpretation of *ch'eng*, 356 n.23; on Han Yü's style, 250–251; understanding of *li*, 352 n.107

Chu I-tsun 朱彝尊 (1629–1709), 62, 113, 273–274, 321 n.37

Chu-jung Peak 祝融峯, 67

Chü-lü Mountain 岣嶁山, 65–66. *See also* Heng-shan

chu-su 著述 "narrative mode," 225–226

Chu T'ao 朱滔 (d. 785), 107, 310 n.206

Chu Tz'u 朱泚 (742–784), 107, 334 n.108

Chü Wen-chen 俱文珍, eunuch acquaintance of Han Yü, 61, 286 n.33, 296 n.110, 322–323 n.47

Ch'ü Yüan 屈原 (332–295 B.C.), 34, 170, 228, 231

chuan 傳 "biography," 216, 266–267

ch'uan-ch'i 傳奇, genre of fiction, 265–267, 370 n.130, n.133, n.134, 371 n.136

Ch'üan-chou 泉州, T'ang prefecture in modern Fukien, 95, 335 n.4

ch'uan-fa 傳法 "transmission of the

fan-an 翻案 "reversing the case," 58
Fan Ch'un-jen 范純仁 (1027-1101), 340 n.33
Fan-shen lu 反身錄 *Record of Returning to the Self*, 331 n.83
Fan Tsung-shih 樊宗師 (d. 824), 72-73, 78, 247-248, 257, 259-260, 362 n.67; surviving works, 365 n.92
Fan-yang 范陽, T'ang city, modern Peking, 34
fan-yung 翻用 "reversed allusion," 309 n.195
Fang Shih-chü 方世舉 (1675-1759), 239
Fang Sung-ch'ing 方崧卿 (1135-1194), 285 n.25, 311 n.216, 312 n.218
Fang Tung-shu 方東樹 (1772-1851), 66
Farquhar, David M., 319 n.23
Faust, 33
Fei River 淝水, 264
Feifel, Eugene, 299 n.132, 321 n.30, 323 n.47, 359 n.41
feng 風 "indirect criticism, comment," 226-227
Feng-ch'eng gardens 奉誠園, 287 n.37
Feng-hsiang 鳳翔, T'ang military district, 25, 84, 288 n.46
feng-sacrifice 封, 91
Feng Su 馮宿 (767-836), 286 n.31, 288 n.43, 302 n.157, 304 n.167
Feng-t'ien 奉天, T'ang county in the metropolitan prefecture, 239
fiction, Han Yü and, 265-267
filial piety, 193
Fish, Stanley E., 373 n.160
fishing, as metaphor for enlightenment, 100
Four Books. See *Ssu shu*
"Four K'uei" 四夔, 21-23, 284 n.16, 333 n.93
Frankel, Hans, 282 n.6, 301 n.144
Frodsham, J. D., 300 n.142, 373 n.158
fu 復 "return," 143-144, 164-165,

187; definition of, 218; "The Return" (hexagram), 208, 218, 351 n.103
fu 賦 "rhyme-prose," 258, 260-261, 289 n.48, 350 n.97, 355 n.15; techniques in Han Yü's poetry, 271-274, 373 n.154. See also *lü-fu*
fu ch'i hsing 復其性 "to return to the true nature," 350 n.98
Fu Hsi 伏羲, legendary Sage-Ruler, 229
fu-hsing 復性 "to return to one's true nature," 218, 228-229
Fu-hsing shu 復性書 *Writings on Returning to One's True Nature*. See Li Ao
fu-ku 復古 "to renew Antiquity," 134, 168-169, 217-220, 334 n.102, 359 n.46; contrasted with *pien* "change," 220, 357 n.26; Han Yü's understanding of, 217-220; T'ang usages of, 220
Fu Lo-ch'eng, 314 n.2
Fu-li 符離, T'ang village in Hsü-chou, 40
"*Fu* on the Swallow and the Sparrow," 364 n.76
fu-ping 府兵 "militia troops," 120-122, 124, 316 n.6
Fukien, 124
"function." See *yung*
Fung Yu-lan, 179, 335 n.1, 337 n.17, 342 n.40, 345 n.67, n.68, 346 n.70, n.71, 360 n.57

Gaṇḍavyūha-sūtra, 346 n.73
genre. *See* literary genre
genre cross-fertilization, 215
Gernet, Jacques, 156, 328 n.67
Goethe, Johann Wolfgang von, 16, 33
Gomez, Luis O., 346 n.73
government, Buddhist and Taoist conception of, 136-137; Han Yü's conception of, 11, 131-145
Graf, Olaf, 210, 281 n.24, 332 n.93, 347 n.78, 352 n.109

Huang Tsung-hsi 黃宗羲
(1609–1695), 340 n.33

Huang Yün-mei, 277 n.5, 330 n.78,
355 n.12

hui 毀 "to break, destroy," 334 n.103

Hui, King of Yen 燕惠王, 324 n.55

Hui-chou 惠州, modern city in
Kuangtung, 90

Hui Hung 惠洪 (1071–?), 354 n.10

Hui-lin szu 惠林寺 Forest of Wisdom
Temple, 44

Hui-neng 惠能, sixth Ch'an patriarch,
23

human nature. See *hsing*

Hun Chen 渾瑊 (736–799), 25–26, 27,
286 n.33

Hunan, 87

Hung, William, 283 n.9, 287 n.38, 295
n.102, 344 n.60, 357 n.27, 358 n.35,
360–361 n.58, 363 n.69

Hung Canal 鴻溝, 82

Hung Hsing-tsu 洪興祖 (1090–1155),
273, 286–287 n.35

Hung Mai 洪邁 (1124–1203), 361
n.62, 367 n.109

Hurvitz, Leon, 349 n.94

i 義 "sense of justice," 134, 152, 154,
157, 205, 225, 350 n.96, 365 n.82

I 夷 "tribal name," 120

i-chao 遺照 "passing on the image,"
351 n.102

I-ch'eng 義成, T'ang military district,
28

I-ch'eng 宜城, T'ang post station in
Hsiang-chou, modern Hupei, 88

I-ching 易經 *Book of Changes*, 15,
94, 173, 180, 187, 189, 191–192,
194–196, 202, 204, 207–209, 225,
342 n.42, n.43, n.44, 343 n.52, n.53,
344 n.60, n.61, 348 n.82, 350 n.94,
n.98, n.99, n.100, 351 n.101, n.103,
n.104, 356 n.23, 365 n.85, 368 n.113

I-ch'iu 奕秋, ancient chess player, 222,
358 n.34

I Chou shu 遺周書 *Writings Remaining
from the Chou Dynasty*, 333 n.96

I-li 儀禮, 336 n.7

i shih wei wen 以詩爲文 "to make
prose from poetry," 217

i-ti 夷狄 "barbarians," 128, 148–149,
158, 314 n.2

i wen wei shih 以文爲詩 "to make
poetry from prose," 214–217,
268–271

Ichihara Kōkichi, 357 n.27, 359 n.144

iconoclasm, 7, 34

Iguchi Takashi, 365 n.90, 372 n.146

Imperial University 國子監, 43, 68,
100–102, 164, 309 n.197, 332 n.87

Inaba Ichirō, 341–342 n.35

Indo-Europeans, 317 n.11

Indra, 96

Inge, W. R., 328 n.66

"inner strength." See *te*

"integrity." See *ch'eng*

Iriya Yoshitaka, 357 n.25, 373 n.162

irony, 309 n.195, 349 n.89

Itō Jinsai (1627–1703), 332 n.90

Jan Po-niu 冉伯牛, disciple of
Confucius, 188, 347 n.76

Jan Yu 冉有, disciple of Confucius,
184, 188

Jao-chou 饒州, T'ang prefecture in
modern Kiangsi, 54

Jao Tsung-i, 324 n.54, 372 n.146

jen 仁 "sense of humanity," 152–157,
169–170, 183–184, 205, 326 n.61,
328 n.63, 333–334 n.101, 350 n.96

jen i 仁義 "humanity and justice," 59,
169–170, 186, 214, 242–244, 247;
and literature, 214, 242–244

jen li 人理 "Principle of men," 347
n.79

jen tao 人道 "Way of men," 347
n.79

Juan Chi 阮籍 (210–263), 50

Jun-chou 潤州, T'ang prefecture in
modern Kiangsu, 22

Jung 戎, tribal name, 119, 130, 159,
315 n.4, 320 n.26
Jung protectorate 容管經略軍, 103

K'ai-feng 開封, Sung dynasty capital
in modern Honan, 241; T'ang
county in Pien-chou, 71
Kai-hsia 垓下, Han place name, 82
Kao Chien-li 高漸離, 325 n.56
Kao-hsien 高閑, Buddhist monk,
acquaintance of Han Yü, 222–223
Kao Pu-ying, 282 n.61, 298 n.128, 302
n.156, n.157, 303 n.161, 304 n.165,
310 n.208, 311 n.214, n.217, n.218,
317 n.8, 323 n.48, n.50, 324 n.5.,
325 n.57, 329 n.71, 335 n.109, n.2,
336 n.10, 338 n.23, n.24, 346–347
n.75, 358 n.36, 364 n.79, 365 n.93,
n.94, 368 n.118, 369 n.119, n.120,
370 n.134
Kao Shih 高適 (706?–765), 315 n.4
Kao-tsu, Emperor of Han 漢高祖
(247–195 B.C.), 82, 314–315 n.2. See
also Liu Pang
Kao-tsung 高宗 (r. 649–683), third
T'ang emperor, 238
Kao Yao 皋陶, minister to Shun, 231,
360 n.52
Karlgren, Bernhard, 284 n.17, 329
n.72, 333 n.100, 343 n.45
karuṇā "compassion," 155
keng 庚, rhyme category, 329 n.71
Keng Yü 耿裕 (1430–1496), 282 n.8
Khitan, 124
Klöpsch, Volker, 354 n.10, 372 n.140,
n.141
Knechtges, David R., 249, 363 n.70,
n.72, 365 n.88, 367 n.112, n.113, 368
n.115, 369 n.124, n.126
ko 歌 "singing," 284 n.18
ko 格 "to arrive at," 196
ko-i 格意 "matching the idea,"
155–156, 328 n.66
Ko-shu Han 哥舒翰 (d. 756), 315
n.4

ko-wu 格物 "investigation of things,"
and ch'iung-li, 196
Konishi Jin'ichi, 360 n.49
ku 古 "Antiquity," 8, 10, 14, 32, 66,
91, 119, 125, 130, 132, 134, 144,
150–151, 163, 174–177, 181–182,
186, 216, 218, 229, 233, 242, 244–
245, 247–249, 254, 300 n.135, 331
n.82, 336 n.8, 343 n.46; as spiritual
state, 217–218; Han Yü's view of,
8, 151, 217–218
Ku I-sheng, 367 n.108, 373 n.154
Ku Li-san, 287 n.38
Ku-liang chuan 穀梁傳 Ku-liang
Commentary, 246, 365 n.86
ku-tao 古道 "Way of Antiquity,"
175–177, 183, 213–214, 219, 221,
245, 358 n.30
ku-wen 古文 "literature of Antiquity,"
3, 13–15, 38, 164, 213, 216–218,
220–225, 240–241, 251–252, 256,
266–267, 270, 274–275, 286 n.33,
353–354 n.4, 359 n.42; acceptance
of colloquial speech, 240; and
ch'uan-ch'i, 265–267; as unified
style, 14–15, 212–217, 279–280
n.23; contrasted to p'ien-wen, 364
n.77; defined, 220–225; difficulty
of, 241; Han Yü's understanding of,
220–225, 359 n.41; history of term,
357 n.27; identity with ku-tao, 221–
224; misconceptions about Han Yü's
idea of, 224, 359 n.41; opposed to
shih-wen, 220–221, 240–241; origins
of, 216–217; relation to ch'i, 256–
257; revival by Ou-yang Hsiu, 241;
Sung authors of, 355 n.12; verse a
part of, 224–225
"ku-wen movement," 29, 176, 217, 359
n.43, 370 n.130
Ku-wen shang-shu 古文尚書 Book of
Documents in Archaic Script, 357 n.27
ku-wen style, 13–15
k'ua-to tzu 夸奪子 "loud disputants,"
34

Ministry of Justice 刑部, 83, 88, 100
Ministry of Personnel 吏部, 29, 31,
 78, 102, 109–110, 113, 138, 143
Ministry of Rites 禮部, 158, 287 n.38
Ministry of War 兵部, 76, 105, 110
minting operations, 17–18
Mirsky, Jonathan, 310 n.203
Mo-tzu 墨子, 152–153, 176, 180, 231,
 292 n.86, 326 n.61, 326–327 n.62,
 368 n.113; teachings on political
 order, 326–327 n.62
Mo-tzu, 50, 326 n.62
"modernity." See *chin*
Mohism, 147, 152–155, 326 n.61,
 326–327 n.62
monarchy, 131–140
monasteries, 123
monastic estates, 146
monasticism, Buddhist and Taoist, 151
mondo 問答, 99
"moral Way." See *tao*
Mori Kainan, 286 n.32, 289 n.49, 290
 n.59, n.63, n.64, n.67, 291 n.75, 293
 n.87 294 n.94, 296 n.105, n.112, 297
 n.114, n.117, n.118, 298 n.123,
 n.127, 369 n.129, 371 n.139, 372
 n.150, 373 n.157
Moses, Larry W., 317 n.10, n.11
Mount Sumeru, 97
mountains, as figure for the state, 51,
 133; as metaphor, 155
Mu, Duke of Ch'in 秦穆公 (r. 659–
 621 B.C.), 171
Mu Hsiu 穆修 (979–1032), 241
Mu-tsung 穆宗 (r. 820–824), twelfth
 T'ang emperor, 100, 108, 110, 133;
 death of, 111, 309 n.197, n.199, 310
 n.208, 311 n.210
mundane. See *fan*

nan 難 "difficult," 364 n.80
Nan-ch'üan P'u-yüan 南泉普願
 (748–834), 193
Nan-hai 南海, T'ang city, modern
 Canton, 59

Nan-yüeh Huai-jang 南嶽懷讓
 (677–744), 248 n.88
narrative verse, Han Yü's, 40
nature. See *hsing*
Needham, Joseph, 313 n.223
nei-t'ing 內庭 "inner court," 136, 140,
 334 n.106
neng pei chung t'i 能備衆體 "ability to
 attain perfection in all styles," 267,
 371 n.136
Neo-Confucian outlook, 8–9
Neo-Confucian synthesis, 12, 174
Neo-Confucian unity, 9
Neo-Confucianism, 5, 151, 155, 160,
 165–166, 169, 173–174, 183, 185–
 186, 195–199, 203, 209, 222, 224,
 251, 279 n.19, 285 n.22, 326 n.61,
 347 n.78, 350 n.98, 350–351 n.106,
 n.107, 354 n.4; and Buddhism, 278
 n.15, 306 n.181, 339 n.33; and *ku-
 wen*, 14–15; conception of the
 physical world, 166; debt to
 Buddhist literary tradition,
 269–270; literary world of, 227;
 understanding of Han Yü's literary
 art, 15, 212, 269–270
Neo-Legalism, 131, 320 n.28
New T'ang History. See *Hsin T'ang shu*
Nielson, Thomas P., 357 n.25
Nienhauser, William, H., Jr, 266, 294
 n.93, 297 n.115, 305 n.179, 355 n.14,
 370 n.132, n.134
Nine Doubts 九疑, mountain range in
 modern Hunan, 63, 297 n.114
nirvāṇa, equated with *ch'iung-li chin-
 hsing*, 344 n.55
Nirvāṇa sutra, 308 n.189
Niu Seng-ju 牛僧孺 (779–847), 311
 n.210
Niu Yüan-i 牛元翼 (d. 823?),
 105–108, 310 n.204, n.208
nomadic customs, 316 n.5, 318 n.13
"non-Chinese." See *Hu*
Northeast, separatist provinces of, 23,
 74–75, 79, 104–108, 123–128

qaghan, 314–315 n.2
Qapaghan Qaghan, 318 n.15
Qutluq Elterish, 317 n.10

rain divinity cult, 53
*Random Notes on the Analects. See Lun
yü pi-chieh*
"reality." See *shih*
Record of Rites. See *Li chi*
"rectification of names." See *cheng-
ming*
regionalism, 9
Rickett, Adele Austin, 363 n.68
Rickett, W. Allyn, 320 n.26
Rideout, J. K., 304 n.166, 305 n.176,
334 n.103, 339 n.33

Sage, as *bodhisattva*, 186, 198; as
metaphysical Absolute, 178, 210;
description of in *Doctrine of the
Mean*, 188, 210, 351 n.106; identity
of with common man, 190–191,
331 n.83, 343 n.50, 351 n.106; mind
of, 14, 256; Neo-Confucian, 185–
186. See also *sheng-jen*
Sagehood, and literature, 218–220,
227–229, 243, 257; Han Yü's conception of Absolute nature of, 190,
195, 210; Han Yü's two paths to, 203
Sakata Shin, 176, 337 n.11
Salt and Iron Commission, 68
salt monopoly, 109
samadhi, 308 n.189
san fen 三墳, 289 n.51
san kuan 三觀 "three insights," 187
san kung 三公 Three Lords, 142–143
San-p'ing 三平, disciple of Ta-tien, 98
san ti 三諦 "three truths," 187, 342
n.39
sao style 騷, 260, 289 n.48
satire, 266
Sawado Mizuho, 304 n.168
Schafer, Edward H., 283 n.11, 294
n.94, 295 n.102, 297 n.114, 305
n.178, n.179, 309 n.200, 313 n.223,

369 n.120
Schmidt, Jerry, 299 n.133, 301 n.145,
321 n.39, 372 n.147, 373 n.154
scholarship, 174–178
Schurmann, Franz, 329 n.69
*Scripture of the Lotus Blossom of the Fine
Dharma*, 349 n.94
se 澀 "asperity," 247
Secretariat of the Right of the Heir
Apparent 右春坊, 80
"self-presentation." See *tzu-chin*
Seng-chao 僧肇 (384–414), 193;
Nirvana Is Unnameable, 344 n.55
Seng-jui 僧睿 (352–436), 344 n.54;
"Preface to the Smaller *Prajñāpār-
mitā-sūtra*," 193
separatism, 9, 19, 23, 74–75, 77,
79–83, 104–108, 124–128, 135,
140–145, 212, 226, 262, 318 n.13.
See also Northeast
separatist rebellions, 23, 24, 140–141,
285 n.28
sexagenary cycle, 143–144, 218
Shan-nan East 山南東道, T'ang
administrative district, 69
Shang-chou 商州, T'ang prefecture in
modern Shensi, 69, 87, 100
Shang Chü 商瞿, 180
shang hsien 上賢 "elevation of the
worthy," 326–327 n.62
Shang-nan 商南, T'ang county in
Shang-chou, 88
Shang-shu shih-wen 尚書時文 *Book of
Documents in Contemporary Script*,
357 n.27
shang t'ung 上同 "unity with the
superior," 326–327 n.62
Shang Yang 商鞅 (d. 338 B.C.), 130
Shang-yüan 上元, T'ang county in
Sheng-chou, 21
Shansi, 316 n.5
Shao-chou 韶州, T'ang prefecture in
modern Kuangtung, 22–23, 90, 99,
115, 285 n.25
shao music 韶, 231, 360 n.53

**Library of Congress Cataloging-
in-Publication Data**

Hartman, Charles, 1946–
Han Yü and the T'ang search for unity.

Bibliography: p.
Includes index.
1. Han, Yü, 768-824—Biography.
2. China—History—T'ang dynasty, 618-
907. 3. Authors, Chinese—Biography.
I. Title.
PL2670.H37 1986   895.143 [B]   85-16885
ISBN 0-691-06665-5 (alk. paper)